METAPHYSICAL JOURNAL

GABRIEL MARCEL

Metaphysical Journal

Translated by Bernard Wall

A Gateway Edition
Henry Regnery Company • Chicago

FIRST PUBLISHED BY LIBRAIRIE GALLIMARD
PARIS, 1927

TRANSLATED INTO ENGLISH BY
BERNARD WALL

COPYRIGHT 1952
HENRY REGNERY COMPANY
CHICAGO, ILLINOIS

MANUFACTURED IN THE USA

TRANSLATOR'S NOTE

THE *Metaphysical Journal* of Gabriel Marcel is not an easy
book to translate into English and not an easy book in itself.
The English reader must prepare himself for some formidably
abstract thinking, especially in the first half of Part I, where the
author is concerned with straightening out his judgment on
Idealism.

The translator wishes to express his gratitude for advice on
various points to M. Marcel himself, to Professor D. M. Mac-
kinnon and to Mr. Montgomery Belgion. He has been able
to avail himself of many of their helpful suggestions.

AUTHOR'S PREFACE
TO THE ENGLISH EDITION

I WOULD like to try to say here what the *Metaphysical Journal* represents for me, considered in the light of my subsequent writings.

Jean Hyppolite, author of one of the best contemporary books on Hegel, is of the opinion that all that I have written since is in fact contained in the *Journal*. I myself am unable to endorse his opinion as it stands. I would even go so far as to say that as I see things in the perspective of my philosophical thought, this opinion is inadmissible; for it presupposes that since that time I have done no more than develop the views expounded in the *Journal*. But we must be careful about that word 'develop'. It can only indicate the analytical process by which thought is limited to disentangling the implications contained in ideas stated at the outset. But in fact I think I can affirm that my thought has never proceeded in this way. And, moreover, it certainly cannot be said that the *Metaphysical Journal* ended by stating ideas from which such a development would have been possible.

It is true that while I was keeping my *Journal* I had no idea that one day it would be published as it stood. I thought of it as a preparation for what would one day be a systematic exposition. But subsequent events made that seem an optical illusion. For towards 1923, or at a slightly later date, I became aware that I would be being unfaithful to myself if I tried to set out in a systematic form what had occurred to me in quite a different way. Hence—this by way of parenthesis—the feeling of anguish that I experienced much later when, in 1948, I was invited by the University of Aberdeen to give the Gifford Lectures. For I wondered whether I would not be guilty of a kind of intellectual treason if I adopted a mode of exposition which did not correspond with the true nature of my thought. Moreover, in the lectures themselves, though I tried to bring to light the fundamental connections between different aspects of my thought, I took care to avoid giving my thought anything resembling a systematic form. The term 'concrete approaches' that I made use of to describe the meditations on the mystery of being that I originally published immediately after *Le Monde Cassé* in 1933, remains applicable both to the Gifford Lectures and to the *Metaphysical Journal*. It may well be useful to be a little more exact about how that expression should be understood.

It seems to me best to proceed negatively and to bring out what is *excluded* by deliberate recourse to a method of 'concrete approaches'. Obviously we exclude establishing ourselves on a fundamental certainty that could serve as point of departure either for a deduction of the Spinozist type, or for a dialectic like that of Fichte or Hegel. In philosophies of that kind the notion of 'approaches' is bound to be meaningless. But it should be noted that the same holds for pure empiricism—so much so that nothing of the sort can exist; for pure empiricism excludes any idea of *direction*; under pain of giving the lie to its definition, it can only *drift*. To be able to speak legitimately of 'concrete approaches' there must at least be a presentiment or 'forefeeling' of something regarding which we can say: "This is reality". But such a way of expressing ourselves still remains unsatisfactory. For to say "This is reality" is to *indicate* something; the designation can only bear on objects. Now the central theme of the *Metaphysical Journal* and, of course, of subsequent works, is precisely the impossibility of thinking of being as object. This criticism of objectivisation, made also by Berdiaev in a parallel way in his principal writings, is, if I may so express myself, the backbone of the *Metaphysical Journal*. Being can not be indicated, it cannot be *shown*; it can only be alluded to, a little as some third person now disappeared is alluded to amongst friends who knew him formerly and keep his memory green. The comparison is acceptable only if the evocation does not convert the being who has disappeared into an object about which we are discursive and ratiocinative. The being in question, who has become active subject, must magnetise a certain silence charged with memory and affectivity.

But we see clearly how inadequate our current language is for translating an experience of this type. In itself it tends to 'objectivise' and when it attempts to transcend objectivity it seems to be pulling itself up. The undeniable difficulty of a book such as the *Metaphysical Journal* (I could say the same of Heidegger's *Sein und Zeit*) comes precisely from this. Heidegger thought it necessary to create an almost entirely new terminology. I have adopted a different course. I must confess that I have never been fond of neologisms in metaphysics. They always seem to me barbarous; and perhaps it would be worth asking why, though until to-day I have never put the question to myself. May we not say that the mode of current expression, by the very fact that it has served for a multitude of different cases, has become charged with a genuine potential that neologisms lack? I am using the word 'barbarous' as meaning 'strange' in the absolute sense of the word. The mind, that is to say, does not feel that it is "at home"; it feels that it is "nowhere", as in certain modern edifices that lack a past and a style.

Yet here we must point out a difficulty. The potential in question carries with it a sort of negative counterpart. The word that has been overused has for that reason often lost its value; it is devalued as money is devalued. So we have to revalue it. I have always been deeply concerned about revaluing words, though I would hardly go so far as to affirm that I always had this in mind when writing the *Metaphysical Journal*. What can be stated, I think, is that my concern is closely bound up with the method of 'concrete approaches' considered in itself. Here again negative thought allows a glimpse of what cannot be grasped directly.

On many occasions I have denounced the fatal consequences of the spirit of abstraction, notably in politics, and have tried to show that that spirit leads to fanaticism, in other words, to idolatry, and that such idolatry is invariably accompanied by a paroxysm of objectivisation (this applies equally to Marxist materialism and Nazi racism). But it is manifest that when I set about revaluing words, that is, set about rediscovering their original and concrete meaning, my thought is proceeding in precisely the opposite direction. Hence to-day I am inclined to accept Heidegger's formula to the effect that language is the domicile (*das Haus*) of being—Rilke's *Duino Elegies* throw light on this formula.

At the time I was writing the *Journal* I do not know what I would have thought of that formula. I suppose it would have made me uneasy. Yet perhaps the intuition that it expresses already dominated my thought, though I must specify, as I did in *Etre et Avoir*, that intuition in an existential philosophy such as this is not something that lies at our disposal, something we have, but rather it is a source, in itself inaccessible, from which we set out to think. It is what I have called a blinded intuition; moreover, it is also a 'forefeeling' or premonition, and without it as I shall recall further on, there cannot be 'concrete approaches'.

The metaphysical difficulties raised by this position must not be underestimated, and I do not think I have to reproach myself with having ignored them. In fact it seems that, wherever we are concerned with being in the strict sense, human thought can only be vacillating; that is to say, affirmation has not at its disposal that 'grip' that the object as such assures it. Instead what happens makes it seem as though the affirmation had to be inverted on to its own non-formal conditions of possibility. In the field of objectivity I always limit myself to ratifying or to putting an official seal on relations which are proposed to me; that is to say, I behave as if I have something in front of me. But as F. Alquié has admirably shown in his remarkable book *La Nostalgie de l'Etre*, the aim of being, the ontological aim as such, cannot fail to pass beyond the point of opposition between me and what confronts me. This, moreover, is the central point of the opposition between problem and mystery as I stated it in *Etre et Avoir*. Though this does not figure terminologically in the *Metaphysical Journal*, I am sure I am not deceiving myself when I say that it is no more than the formulation of a distinction that is necessary to make the *Journal* intelligible. For what is the unverifiable, of which so much is said in the first part of the *Journal*, if not mystery itself? This may be the proper place to make yet a further remark. To-day I would no longer admit that being should be given a place beyond truth, as I tended to do at the time when I wrote the first part of the *Journal*. That formula now appears to me either as meaningless or else (if interpreted in a Nietzschean way) as extremely dangerous. As I wrote in *Homo Viator*, I consider it indispensable to distinguish carefully between a particular truth that is inevitably presented to us as susceptible of being acquired and transmitted, and hence can in some degree be compared to a *having*—and truth taken in itself which, as such, can in no way be *thought* (or degraded) in that way. And in the measure precisely in which truth cannot be possessed, in which no one can claim to be the repository of it, it tends, negatively, to be confounded with being. Truth is and can only be, mind. But the meaning of that formula can only be revealed *indirectly* or negatively. The fanatic, for instance, whatever his fanaticism, is like a troglodyte who has dug a home for himself into which mind is unable to penetrate. And that is all the more true in the measure in which the fanatic claims to be inspired by what he calls a principle or a truth. The idolatrous one-track mindedness whose champion he becomes turns into a screen between him and the innumerable appeals that mount up from reality to the man who has kept his power of reception whole. It is not enough to say that such power is systematically held suspect by the fanatic; he is muzzled once and for all, and as a result he is atrophied to the point of non-entity.

But it is only proper to add that docility to the solicitations of the real may itself have a deforming character if it is not compensated by that courage of mind that is necessary if consciousness is to avoid being wasted in superficial and sterile dilettantism. And before all else we must elucidate the nature of such courage. The truth is that it is bound up with value, that it is, so to speak, the active and concrete safeguard of value—in contrast with exhaustion in all its forms. Value, moreover is polymorphous because it can be presented as truth or as justice, and it concerns different aspects for the artist as for the believer. I have sometimes asked myself in the course of the last years whether the use of the term value was in last analysis quite satisfactory and whether it did not correspond to an effort to transpose—into the domain of spiritual realities—a notion that only fully exhausts its significance in the economic order. The sophisms of which Sartre has been guilty have helped to throw light on the dangers we are exposed to when we make an uncontrolled use of the idea of value: I am alluding to the entirely false thesis that man chooses his own values. But by this route we are led back to the idea of an

ontological participation that takes the mind beyond the opposition that Sartre erects between *being in itself* (*l'être en soi*) and
being for itself (*l'être pour soi*). Meditations on the implications of
the word 'with' and on metaphysical fruitfulness must in my
opinion be counted among the most valuable contributions of
the *Metaphysical Journal*. Later, in the collected writings published under the title *Du Refus à l'Invocation*, I was to submit
to similar analyses the relations, or rather the super-relations,
implied by the French word 'chez'. Here, unless I am mistaken,
I made use of the word super-relation for the first time. The
vigorous criticism made by F. H. Bradley (in *Appearance and
Reality*) of the current notion of relation—considered as pure
makeshift—is there extended, and I think I will never be able to
recognise too explicitly what I owe to that great thinker. In my
eyes his mistake may well have been—that, at least, is what I
suggested in my Gifford Lectures—that of remaining too faithful
to the traditional notion of totality and of the possible inclusion of
appearances in the whole. For my part I have tried deliberately
to do without the, to me, fallacious props that these notions—in
reality inapplicable to the domain of the mind—have the appearance of furnishing to the metaphysician. But it is evident that in
that way I automatically renounce setting up what until now has
been called a system; for no systematisation is possible without
constant recourse to the notion of totality. From this standpoint
it can clearly be understood why the *Journal* and its dependent
writings on the one hand, and drama on the other, were my
favourite and even rather exclusive modes of expression. And
this motive explains why researches which I originally thought of
as preparatory work should in the end come to stand by themselves. Doubtless those who have tried to expound my thought
have often yielded to the temptation of systematising it, and in the
Gifford Lectures I too may have succumbed up to a point to that
temptation. What matters, above all, in an *exposé* of this sort,
is that it should be carried on in such a way as to provide an
irresistible invitation to the reader or the listener to break out of
his strait-jacket and plunge directly into that current of personal
and passionate research which is the very heart of my thought
in its original impulse.

One of my pupils once asked me whether my philosophy

could not be considered to be a kind of neo-Socratism. The expression struck me very much, and on reflection I wonder whether the description would not be the least inexact that could be applied to me. The term existentialism brought with it the worst of misunderstandings and I now consider I have repudiated it once and for all. I pointed this out in Milan several months ago—and it was in Italy that the label of 'Christian existentialist' was first attached to me.

What the term neo-Socratism implies is above all the—in no way sceptical—attitude of interrogation that is a constant with me, and appears perhaps even more clearly in my stage plays. It also and co-relatively implies an emphasis on communication as realised by dialogue, by addressing oneself to a Thou and counting on him and thus giving him credit. It implies, finally, the adoption of a negative attitude to the results we can hope to reach through any kind of physics because physics can never escape from the objective categories. Viewed in this perspective my thought should appear as the prolongation of a fundamentally anti-dogmatic tradition; and if it is linked up with Bergson that is in the measure in which Bergson himself gave us the means for proceeding beyond him when in his last work he made use of the category of the 'open' (which is also to be found, though admittedly in a very different way, at the end of the *Duino Elegies*). I do not think I am deceiving myself when I say that though I did not realise this in the beginning, my researches have bearing on all the conditions that permit us to maintain thought in the state of 'openness', in contradistinction to a systematised dogmatics closed in on itself. It is in this sense, it seems to me, and in this spirit, that the reader should approach this difficult and, in places, disconcerting book that is now presented to the English speaking public.

Autumn, 1950   GABRIEL MARCEL

CONTENTS

PART I

METAPHYSICAL
JOURNAL

January 1st, 1914

ON ONE plane the world is not only devoid of all meaning, but even to raise the question of whether there is a meaning is a contradiction. This plane is that of immediate existence. It is of necessity the plane of the fortuitous, of the order of chance.

By reflection we can raise ourselves to successive planes on which things become intelligible. The question I have set myself is whether it is possible to establish the existence of ontological differences between such planes. The orders are really differentiated by their respective potentials of intelligibility, that is to say they are unequally explanatory. From the standpoint of immediate existence nothing can be explained or even understood. Empiricism, in that it is a philosophy of the immediate, is self-destructive. The immediate is the very reverse of the principle of intelligibility.

From the standpoint of the higher planes the immediate must no longer be defined as a datum but as infinitely mediable. This does not mean that it ceases to be a datum, but that the category of datum is not here the essential thing. The relation of the *Gegebensein* on which in the beginning all, it was claimed, could be built, is shown to be entirely devoid of intrinsic significance, in the sense that it implies an empirical subject who himself enfolds an infinite. This relation is presented at the outset as immediate and absolute only because immediate consciousness sets aside the determinations that qualify it as subject. Whereas, in so far as immediate consciousness becomes self-aware as a definite empirical subject, it is constituted as pure reflection. (I am tempted to express this by saying that a mind is only really what it itself makes itself.) The act by which reflection is defined as such (for the philosopher, i.e. for the νοησις νοησεως) is the act by which consciousness thinks itself as empirical.

January 5th

I am of the firm belief, and my conviction is not of recent date, that philosophical truths are relative to the requirements (*exigences*)[1] of the thoughts that constitute them. The hierarchy of truths is defined in function of the hierarchy of the requirements. The only problem lies in finding out in relation to what these hierarchical planes of thoughts are ordered. Thinkers like Leibnitz or Hegel believed that they were ordered in relation to an absolute plane which was the plane of being itself—the plane on which reality is what it is, the plane on which God sees reality. (Here, as we can immediately see, the question of divine transcendence has no bearing.) This way of thinking is involved (in the most confused and implicit way) in every affirmation that starts out from the postulate that philosophy has an exterior object whose faithful reproduction it tends more and more to become; thus with anyone who thinks he is in a position to talk of the truth or falsity of a system. But in my opinion this hierarchy neither should nor can be defined in function of an ontological order posited in an idealist way. The criticism of absolute knowledge ends in a condemnation of this way of looking at things. So the problem I am induced to raise amounts to asking how the hierarchy can be thought of independently of this idea.

January 7th

The problems by which I am preoccupied at present are for the most part problems of method. Here are the main ones. First of all there is the problem of founding the hierarchy of philosophical thought while avoiding both realism and pure subjectivism (which is, moreover, contradictory; to posit systems as subjective interpretations is to consider them as relative to an entirely objective order that is relegated to the domain of the unknowable). Then I would like to define my attitude to the philosophy of history in relation to Hegel's. The Hegelian paradox lies in the idea that the

---

[1] *Exigences.* There is no completely satisfactory translation of this word. The German word would be *Forderung*.

systems illustrate the dialectic even before begetting it, that the mind only exists on conditions that it creates itself, that the *Fürsichsein* supposes the *Ansichsein;* in other words that the moments of the dialectic have to begin by being posited as absolutes (the positing of the moments as absolutes is itself a moment that necessarily precedes the positing of the moments as moments). I am not satisfied with this dialectical realism. But why not? Is it because I have not freed myself sufficiently from the realism of time which, so to speak, hypostatises the before and the after?—I am led to raise the obscure and badly defined problem of the reality of time. Yesterday I was wondering (perhaps some light will finally emerge from all these problems) whether we know exactly what we mean when we posit a problem of the *a priori*. In what sense is it true or false to say of an idea that it is *a priori?* Does not the question go completely beyond the system in which such categories have a meaning? Is not its significance restricted to that lower stage on which what is innate and what is acquired are conceived in some physiological way? Here we have an important problem which no one, I think, has noticed. I also asked myself whether there might not be a way of defining the conditions under which the reflection of a thought upon itself could be creative (and not be a mere reproduction or sterile double). But I still see no solution.

To return to the problem of time. Ought we not to distinguish two planes (I still see this very confusedly) according as to whether the mind is aware or not aware of the relativity of the before and the after? I will go into this later.

January 8*th*

There is an immanent connection between the reality of God and the realisation of God by the saint. But to the saint the reality of God can only appear as that in which he (the saint) participates —there would be no truth in a statement that claimed to transcend the need to posit participation. On the other hand we should notice that the saint's realisation of God is not a matter of historical immediacy, susceptible of being somehow a *datum* for further consciousnesses; it can only be re-thought and re-constructed. In this way the historical uncertainty which must needs have weight in the life of a saint is justified in reason; sanctity, which is itself constructed, has to serve as foundation for further constructions, etc. These further constructions will not be false, for it is not the historical material that matters in the life of a saint, or rather it is arbitrary to dissociate such material from the religious content. And the dissociation is only possible for the unbeliever. The unbeliever who claims to make a historical reconstruction goes beyond the frontiers of all that which is. Analysis, here, can only be brought to bear on the void and can only discover the void.

January 9th

I seem to see clearly how the idea of divine creation is justified (faith in God as creator). From the standpoint of science I see myself as conditioned causally in an infinite degree by the biological development that preceded me, and this seems to pulverise my reality. But can I conceive this truth regarding myself (it is anyway unthinkable) as final? I could only do so if I made this truth real by an arbitrary act. Notice that were I to accept this infinite determinism I would necessarily reach the point of positing a radical dualism between what I am in so far as I am thought (which seeks being and the good)—and the purely contingent matter that makes up my empirical self. If I affirmed this dualism seriously I would be destroying all action or rather would be rendering it impossible. Only in so far as I deny this dualism can I act; action itself is the negation of it. But what do I discover if I reflect on what the negation of this dualism requires? I discover that I must posit that the relation between myself, inasmuch as I am thought and will, and my empirical self, is not a contingent relation. It is *beyond knowing* that I must think the unity of this dualism.

The unity can only be thought outside time. I must refuse to think myself as contingent (that is, as determined in infinite degree). This means that I must think myself as willed by a non-temporal act which is bound up with me without any intermediary. And from the thought of the God who willed me and in virtue of the immanent connection that unites me with the world and makes me exist, I must pass on to the thought of the God who willed the world.

This could be systematised if we thought of God predetermining the series of causes at the beginning of time, but in that way we would be setting aside the essential element of the demonstration.

(This leads me to a reflection on method. I can ask myself about the conditions under which I can think myself as created. But that method is no more than heuristic because that whose conditions I am seeking can still be thought to be a pure and gratuitous hypothesis. Whereas if, later on, the conditions come to seem real to me and as of necessity involving faith in a creating God, then I shall have achieved the real demonstration.)

This is bound up with the problem of time in the form in which I have already raised it, and leads, I believe to the solution.

First of all we must posit in principle that the real consumption of time is bound up with the existence of a world in becoming, that is, of a world subject to causality. I believe that causes are abstractions and that in this sense causality itself is no more than a purely artificial rationalisation of a totality of becoming; but that does not matter here. If such be the case it is only if the mind can transcend the order of causality itself that we can conceive the ideality of time. But on what conditions could such ideality be thought as truth? In other words, do the conditions under which a notion can be thought as truth apply to the ideality of time? For that to be so it would not only be necessary that empirical thought should be capable of elevation to a viewpoint at which it would appear to itself as appearance (in so far as it was bound up with a world in becoming) but also that this viewpoint and order should have characteristics which in a general way define a truth.

January 12*th*

This morning I was wondering whether, if faith cannot be identified with a judgment of existence, it would be possible, inversely, to see faith in the judgment of existence; that is, to justify in function of religious thought the irreducible character of the judgment of existence—that pure immediacy which ordinary thinking has set aside (since it converts the judgment of existence into a confusedly stated judgment of relation). That remains to be seen. Along that way the theory of participation would lead to a new metaphysic based on religion. But obviously such an idea is dangerous.

January 13th

Regarding the ideality of time the first problem we should have raised is about the conditions which alone can make it thinkable.

In my opinion the reasons in favour of ideality are not those given by Kant. We can only deduce transcendent ideality from empirical reality if we posit implicitly a relation of experience to reality which may well be unacceptable. The process of argument supposes that the idea of the thing-in-itself acts as a substratum of experience, and, as is well known, this idea is difficult to admit. As I see things, the ideality of time can only be demonstrated with the help of an internal criticism whose object is to make explicit the contradictions immanent in the idea of time. In this sense one should see in the Antinomies the true and only demonstration that Kant has made (although he thought he had done it in his *Aesthetic*). I leave aside the question of continuity and restrict myself to taking up once more the principal difficulties inherent in the idea of time (as regards the problem of a beginning). When we posit a beginning to time we are in reality thinking nothing at all. For a "before" remains conceivable and even of necessity has to be conceived. We are exclusively positing a beginning of *what is in* time. Is this a real or merely a verbal solution? It could be said: time itself as ideal form has no beginning, but that which is in time may have one.[1]

But this is either straightway unintelligible, or else comes back to thinking a relation between what is outside time and what is in time; and this relation is unthinkable (unless we surreptitiously convert what is outside time into temporal reality). The solution is thus purely verbal. Moreover, can time be really thought of as purely ideal? As the duration of nothing kept in duration by nothing?

January 14th

On the other hand, to think of time without a beginning is also

[1] Perhaps the first question we should ask is whether the mind can reach certainty on this point, or whether such a solution is not a figment and really boils down to imagining a historical fact (i.e. that can be regarded by the mind as contingent, as not bound up with the act by which it defines and thinks itself).

impossible, for the reason given by Kant. Moreover, it is no real solution, it is an answer that only puts off the answer indefinitely. And so we are forced to admit that the problem is insoluble. Why? Not for a reason of fact, but only because thought has no right to realise time, to treat it as an object about which one can reason. Time is a formal condition under which objects can be presented to us, it is not itself an object. The problem is insoluble because it is not a legitimate one. How can we get from here to the idea of time as mere phenomenon?

It seems to me that the transition can be made as follows. There is a solidarity between time and temporal reality. To prohibit ourselves from raising the question of the origin of time means to prohibit ourselves from raising the question of the origin of the world (inasmuch as it is bound up with time and is its real aspect). But if it is equally absurd to affirm or to deny that the world had a beginning, this is because the world (as such) is not in being, because the world is pure appearance. And from the ideality of the world (inasmuch as temporal) we deduce the ideality of its form, which is time. In other words I believe that we cannot directly infer the phenomenal character of time from its formal character, and that, as intermediary, we must have recourse to the idea of the solidarity of time with what exists in time. But the (negative) answer which is clear as regards time, is very obscure as regards what exists in time. It seems unthinkable that both alternatives regarding the world can be false. In fact the only way of avoiding the contradiction appears to consist in saying that the true world is outside time; and that the contradictions we have to face are bound up with the non-adequation of time as a form with a reality which is itself (in itself) non-temporal. The subjectivity of time will serve as an explanation. We can say that it is because of the weakness of our finite consciousness that we can only grasp reality in a temporal way, and so we get involved in the antinomies already mentioned. Such, I think, are the principal lines of the process of argument. (It is important to see that, even if we admit the Bergsonian theory of time, the problem still stands absolutely, and that, even if real time is only the duration that gives rhythm to the *élan vital*, the dilemma remains unchanged. For the *élan vital* began in time; and it does not seem to me possible to escape the question of the "before".)

What are we to think of the idealist solution so defined? Before we tackle it must we not ask ourselves whether a refusal to realise the historical "becoming" of the world would provide an escape from it? We have to give up the illusion by which we compare the world to a person whose past (so it seems) can be completely realised. It can be objected that there is no reason why the mode of thinking valid for a part of the world should not be equally valid for the world itself. To this we can answer that if it is possible for us to "realise" a person's past, that is because in an arbitrary way we envisage a discontinuous section of the "becoming", a section in reality bound up absolutely continuously with all the becoming that went before; we realise the past in question because we are only considering a fiction. And hence we should never view the world's past under the aspect of datum— for under this aspect it is inevitably contradictory and unthinkable. We should only regard it as the material of an infinite rational development (a development conceived as potential and future and hence not contradictory). By the conversion of the past into the future we escape the disastrous contradictions of thesis and antithesis (obviously the germ of this solution can be found in Kant). By viewing the historical past of the world in function of the infinite activity of mind which progressively extracts its truth, we manage to eliminate the irrational elements which, it seemed, only the idea of a non-temporal reality could dissipate. Can we accept a solution of this kind, one at once idealist and critical? Notice that we have been speaking of the development of a thought which progressively constitutes a truth. But a truth can only be constituted in co-relation with an intuition (at least as ideally reproduced). If it is abstracted from intuition the thought by which truth is defined is stated to be incapable of verification. So the solution is shown to be vain. There seems to be only one way of escaping from this difficulty. It consists in saying that the thought in question has bearing on laws and not on past facts. But here we have two alternatives: either such laws are posited to be outside time (interpreted in a Platonic sense) and in that case we cannot evade positing the non-temporal, or else they are thought of as immanent conditions of the empirical, and then they are not dissociable from the world as subjected to time. And so we fall back into our earlier difficulties.

Hence it looks as though we cannot escape from the dilemma of, on the one hand, a reality involved in time, and on the other of a non-temporal reality (in which the order of becoming seems to be mere appearance). What about the second alternative? It forces us to raise the general problem of the relationships between appearance and reality. Do we really eliminate the contradictions inherent in time by conceiving a non-temporal reality of which time is the appearance? It is clear that there is no real meaning in positing the objective production of time by the non-temporal. We need to have recourse to the roundabout way of subjectivity and say that appearance is bound up with the existence of finite thought.

January 15th

I have shown elsewhere the vanity of the attempt of the Absolute Idealists to integrate phenomenal appearances into the absolute (whether or not the appearances are conceived in function of thought that is tainted with subjectivity). And so if we posit the dualism of what is in time and what is outside time, we should not do so with the hope that we will, later, be able to unify the two orders. The logical faith with which a philosopher such as Bradley posits the unity and the transmutation of appearances in the heart of the real is only an appeal to the unintelligible. To the logical optimism of the neo-Hegelians we need to oppose the logical pessimism of a philosopher like Spir who denies both the possibility of establishing a co-ordination between the norm and the anomaly and the possibility of deducing the anomaly from the norm. It seems to me that Spir's dualism contradicts itself in so far as he admits that the action of moral causes "cannot cause any derangement in the order of the world, *because it is exercised in virtue of one of the fundamental cosmic forces.*"[1] But is Spir's ontological dualism tenable? No doubt Spir would not like to see his doctrine called an ontological dualism, because for him only the norm has an ontological character. "The norm of thought," he says, "being the notion of the normal and absolute nature of things, is the foundation of all ontology."[2] He tries to demonstrate the objective validity of this norm so as to show

---

[1] (*Nouvelles esquisses de philosophie critique* p. 113).
[2] *Loc. cit.* p. 91.

that it must be thought of as being of the very nature of objects. It would be useless to go into it here, but when we examine his demonstration[1] we see that the—often very vague—reasons he adduces militate, not in favour of his metaphysical realism, but in favour of a doctrine of a critical type in which thought is conceived as applying certain formal criteria to things, and hence in need of rediscovering the tracks of its criteria in objects. I seem constantly to see in Spir's thought a confusion between the object of thought (in so far as it is the object of thought) and what could be called the absolute object. Doubtless Spir would deny the legitimacy of this distinction, but, if he fails to make it, he does not even touch the critical problem; and his solution is meaningless because it falls short of the issue. Moreover, if the norm is posited as reality, we are obliged, also by means of an act of equalising, to posit the anomaly itself as reality. Or else, if we do not posit the norm to be reality, but only to be appearance, at least that appearance must be the appearance of a reality. Now either this is meaningless or else we must posit a relation (an incomprehensible one) between norm and anomaly. Were we to admit something which was neither reality nor appearance, we would merely be playing with words. Can we admit two realities? If we posit them as equally real, we destroy the very nerve of the ontological argument (which consists in the transition from the intelligible to the real) since the irrational also has a reality.

So the conclusion of this dialectic is that the norm and the anomaly should not be posited as realities (neither *one nor the other* nor *one and the other*); and that the dualism ought not to be and cannot be conceived in an ontological sense. And this obtains for any conception whatsoever of appearance and reality. The dualism can only be thought to be entirely relative to the movement of the mind that posits it. Moreover, when we conceive the ontological norm, it is only too clear that we profit nothing and, futhermore, that we are thinking nothing concrete.

January 16th

I return, then, to the problem of the ideality of time. From what I have said already it follows that if time can be posited as ideal, this is in no way by opposition to a reality not subject to time and

[1] *Loc. cit.* pp. 85-90.

the temporal order of which is subjective appearance. It is in this sense only that the problem of reality *cannot even* be posited as regards time. Thought, in its interior progress, is led to ask itself certain questions which at first sight seem to have a possible bearing on the world and its conditions but which, on analysis, are shown not only to be insoluble but even inapplicable on that plane. To posit the ideality of time and of the world in so far as it is subject to development in time (this development being the real correlative of time) is thus merely to say that: *metaphysical problems can only be raised in an order abstracted from all relation (even a negative relation) to time*. We may also ask ourselves whether the negative relation, in whatsoever way we conceive it, does not also imply a positive (and incomprehensible) relation— for my own part I am convinced it does. It seems to me that apart from this solution and those we have already set aside there is only one further solution that is theoretically possible. Namely, the positivist solution which consists in saying that as these questions cannot be applied to the world of experience, they ought quite simply to be excluded. But that solution is purely verbal. Questions regarding the origin of time (and of the world) arise inevitably and precede all criticism. And the only criticism which can demonstrate that they are illegitimate requires a real employment of pure thought (which is constituted by this very employment) and that transcends all positivism.

So the progress we are describing is not the synthetic Hegelian progress that at one and the same time surpasses the thesis and antithesis and unites them in the synthesis; it is the progress of a reflection that transcends what it itself has posited. Whereas progress as defined in the Hegelian way must needs claim to have an ontological significance, but because of this raises the insoluble question (which cannot be avoided but only conjured away) of the independent reality of the inferior moments—dialectics as I conceive them are purely ideal, they bear exclusively on the modes of statement, consequently they do not claim to be valid ontologically, and so do not come up against the above difficulty. It can be objected that, as there is no integration, the exteriority of the successive moments in relationship to one another still subsists. But I reply first of all that such exteriority always subsists implicitly, and that, moreover, assimilation or real integration is not the aim I am pursuing and there would be no point in achieving it.

A further objection is that a synthetic dialectic is only valid if it is therefore—at least ideally—analytical, that is, if it requires its term as its principle; and that is only possible if its term is posited at the outset as absolute synthesis, as totality completely realised. But I reply that this only applies to a dialectic that claims to reconstruct, and not to the dialectic of a reflection that rises to ever higher planes of intelligibility.

Yet a further difficulty could be raised regarding the relation of dialectics to their matter, their object. But such a problem is not absent from Hegelianism itself, and moreover it does not seem to me to present special difficulties. What is certain is that the relation of thought to its object appears differently to thought itself following the manner in which thought conceives the object. This needs further elucidation.

There is still one further difficulty, that of understanding the relation of the dialectic to time. But that difficulty is strictly non-existent because we are not positing the reality of the non-temporal but only the transcendence of the real in relation to the opposition between the temporal and the intemporal; that is to say, "the irrelevancy of time."

I note that Spir's pessimism is defined in relation to the idea of a potential resolution[1] of the dualism and that the resolution is posited in an ontological sense. But that is precisely the refuge I cannot admit, and for this very reason I am unable to admit Spir's point of view. If there is ground for adopting logical optimism this is not, as the neo-Hegelians think, because in the absolute all is good and contradictions are reconciled, but because thought experiences itself as the potentiality of mediation and conciliation. But here we seem to be up against another difficulty. Are we not confronted with the idea that reconciliation or mediation is an infinite task, an infinite "*Sollen*"? And are we not overlooking the Hegelian demonstration of the relativity of the point of view of the "*Sollen*" (which implies the "bad infinity")? Before going into this question I feel we need to note that there is no contesting the fact that all contradictions cannot be thought of as being reconciled in the absolute. The contradictions inherent in time can only be reconciled by substitution, not by synthesis.

[1] Theoretically, not actually.

But, if we look closer, the neo-Hegelian method will be seen to be identical with mine as regards all that is concrete in it.

A way that allows us to proceed further is opened up, I think, when we ask ourselves what we mean when we question ourselves about the *existence* of truth. We can imagine (I do not say *think*), a type of pure and absolute scepticism which denies all truth; but it is plain beyond need of emphasis, that this type of scepticism is in every way destructive of itself. I am not saying that a certain scepticism may not be legitimate; but it is not the kind that denies all truth—the latter kind is in no measure a thought. But then it will be enough if we admit that there is an order of the true. What do we mean, as regards this order of the true, when we raise the question of existence and ask if the true exists? If we are not asking whether affirmations exist which can be qualified with the epithet true, what are we asking? I take it we are applying to truth the requirement of imaginative thought which insists that objects should "exist outside ourselves." Only we should note that this requirement as regards objects is itself very ambiguous. Do we mean that the objects ought to exist outside our body?—something that has ever been contested by the idealists. Do we mean: outside thought (representation)? But as imaginative thought identifies the thinking subject with the body, I believe that the distinction between the two questions has no clear meaning for it. Note, moreover, that imaginative thought affirms the identity of the real object and the object represented, it would never occur to it to affirm that they are dual. Hence I think that the problem of the reality of the external world is one that cannot even be raised by imaginative thought. If it is so raised it is as regards the body, and in that field it is meaningless. And even if it were raised on genuine grounds, imaginative thought would clearly prefer idealist theory to the admission of a dualism between the real and what is represented. Furthermore it would object to conceiving this identity (of the real and of what is represented) in the interests of what is represented, on the grounds that such a solution seems to compromise the reality of the object (its independence in relation to its *percipi*).

January 17th

The solution clearly consists in positing that the object is constructed as object; that is to say—and by definition—as independent of the perceiving subject. Its construction is not posterior to experience, as maintained in a contradictory way by the Empiricists, nor anterior to it, but identical and co-extensive with it.

What do we mean by existence when we attribute it to an object?

Until now I have been much tempted to identify existence in this connection with the immediate thought apart from which we can only establish purely abstract reflection. I have defined it as posited (whether ideally or not) in relation to an actual consciousness, that is, as the link in the heart of an experience to an actual content of consciousness. During the summer I wrote: "When I say: Caesar has existed—and I take my example from the past because it is there that definition seems to be *most* subject to discussion—I do not only mean that Caesar could have been perceived by me; I also mean that between the existence of Caesar and my state of consciousness, my actual awareness, lies an (infinitely complex) series of relations in time which is capable of being determined in an objective way. My actual state of consciousness, which is bound up with the position of the organic body that it expresses, is the landmark in relation to which the infinite multiplicity of what can be thought by myself as existing is ordained. All existence can be traced back to this landmark, and outside of all relation to it, it is only by an abstraction that we can think existence. To think a thing as existing is to think oneself as the perceiver, it is to extend one's experience in such a way that it comprehends even that which it appeared to leave outside itself. This does not imply the kind of subjective idealism which attributes a privileged value to the immediate data of perception, but only the affirmation that existence supposes a relation to an immediate thought in general, that is to say, to *my* thought."

Clearly at first sight this does not satisfy the mind. The ideal relation in question appears to be only the indication of existence. There would thus seem to be a reality of existence of which the relation is only the phenomenon. Has this any meaning? We then need to distinguish between the content of the notion, the existence in itself of this content, and the indication (for us) of this existence (the fact that it enfolds a potential relation with an actual consciousness). But what is existence in itself here? If we posit its unknowableness, its absolute indeterminability, we are clearly saying nothing and even ruling out the notion itself. Ought we to regard it as a characteristic intrinsic in the notion? But that is impossible because the thing can be thought of as non-existent. And if it is an external characteristic of the notion it comes back to the general relation we have already defined. Only a psychological metaphysic could provide a solution by saying that existence defined as relation to experience is only the indication of the fact which consists in being *for itself*, in being a *datum for itself*. Thus the existence of other consciousnesses could be said to be not exhausted by the fact that these consciousnesses are data given to an actual consciousness as bodies. And in this example, the only one that can be adduced in favour of the pan-psychist theory, there is a latent claim to discovering the proof of the dualism of existence in itself and of existence for us. But the argument is extremely superficial. A consciousness only exists for me in the measure in which it is revealed to me objectively (that is, through the medium of a body.) I then proceed to think of this consciousness as a consciousness by analogy with myself.[1]

Provisionally I will leave this point aside so as to turn back to a potential difficulty. Do hallucinations exist? Anyway, they do not exist in the same sense as a physical object exists. Three solutions are possible. We could say that existence is relationship to an immediate consciousness (an individual consciousness, since the relation is not capable of being generalised). Or we could say there are degrees in existence. Or we could say that existence is this relationship, but to an actual consciousness in general (which would amount to saying once more that there is only existence for what is objective). It seems to me evident that we must posit *a priori* a plurality of planes of existence each defining itself by the system of conditions which govern the ways in which one and the same content can be given to the immediate consciousness (which is itself defined in function of these planes, and hence on planes that are themselves in a hierarchy). I will.

---

[1] (1925). Nowadays I should make the most express reserves about this interpretation. But in what sense do I think myself as existing?—there lies the whole question. Here we are touching on an essential problem.

return later to the difficulty of understanding what becomes of the identity of content.

But now we come against two fundamental problems. The first is to find out in relation to what the hierarchy in question is defined, what is its principle. The second regards the nature of the *identical content* which is given as apprehended in different ways on the different planes of consciousness. It is clear, to begin with, that if we use the word content in its common meaning, the content is not and cannot be identical. So under the distinct contents we must subtend a content differentiated from them yet conceived as being substantially the same. But then all the difficulties I have already pointed out reappear. Either this content is a logical form (the very unity of consciousness) or else it is indeterminable, contradictory and fictitious. It might nevertheless be claimed that this content may possess determinable and definite characteristics though they are differentiated according to the character of the mode of consciousness which apprehends it (this content). Contradictory or not, this interpretation at first sight seems natural enough. Can we accept it? It is plain to begin with that as regards the problem of existence this interpretation in no way modifies the situation we have already noted. For either we identify existence with the characteristics which make up this content (which means making existence a predicate), or else we attribute existence to this content because we posit it as ideally given to the consciousness which thinks of itself (in an undetermined way) as the perceiver. What matters in the foregoing process of argument is that it establishes that existence cannot be conceived as the substratum common to the different contents we apprehend.

So if we posit a common content, it can only be on condition that we do not posit it as existing (in the sense in which preceding contents *existed*) because it can only exist by the same right as preceding contents (in virtue of its relation to immediate consciousness) and it has no ontological privilege in relation to them (no pre-eminence from the standpoint of existence). This is to say that the content can only be posited as having no relation to immediate consciousness, as not being *given* to it; it can only be posited as thought, that is to say as ideal (in opposition to the contents of sense—data which were, on the contrary, existent).

And so if we adopt the word existence in a univocal sense, we must maintain that in so far as sense contents exist, laws do not exist (or vice versa).

From this it follows that the datum should be thought of as contingent. For we have already seen that if existence belongs to the world of sensation, it cannot be said to belong to the rational order. But it follows that the world of sensation cannot be deduced from the rational order, for the profound reason that thought, inasmuch as it is thought (and non-immediate), is not deduced from immediate consciousness. If the order of sense cannot be deduced from a rational order we are forced to admit that an individual thought must appear to itself as situated in a contingent whole—because this thought itself can only define itself as rational by transcending the whole (which rational thought, far from justifying, presupposes).

January 18th

I come back to some of the points I touched on yesterday. I feel I can now view as established that we can only speak of existence with regard to objects given in an immediate relation to a consciousness (which is at least posited as possible). As we can conceive a multiplicity of ways in which one and the same object (the same content) might be given to consciousness in an immediate relation, we must conceive an infinite series of planes of existence relating to the possible modes of apprehension. The external world (in the usual sense of the word) is posited on a special plane of existence which corresponds to the special system of conditions which govern human perception, and it is certain that in the measure in which, to take a particular example, we introduce instruments to modify these conditions of perception we in some way violate the unity of *this world* and introduce a principle of equivocation. We have seen, moreover, that the relation that we must establish between these planes of existence is extremely difficult to determine, that the unity that we can subtend beneath them is not that of a thing existing; that is to say, even if it is the unity of an object, this object cannot be thought as being in immediate relation to any consciousness whatsoever (even potential). If, then, we supposed there to be conscious beings differently organised from ourselves and perceiving qualities that we do not suspect, we ought not therefore to allow ourselves to posit a substratum—itself endowed with qualities—which, though diversely apprehended by distinct consciousnesses, would possess in itself certain determinations. Such a substratum cannot be thought of as fundamental reality, as objective basis of two distinct systems of perception, unless it is thought of as being itself removed from all the conditions of perceptibility for any consciousness whatsoever; that is to say, as an intelligible, as something can only be thought or constructed but cannot be a datum. All the spurious problems that are posited on the relation of laws to things (existences) are precisely due to our failure to make this capital distinction, to the fact that we refuse to situate them both in orders that are irreducibly separate. If, by the contingence of one order in relation to another, we understand the impossibility of deriving the former from the latter, we must in consequence posit the absolute contingence of existences in relation to any rational order whatsoever.

But then, to leave aside the primary problem and to return to an earlier question, we have to ask ourselves in what sense a consciousness can be thought of as existing. It is clear that it can only be so thought in the measure in which it is given in an immediate relationship either to itself or to another. And as soon as we state the problem in this way we are on the road to a solution. For it is clear that the datum common to my consciousness and to other possible consciousnesses is my body. I cannot think of myself as existing save in so far as I am a datum for other consciousnesses, that is to say in so far as I am a datum in space.

January 19th

At this point we reach a dangerous and obscure point in the theory. There seems no denying that I can be a datum to myself otherwise than in space, for instance as affectivity. From there on we have a new mode of existence whose relation to the spatial mode of existence seems singularly difficult to determine. Of course my consciousness cannot be a datum given as a whole either to itself or to other consciousnesses except as body. But, on another plane of existence, might it not be a datum for itself—exclusively? It is plain that this means raising the whole problem of what is commonly called the relations of soul with body.

From the standpoint I have adopted, can I throw some light on this?

It seems impossible to set aside absolutely the following problem at least. There is an immediate relation between my consciousness and my body in so far as the latter is a datum in space (of course this does not exclude the idea of a construction of the body's image; what I mean here is that the relation between my consciousness and my body is given as immediate, and that is all we need take into account).

But between consciousness and body there is another relation inasmuch as my body is a datum given to internal perception (*coenesthésique*); and here, it seems, we are dealing with two absolutely distinct modes of existence. One is by definition objective, that is to say it applies to any consciousness endowed with conditions of perception analogous to ours; the other is by definition purely individual, i.e. bound up with my consciousness. Of course, inasmuch as I abstract from myself as ego and adopt the point of view of a consciousness in general, I identify the reality of my body with what my body is for perception. But that can be regarded as arbitrary. These two modes of existence are irreducibly distinct. We have seen that if a content be subtended under them, it is on condition that this content is not itself thought of as susceptible of being a datum for a consciousness in an immediate relation. It is an intelligible, that is to say, a totality of relations that can only be thought (only in virtue of an illusion could this totality be converted into a metaphysical entity). I can, if I wish, call this totality unconscious, but only in a critical sense and neither metaphysically nor psychologically.

Between the respective data of what I shall call the subjective consciousness and what can be called the perceiving or objective consciousness we must conceive a harmony; but we must not allow ourselves to think of this harmony as susceptible of being a datum for any consciousness whatsoever.

As I see things, all we have the right to conclude from the foregoing (which seems to me myself full of mysteries) is that from the moment that the body is a datum given to the consciousness in two irreducibly different ways, any reduction of the reality of the body to a purely spatial (mechanical) whole, must be regarded as only having a phenomenal character. Hardly any reflection is needed, I think, to make that quite clear. Inasmuch as I think, that is to say, that I transcend these two modes of existence of myself, and I do not allow myself to regard them as appearances of an existing content, I posit the reality of an entirely intelligible content which itself necessarily transcends this reduction.

But does this authorise us to posit the possibility of isolating these two modes of existence, to posit that consciousness can be a datum for itself in a purely internal relation? I do not think so. It seems to me evident that these two modes are in fact indissoluble and that they complete each other. It is perhaps even possible to maintain that the body can only be a datum for me in an internal relationship because it is a datum for me spatially. Here we have a question of genetic psychology which does not concern the philosopher. However it may be, I prefer to affirm the indissolubility or close solidarity of the two modes of existence.

Then how is the thinking subject defined in function of this datum? And over and above the physical datum which is not perceived exclusively from within, is there not a psychical datum of an exclusively external character?

I will begin by replying to the second question. It is perfectly clear from what has already been said, that we cannot speak of an internal physical datum; there we have a mode of reality of something which, as we know, can only be *thought* (henceforward I shall call it an Idea). But this simple remark should be enough to show that the question we are asking is in reality complex and even obscure. It clearly follows from what we have said that the denominations 'physical' and 'psychical' do not enlighten us on the nature of the Idea; or rather that as the Idea, inasmuch as it is thought, is not reduced to a datum of any kind whatsoever, it can neither be defined as psychical nor as physical. If, then, there even exists a datum which is purely psychical, that is to say one that does not correspond to a physical datum—in other words, even if, in the end, the correspondence that I have indicated between the two modes of existence cannot be admitted—it will nevertheless remain that this purely psychic datum must be regarded as the expression of an Idea which in itself only defines itself as Idea (and hence not as psychical). Of course at the outset it is not possible to determine the relation between the Idea which now appears to us and the preceding Idea. But, it may be said, the necessity of admitting an Idea of the psychical seems in no way evident. I experience a feeling; whether this feeling has or has not an organic correlative (datum for a possible consciousness), inasmuch as it is psychical it suffices in itself; there is no need whatever to subtend an intelligible substitute for the psychical datum. The answer seems to be as follows: if we admit that the psychical datum in question suffices in itself, and there is no need to appeal to an intelligible content, how comes it that this was not also true previously? Are we to see the explanation in the fact that previously we were in the presence of two modes of existence that needed unifying (in the intelligible); and that now, on the contrary, we are only in the presence of a single mode of existence and in consequence the difficulty collapses? This answer is invalidated in the following way: first of all it seems dangerous to deny dogmatically all remaining correspondence between the two modes of existence; then, if the psychical here functions as reality, why could it not similarly function as reality at the preceding stage? True we have seen that this was impossible (because the two modes of existence are irreducible) but then why the change? To justify it, we would need to establish a difference of nature between data which, as data, do not appear to have any distinction. Moreover, as an exact analysis of psychical life would easily show, it is necessary to interpret an effective development in function of the individual logic (itself Idea) which is translated into it.

And so we reach this general conclusion that there exists between immediate consciousness and thought (the thinking subject) the same relation as between the datum (whatever it be, even if it be purely psychical) and the Idea, that is, the intelligible content, not posited as existing, which while still maintaining its contingent character, alone can justify the datum.

Note that in view of the critical way in which we have been led to think the Idea, from our present standpoint it is quite impossible for us to speak either of a single Idea or of a world of Ideas. What makes the question confused even in its terms is that clearly from the spatial point of view the body is in relation to all that surrounds it, it is prolonged, so to speak, in its surroundings. And on the other hand our internal perception does seem to bear only on the states of the body. And so if from one viewpoint it seems unreasonable to posit an Idea of the body, from the other it seems certain that the content ought to present a certain character of individuality.

All that we know and all that we can legitimately affirm so far is this: In so far as my consciousness transcends itself as immediate it is obliged to think an intelligible content which does not participate in existence; and this content has the ambiguous character of being itself and at the same time issuing out from itself (to pass into its other, as Hegel would say). It seems to me that this only becomes intelligible if we posit the absolute solidarity and even the identity of these two aspects; if, that is, we understand that this content is only *in itself* when *it issues out from itself*. It is only by the movement of its parts (relatively immanent action) and the actions taking place between the spatial datum (the body) and what surrounds it, that internal perception is possible. This ought not, I must repeat, to be understood in a causal way. As we have already seen, the modes of existence are radically distinct. The correlation itself can only be conceived through the medium of the intelligible unity that founds it, that is, thought needs to posit a subject of this double becoming, a subject placed in some way at the intersection of this double becoming. Only this subject is not existent; it can only be thought. A critique of the notion of this subject can only be made when we forget it is a notion, that is, when we show that the subject thus posited presents no psychological or sense characteristics (no qualitative determination) and as nothing exists save what has quality, we conclude that it is nothing—and that because we forget the fundamental distinction between what is existing (i.e. in relation to immediate consciousness) and what is real (i.e. only defined for thought).

January 20th

Only a little examination is required, I think, for us to see that, as thus stated, things are still too simple and too schematised; and that the dualism of what I have called the immediate consciousness on the one hand, and of thought strictly speaking on the other, is not really in accord with my definition. For, in fact, from the moment at which judgment takes place, immediate consciousness is revealed to be nothing but an abstraction contradictory in itself. I have proceeded thus far as if the datum itself required no construction. But it is clear that a series of existences (a succession) requires, as Kant saw, an activity to form the data into a complete whole and so, as a result, is not reducible to immediate consciousness—for the latter, on the contrary, is only apprehension of the instantaneous; and in the measure in which the instantaneous really supposes a whole that conditions it, it negates itself, and with it immediate consciousness is also negated. For the dualism previously posited between modes of existence corresponding to immediate consciousness on the one hand and to the intelligible content opposed to these modes—in some way as substance to accidents—on the other, we now seem to have substituted the idea of a constructive activity which is realised at one and the same time in the two orders and even makes possible what appeared to depend exclusively on immediate consciousness.

But here, I feel, we must take care. For in this relation to immediate consciousness from which we started out, are we not tempted to view existence itself as a sort of phenomenon begotten by the intelligible movement of that activity? Instead of on the one hand the order of what exists and on the other the order of what is above existence, we might end up with something like the re-absorption of existence into the womb of constructing thought. But has not thought already been defined by the very act by which it transcends immediate consciousness, and does it not negate itself in the measure in which it claims to make an abstraction of the immediate consciousness? Here we must try to dissipate a whole series of confusions.

My consciousness is actually 'occupied' by a certain perceptive content that it *ipso facto* posits as existing—and perhaps we are already up against the question of what is the relation between this judgment of existence (by the way, is it a judgment?) and the datum itself. Is this judgment constructive or does it really make explicit? And even if it serves to make explicit ought we not to say that it is for thought that it is constructed as making explicit, in relation to something explicit constructed similarly? Before trying to answer I think we should ask ourselves whether it is legitimate or not to set aside the fact that the content is already a (psychologically) constructed content. The chairs, the table, the fire etc. that I see in front of me are defined in function of the awarenesses of the potential consciousness (awarenesses of the consciousness that remain virtual); while the wood on which my paper rests, and that my hand touches, is itself as actual for me as it is susceptible of being, because it is in direct contact with a part of my body. It is evident that wherever there is no direct contact there occurs a construction of a state of consciousness that would correspond to the contact; and that this state of consciousness generally condenses itself into a sort of abstract symbol. But where there is contact I think there is a positing of an existant, an entirely spontaneous positing that cannot really be called a judgment. The accord of the senses may well provide a check, but nothing more, for the spontaneous positing is realised before the check has necessarily functioned. What relation is there between this positing and the datum?

Here it seems to me essential to note that the problem when raised, by the very fact of being raised, transforms its terms. It is presented in the form of a question bearing on a relation between distinct terms. But the terms are only distinct because the problem is raised. There is a solidarity between the distinctness of the terms and the very fact that the problem is raised. As soon as the problem is raised we are led on to say either that the positing, as existent, only makes something explicit that must lie *under* the datum (i.e. the very foundation of existence) or else that it is an addition made by thought. But a little simple reflection is enough to show that both solutions are equally inacceptable, because the very act by which we question ourselves on the basis of the union of the terms is precisely that which separates them. (It is probable that at the root of the equivocation that I have just indicated there lies a confusion between existence in general and spatial existence or externality.)

In this way we escape, I think, from the dilemma by which existence is turned either into a predicate or else into a sort of ontological quality that comes from outside and is added to that which exists. The notion of a judgment of existence bearing on an object is only substituted for the positing of a datum as existing achieved by the intervention of thought.

But it is important to understand that the immediate consciousness in which there is as yet no dualism between the datum and a form (?) of existence, can only be posited by an act by which reflective thought becomes aware of that which came from itself in the preceding act, and sets about making an abstraction of it.

Henceforward I will call this positing as existent (in which existence is not defined as a predicate) experience-limit; and say that experience-limit can only be thought by an act of reflection brought to bear on the dualism of the judgment of existence and of that on which this judgment is made. This experience-limit, inasmuch as the reflecting subject claims to disentangle its objective content, is reduced to a contact between a body bound up with a perceiving consciousness, and an external datum. Reflective thought thus posits the judgment of existence as being the transposition of the experience-limit into the intellectual order (where there are objects and judgments bearing on those objects); and this goes for any judgment of existence whatsoever. From this standpoint we can see how only that which is capable of entering into relations of contact, i.e. spatial relations with my body, can be said to exist. That may serve as a definition.

It is important to know how I am led to posit the judgment of existence, to dissociate existence from that which exists. To account for this I think we need to have recourse to the phenomena of becoming and also to illusions (hallucinations).

It is plain that it is only when reflective thought is brought to bear on it that the experience-limit reveals its spatial content. In itself, so to speak, it is the immediate considered in all its purity. But inasmuch as it reflects itself, it is necessarily converted into an affirmation regarding spatial data. To say that nothing exists save what is in space is merely to say that the experience-limit can only be translated into thought on condition that it is converted into an affirmation regarding spatial data.

From this point of view we can see how the problem of the existence of the external world strictly speaking has no meaning at all, for the external world is implicitly posited as something which exists (or does not exist) amongst other things.

And so if we can speak of thinking existence, it is solely in so far as consciousness—if it can so be expressed—can project itself backwards and itself conceive itself as realising the experience-limit as translated into a historical judgment. In this sense it can be said that imagination (conceived as the faculty thanks to which consciousness can be projected or transposed) is the transcendental condition of history.

So henceforward we must consider all claims to attribute existence to what cannot be represented in space as completely meaningless.

But then if we conceive of consciousnesses organised differently from ours, consciousnesses whose different sensorial apparatus enables them to apprehend data inaccessible to us, can we conceive the data in question as non-existent? To this we must reply that we can only represent such data to ourselves as in some way situated in space, and that hence there is no reason to deny their existence. Here I am tending to modify what I said earlier about the modes of existence in order to simplify it; but in last analysis there is no real difference between what I am saying here and what I said previously.

It would obviously be absurd to view all this in terms of a realism of a spatial character. As is immediately clear, the whole theory is in accord with Kantian idealism.

When we say that the experience-limit has a spatial foundation we only mean that, corresponding to each positing 'position' of a datum given as existing by whatsoever consciousness for another consciousness, there should be a determination of the spatial or physical relations between the organic body with which the first consciousness is bound up and the external world. These relations can be called the truth of the experience-limit. Of course the distinction between the two consciousnesses cannot present an empirical character but only a transcendental one; we have only stated the harmony between the immediate consciousness (experience-limit) and the reflective consciousness which determines relations in space, though the latter may be elsewhere or may be not actual.

January 21st

I can see the problem that now arises very clearly. Is truth possible regarding what is not manifested in space? The question itself involves a dilemma. Either there can be truth regarding that which cannot be posited as existing, or else we must admit a judgment of existence that has no bearing on spatial relations. If we reject the dilemma, we have to deny that truth is possible regarding what is not realised in space.

January 23rd

On what conditions can we think something to be truth? First of all we must determine the exact meaning of this problem, and the limits within which it can have a meaning. We are not concerned with finding a standard by which we can determine whether an idea (for instance) is true or not; but with knowing the conditions which an order must satisfy to permit of truth. But it may be claimed that as soon as we raise the problem we have already solved it, and that we have done so in a contradictory way that is equivalent to positing that it is insoluble. For we are involved in positing the transcendence of thought in relation to truth. But if thought is not in itself a form of truth, then truth has no existence, and if it is in itself a form of truth this determination is impossible. This reasoning seems to me only valid in appearance. Even if in itself thought is the form of truth, it still remains that this form must be separated for itself from the ore of contingency that encloses it; and that, on a higher level, posits that thought is not involved in the dualism in question.

January 24th

What relation are we to establish between the true and the thought that verifies it? Ordinary thought posits that the activity of veri-fication is contingent in relation to what is verified. It defines the true as being anterior to its verification. But is it absolutely inde-pendent of it? And what, strictly speaking, is the exact meaning of the question? If we are told that the capacity for verification enters into the very definition of the true, the first objection aroused in our minds is that some things are true though they have never been verified, and indeed are incapable of being veri-fied. (For instance historical events may have occurred without leaving a trace, and these are none the less true for being unveri-fiable.) So if we are to define the true in terms of its verifiability, it is on condition that we make a distinction between the material conditions of verification that may be lacking, and conditions that are purely ideal. But is this distinction valid? If not, then we must either give up defining the true in terms of the verifiable, or else think the true purely empirically in function of thought subject to restrictions of fact (and not merely of right). But this last alternative is plainly unacceptable. We are not prepared to accept the denial of the historical truth of something which, for factual reasons, we can no longer determine. And the reason for this is that we admit the existence of a link between what in practice can and what cannot be verified. Between one group of data and the other there is only a purely superficial difference, a difference that thought, out of duty to itself, must treat as negligible. The same applies to whatever is thought in space though escaping the observation of our present instruments. And so if the distinction between conditions of fact and conditions of right is invalid, we are forced purely and simply to abandon the possibility of verification as part of the definition of the true. In other words, if between what is relatively and what is absolutely unverifiable there is only a difference of degree—because that which is only relatively unverifiable cannot fail to be thought of as susceptible of truth—we are bound to recognise the possibility of truth even regarding what evades verification by definition. But has this any meaning? That which by definition evades verification is not that which cannot be reproduced but that which is not inserted into a whole that thought can reconstitute, that which is not in a determinable relation to the rest of the content of thought. Here again in what sense can we speak of truth?

Inasmuch as it can be predicated of the unknowable, truth is here confounded with existence, it is nothing more than an abstract denomination without content. If, then, anything is absolutely unverifiable it cannot be thought as susceptible of truth, it cannot be regarded as being distinguished only by the degree of what is relatively unverifiable. And in consequence no real (and formal) objection can be opposed to the idea that verifiability is a constituent of truth (since the factual and ideal conditions can be regarded as distinct).

But if nothing is absolutely unverifiable (here the meaning of the question itself is far from clear), does not the idea become purely tautological? And how can we continue to dissociate factual from ideal conditions? Supposing everything were verifiable ideally, yet we were unable to determine some particular point, this could only be for factual (hence contingent) reasons.

We could certainly affirm the identity of truth and of being; and the finiteness of thought, for which there are still things unverifiable, would reside in contingent circumstances with which thought is bound up. In this sense thought would have a double nature; an intelligible nature affirming the identity of being and the true (universal verifiability) and a contingent nature noting the factual restrictions which, according to the affirmation of the intelligible nature, in no way concern the rational content.

January 26th

To return to the problem I raised the day before yesterday. We know that ideal and actual conditions cannot be regarded as really separable unless *there is* something absolutely unverifiable. Only what does *there is* mean? For, as we can see immediately, this unverifiable something should not be thought to be unverifiable for reasons of fact. Hence it cannot be in space or even in time for, were it so given, reasons of fact alone might make verification impossible. But, if there are grounds for what I have already said, we cannot, strictly speaking, attribute existence to this unverifiable something (since existence resides in the relation to the immediate consciousness, posited ideally at least). And in this way the question of the relation of truth and of existence is resolved. For we have seen that truth implies the possibility of verification and on the other hand we have had to admit that what is outside space and time (that is, what cannot be thought as existent) is non-verifiable. We are incapable of not thinking truth about that which exists, but to speak of truth regarding what is outside existence is a contradiction in terms. This is a cardinal point and seems to me to be the very key to my thought. Meanwhile if the *there is* cannot be taken in an existential sense, either it is meaningless and we cannot speak of absolute unverifiability, or else we must define the meaning that it is possible to attribute to it.

I note that the agreement between what I am saying here and the Kantian view extends a long way. In fact, in both, truth, far from being defined as a logical form, is a function of what can be called potential experience. Kant's only mistake lay in his failure to see all the implications of this position, and the fact that he treated things-in-themselves as susceptible of a truth which cannot have being for our thought, which is a contradiction.

We cannot speak of absolute unverifiability unless we can in some way think a 'beyond' of existence. Notice that this 'beyond' is implied in the very notion of truth which just now seemed to us correlative with the notion of existence. The fact is that truth is only possible for thought when it liberates itself from the conditions of time and space. Truth only regards what is in space and in time, but a truth is only *for* thought which is defined non-spatially and non-temporally. Such thought cannot without contradiction posit itself as existing; and that is equivalent to saying that it is free.

Freedom, which is the condition of all verification, cannot itself be thought save as radically unverifiable, that is, as liberated from the conditions of existence which an object must satisfy if it is to be an object of verification (determined as truth).

When we speak of the Truth, of the Idea of the True, we involuntarily confuse the objective whole that seems to compose the integral system of the determinations of the true for our imaginative thought, with the free thought on which all verification depends.

In this way we find we have entered the realm of mind which is the realm of freedom.

But we need to be more specific. How can we justify or even merely describe the judgment by which we bind up the verification (the act of verifying) with thought that is transcendent in relation to all verification? The judgment in question, it seems, must be true or false. But then we fall into a contradiction. So we are forced to deny the dilemma absolutely and maintain that the judgment belongs to an order in which we can no longer talk of truth or falsehood. For the mind the true is defined as independent of the mind. This may be an illusion but for all that the mind is bound to posit truths as subsisting independently of the knowledge it has of them. Whereas the act by which the unverifiable is thought really constitutes it. This needs to be gone into more deeply. When thought reflects on the movement by which truths are constituted, it recognises the necessity of thinking that movement in function of a purely intelligible activity. But does this mean that that activity appears as a factual condition, as existent? Obviously not. The factual conditions that govern the search for truth should be capable of being defined psychologically. We can conceive the possibility of a psychology of the search for truth which would take all the subjective factors into account (interest, curiosity, desire for glory, etc.). . . . Strictly speaking all this can be regarded as object for verification. But the pure activity about which we are speaking is only capable of appearing to a reflection that itself bears on the conditions of the possibility of the true (not on the motives an individual follows when he is seeking for the truth). It is pure reflection, then, that introduces the idea of this activity—which is equivalent to saying that it brings it into being and creates it, because it itself is the very activity in question and is only capable of thinking itself as identical with it. The act by which I think freedom is the very act by which freedom comes to be. Here the ego seems in some sort to be the intelligible medium by which freedom effects the transition from idea to being. But it is clear that this act of creation is nothing save the *cogito*. Thought creates itself when it thinks itself; it does not discover itself, it constitutes itself.

Moreover, elementary reflection on the possible nature of an absolutely unverifiable something permits us to establish that this is only unverifiable when it constitutes and creates itself. Otherwise it would be a pure datum, a pure existant.

It must be noted that if the unverifiable in question is *a priori*, it can only be so inasmuch as it is constituted in opposition to an experience and in relationship with it.

When we suppose we are positing (in existence or still only objectively) the absolute independence of God, we are really on the contrary only binding up God with immediate consciousness. I never saw the antinomy so clearly. It amounts to saying that the problem of the existence of God can only be stated in mystical terms, in terms of experience. But on that plane it is destined to be answered negatively, because when the unverifiable descends into existence, it substitutes itself for existing causes, and when reflective thought comes back into it, it is obliged to operate in an inverse way and reintroduce the causes. Here lies the real dialectic of divine existence. Divine existence only is in immediate relation to empirical consciousness, whereas the relation is defined for reflection as action of an existant upon an existant, that is, as not of the divine order.

But we are anticipating what is to follow. All that I am

positing for the moment is that thought raises the problem of the existence of God by a contradictory step. Existence, to speak generally, is that from which all thought is able to set out, in the sense that thought cannot define itself save by the movement by which it transcends the immediate datum. Hence existence cannot at any level be regarded as a *demonstrandum*, a point at which we end up. As thought is unable to lay the foundations of the immediate relation—it can only surpass them—the idea of the demonstration of the existence of God involves a contradiction and collapses. If there is an experience of God (and only in this sense can we speak of the existence of God) that experience must be a point of departure and no more. Moreover, we know that the experience must, as such, seem to reason to be self-destructive.

It is perhaps time to recall that, though existence is the immediate relation, it is the immediate relation as it negates itself as such (and is posited as the suppression of the relation). To posit the existence of God really means positing a relation between God and the immediate consciousness, but explicitly it means denying that relation.

But how can thought affirm God without positing him as existing, in other words without even affirming him as a truth? Obviously it can only do this on condition that it is faith. Only here we need to dispel a whole crowd of ambiguities. We have to free ourselves of the idea that between faith and knowledge there is the same relation as the relation between probability and certainty. Faith is not an act by which we *approximate* to a judgment of existence which cannot be formulated as such (in view of our finite nature). Only if it transcends knowledge can faith justify itself—otherwise when we assign existence to God we are realising him in space and time.

January 27th

We need to define more accurately the kind of affirmation that has the character of faith. To begin with I note that if existence cannot properly be ascribed to God (from the standpoint of thought) neither can non-existence. To deny the existence of something is in fact to affirm that, for empirical reasons, that thing is not realised in experience. I believe that we must distinguish this radically from the act by which we affirm the impossibility of a given object. A square circle, for instance, is denied as essence before it is denied as existence, and the negation of the essence is alone important. But to deny the existence of God would not be to think of God as contradictory, it would be to say that God is not manifested to experience. So we perceive two radically distinct ways of denying the existence of God (always on the plane of thought). One of them comes back to treating God as an empirical object and saying "This object is not met with in experience." The other consists in the statement that God cannot be treated as an empirical object and that by consequence existence cannot be attributed to him. These two affirmations are more than distinct, they are inverse. The philosophers who admitted the ontological proof had the immense merit of seeing the absurdity of the first way of denying the existence of God. It is even absurd in virtue of its postulate; in that it posits God ideally as an empirical object, only then to deny him. The philosophers in question saw that the existence of God cannot possibly be denied on empirical grounds. They concluded that it was necessary to affirm his existence. At a deep level I am convinced that the argument is valid and that it is only in its form that it cannot stand. Because the reasons which render the negation of the existence of God impossible are the very reasons which militate against the affirmation of his existence. The real contradiction comes if we think of God as an existant—it is a useless contradiction that vitiates thesis and antithesis alike. Hence we must cease to base the denial of God on reasons of an empirical order (if God is not an empirical object it is obvious that he is not to be met with in experience). Nor can the denial of God be based on considerations of essence—on saying, for instance: "As the divine essence implies a contradiction it negates itself as essence." Here, I think, Leibnitz' argument can be accepted as genuinely making such a demonstration impossible. But I think we must tackle the question in another way. For our concern must be whether there can be essences which do not manifest themselves as existences. Of course it is possible to say that the existence that corresponds to the divine essence is that of the world itself. But that is either vague and inappropriate or else it is contradictory. As I have said elsewhere, existence cannot be attributed to the world in that the world is the *site* of things that exist.

At this point let us recall that essences are defined in function of thought, and hence of the movement by which thought elevates itself above existences. It seems to me that to set aside the negative but real relation which unites essence with that which exists is to suppress a perfectly real moment which is constitutive of essence and to make it something purely abstract. So it can be maintained that to deny God as existing is indirectly (but absolutely) to deny him as essence. Is this an absolute denial? Or can the negation of God as existing be converted in some way into an affirmation? We must return to this cardinal point.

To deny God as existing, in our sense, is to refuse absolutely to treat him as an empirical object, and at the same time and in consequence to deny (and the negation is transformed into a negation of itself, that is, into the negation of a negation) that anything in experience, that anything in that which exists, can be *incompatible* with God, can *exclude* God. In this way the negation of the existence of God is converted into an affirmation of the power of God as transcendent as regards all that is empirically possible. This links up with Leibnitz.

But obviously here we have to face some serious objections. Setting aside all subsequent difficulties it may be argued at the outset that the foregoing process of argument is fundamentally vicious. On what grounds have we posited that from the standpoint of thought, existence cannot be attributed to God? Is it not because we think that existence as defined in a particular way is incompatible with God himself, who is viewed as a determined content (as essence); and does not the whole pseudo-demonstration rest on an ingenious arrangement of concepts? Here we must take care. I maintain, first of all, that we are not free to think of existence as anything other than I have said, that is to say, other than the relation to an immediate consciousness (negating itself as such, moreover, inasmuch as it is not thought). But the weightiest objection is still to come. Do we not set out by defining God in a special way only so as then to deny him existence? This objection does not seem to me to hit the mark. In whatsoever way thought thinks God, it is unable to posit him as a datum given to the subject in an external way. I do not say that it is impossible that an empirical relation should appear to be established between God and the subject. What I say is that this occurs not from the standpoint of thought but from the standpoint of the immediate consciousness, a very different matter. Notice, moreover, that even in order to deny God we must first of all think him in some way—otherwise our negation is purely indeterminate.

But there is another difficulty that seems to me much more serious. If, from the fact that nothing in experience can exclude God (be stronger than God), we conclude that God is at least power, are we not playing with words? And what meaning can we attribute to the word power?

We have seen that God is beyond even essence, which amounts strictly speaking to saying that there is no divine nature. But in that case are we not making him indeterminate? Does not 'being' mean 'being something'?

At this point we need to subject the result we have reached so far to rigorous examination. We have said that the negation of God as existing entails the affirmation of God as transcendent. This means that we must think God as transcending every determination whatsoever. Are we going to end up with the Alexandrian *One*? We must recognise, I think, Plotinus' idea that God *is* veritably for us only in so far as we participate in him. But it is important that we should transpose the surviving elements of objective emanationism in Plotinus into the order of mind, the subjective order. I do not think that Alexandrianism can really help us to resolve the difficulties we now have to deal with.

We know that if God can and must be thought as power, it is only on condition that by power we do not understand an existing power susceptible of functioning as cause amongst other causes. But how are we to conceive the relation of such transcendent power to the order of things existing? It is clear at the outset that the possibility of a direct relation between one and the other must be denied absolutely. An objective doctrine of creationism must be rejected out of hand. As I see things, the process we adopt so as to demonstrate the legitimacy of our affirmation of God implies the rejection of creationism. Further on we shall see whether creationism can and must reappear in a deeper sense (the idea of divine fatherhood preceding and justifying the idea of creation). If, then, God is conceived as a freedom it is on condition that that freedom is not thought of as creating the world.

But is it not possible to object that the proof by means of the idea exhibits the same defects as the other proofs? If the idea is denied, what remains of the proof? I believe that this will take us much deeper into the question. The objection rests on the implicit postulate that the idea can be false, that it participates in the order of the true and the false; that hence it supposes a transition from the idea to the *ideatum*, a ticklish transition whenever the idea is not constructed as in mathematics. But here we must bear in mind how very unacceptable that postulate is. The affirmation regarding God is not, cannot be, and must never be regarded as an idea. It essentially partakes of what, earlier, I called the 'absolutely unverifiable.'

January 28th

But if we are dealing with the unverifiable, are we not also involved in the arbitrary? So as to guarantee ourselves against the risk of criticism it looks as though we ought to be able to establish a link between the unverifiable that is the cogito and the unverifiable that is God. Thus stated, the problem takes on terms that are almost Cartesian. But is it not insoluble? For either we have an implication of notions and do not depart from the logic of essence —but that is impossible because the cogito itself is not an essence —or else we seem forced to abandon the discovery of any necessity whatever, any basis of mediation. The problem could only be solved were it possible to determine the conditions of what I have elsewhere called a logic of freedom, that is, an order assigned by freedom to itself. But are we in a position to deduce such an order from the cogito? There seems to be a hiatus between the cogito and the affirmation regarding God. Can it be bridged?

The first moment of the solution seems to me to be as follows: I have already said that the unverifiable which is the cogito— that is, that which can be called formal freedom—is only for the free act that apprehends it. Here we must avoid being taken in by the image we use, the image of discovery, which is fallacious. Thought does not discover itself, it is constituted, and the cogito which is the very act of discovery (rather than an object susceptible of being discovered) is identical with the reflection on the cogito, it only *is* for this reflection and it only is this reflection (inasmuch as it is act). The 'I think' is neither a datum nor a form, it is an act. Here I think Descartes penetrated more deeply than Kant. The unverifiable, then, is a function of the free act, it is the track of it, it is the entirely negative expression of the fact that the free act becomes for itself a mystery as soon as it is transformed into objective thought (it being characteristic of objective thought that it negates itself for the benefit of its object). I do not think we can go further than this in determining the idea of the unverifiable.

But how can we get beyond that first free act—which seems likewise to be the last? At first sight this difficulty appears inextricable.

Note that we have made some real progress, for we have broken with formalism. We are no longer taken in by that post-Kantian formalism that hypostatises the *I think* and so turns it into a sort of timeless form (I am thinking especially of T. H. Green). But for all that are we not still the prisoners of some sort of ambiguous and sterile subjectivism?

We already know, at least, that the unverifiable is far from arbitrary, that, on the contrary, it is the source of every rule and the principle of any order whatsoever.

The first link between the cogito and the affirmation of God is, I think, manifest even to purely external reflection, reflection limited to bringing together the terms on which it bears. We have seen, in fact, that God can only be defined as the affirmation of absolute freedom. Now a freedom can only be affirmed by a freedom. As long as thought is not raised to the level of the cogito, as long as it does not think itself as freedom (as free act thinking itself) it can have no real freedom and hence there is no divine freedom.

But this takes us more deeply into the problem. Does not all that we have so far said about divine power (posited as non-existing) also apply to the cogito which likewise transcends all experience, all possible existence and even all truth? When we dissociated the cogito from the affirmation regarding God, were we not being taken in by words? Moreover, does not the distinction between two freedoms now seem absurd? At the heart of thought thinking itself (which is neither my thought nor the thought of a God but simply Thought) are we not obliged to identify two moments that reflection when superficial allows us to dissociate?

What makes the question particularly obscure is this. We have said that God, by the fact that he could not be posited as existing (on the plane of thought), needed to be thought as transcending even the world of essences. But what is the God with which the process of our argument is now involved? If he is an essence, the process of argument destroys itself; if he is not an essence what is he? Must we admit that the process of argument on the whole tends to make explicit the initial content on which it bears (in the sense in which even the Hegelian type of synthetic dialectic can be regarded as a 'making explicit')? If God is not an essence, he remains an affirmation (an act): but how, in its turn, is this affirmation qualified? It seems it must have been in virtue of an intrinsic qualification of the affirmation that we looked on ourselves as being correct in our denial that the affirmation bears on an existant. Does not this qualification (by the very fact that it exists) convert the affirmation into an essence? If, on the other hand, the qualification is lacking we cannot see on what the negation, which is the nerve of the process of argument, can rest. This point is really vital. Unless it can be elucidated argument is not only invalid, it is meaningless.

I think we can set aside an initial difficulty which would be insurmountable if admitted. Up to a certain point it is possible to be in the order of the qualified without being in the order of essence. To grasp this we only need to introduce the notion of the mode of affirmation (we can conceive pure, absolute affirmation, the verb; qualification, not essence). In that way we posit the problem in more precise and clearer terms, and realise that the initial difficulty lay in the grammatical form in which the argument was formulated. What we must say is: the affirmation regarding God is defined by a particular mode which is incompatible with the notion of an existant, etc.; in other words *faith* (which is what we shall call that mode) belongs to the order of affirmation which, etc. . . .

If anyone says that that mode of affirmation is only defined in function of an object, an essence, we can answer that the real (valid) relation is the inverse; that the object is only the translation into the language of knowledge (of that which is posited) of the privileged act that is faith. In this way the problem of God makes way for the real problem which is that of faith.

But here traps still lie in wait for us. Obviously the faith we are talking about here is not a psychological state. Moreover, we must be clear that faith cannot be thought as a form, it must be thought as bound up with a reality. Here the difficulty and even the danger of my attitude becomes clear. We are unquestionably concerned with thinking an affirmation (as we are speaking of faith), but it is an affirmation which cannot and must not be dissociated from that on which it bears. In so far as faith is denied for the benefit of what it affirms (which is then treated as an object), faith is converted into theoretical thought and is suppressed. The act by which I think faith should be the act by which I deny the dissociation; by which, in consequence, I deny both subjectivism and realism alike. We must grasp that the realist and subjectivist attitudes both imply the possibility of such a dissociation (in the first case the accent is on one aspect, in the second on the other). There is no internal distinction between them. The distinction is purely one of opinion (*Meinung*).

Hence to think faith is to think faith in God. When I say that faith bears on God I add nothing to the idea of it. Here there are two aspects that I must posit as conjoined. If we like we can say that God is the reality of faith, but on condition we do not interpret this in an objective sense.

In this way we dispose of a whole series of difficulties and, furthermore, we state the problem of the metaphysical justification of faith.

Even the terms of this problem must be precisely expressed. We are concerned with justifying faith as faith, that is, faith that is not converted into certitude. On what conditions is this possible? Clearly justification must not go back to establishing an implication of notions (cf. what was said above). Naturally what was said earlier regarding the transition from the cogito to the affirmation regarding God also applies here. To put it briefly we have to ask ourselves how the mind can effect the transition from the cogito to faith, from the *I think* to the *I believe*; that is to say, how one free act can depend on another free act (as the link between them cannot be derived from a logic of essence—this last term being given the meaning it bears in current philosophy, not the strict Hegelian sense). Or, to put the question in another form, how can such dependence have value (*gelten*) without being either logical in the strict sense or objective? The difficulty of determining what *value* is, is bound up with the fact that in the theoretical or even in the ethical order (which is only a transposition of it) the current meaning is manifestly of no value.

It seems there cannot be value (*gelten*) for thought outside a certain formalism, but it must be noticed that the formalism that can concern us here must not bear on thought in general (otherwise we would remain in what I have called the logic of essence). Here there can only be question of what, for lack of a better term, I shall call an individual formalism. Faith is only possible on condition that from the cogito there springs forth that which is individual.

January 29th

I maintain—and this is a cardinal point—that, in the *I think* and in the *I believe*, the subject does not play one and the same part. I have said that the ego is the medium of freedom, that is to say, with the cogito the ego expresses the act by which freedom posits itself. But this ego is universal, or it is at least suppressed in the universality of the thinking subject. Inasmuch as I think, I am universal, and, if knowledge is dependent on the cogito, that is precisely in virtue of the universality inherent in the thinking ego. In faith there is nothing of the kind. It is precisely the absence of this clear distinction that causes the equivocations which have always played around the idea of a '*Vernunftreligion*'. Either religion is reduced to a totality of purely rational affirmations, that is, assertions valid for thought in general, and so is no more than an abstract and empty deism (and is arbitrary as well—I shall return to this point); or else it ceases to be based on a universal and is thus no more than a sentimental and purely subjective scaffolding. The true road lies between the two.

The subject of faith is not thought in general. Thought in general in so far as it is reflected (and, as a result, is objectified) appears to itself as purely abstract, purely indeterminate, a formal condition and nothing more. The subject of faith, on the contrary, must be concrete. Does that mean that the subject of faith is the empirical content which I have called individual? Without going back over the ambiguities of the idea of the ego conceived in a realist sense (James, Bradley), it is worth observing that the subject of faith cannot be a datum given—in any case it would only be a datum that would suppress itself as datum, setting itself aside in an effort at reconstruction. Just as we cannot accept the objective relation between faith and God (cf. above) so, as regards the rôle of the ego in faith, we must be careful over the insufficiency and even the unreality of the relation of subject to act.

I am tempted to say at this point that, in the measure in which sociology has reacted against moral and psychological atomism, it has smoothed the path for a religious philosophy such as the one I am trying to define.

This is as much as to say that if faith cannot be conceived as a relation of forces (a sort of dynamism operating between objectively realised terms) neither can it be assimilated in any way whatever with the act by which a subject determines an object.

Still speaking very roughly, faith appears as the act by which a thought, which denies itself as fixed and existing subject, re-constructs itself as (willed and created) subject by participation in God (who seems to be defined as the mysterious medium of this re-creation).

This is very obscure and the heavy task of working it out still lies ahead. But the first point consists in finding out how the complex act that is faith (which for us has taken the place of the objective demonstration of a divine existence or essence) can be regarded as bound up with the cogito. The question comes back to this: how can the cogito surpass itself? It is clear that the individuality that is realised in faith must be beyond the purely abstract universality of the *I think*, it must comprehend it and surpass it.

We know already that there can be no question of discovering a principle of interior necessity by which the cogito can surpass itself. We are in the order of freedom, that is to say, in the order of that which is capable of not being. I must repeat that were faith converted into certitude it would be denied as faith, and all the determinations I have given to it so far would lose their meaning. But how are we to escape from the realm of the arbitrary? For thought is extremely distrustful of what is capable of not being. Note, however, that the cogito itself does not escape from this contingency. The reflection of thought upon itself may well appear to itself as necessary, but for all that it is impossible to discover an internal link that allows us to account for the passage from pure physical becoming to the act in which thought is created by thinking itself. The universality appertaining to the *I think* is not even—we must take care here—the purely hypothetical universality that appertains to a law. It is unconditional. And unconditionality is the mark of freedom. Thus we have a reassuring example—we should keep reminding ourselves of it— of the possibility of thinking a free act which is nevertheless not arbitrary (the appearance of arbitrariness only arises when abstract thought claims to deduce the free from the necessary and the unconditional from the derivative, because in the necessary and the derivative it takes its point of departure).

So even if we limit ourselves to the cogito we are for all that in the metaphysical order, that is to say the order of freedom (I would be inclined to say that contingency is freedom regarded from the point of view of the object).

On what conditions can the cogito transcend itself? And, first and foremost, what makes the act of transcendence possible (in general, i.e. independently of its particular determinations)?

Light can be thrown on this question, I think, by some further considerations. We have seen that the *I think* could be converted into a form, and we have denied the legitimacy of this conversion. But even the fact of the possibility of this conversion is instructive (nothing informs us better about truth than error: or rather the conditions that make error possible must be closely linked with the conditions which make truth possible; and the same holds for good and evil). The conversion was only possible through the medium which confronted the *I think* with the empirical material and hence in some way interpreted their relation. As a result the cogito was already in some fashion transcended. But the two terms were only brought together in a quite superficial way which left the question of how they could co-exist untouched. Between the empirical content which is the datum given to the *I think*—and by reflection on which the *I think* is constituted—and the *I think* itself, no relation is thinkable. And in this way it seems that the thought that reflects the cogito is driven on to the rocks of Spir's radical dualism which places an intelligible nature and an empirical (irrational) nature in absolute opposition to one another (at least inasmuch as it is consequent). Can such a dualism be avoided, and if so on what conditions? Pure formalism, which we have already rejected, has the extremely serious defect of being unable to account for the act that makes it possible, for the act by which the conversion of the cogito into form is operated—and indirectly for the cogito itself. Can we now remain content with a philosophy that denies the possibility of transcending the cogito, and is satisfied with positing it as irreducible to any empirical content whatsoever? We should observe, I think, that, though what is posited here does not imply a contradiction, it cannot be regarded as satisfactory. What relation can I establish between myself as thinking, and myself as empirical, (that is to say, in so far as I enfold the universe, for between me and the world there are infinitely complex relations in which, in last analysis, all reality is involved)? Can I deny that there is a relation? Or can I try to derive the thinking ego from the empirical ego? This last solution, as we already know, is not acceptable. It takes on a semblance of coherence only by substituting for the act of *I think* a complex psychism with which this act (inasmuch as it is intelligible and unverifiable) cannot and should not be confused. To be possible, the truth of the relation that we are claiming to establish requires the cogito itself, and the problem consists in integrating the cogito into an empirical synthesis. And as I see things this is enough to refute any empiricism whatsoever. Moreover, we know that thought cannot negate itself for the benefit of the immediate consciousness. To that extent we seem to be cornered in a dualism. But here one observation is imperative. If we deny that there is a truth in the relation of the cogito to the empirical ego, do we not in some way re-establish that truth? By positing the truth of the dualism do we not thereby reconstitute the very thing we claimed we are denying? Does not the dualism lead us to this dilemma: either we genuinely think two realities, which yet inasmuch as they are realities must have some common measure and so partake in an intelligible whole, or else we posit one of these realities as pure negation (and hence self-negating even as dualism)—unless we posit the transcendent possibility of a synthesis of that which for us is dialectical, which amounts to thinking a truth of this relation while denying ourselves the right to think it.

From this we would have to conclude that thought must posit the relation of the *I think* to the empirical order as unverifiable; that is, it must affirm the absolute impossibility of an objective definition (even, in fact above all a dualistic one) of such a relation. Of course there is still Fichte's solution, consisting in the deduction of the empirical from the *I think*; but unfortunately that deduction seems to imply the reduction of the contingent to the rational (which, as we have seen, is absurd, for thought cannot affirm itself and constitute itself save by the movement by which it transcends an existing datum which must needs appear to it as contingent). We must note, furthermore, that the deduction necessarily stops at the point at which empirical individuality— the only individuality that matters here—is posited. If, then, the relation of the cogito to the empirical ego is unverifiable (that is to say, not susceptible of truth), we posit at least the possibility of faith. It might possibly be maintained that the transition from absolute indetermination to the act of faith constitutes a *saltus mortalis*. The only truth in this observation is that the transition must be regarded as entirely free. To speak of the transition as arbitrary is to treat faith as a hypothesis without justification on to a state of doubt and objective indetermination. Now faith is nothing of the kind. Faith is not a hypothesis —it is essential to grasp that point. Faith is the act by which the mind fills the void between the thinking ego and the empirical ego by affirming that they are linked transcendentally; or, rather, faith is the act by which the mind is made, the *mind*—i.e. the mind as a living and active reality, the mind as distinct from the thinking subject. Doubtless the dissociation of these various moments can and must seem arbitrary. It is only by abstract analysis that we can recognise them, single them out and give them names.

But how are we to comprehend the transcendent unity of the thinking ego and of the empirical ego that the mind affirms so as to be mind? The unity is in function of the freedom that wills it. Here we return to what we have already said regarding non-existence, and it is here that the demonstration we then sketched out belongs. Now the transcendental unity is capable of appearing as non-arbitrary, as *valid*, but only as valid for the mind, that is for thought which has transcended itself, for the being that wills to be mind. In this way we can at last conceive the relation of human freedom to divine freedom which is the central mystery of the Christian religion; and we can finally grasp how the individuality that faith requires as its pivot is created. I would be prepared to say that by the act of faith that posits the non-contingence of the empirical ego (and hence of the whole world) the mind actualises that principle of freedom which in the cogito was still only virtual and even ran the risk of being converted into a pure form of necessity.

It seems to me that, however general they are, these first indications already give us a glimpse of the real relation between science and religion. While science is the concern of the abstract ego, the cogito, and as a result reposes on the act of a freedom which has not yet reached the stage of being for itself, religion is based on the very mind itself, that is to say on the individualised thought which has posited an intimate relationship between itself (as abstract) and its integral experience, by means of the act of faith. Through faith I affirm a transcendental foundation for the union of the world and of my thought, I refuse to think myself as purely abstract, as an intelligible form hovering over a world which is what it may be, and in which necessity is only the reverse of contingency. Thus the order of science is relative to faith in the measure in which the *I think* is subordinated to the *I believe*—where abstract thought (the thinking subject) is subordinated to the mind.

But is this not ambiguous? Are we not now confronted with two alternatives: either this transcendent truth is that of a cause, or else it is so indeterminate that it serves no purpose. (In the first instance it remains objective and has no validity.) But that objection implies an absolute misunderstanding. We are not concerned with explanations, there is no question of hypothesis. The freedom realised in the act of faith is no longer the virtual freedom of the cogito which is suppressed in its object, it is actual freedom, freedom for its own sake. The only thinkable link between God and the world is established in faith and by faith, that is to say it resides in the perpetual mediation of the believer.

But are we not making divine reality dependent on the act that thinks it? Is not God consumed in the subjective affirmations that seem to beget him? This is important and must be emphasised. The mind, as we have said, is only created as mind by faith in God. But this faith in God involves the affirmation that it is itself conditioned by God, that is to say, the affirmation of the divine fatherhood. Which means that *the mind posits God as the positer*. Can this be called pure illusion, a kind of phenomenal game of reflection, which in reality comes back to the positing of the mind by itself? But it would be necessary to begin by asking whether, in the order of mind, the distinction between appearance and reality can continue to subsist. I think it is possible to show—I have done it elsewhere, though from a rather different standpoint—that that distinction is entirely relative to the movement of thought. The distinction is suppressed in the act of faith which restores to the world its reality. By that act, in fact, abstract thought grasps itself as moment and brands with invalidity the condemnations it brought to bear on things when it took itself as indication of reality. In the kingdom of heaven there is no room for illusion and error, and I would be tempted to say (perhaps this needs to be verified) that the rationalist criticisms that are made against thaumaturgy are both well founded (in the sense that from the standpoint of rational thought a miracle is impossible), and also absolutely pointless because they come from outside and are external to what they bear on (by the very fact that they are criticisms) and because they imply the dualism that is suppressed when the order of faith and of the miraculous is posited. It follows that the problem of the miraculous must be resolved in a negative way for anyone who is not a saint. The possibility of the miraculous is capable of becoming apparent to whoever conceives the distinction between the two orders, but possibility is superseded by reality for the saint who accomplishes the miracle, and for those whom he enables to participate in the grace that has touched him.

But the saint is only really *for himself.* For anyone who reflects on sanctity, by an analytical necessity sanctity is suppressed. In this sense we can say, I think, that the saint can only be the object of a cult—cult being defined here as the partici- pation of a mind in another mind which it does not accept as an object or datum. It must be emphasised that the science of religions *discovers nothing*, for its very definition involves the suppression of its object. A cult some humble person devotes to a saint of whom he knows nothing and of whom, doubtless, he forms an image which is gross and inexact historically, has more *being* than the volumes piled up by men of learning so as to reduce the saint to normal proportions or even to establish that he never existed. Yet here a difficulty arises, which we shall certainly come across in a more general form. Does not the religious cult purport to depend on objective affirmations? Are not the miracles posited to be facts? Yet in the order of facts and objective affirmations there is evidently room for illusion and error, and hence the possibility of illusion and of error seems to be introduced into the heart of religion. Here we come up against the question of the measure in which historical elements may intervene in the field of religion.

There can be no question that in so far as it is claimed that the affirmations of the religious consciousness are supported by historical certainties their meaning is profoundly changed and they run the risk of being swept away in the maelstrom that inevitably carries such certainties away. In so far as those certain- ties are presented as objective they have no characteristic by which they can escape investigation, that is, dissolution; and in so far as they are affirmations of a cultural kind they are not objective. But can we agree that the historical factor should be excluded entirely from religion? I think that would be a dangerous mistake. For it implies that very dissociation of empirical from rational elements which, as we have already seen, involves the absolute negation of religion (specifically considered). But does this not lead us, by a roundabout way, back to the subjectivism that we have already denounced? If, independently of the empirical or historical reality possessed by its object, worship seems to me to justify itself, is it not because the object does not really matter, because the essence of worship resides in the act itself, because the act, in opposition to the illusions of appearance, has a truth in itself (in appearance the act is subordinated to the object, in reality the object is ·only the purely contingent expression of the act)? This difficulty is very serious. It looks as if we must either re-establish the dualism, or else posit for the object an ambiguous reality which is non-empirical. Clearly we cannot affirm dogmatically that the origins of any particular devotion invariably provide it with a justification. Such an affirmation would lack any valid guarantee.

This is the worst difficulty I have come across so far. For it turns on conciliating the fact that in the realm of religion there are objective affirmations—and hence the danger of reintroducing the dualism of appearance and reality—and of the fact that by its very nature the realm of religion excludes any such dualism. The difficulty is that if we suppress the element of objectivity we re-establish the dualism absolutely. Just as it may well be that the incorruptible soul is only revealed when it is incarnate in a corruptible body, so it looks as though religion can only become reality when it is manifested in affirmations that preserve their relation with history and thereby involve seeds of death. But I can see a solution. For the saint, for whom all is actual, and with regard to whom all is ordered, (Christ posited as Idea), the historical basis is not necessary. Eternity is embodied with the actual, it is actual. Whereas for someone who only participates in sanctity in a purely empirical way, history and time become important, bringing with them that relation to an objective element which has within it the seeds of death. In other words, the difficulty would be resolved for anyone who could see that the state of affairs that provokes it is itself relative to a moment which cannot at any level be viewed as ultimate in the development of the religious consciousness (a development posited by thought as soon as it conceives a saint). In the measure in which the dualism of appearance and reality is not entirely overcome (and it can only be absolutely overcome in the saint, the absolute mediator) it is natural and necessary that the non-eliminatable element of objectivity should survive—the existentially posited element that is the defect of the ordinary believer's religion. The real believer has no need to touch (i.e. to know) in order to believe. As long as devotion still implies objective affirmations we have a failure to realise absolute religion—the religion of the saint for whom all is pure actuality, all is revelation, for whom, in a word, subjectivism has no meaning and is confounded with an objectivism of the most artless kind—because ideality is entirely absorbed in spirituality.

January 31st

I feel the need to return more methodically to the series of questions I only touched on yesterday, for it is important to visualise them clearly. The transition from the act of faith to a historical religion is far from clear to me. It means raising the question of the relation of religious philosophy to the historic religions. We are not concerned with constructing the historical religions. The Hegelian idea of a parallelism between dialectics and history is one better entirely rejected. At all events it implies a metaphysical postulate that I do not admit. But that being so it appears that religious philosophy must either construct a rational religion without relation to history, or else receive its historical material from outside. The first solution has already been rejected. The idea of a rational religion excluding all relation to history is the very negation of the act by which the mind wills and creates itself. But what then? The historical material we are obliged to adopt seems incapable of adjustment to the framework of reflection save by a procedure that is arbitrary and purely superficial. Beyond question this second solution is even more unacceptable than the first. Furthermore it implies the very dualism of history and reflection that the act of faith, when realised, negates. But how are we to establish a hierarchy in the religions that exist? If it is objective such a hierarchy can have no metaphysical value; it must needs be based on a principle whose very essence is extra-religious. At the threshold of the act by which a mind adopts a historical religion the philosopher's task is over. But in this way are we not ending up at a new kind of historico-religious formalism which posits the necessity of some sort of historical landmark? Are we not recreating that very dualism of matter and form which we seemed obliged to exclude from the realm of religious thought? On what does this apparently insurmountable difficulty depend? Strictly speaking it seems to me to depend on the fact that, when pushed to its furthest extent, reflection on religion negates itself. Such reflection only achieves the entire suppression of the dualism of matter and form when it is itself suppressed and is converted into belief. For reflection is inseparable from some kind of dualism. The formalism we have now attained, however transcendent, is still formalism. Only in so far as reflection achieves a grasp of the intimate solidarity that exists between itself and formalism in general can it manage to recognise the relativity of this attitude, to think of itself as suppressed, and to pass over to faith. In this sense faith appears as reflection that has reflected itself, and as a result has been negated. The mode of thinking proper to philosophy is the only one that possesses in itself a sufficiently active and sufficiently conscious principle of reflection and negation to be capable of suppressing itself. The plurality of religions only seems existent to reflective thought when it has not yet been elevated to the level of faith— when faith still remains an exterior object for it. From the standpoint of faith there is only one religion and there can only be one.

Here an objection forces itself on us. It consists in saying that such a unique and absolutely individualised belief appears to a knowing subject as function of a whole series of social and historical conditions by which it is completely determined. But this point of view, as we have already seen, is relative. The critique of absolute knowledge as I have outlined it elsewhere allows us to grasp that, as the plane of scientific knowledge is a subordinate plane, it is impossible to maintain that the historian of belief can transcend the belief that he studies (because he denies it).

So genuine belief appears to reflective thought as that which reflective thought turns into when it is negated. Here I think I have just given a definition of grace. For inasmuch as such self-negation is an object of reflection it is destroyed, that is to say reflection is reborn from its own ashes. The genuine negation of reflection seems possible only by the intervention of a transcendent power. Conversion is only thinkable by the intervention of grace. But is conversion thinkable? From the point we have reached it is clear that there can be no question of practical observation and confirmation. Conversion does not create conversion, or rather, if it does so, it is only by purely internal action and not because it is example observed (in the sense in which the observation of a physical fact begets belief in the fact).

February 1st

But what I have said must be subordinated to the question of whether conversion is really thinkable (other than as a pure empirical datum which, as we know, is nothing). If conversion is thinkable it must be something that is in no way a datum given by the fact that it is thought.

February 2nd

What reasons can we have for thinking something of a given thing? Notice that the hiatus between the *Gedachtsein* and the *Gegebensein* occurs equally for all that goes to make a nature, for all that is empirical. So may not what we have called grace be capable of reduction to the totality of the practical conditions, of the favourable conditions, that determine a conversion? Were we to admit this, either we would have to deny that conversion creates a new intelligibility, or else we would have to realise that intelligibility, interpret it psychologically and render it dependent on the factual conditions we imagined we had discovered. The latter solution seems to me purely verbal. An order is not defined in function of psychological conditions. So we must purely and simply deny that conversion creates a new intelligibility, and see mere appearance there—in other words, for the illusion undergone by the believer we must substitute the real intellection of the psychologist for whom the illusion is object. Has such a substitution any value or even any meaning whatsoever? It implies the negation of all that we have taken so much trouble to establish, it supposes that the dualism of appearance and reality is capable of a meaning in the order of faith, or else—which comes to the same thing—it posits that the thinking subject in general is transcendent in relation to the real individuality who is the subject of faith. Indeed it is based on an utter confusion of categories. To deny the reality of conversion is almost equivalent to denying the validity of the description someone makes of what he sees, hears or imagines, and substituting instead a description of his cerebral condition. But for all that it must be admitted that if we posit this a serious difficulty arises. Does not the argument prove too much? From this standpoint could we not claim that all visions (even hallucinations) are transcendent in relation to the psychological explanation we claim to give of them? How, in a word, can we establish a discrimination in the heart of experiences without recourse to objective criteria, criteria analogous to those we would use in demonstrating the intervention of some kind of cause? It seems as though either we are bound to remain forever in the realm of objective psychologism, or else we are obliged to deny it on all counts—which would result in a sort of untenable mysticism; or—third alternative—that we must make a discrimination the basis of which we cannot see. Here as previously it is easy to see the empirical function that could appertain to the Church. Just as the Church guards the deposit of history, so it claims to be alone competent in the matter of discrimination. In both it appears as the incarnation of religious objectivity—hence its grandeur and at the same time its weakness. But this is no philosophical solution. The philosophical question concerns the criteria that can be recognised as valid. And, moreover, what is a criterion of value in these matters? We know (cf. as I have already said) that it can neither be strict moral efficacity, nor evidence conceived in an objective sense, nor in general any of the criteria that can be used in the theoretical order. As the simplest reflection shows the problem cannot even be stated in elementary criteriological terms. There can be no question of discerning amongst possible causes, for we already know that divine action cannot be thought as a cause amongst other causes, and it is therefore absurd to ask what are the signs by which we can recognise whether it is a given cause and not some other that has operated in a particular case. But then are we not victims of the superficial subjectivism that posits the transcendental reality of all experience as experience? For now we seem to be forced to a choice between metaphysical phenomenalism of that type and a doctrine of objectivity whose impossibility we have just seen. But in reality this superficial subjectivism is nothing or rather it is an imperfect realism; for under the cloak of subjectivity it posits no more than an incompletely thought-out objectivity, it does no more than realise experience improperly. Now the fact that such realism is impossible has been established by all the foregoing inquiries. Only if we set all realism aside can we think the act of faith. There is not a faith of x and another of y. There is only faith. The act of faith is indivisible. The individuality realised in and through it is not the immediate and atomic individuality which overcame and negated itself in the *I think*, it is the individuality that has transcended the *I think* and has recovered possession of itself in a creative synthesis. The faith of others *is not* quite absolutely for me. I think it possible to establish that a universal religion or, more simply, a religion, can only be founded on the kind of preliminary solipsism (elsewhere I have called it practical monadism) by which an individuality is created. And hence the problem of grace can only be posited in infinitely more complex terms, those I began to suggest the day before yesterday, terms that transcend all psychology. I would like to make those terms more definite.

Note that the question of how conversion can be regarded as thinkable has not yet been answered. We came up against a contradiction which was, at least seemingly, insoluble, namely that when reflection negates itself it remains its own object, and hence the free act does not achieve real self-realisation. If it can be thought as realised, that is only because of the intervention of grace. But granted that an appeal to an objective and external causality could only be an absolutely sterile subterfuge—what does this mean? How can we think grace?

It seems to me that I have not yet at my disposal a method that allows me to throw adequate light on the problem. Hence I can only proceed in a stumbling and provisional way. Grace implies the absolute irreducibility of the strictly religious mode of intelligibility in relation to all objective intelligibility, and in consequence it also implies an absolutely discontinuous transition from the cogito to real individuality. In this way, it seems to me, we can understand the gulf that still subsists between the act of faith, as I defined it earlier, and grace as it presents itself to us now. The act of faith is indeed reflection negating itself (in that it denies the dualism between itself and the empirical world), but in so far as the negation of reflection is itself converted into an object of reflection, the act of faith appears to it as a sort of transcendental auto-suggestion—and inasmuch as reflection triumphs in its effort at self-negation, it seems condemned to see grace as the objectivised product of this effort considered as illusory, as the arbitrary suppression of the re-establishment of possession over itself, by which it has converted the negation of itself into an object. I confess I do not find it difficult to think of reflection's return on itself in terms of a relapse; the act by which I think it as such is necessarily posited as transcendent in relation to the return—but for all that the act itself is in danger of becoming an object again, and so on.

The question, then, is how grace can be thought as real, how thought can manage to condemn as invalid the act by which it can claim to see grace as the illusory and fixed expression of an activity that is unable to be *for itself*. Even before this question there arises the question of what 'real' means here—and whether we are not re-establishing beyond grace some kind of norm to which we could claim to reduce it. And going even further— we need to know whether this reduction is not contradictory. Now here the answer is simple. To speak of reality in connection with grace is to say nothing whatever, it is to posit irreducibility in function of a system of reduction and be involved in a contra- diction in terms. In that way the further questions immediately undergo a complete transformation. For we have to say that the question of reality cannot be posited regarding grace, for grace lies outside the categories of modality. Just as from divine non- existence we can deduce the validity of the affirmation of the divine, so here, and in a similar way, grace is posited as beyond the categories, because a negation would restore it to a plane from which it has been excluded.

February 3rd

But is this more than mere sophism? For on what plane are we affirming the reality of this power? If it is on the plane of the real in a modal sense, the reasoning seems to be vicious. If it is outside reality in the modal sense the reasoning may be regarded as valid and even as analytical, but it is sterile.[1]

I would argue as follows. If conversion is possible, this can only be by the intervention of grace. But inversely we should be able to establish the possibility of conversion had we a means of showing that grace is posited when conversion is thought. Though this last point at one time seemed agreed, now it looks as though it is doubtful. The logical regression has not yet led us to the point of evidence at which a new progression can begin. All that we have seen is that there is a sense in which the question

[1] Since I wrote the above I have defined my method by saying that it starts out from the superficial positing of a problem, so as to derive a negative conclusion from it which emphasises the new terms that furnish the elements for positing it anew (this time as real); and this, in its turn, makes possible a positive solution.

of grace is absolutely incapable of being posited. It is absurd to ask whether it is legitimate to think grace, for grace, by definition, falls outside the norms of reflection. From this point of view we can say that grace is the absolute fact. Do we end up, then, with a sort of transcendental empiricism which defines grace exclusively in function of an experience (which in itself is incapable of being objectivised)? That, put in a phrase, would mean that there is no way of thinking grace, that strictly speaking grace is not even possible, that it can only be conceived in function of a particular experience which can only be actual (it cannot be in any way represented to anyone who has not received it). But here I see a grave ambiguity. For to posit grace in this way still means to think it. Everything depends on whether the act by which it is thought remains explicit, or whether we extend the inconsequence so as to set it aside (which would amount to falling back once more into the philosophy of pure immediacy). Let us see if we can adopt the first way. As the question of legitimacy has no meaning if applied to grace, it is plain that our business does not lie in knowing whether grace can be used as an explanation of the transition from my (actual) given experience to another experience which is merely conceived. Hence we at least admit the possibility of a naturalistic or psychological explanation which can account for the transition.

On the other hand I cannot conceive any direct relation between what I am and grace. Strictly speaking, what I am capable of thinking is a subsequently established relation beginning with the new experience which itself can only be defined in function of grace, in function of the affirmation regarding grace. But in that case there is reciprocity between grace and the experience which we affirm to be made possible by grace, it looks as if we have to abandon all hope of transition from the idea (?) of grace to the idea of conversion. "This", it may be said, "is a pseudo-problem, for conversion is only thought because experience shows us examples of it; it is impossible to posit at this point a problem that is strictly critical. For we are in the realm of the pure empirical". This way of looking at things may be very prudent, but it does not seem to me justifiable. We are not concerned here with knowing what the conditions are under which the idea of conversion may be presented to a mind. Such are evidently mere conditions of fact; conditions that are entirely contingent. We are concerned here with knowing under what conditions I can think myself as converted (let us not forget that we have passed beyond objectivity and plurality). Inasmuch as I am a thinking subject and inasmuch as I remain external to myself I can easily imagine objective reasons for my conversion; but inasmuch as I overcome the dualism of the thinking subject and the empirical ego, conversion appears to me to be an insoluble problem—I can think only of its being resolved by grace, but on the other hand I know that grace cannot be thought as objective cause, that it can only be affirmed after conversion; to think of grace objectively is to deny it absolutely and for certain. *This is as much as to say that conversion cannot really be thought as yet to come* (here the word 'really' means by oneself as individual, as thinking subject transcended). At this point, though now on an infinitely higher plane, I think we come once again upon the problem of time, and approach the idea of an absolute present.

February 4th

I would like to attempt to state precisely what I only sketched yesterday. First of all, doubtless, there is a relation between the fact of surpassing the categories of modality and the fact of positing an absolute present, i.e. of denying the homogeneity (and hence the reality) of time. I think we need to define this relation exactly.

I was led to say that we cannot attribute any of the known forms of modality to grace when I reflected that the question of whether or not it is legitimate to think grace is meaningless, because it supposes that grace can be thought as a mode of explanation. From this viewpoint, whether we affirm or deny grace, we think it as objective (as objectively true or false), and hence, at least in a negative way, we define what I call absolute freedom (that which is transcendent in relation to the categories of modality). Thus defined, absolute freedom does not belong to the order of what can be posited (in the sense that the objectively possible is only the existant as problematically posited); it does not belong to the order of the existential (cf. my whole criticism of existence—moreover the objective determination of that which exists is based on internal necessity), it does not belong to the order of what must be posited, for all necessity is defined in function of an explanation or of an integral experience of what is given. It can be described as the form of the judgment of existence least ill-adapted to the act that posits it—provided that the existential is thought independently of an objective substratum (which, doubtless, is contradictory).

So we cannot really think grace. Or rather we can only think it as unthinkable (inasmuch as we associate the act of thinking with the idea of an objective content). From the standpoint of the *I think*, of the thinking subject, grace must be rejected out of hand. But in the measure in which the *I think* is capable of transcending itself, and of becoming faith, at least a distant communication seems possible. As we have said, to think grace is to deny it. It remains to be seen whether that negation converts itself into an affirmation. In other words we have to ask ourselves whether the act of faith itself does not involve positing grace; and whether the negation of grace is not equivalent to the self-suppression of faith, that is to say to the suicide of a freedom which can only be negated when it is exercised. Divine transcendence would be affirmed by the very act in which the freedom of the creature is realised. Is that the case?

It is clear that, as I have conceived it, the act of faith implies positing God as independent of the act that posits him. In that sense the act of faith enfolds another act by which thought prohibits itself from reflecting the free act. What does this suppose? What if it be said that such a prohibition is unjustified? Obviously this would re-establish, beyond the act of faith, a world of truths that the act of faith transcended when it was constituted. What if we said that in this way thought posits itself as trans-subjective, that is, that the act of faith is the very act by which God thinks himself? But that implies a metaphysical transposition of the cogito which seems to me illegitimate. It remains that faith posits transcendence in the strictest sense; i.e. grace, i.e. a radically independent power (and in my view this is the foundation of what can be called the divine personality). But does this not involve us in thinking a possible (or necessary) relationship between ourselves and that power? We are obliged by all we have said to answer that it does not, that is, we are obliged to deny the legitimacy of any kind of modal qualification of such a relation.

I can say no more than that between God and me there is the relation of one freedom with another. That relation is involved in the act of faith—as affirmation. In other words, between God and me there must be a relation of the kind that love establishes between lovers.

February 5th

And so, side by side with faith we posit love. I have said elsewhere that love is the condition of faith, and in a sense this is true. But it is only one aspect. I believe that in reality love and faith cannot be dissociated. When faith ceases to be love it congeals into objective belief in a power that is conceived more or less physically. And love which is not faith (which does not posit the transcendence of the God that is loved) is only a sort of abstract game. Just as the divine reality corresponds to faith (the former can only be thought in function of the latter) so divine perfection corresponds to love. And the union of reality and perfection in God, far from needing to be understood in the old intellectualist sense (*ens realissimum*), can only be grasped in function of faith and of the union of faith and love that I have just emphasised. I cease to believe in God the moment I cease to love him; an imperfect God cannot be real.

This, it may be said, is pure phenomenalism. Does it not resolve the divine reality into the purely phenomenological 'becoming' of the consciousness that thinks it? We know that, to thought, faith is presented as that which thought only transcends in an illusory and provisional way. Faith, in so far as it is not really thought, seems no more than a game of subjective appearances. In other words, in the name of faith as ideally conceived, thought must see the gulf that separates belief that is still purely intellectual from sanctity (absolute belief); and it must recognise the absolute impossibility of maintaining the validity—only possible at the lower stages of speculation—of the dualism of appearance and reality.

Hence we are once again up against the question of grace. For grace is presented to thought as the order in which the dualism no longer occurs. The basis of the separation between God and the creature seems to reside in the act by which the creature posits, beyond faith, an ideal knowledge capable of disentangling the truth of faith. On the other hand we have seen that grace can only be thought as unthinkable, that is, as the divine suppression of that act. But does not this oblige us to convert grace into a sort of truth of faith, into a sort of mysterious, ideally posited landmark by which we can measure the distance that still separates us from our goal? It is only too plain that if we so conceive grace we are abandoning all that we have previously posited. We must go back to what was said earlier, namely that grace cannot be thought as Idea without being denied. The ideal convergence which is characteristic of knowledge cannot apply in the order of faith. To think grace as required, as postulated by the act of faith seems inevitably to posit grace as a sort of ideal; and consequently it means denying that very divine freedom on which alone it can be based. Ought we then to say that we have the idea of grace within us, but that that is a contingent psychological fact, and the idea is necessarily dissolved by dialectics? But, as we have already seen, human freedom is veritably *for itself* only in the measure in which it is suppressed when it thinks divine freedom, when it renounces seeing anything in itself save the anticipation of an action which could not emanate from itself. If it aims to be more it collapses, and becomes the illusory game of a reflection that seeks for self-forgetfulness in the womb of its non-activity, busied with limiting itself to independent products whose origin it insists on ignoring.

Here the relation between my views and the philosophy of Fichte appears clearly—and also the enormous difference between them.

Grace indeed remains the postulate that is transcendent and incapable of being objectivised—of the act of faith. I would express this in another way by saying that by the act of faith I posit between God and myself a relation that completely eludes the categories of my thought (I think it as unthinkable but as absolutely involved in the act of faith).

February 6th

Thanks to a conversation I had yesterday with A—— I think I now understand.

Grace, I said, must be thought as unthinkable. That must be made explicit. There is always an advantage in making things explicit, anyway we gain nothing by not making them explicit. But—and this will reveal results—the transcendence of grace thus thought as unthinkable remains a function of the stage of reflection. A relationship of tension in some way subsists between reflection that thinks the impossibility of negating itself absolutely and the transcendent (supermodal) order that would make this negation possible. In this sense to think grace as absolutely not relative to myself is to make it once again in some manner relative. In the measure in which I become aware of the dependence that subsists in spite of everything, I can say that "to affirm grace is to deny it." In other words, for the saint, strictly speaking, there is no grace. If grace subsists for the convert it is inasmuch as he claims to explain to himself the transition from one stage to another, inasmuch, that is, as he identifies himself in some way with what he was before his conversion. So grace remains as function of a development in which a discontinuity has survived. As I have already said, it is defined less in relation to the conversion that has been achieved than in relation to a persisting dualism between the two modes of experience (of intelligibility), which are posited as discontinuous.

In this sense I am absolutely incapable of positing the problem of *my conversion*; to admit the possibility of an action of grace is at least to construct a fictitious causality—and it is nothing more. If grace can only really be thought as unthinkable, I have no actual measuring rod for the spiritual condition in which I find myself. Grace is no more a norm than it is a cause. From the critical (or transcendental) standpoint it is only the act by which the convert posits the impossibility of reducing the new intelligibility to the previous modes of his reflection—though this act is only possible inasmuch as the modes in question still subsist in him. And hence at one and the same time we see the necessity of a dualistic basis for grace and also the relativity of grace. Grace is not the adequate expression of divine freedom, it is the expression that that freedom takes on for a thought dissociated from itself. This dissociation from itself I shall henceforward call the Fall.

February 7th

I do not intend to go on with the foregoing reflections directly;

I think that they will be cleared up little by little as we proceed. It is better to emphasise aspects more easily capable of direct elucidation.

I would like now to take up the question of the relation of individualities to one another. I have already pointed out elsewhere why the monadistic solution seems to me unacceptable. Thought only has grounds for denying communication between individualities inasmuch as it posits itself as thinking (universal) subject; from that standpoint a plurality cannot in any way be conceived. This is as much as to say that if we still conceive that plurality is possible we have no reason to deny that interaction is likewise possible. Nevertheless, equivocations arise at this point owing to the chronic danger of confounding the empirical content that must be transcended for the cogito to become possible, with the real individuality which is the act by which the mind is constituted when it makes actual the freedom immanent in the *I think*. Doubtless we can and must agree that the *I think* is presupposed by the empirical content, in that the latter is inserted into an experience (my experience) which implies the formal unity of the thought that constitutes it. But for all that the *I think* as form does no more than translate for reflection the *I think* that is act. Yet that is unimportant. What is plain is that communication between empirical contents must be regarded as possible. We must not forget that bodies are the site of existence; that is, of causality (or of *Wechselwirkung*—inter-action). Now if the *I think* becomes *for itself*, such communication seems pure illusion. Inasmuch as it is unverifiable, the cogito is posited as transcending any possible communication. But, I repeat, this can only be converted into a monadistic affirmation if we posit centres of thought, and that would be radically contradictory—as the plurality of the centres remains relative to the act that thinks the plurality. So at this third stage, at which individuality is constituted, we have to ask ourselves in what sense a plurality once again becomes possible. There are grounds for seeing an important signpost for the solution in the fact that individuality only *is* when it depends from an act of creation, a freedom distinct from it—the absolute negation of solipsism is the preliminary condition of all spiritual life. And we already know that faith consists in, or is translated for intelligence into, the refusal to insert that negation into a solipsist system. From this standpoint, to adopt the words I put into the mouth of Clarisse,[1] God is that in which thoughts communicate, the real foundation of the communication between individualities. And if this by its nature is bound to seem fundamentally ambiguous, it is because, apart from the spiritual communication of love, there is another kind of purely mechanical communication which is like a parody of it (it appears as its symbol only to faith), which is due to the fact that individuality itself is only constituted from the starting point of that which exists. In so far as purely mechanical communication is established between individual thoughts the latter are negated and destroyed as individual, and they fall back into the order of pure existence, which by definition is indifferent in relation to all values whatsoever. There can be no real externality in the world of existence (the world of mechanical communication), because there is no interiority either (before one gives oneself one must belong to oneself). It is only from the moment at which individuality has an interior that it can think itself as really distinct from another individuality (and that love becomes possible). Now such an interior has itself to constitute itself or rather (as individuality is not really a form), individuality is the very act by which the empirical content becomes interior.

What I have elsewhere called real interiority is thus involved in every act of love—and, inversely, real individuality is essentially defined through love (or, strictly speaking, in aesthetic creation which makes possible the communication of individualities). Hence the meaning of my statement that love creates its object can be seen more clearly. It must not be understood in a superficially subjectivist and solipsist sense. The reality of the beloved one is essential to love—no (subjective) truth can transcend that reality. In this sense it is perhaps true to say that only love is real knowledge and that it is legitimate to associate love and adequate knowledge, in other words that only for love is the individuality of the beloved immune against disintegration and crumbling away, so to speak, into the dust of abstract elements. But it is only possible to maintain the reality of the beloved because love posits the beloved as transcending all explanation and all reduction. In this sense it is true to say that love

[1] In *Le Palais de Sable*.

only addresses itself to what is eternal, it immobilises the beloved above the world of genesis and vicissitude. And in that way love is the negation of knowledge, which can only ignore transcendence. Of course we need not conclude that love is necessarily blind, that to love means to exclude judgment. As soon as love is knowingly dissociated from knowledge it ceases to be love—from that moment love is no more (for itself) than an illusory and voluntarily idealised knowledge. Love needs to appear to itself as perfect knowledge, and in the measure in which it is now no longer permissible to dissociate being from appearances we can say that it *is* perfect knowledge. For all that, reflection is bound to distinguish it from knowledge, and it cannot be defined save as being beyond all knowledge. Reflection (which, as I said elsewhere, cannot manage to get away from formalism entirely and from the dualism of appearance and reality) posits love as that which both experiences the need to justify itself and is itself alone capable of justifying. But how is it that love is not an illusion? If it requires justifications and if the justifications are purely fallacious, what is its value? To this we must answer that the dualism of love and of the principle of justification can only subsist in the finite order, that is, where reflection fails to negate itself completely—for God this dualism is suppressed, for God's love does not meet with any truth that it is powerless to recognise. Is it possible to maintain that this is tantamount to seeing love as an illusion which, when bearing on creatures, is hindered by reality but when it bears on God, that is, on a pure construction, has full play and nothing to fear from experience? But we know already what to think of this kind of realism regarding the true. It would be child's play to show that it implies a misunderstanding of all that has so far been established. We know full well that genuine love, even when directed towards human beings, does not allow itself to stop at knowledge; it affirms the value of its object beyond the merely relative and contingent order of merit and demerit—for love has partaken of divine mediation.

February 9th

I continue with the principal ideas I referred to the day before yesterday. Then I said that love appeared to itself as perfect knowledge and that, as the dualism of appearance and reality only exists for reflection, in so far as reflection thinks itself as suppressed it needs to affirm that love is in reality what it is for itself. Only, of course, beyond reflection there is no longer a place for what can be called the true. And, in consequence, if the expression knowledge be applied to love it is misleading, for knowledge must be thought as referring to a truth. This will become clear later. Love, then, is not addressed to what the beloved is in himself, if by what he is in himself we understand an essence. The contrary is the case. As I have already said, love bears on what is beyond essence, love is the act by which a thought, by thinking a freedom, is made free. In this sense love extends beyond any possible judgment, for judgment can only bear on essence— and love is the very negation of essence (in this sense it implies faith in the perpetual renewal of being itself, the belief that nothing ever is, that nothing ever can be irremediably lost). Doubtless, inasmuch as the lover is a thinking subject, and the beloved is the object for this subject, the lover cannot fail to judge, but he can only judge the beloved inasmuch as object, that is, in the beloved's actions. Inasmuch as he loves (that is, inasmuch as he converts the object into subject) he must absolutely forgo making a judgment. The *Thou shalt not judge* of Christian morality must be viewed as one of the most important metaphysical formulae on earth. And it is in that sense that love necessarily places the being himself above all determinations of merit or lack of it. (The point, of course, needs developing.) But now two quite different questions come up before me. First of all, in what measure does the forgoing render a real communication of minds thinkable? And secondly, if, as is clear, the way in which God has been thought makes a judgment on God impossible and radically illegitimate, has this impossibility the same sense as when we are dealing with creatures? I will begin by examining the second question.

God cannot and must not be judged. For judgment is only possible regarding essence. That explains why every kind of theodicy must be condemned, because a theodicy necessarily implies a judgment, it is a judgment, a justification. Now God cannot be justified. The thought that justifies is the thought that has not yet been elevated to love and to the faith that claims to transcend the mind (belief). Theodicy is atheism (cf. Brunschvicg). But does this imply (in any way whatever) that we should think God as being beyond good and evil? No expression is more ambiguous than that. Nature is not beyond good and evil, it falls short of good and evil, it is below the level at which we can speak of good and evil. Between good and evil there is a profound solidarity that Christian philosophy has been able to detect better than any other. So if we maintain the expression, we must be careful about the sense in which it can be regarded as legitimate. We have already seen that divine perfection is defined in function of love. But from that very fact we must conclude that divine perfection cannot really furnish the criterion of goodness that certain rationalist systems of morality would like it to. At this point the difficulty can be clearly seen. Either such perfection is identified with the good in general—which is ambiguous and dangerous—or else it seems to be reduced to a kind of beyond which is purely abstract and lacks all communication with our life. We must go into this further. We have already seen that God is nothing less than a notion, and in that sense he clearly cannot provide us with a criterion. Moreover, the true God is a living God—not merely the logical God required by some perfectionist moralities. To identify divine perfection with the good is an ambiguous step, because either we are only being tautologous or else we are claiming to base love on a previous (ethical) content and are vitiating profoundly what is essential in the act of love. It is here perhaps that we can discover the purely negative meaning we must attribute to the affirmation that God is beyond good and evil—that is, that there is no common measure between the statement concerning God and any kind of ethical judgment (and in consequence the statement can no longer serve as standard for such a judgment). But then are we not guilty of hypostatising this perfection into a sort of metaphysical solitude in which it is immobilised? We must grasp the very contrary, namely that if it is possible to think a divine action it is on condition that God is concrete and personal (in the sense I defined earlier); and God can only be that if we are free to reject the interpretations previously laid down.

So it seems that between God and the believer we can trace relations strikingly analogous to those that unite creatures in the realm of love.

But here we must avoid taking the wrong step. I think we must begin with the fact that it is impossible for the lover to judge the beloved, and ask about the conditions on which it holds. I have already said that the love which prohibits all reflection has been subject to divine mediation. In other words, in so far as the beloved is thought as participating in God he is situated in the order that transcends all judgment and is conceived as absolute value. Or rather (to exclude all psychologistic interpretations) the justification of the act which affirms the transcendence of the creature consists in that which postulates his divine filiation.

The solidarity which is now apparent between the relativity of any ethical characterisation regarding the individual and the positing of the divine paternity, will perhaps help us to disentangle new problems and to see the question of "real communication" in a new light. We should perhaps first of all ask ourselves about the exact relation between the act of faith as defined in the beginning and the participation of other minds in God. We have seen that with the act of faith I set myself free by thinking the divine freedom and by affirming, through love, other freedoms that depend from the divine freedom, (the basis of what I have called the communication of minds), I only participate in God (I am incapable of thinking myself as participating in God) inasmuch as I have faith in him. Such participation has no truth that is transcendent in relation to faith. But the participation of other minds in God is implied absolutely in the act of faith and as the faith of others cannot in any way have being for me we seem here to be obliged to effect some kind of dissociation between participation and faith—which brings serious difficulties in its train. Participation is here manifest as a fact.

February 10*th*

To return to the subject. By faith I affirm that God is the father of all men. On the other hand I can only think myself as participating in God in so far as I have faith in him—in other words, such participation cannot and must not appear to me as a fact of which I can become aware or be unaware as the case may be. As regards others I am obliged to dissociate participation from faith—for the faith of others is nothing for me, it is in no manner thinkable. But inasmuch as by reflection I think myself as a simple unity amongst other unities, by a sort of inversion I reach the point of positing myself as participating in God *in fact*. I scarcely need to point out the illusion here. But for all that it is difficult to understand the dualism between the way in which I need to think my participation in God, and the way in which I conceive the participation of other minds. This point must be emphasised. First of all we must throw some light on the nature of the relations between participation and faith for myself. Obviously there is no strict sense in which I can make the divine transcendence dependent on the act of faith; yet an individual relation between them remains, in the sense that I dispossess myself of any right to affirm the divine transcendence in so far as I have no faith in it. In other words we must not only distinguish but even allow a radical opposition between the relation between faith and its object and the relation that exists between the perceiving subject and the object perceived. In one instance, under penalty of contradicting myself, I need to affirm that the act of perception can and must be thought as contingent in relation to the object perceived—the dissociation can and must be made. In the other instance I need to affirm that the act of believing is constitutive and that the dissociation cannot and must not be made. We must go into the matter more exactly. We will find a sort of 'realism of the object' and a sort of 'idealism of faith,' though these terms can only take us astray. I say that the idea of the independence of the object perceived in relation to the subject perceiving is constitutive of the idea of truth (this implies no metaphysical statement regarding the reality of the object in itself); on the other hand I say that the idea of the indissoluble unity of faith and of its object is constitutive of the religious affirmation. But just as in the first case I do not realise the object metaphysically, so in the second I do not claim that the divine reality is reabsorbed in a purely subjective process. Here we are in the realm of criticism and I do no more than point out that the conditions that form a basis for any affirmation regarding God are the inverse of those that render objective certainty possible. Doubtless faith is affirmed as contingent in relation to God, but such contingency is itself relative to faith. The reflection that is brought to bear on faith (and suppresses it) cannot allow the transcendental reality of that on which faith has bearing; such reflection converts the transcendental reality into question into a sort of *caput mortum*, into conceptual material lacking all content. The act that thinks faith is also the act that postulates divine transcendence; if the former is abolished the latter cannot subsist. But to make divine transcendence depend (in a subjective sense) on the act of faith means realising the act of faith in a psychological way, it means turning it into a sort of projection of imagination; it means denying it and in consequence making an affirmation the very terms of which have been completely eliminated.

Before deducing from this the conclusions that interest us, I think it is necessary to elucidate a difficulty. I have just spoken of the act that thinks faith (as faith), and which, in consequence, we do not reduce to reflection on faith. But what is this act? What is its relation to the act of faith in the strict sense? Obviously this is a major issue—in what measure does thinking faith already imply belief? I have described the act of faith as that by which the cogito transcends itself, that is to say the act by which the mind is constituted by positing in God the unity of the *I think* and of the empirical content with which the *I think* is bound up, (that is to say, the world). What is the relation between this act and the act that thinks it? The question is rather obscure. I think we must answer that in the end the two acts are doubtless identical. But inasmuch as the act of faith is still attributed to the *cogito* (the universal thinking subject), it is inevitably defined as a kind of plausible hypothesis, it is not really faith— it is still as it were in function of a truth, and appears as its potential approximation. In this sense thinking faith does not mean believing (for faith is still subordinated to the *I think*). Belief in the strict sense suppresses all such preliminary dialectics; and, inversely, the dialectics are only possible when pure belief is not achieved. As long as belief remains the thought of belief and in consequence depends on the *cogito*, it is prohibited from being really itself. Doubtless dialectics are entirely directed towards the self-renunciation of the *I think;* but, for all that dialectics are the work of the *I think*, the *I think* subsists even in the act by which it aspires to its own renunciation; in that sense, as I have already pointed out, reflection on religion is shown to be contradictory, it sees itself as necessarily fettered by an obstacle that by definition it is incapable of removing—and the act itself, the transcendent act which would suppress this obstacle (I have called it grace) that it goes so far as to conceive, remains relative to the movement of thinking (precisely in that it is thought as transcending it).

And so I think we can see clearly the distance that divides the act of faith from the act that thinks it. But one difficulty still remains. How can this distance be really thought? Do we not need another act which really thinks faith and is distinct from the first? And does not this involve us in an infinite regression? We will get our answer if we remember that we must not be taken in by abstractions. Like all thought of whatsoever kind the act that thinks faith is doubtless capable of reflecting itself. And when it reflects itself it makes explicit its own conditions and must needs appear to itself as distinct from what it was for itself at the outset (as it was *for* itself from the outset but not as it was *in* itself).

This reflection makes explicit the intervention of the *I think* as subject in the act which was given as datum to itself as that by which the *I think* was transcended and negated for the benefit of faith. It is thanks to this reflection that the confrontation of what the act really was and what it aimed to be is rendered possible. Such reflection in consequence sheds light on the dualism of the act of faith and the act that thinks faith. But in the process the act of faith seems to be pushed back beyond all limits (beyond a reflective process that is necessarily endless), and it seems to reflection that it could only put an end to the regress by self-suppression. Hence the idea of grace, of a power that limits reflection by suppressing it from without. But inasmuch as this idea in its turn remains subject to reflection, it must needs appear as purely relative (in the sense in which the beyond itself is relative). In this way we seem to be defining what could be called a monism of pure reflection which would go so far as to incorporate its 'beyond.' But when reflection reflects itself it conceives its nothingness. It destroys itself. It is the free act—act in which, doubtless, reflection runs the risk of being reborn so as to negate it reflectively, but which subsists as transcending what precedes it and what follows it, and which suddenly lights up the nothingness of its genesis and its posterity. It discovers that it is in the path of being, because the act by which reflection denies it will itself still be the negation of itself, will be, so to speak, changed as regards indication, but still itself. Here, if such be insisted, I will mention intuition. In that way light is also cast on the act of faith. And the negation of the act of faith is defined as being itself a free act—but as the fatal act, the act that is the inverse of faith (which is freedom self-affirming, freedom self-actualising), the act by which freedom is denied— as the Fall (freedom negating itself freely, that is, only continuing to affirm itself for another—positing this otherness *which is nothingness*).

I shall have to take up several of these themes again. How is the free act posited? And how does the negation of itself appear to it as identical with itself? These points need more elucidation. I will restrict myself to a comment on the two dialectical moments. If reflection is all (i.e. what I have called the monism of reflection), then it turns back on itself of necessity.

February 11*th*

I would like to elucidate this further. In what has been said there are equivocations and obscurities. They lie in the very nature of the problem. The problem was how to determine the relation between the act of faith and the act that thinks faith. And in answering this question another question necessarily arose— regarding the conditions under which the dissociation is possible. But first of all is such a dissociation (dualism) really given to us as a fact? That seems hardly capable of being answered directly. It seems as though we must look for the conditions that make the dissociation possible, establish that once these conditions are given the dissociation is also given, and see if they really are given.

Under what conditions can the dualism be thought? It can only be thought if the act by which faith is thought is revealed (to itself), when it reflects itself, as not identical with that for which it was itself originally given. Thus it must be admitted that though the act is already initially for itself, when it reflects itself it sees conditions made explicit which were not apparent to it in the first *Fürsichsein*, and discovers that it was not really what it purported to be (that it was not in itself what it was for itself). It is only thanks to reflection of this kind, and after it, that the act of faith and the act that thinks faith can be dissociated. In other words the thought of belief is given to itself as being belief, and it is only when reflecting on itself that it makes explicit what in it is not belief—what, that is, is universal affirmation (*cogitatio*). The act of faith is identical with the thought of faith inasmuch as the latter remains (as thought) implicit, it is distinct from it inasmuch as it recognises itself by making itself explicit as thought strictly speaking. It cannot make itself explicit as thought without positing itself as distinct from what it was inasmuch as it was implicit.

The act of faith, as I have already defined it, is thus shown to be distinct from the act that thinks it, because the latter, when it reflects on itself, reveals the cogito that still remains in it. As long as the act of faith is posited for the *I think* it is defined as hypothesis, as the positing of knowledge (of a causal relation), and from this viewpoint faith remains an inaccessible 'beyond'. I call this *I think* reflection inasmuch as here it subsists as that for which the act of faith is posited. From this standpoint faith, strictly speaking, appears as that which cannot be thought save on condition that it is posited by a power that transcends all reflection, by what I have called grace. But in its turn the dualism of religious reflection and of grace still subsists for the reflection that denies it (as relative to itself). This is what I have called the monism of pure reflection. Only—and this is the essential point— such monism is by definition unstable. For all reflection is (at least potentially) reflection on itself. Reflection is at one and the same time each particular moment and the power of transcending that moment. But this power of transcendence is only on condition that reflection is for itself, and, in consequence, that it posits each particular moment as transitory and as suppressing itself. Such power of transcendence I call freedom. Inasmuch as reflection comprehends itself as free, it is free; but the free act, (the apprehension of self as freedom), when treated as a particular moment, brings about a further moment that annihilates it; and in that way, by virtue of its ambiguous nature, reflection negates itself as freedom. But in the measure in which self-consciousness as transcendent (I have called it intuition) is bound up with every act of reflection, it is the negation of this freedom converted in its turn into free act (inasmuch as the moment is negated as moment for the benefit of the power that supports it). If the monism of pure reflection is not converted into an endless chain of moments which suppress one another, it is transformed into the unique act by which freedom is posited.

In this way the intellectual dialectic which threatened to eliminate the act of faith by making it the ideal term of a perpetual regression, is eliminated.

What is the result of this inquiry? It is now clear that the dissociation between belief and the act that thinks belief involves us in a reflective dialectic which suppresses itself as soon as it is transcended (that is, is comprehended). Thus the dualism is suppressed by the free act. Reflection on faith which posits itself for itself as necessarily distinct from faith, is suppressed in the free act.

But do we not end up with an absolute contradiction? If reflection on faith destroys itself how can faith remain a thought? Doubtless reflection is not purely and simply annihilated, it is converted into what we have called, (by a term, however, that is dangerous) intuitive thought. But what relation can we establish between intuitive thought and faith? Of course any kind of relation that is strictly reflective must be excluded at the outset. But then the difficulties reappear. Intuitive thought only seems capable of bearing fruit if it is prolonged into reflection, that is, if it negates itself. When left to itself is it not used up in one sterile and of necessity unique procedure, that of pure affirmation? It seems to me that the inquiries I have made so far permit at least an indirect solution of the problem. We have said that the free act (intuitive thought), implies the negation of the dualism between faith and reflection on faith; but that amounts to saying that the negation is only of a practical character. And there precisely lies the importance of the conclusions we have reached. If the reflective dialectic suppresses itself it is precisely because (it is as much as to say that) the discussion of the relations between faith and thought regarding it can only be sterile. In practice it is important to deny that there is any real difference between the one and the other. Real belief presents itself with the characteristics of an imperative.

So we do not end up with the contradictory idea of the unthinkableness of faith, but with the affirmation that if we really dissociate belief from thought bearing on it, we are involving ourselves in a process without end, we are freely renouncing our freedom. In the place of the dualism of faith and of thought bearing on faith is substituted the idea of the will to believe, and that will is thought to be bound by an obligation.

February 12th

I am not going to recapitulate the reasons for which a judgment cannot be brought to bear on God or on creatures inasmuch as they are thought as being in his image, that is, inasmuch as they participate in God. It is now clear that faith affirms itself as the will and obligation not to judge. But is there a basis for determining the relations that unite souls reciprocally in the dualism that I mentioned when writing about participation? I have pointed out that we can conceive two orders, of which one only is legitimate. One order consists in inferring participation as fact (for other minds) from participation through faith; the other in taking one's stand on participation as fact by reducing the believer himself to participate in fact. Here we have to find a terminology. Only the first of these orders can be thought—we have already seen why. And hence we posit the idea of the believer as mediator, as constituting, by means of faith itself, a factual order which is without relation (other than mystical) to that faith. The real believer, the saint, in this sense appears as the absolute mediator and at the same time as the redeemer. This means that faith implies the affirmation of an absolute relation between itself and what can be called the totality of the world of minds. And hence, it seems to me, participation is posited at what I would like to call the second degree; i.e. participation in the absolute mediator.

And now a few reflections on method.

It seems to me that all discussions about method in philosophy are obscured by a fundamental misunderstanding that the evolution of speculative thought has never yet dissipated. People persist in positing the dilemma of pure empiricism on the one hand, and, on the other, of reason that finds its own content within itself; and, setting out from an initial truth (on the nature of which it would be hard to make a pronouncement) reason, so conceived, unfolds a whole chain of propositions thanks to its internal spontaneity alone. I believe the latter alternative should be rejected out of hand. What is to be our attitude to a process conceived in this purely rational way? I am convinced that if we want such generation to be possible it is because we are still under the influence of the idea of machinery—we would like to realise, in the order of reason, something analogous to a mechanism which functions by itself, independently of the will—something that moves of its own accord. I feel obliged to protest against any such mechanisation of thought. It may be argued that we should view it in terms of a desire to imitate mathematical reasoning. Yet we begin constructing that reasoning by looking on it as a sort of rational automatism. I note that this goes for every method described as purely rational—everywhere alike we run into a superstitious transposition of mechanism into thought itself. I am convinced that all philosophers who have reflected on mathematical thought, from Descartes to Henri Poincaré, have reacted against this crude way of representing thought. But for all that the fetish has survived all the blows delivered against it. Mechanism is continuously being translated into the order of thought—because mechanism is what imposes itself on us all—and should a hand imprudently touch the machinery it is crushed. In some way mechanism and universality seem to imply one another. If analytical thought was for long able to affirm its primacy that was because it is easy to schematise the mechanism of its development in a way that is in some way spatial. Kant's notion of the *a priori* synthesis, however ambiguous in some of its aspects, has the immense merit of emphasising the fact that rationality is capable of subsisting in its entirety even when a radically unmechanical element intervenes (and even plays a primary part). Freeing mathematics from any kind of dependence on intuition always runs the risk (though here, strictly speaking, there is no *real* solidarity) of entailing mechanisation and this is an error that is dangerous to philosophy. Against the idea of a mechanism of reason functioning, so to speak, quite on its own, our experience—with all its characteristics of contingence and subjectivity which the rationalists have taken pleasure in emphasising—revolts.

February 13*th*

I believe that we must reject this dualism absolutely. However true the idea of a reason that organises experience may be it has at least the disadvantage of appearing invincibly dualistic. It seems to me that reason ought to be accentuated in another way. We need to admit that thought (reason) does not constitute itself as thought for itself save in the measure in which it is realised in experience. And this must not be understood in a purely psychological sense (with which Kantian theory, strictly speaking, could come to terms). In other words, the idea of pure thought anterior—even in a rational sense—to all experience is certainly a pseudo-idea; it is the product of a schematic and illusory reflection. This amounts to saying that it is as arbitrary to pretend to define experience in function of categories anterior to it, as to make thought depend on an improperly realised experience. Thought, it must be understood, is only known and grasped in experience in the measure in which the experience is defined as intelligible. Kantian criticism corresponds to the purely transitory moment in which analysis hypostatises intelligibility and converts it into form.

I am still concerned by the question of the conditions under which religious history is possible. The foregoing inquiries prove that the problem cannot be stated in traditional terms. For, as is obvious, religious history is history in which one believes. And this primary fact suffices to differentiate religious history from history in general. (Of course I am speaking here of belief in the rigorous meaning of the term, not belief in the vague sense of an approximation to certitude.) The relation to the believing individuality is an element constituting the notion of religious history, whereas history in general is characterised by the negation of that relation (like all knowledge history in general implies a relation to the thinking subject who negates himself as individual). The existence of religious history may seem contingent (though in reality it has already been established by dialectics), but if we admit it, does it follow that it must have characteristics (internal ones this time) that differentiate it from any other history—and in particular does it follow that it is subject to laws which are not those of ordinary history? In a word, what is the relation between the strictly miraculous elements contained in all religious history and the fact that such history has reference essentially to the believing subject?

It seems at the outset that if we deny the miraculous elements our act implicitly suppresses the relation. The miraculous elements can only be denied from the standpoint of historical criticism—which brings in the objectivist postulates of science. Inasmuch as the *I think* is substituted for the *I believe* the miraculous elements can be eliminated. But this, it may be objected, only shows up the self-contradictions involved in the notion of religious history. As history, religious history depends on the *I think*. In the notion we are discussing one domain trespasses on to another.

We have already seen that we must regard the idea of a trans-historical religion as inadequate and fruitless. So it does not look as though we can be satisfied with such a simple relation.

But then the question comes up again. It may be objected: "All this supposes that the miraculous elements are given as existing. But that hypothesis must be rejected. If we begin with the *I believe* no deduction of those elements is possible." Here, it seems to me, a grave misunderstanding needs to be dispelled. There is no question of deducing religious history from the *I believe*. The important issue is whether the *I believe* can be posited otherwise than in relation to affirmations bearing on history. This does not mean that such affirmations would be analytically implied by the *I believe*, but simply that faith would only be realised through the *recognition of a history*. We must not forget that with faith the datum reappears; as we have seen, the negation of the datum which is enveloped by knowledge, and on a much higher level by absolute science, cannot subsist save thanks to an illusion, since all rationality of whatever kind is based on the act that transcends a contingent datum. There is thus no question whatever of establishing an analytical relation between faith and religious history—the enterprise would be absurd. We must go deeper. If our conclusions so far are really founded we must entirely give up seeing in religious history the realisation of a dialectic (Hegel) in the measure in which that dialectic still *'would be'* in some way for pure thought (for the cogito). But if this is really so, as we can neither deny faith in the interests of knowledge nor see faith as an absolutely trans-historical act (save, as we have said, in the saint), we seem to end up with the conclusion that the act of faith postulates religious history.

The foregoing reasoning is obscure and I would like to clarify it. First of all I show that if we posit a religious history it is necessarily bound up with the act of faith. Yet we cannot deny the fact that the history in question is given as datum unless we adopt the standpoint of analytical logic (asserting that religious history is not implied analytically in the act of faith), and such analytical logic must be absolutely excluded here, for it cannot operate save from a datum recognised as such.

February 14*th*

In that way some difficulties are unquestionably eliminated. Yet there is still the problem of how the believer can reject a historical investigation into the miraculous without thereby surrendering his sincerity. Is not this a very serious antinomy? Is not the prohibition of reflection on the miraculous equivalent to self-negation as thought? Of course we already know that the believer has to prohibit himself from reflection on God (judging God), but is that of the same order? God can only be thought as transcending all judgment. But the miraculous? If it is historical how can it escape the conditions that make all history possible? Is history on which the mind is not permitted to reflect anything but false history posing as true? Here, as is plain, two attitudes are possible. The first consists in saying that, even judged as history, religious history stands up to its critics—but it is perfectly clear that by definition criticism implies the negation of religious history (and furthermore takes away all ultimate value from its results). It is perfectly clear also that if religious history, as history, is constituted like all other history, it is no longer what we have called religious history (involving, as constituent element, a relation to faith). The second attitude consists in making use of the fact that religious history cannot subsist as such so as to argue in favour of its metaphysical reality. This at least means there is a clear perception of the fact that if history is, strictly speaking, religious it necessarily presents certain characteristics of irrationality. Thus it seems impossible to regard the difficulty, the requirement (*exigence*) we are up against, as contingent and fortuitous. If on the one hand the act of faith involves the recognition of a special religious history, and if on the other such religious history, by the very fact that it is religious—that is to say, that it embraces a relation to faith—must contain some miraculous elements, it follows that the believer, inasmuch as he is a thinking subject, is quite incapable of thinking about such history rationally.

February 15th

Must we maintain that there are categories of religious history? But that is singularly ambiguous. The reflecting mind necessarily posits the unity of history. Can it be said that what matters is not the historical material, but the form, the interpretation given to it by the mind?—religious history being defined by the interpretation faith puts on material in itself indifferent. I do not think that this position is any more tenable than the preceding ones. It implies a dualism of matter and of form which, as we have seen, must needs be foreign to faith. In faith the interpretation cannot in any way be contingent upon the fact interpreted, which amounts to saying that we ought not to speak of interpretation here. The dualism of the fact and of the interpretation is relative to a reflection which dissociates the datum given and the form, so as to bring them together subsequently as best it may. To me it seems unquestionable that the problem of miracles will remain insoluble as long as we fail to posit the absolutely illegitimate character of that reflection. Any reflection on a miracle makes it appear contradictory. That does not mean that the miracle is contradictory in itself, or at least it does not necessarily mean it. It may also be due to the fact that there is an absolute lack of adequation between the miracle and the reflection that bears on it. To be sure, if we make reflection an absolute, nothing can be really inadequate for it, there is no room for anything save moments in hierarchy (unequally elucidated by reflection). But we have precisely seen that reflection cannot treat itself as an absolute without negating itself; and in this sense it seems that the conditions on which the possibility of the free act is based are the very conditions that allow us to conceive the miraculous as transcending all reflection—as individual unity of that which (for reflection) is dissociated into matter and form. Is it possible to proceed further with the definition of what constitutes a miracle? A miracle only *is* in the measure in which our spiritual life is concerned in it (that is to say, that reflection can only negate itself in relation to a spiritual end that is posited as absolute), it only *is* inasmuch as it is a revelation. And in this way I find I am led to asking myself about the way in which revelation can be thought. To say that a miracle can only be understood as revelation is precisely to affirm that, strictly speaking, there is no interpretation for it. Revelation, negatively, is only suppressed interpretation. Revelation is by essence that which cannot be reflected (dissociated), and the problem of the world, in last analysis, comes back to the problem of revelation. Wherever there is revelation the miraculous is veritably present in the deepest sense of the term. And at this point I think it is possible to find a key. If nature is opposed to revelation it is precisely because nature is the order in which the dualism of matter and interpretation has its reign—to such a point that the interpretation appears to some people as the purely contingent garment in which the mind clothes matter in itself indifferent to all form. For in nature we are in the order of knowledge (of pure objectivity). Wherever that dualism is suppressed the miraculous occurs. In this sense genuine art is a revelation, and so, though in lesser degree, is language (the word) inasmuch as in it the physical basis is united with the meaning. Of course it can be said that that is a purely human revelation, that there is no possible analogy between that kind of revelation and a revelation that is, strictly speaking, divine.

Can we agree to conceive revelation in this restrictive way?

Before elucidating the question I think we need to examine an objection. "Doubtless," someone may say, "if the historical material is posited as outside discussion your interpretation stands; but then it follows that the dualism of the fact and of the interpretation in the affirmation of revelation is only suppressed for the believer—for the historian it necessarily remains." But we must not forget that the matter itself is not identical in the case of the believer and of the historian: how then can we say the latter is right and the former wrong? It seems that inasmuch as it is historical, the historical material is the concern of the general methods of history. The objection is strong but I do not believe it is insurmountable. May we not answer that the objection, in the measure in which it implies belief in the possibility of a history dealing exclusively with matter (isolated from interpretation) and so to speak anterior to the alternative, implies the very dualism that it aims to set aside? May we not maintain that in reality nothing is anterior to the alternative, that from the beginning we must choose between the entirely secular idea of historical monism and the idea of religious history that lives on in the womb of indifferent matter like a current in the ocean?

What makes the discussion so obscure is that there is no possibility of empirical or objective discrimination to permit us to make our choice. For it is clear that what I have called historical monism cannot be refuted *on the plane of history*. That monism is the very idea (formally posited) of universal reduction to a certain system of categories.

February 17*th*

I mean that historical monism is defined by the purely formal affirmation that there are universal conditions that are identical for every kind of history, even though the nature of the conditions cannot be so defined (they may be economic, sociological, etc.)— if a certain specification is shown to be insufficient in actuality, it can always be admitted, formally at least, that another would be adequate. From the historical standpoint it is not clear by what a historian could be obliged to recognise the existence of a special domain—that of religious history—defined in function of transcendental conditions without analogy. And this is justified by all that we have seen earlier, for such transcendental conditions have reference exclusively to faith and not to the thinking subject. In consequence not only are we without all hope of establishing the legitimacy of religious history with historical arguments— but, also, history must be regarded as forever obliged to hold such an idea in check. Religious history can only appear intelligible to the philosophical spirit if it is possible to establish that historical monism does not cover the whole field.

Fundamentally the question is whether the historian really occupies a position this side of the point at which an interpretation is grafted on to historical "material"—and, it seems to me, he certainly does not. In reality the historian's pure material already contains an interpretation. To the belief of those for whom things happened in one particular way the historian opposes the affirmation that *in reality* things occurred in another way. For the false interpretation he substitutes an interpretation which negates itself as such because it claims to be the truth. The purely realist idea is that, in opposition to any interpretation grafted on to it, the matter of history in itself carries its form (as datum). That realism needs to be attacked resolutely.

I think we need to set out from the principle that nothing justifies the thesis that there are pure historical data measured by which all systematisation is contingent. The notion of event supposes a whole, it is only defined in function of wholes. And that itself is enough to annihilate what I have called historical realism. Yet we are still very far from a rehabilitation of the idea of the miracle. For it seems that, between an objectively determinable whole (the history of a nation) and a whole that is only valid for believing consciousnesses, a distinction is inevitable. But when we answer in that way are we not slightly displacing the question? Unless it is to have recourse to pure and simple lying, historical reconstruction that is brought to bear on the miraculous must be limited to demonstrating that certain facts have been badly interpreted (either because of the ignorance of the spectators, or as a result of certain abnormal psychical states—collective psychoses etc.). In any case we have the substitution of one interpretation for another, the new interpretation being given as immanent in the facts and, so to speak, co-existensive with them.

I am wondering whether these inquiries can be really fruitful. For in taking this path I am running the risk of coming to regard the truth that tends to disengage itself from historical psychology and exegesis as pure interpretation, so as to go on to say: this interpretation is worth less than the specifically religious interpretation, or rather: if there is a dualism of matter and form it is not for the believer but for the historian. Now I believe we need to distrust this kind of conciliation thoroughly. We must remember that, for reflection on history, there is no truth outside what can be called the *frames* of truth (frames which are doubtless constituted in the measure that knowledge is created, and cannot be considered as a timeless mould, yet of which thought is none the less a captive). If the idea of the miraculous is capable of providing a philosophical content, it is on condition that it is not dissolved in the notion of history. I believe that the idea of the miracle can be given a content through the medium of the idea of the present (of absolute present). The present is the site of religious thought—it is what has been called eternity.

February 17*th*

While religion is the perpetual affirmation of the present, history is the perpetual negation of the present. History only has bearing on becoming, it knows no fixity; nowhere can it find rest or stability, it only sees preparations and consummations (which themselves embrace the beginning of new developments and new preparations). In this sense history can never render the past present for us; in the series of entirely ideal presents which is realised in the representation of historical becoming we never meet with the real present anywhere. If the present has a reality that can only be as transcending historical becoming. It seems to me certain (though so far this is only clear to me *in abstracto*, so to speak) that the miraculous must be regarded as transcending history exactly in the sense that the present transcends becoming. The miracle can only be re-thought as miracle by religious practice—just as the present can only really be re-thought as present by a trans-historical act (which is itself perhaps fundamentally of the order of faith). Hence if we claim to conceive the miracle as miracle without abandoning the framework of history, we necessarily fall into contradiction (in that sense rationalist criticism must be regarded as absolutely established; it permits us to exclude a particular way of conceiving the relations between miracle and history). We could say, similarly, I think, that if we adopt the standpoint of homogeneous duration, the present as such cannot be thought—just as the effort of the mathematician (or of anyone who considers the world in mathematical terms) consists in setting aside the 'here', hicceity. The present transcends such duration, the latter is, strictly speaking, only conceived in function of it. If I am not mistaken, the miraculous should be viewed as regards the matter of events in the same light as the present should be viewed as regards their form; as the present rendered capable of sense perception (which must necessarily appear as the action of the eternal). If conceived in this way the miraculous must necessarily be in function of holiness, because only the saint really lives in the actual. Of course it can be objected that I am juggling away the most irrational characteristics of the miraculous, that I am voluntarily leaving in the shade the question of whether a miracle really contradicts the laws of nature. But that objection implies an absolute misunderstanding of the solution. If we pretend to re-absorb the miraculous into the course of history, clearly we are suppressing it—the real question is whether we are in our rights to do so. Note that the action produced on minds is an essential element in the very notion of the miraculous, and so is the holiness of the person who performs the miracle. Hence a miracle must be defined as a complex relation of a spiritual order which—absolutely—is only thinkable in relation to faith. It would be fundamentally illegitimate to substitute for that relation a purely material phenomenon exclusively characterised by being "in contradiction to the laws of nature."

The attack will be continued, I suppose, with the assertion that either the miracle is a-normal in its content (but this would need to be established by evidence we lack or which can at all times be doubted), or else that its a-normal character is due exclusively to the subjective interpretation made of it by ignorant spectators. Does our solution ignore this dilemma? It is already agreed that we must reject the first alternative, for, as I have said, the very idea of criticism involves the negative results that may be its outcome. But the second alternative is no more acceptable, for once again it supposes the dualism of appearance and reality whose negation is the very condition of faith. If the miracle is thinkable, it is only in function of faith, that is, it is beyond the dualism of objective matter and of subjective interpretation, and similarly beyond the idea of a historical order—in the absolute present (which only is for faith).

February 20th

It seems to me now that we must determine the degree in which a problem such as that of the miraculous has to do with the subject as I have defined it. I have no desire to write a philosophy of Christianity, and so it may be dangerous (as well as tempting) to pick up by chance a notion which is specifically Christian so as to discover what it turns into once it is transposed. I am now wondering about the extent I have succumbed to this temptation as regards the miraculous.

It is clear that the notion of religious history, as I have posited it, has an immediate connection with the most fundamental data of my work. For I think I have established that the believer must needs place himself within religious history (of which, moreover, his faith is the transcendent condition). And there is no doubt that it is here that the difficulties I am up against belong. For the religious history of which I am speaking seems incapable of being other than Christian history, and hence it looks as though I must be inevitably led to state the problem that that history involves. Thus a labour of critical elucidation becomes necessary. Once again we seem to be being carried off, as though by an irresistible current, towards the danger point where reflection on faith passes into faith.

I will restate the difficulty. It appears at first glance as if we cannot escape from what is contingent in a pure and simple Christianisation of religious thought, save by setting up a formalism that defines in the abstract the transcendent conditions that direct all religious thought. Now this formalism, as we have seen, is impossible; it is certain that the determinations characteristic of a religion do not amount to a particular content in which a form in itself universal is specified. Such formalism, supposing it were possible, would only have bearing on the external conditions (sociological or even psychological conditions, for instance) of religious life: the essence of religion would remain completely outside its framework. I have already said that *religion* only is for whoever has already passed beyond the stage at which there are still religions. But the question is even more complicated by the fact that, as we have seen, this religion does not amount in any degree or at any stage to a universal system by means of which the Work of theoretical thought or even of practical reason could be achieved. Religion *is* only for the person who surrenders himself to it. There is no possible transition from a judgment bearing on religions to faith—indeed faith even implies the absolute opposite of the position implied in that judgment. (I recall the expression in *L'Echange*: "There are no other women.") The absolute transcendence of religion (I do not even dare say *his* religion) for the believer is expressed by him in the affirmation that it is true. This expression must be regarded as ambiguous and even as absolutely false by the philosopher. We are here in the domain of being and no comparison is possible. And that explains why I could not admit the statement that all religions are true in the measure in which they are identical: there we would still have some illegitimate rationalism, we would still be claiming to transcend faith in the name of an objective affirmation. Faith must appear to thought as that which cannot be transcended, as that which cannot at any degree be regarded as the approximation to what, for a superior understanding, would be an objective affirmation. This links up with the negative position I have developed elsewhere regarding what could be called transcendental science.

This, it seems to me, is as much as to say that even metaphysically we cannot transcend the idea of salvation (salvation not being taken in a subjectivist sense, since, inasmuch as I am a believer, I must will universality; nothing is less religious than subjectivity in the particularist sense of the term).

"But," it may be objected, "all this is no more than pure fideism. You are only taking up anew the old idea that, whatever object it be applied to, faith is a value for itself; the idea that faith is the only reality and that the intellectual and representative vestments with which it is clothed always remain contingent in relation to it." But I totally repudiate fideism. And that because when it affirms faith it suppresses it in the degree to which it re-establishes between itself and its surround a dualism that it is the mission and originality of faith to surmount. Faith has no truth that permits it to be isolated from the ideal realities upon which it depends. Inasmuch as it postulates such a truth fideism negates itself. "One cannot believe in the abstract, one cannot believe in the void," says my heroine,[1] which amounts to saying that as soon as faith ceases to appear to itself as absolutely bound up with its object it negates itself as faith. It is important to emphasise this realist aspect of faith. If it be said that it is a necessary illusion bound up with the very nature of faith, I answer that I have adequately demonstrated the nothingness of an interpretation that realises faith and converts it into an object (cf. all that was said earlier about the way in which divine transcendence must be thought[2]).

[1] *Le Palais de Sable.*
[2] Cf. note of February 10th.

In this way I return once more to the cardinal idea of my thesis, the absolute centre to which all other ideas must be referred. The relation to God, the positing of the divine transcendence alone enables us to think individuality. This not only means that the individual is himself realised as individual in thinking himself as creature, but also that by the mediation of the believer even those who remain dominated by what Claudel has called the spirit of the earth can perhaps gradually assume an individuality. If we can think divine grace (in the sense of clemency), it is because the believer cannot resolve himself to think that his intervention will be vain and that there are beings irremediably designed for nothingness. The real spirit of universality, which is the religious spirit in eminent degree, is only realised by belief in the divine fatherhood, by the belief in what I have previously called participation as fact—function of the participation through faith which in the religious order should be regarded as the true *primum movens*.[1] I am convinced that the very principle of prayer lies in this tension and living dualism between the two modes of participation that are reconciled in the personal unity of God. And in the measure in which I cannot not think myself as participating in God in the two senses (the factual participation being justified by the 'inverse return' that I pointed out earlier), prayer takes on a profound significance and value.

February 21*st*

Yet the problem of prayer does not yet seem to me resolved or even clearly stated. For in fact prayer appears to the believer (and it is admitted that no extra-religious value could be attributed to prayer), as that which may or may not be granted. But this seems to reintroduce the idea of divine causality.

February 22*nd* (Important)

It seems to me we must set out from the fact that even if the event answers the prayer it cannot appear to be determined by it save to the believer and only to the believer—or, in other words (so as to dispose of an individual interpretation that is illegitimate), to faith and to faith alone. And that is enough to show that we cannot really speak of causality in the strict sense of the

[1] Cf. notes of February 12th.

word; for the judgment of causality is by very definition objective, that is to say, valid irrespective of who enunciates it, valid for a thought in general. Is this enough to refute the religious interpretation? Is it only because we are hard put to it that we localise the action of prayer in the order of faith, because religion, though it did indeed originally aim at giving an objective explanation, has been dislodged from the world of objects? Here I think we must dispose of some equivocations. Obviously we could only formulate the distinction we are now able to establish between objective determination and the religious interpretation as the result of developing speculation at length. But the whole question is whether this development has not resulted in disengaging the very essence of religion more and more clearly; the whole question is whether it must be *regretted*, even on behalf of religious thought, that religious affirmations of a causal order manifestly can no longer have any bearing (in an objective sense). The answer is clear. For the really religious soul no such regret is possible. Religion does not require the confusion of domains, it cannot even adapt itself to them with ease. The "medium" of religious thought, of faith, must needs appear to the believer (inasmuch as he thinks his belief) as an essential and intrinsic condition outside of which no efficacy can be attributed to prayer. The question is whether in that way prayer and the idea of its efficacy degenerate into purely subjective representations and vain illusions. All my work leads to answering this question in the negative. We could not speak here of subjectivity in the pejorative sense of the term unless the event had an objective reality in relation to which the interpretation could be regarded as genuinely contingent. Now we know that this is not the case. There is no ultimate truth of the course of things of which the religious interpretation could be regarded as a deformed and imperfect vision (were it only because time itself cannot be thought as metaphysically real). Yet, it can be argued, if we adopt this standpoint what real efficacy can be attributed to prayer? Obviously this efficacy could only be of a metaphysical order. Can this question be in some way cleared up?

Notice that prayer appears to itself as efficacious—or rather as susceptible of efficacy. Can we say that there are really cases in which it is "of use" and others in which it is not "of use"?

Two other alternatives would be possible. That it is never "of use" or that it is always "of use". We already know why the first is unacceptable; is the second any better?

February 23rd

It seems to me that it amounts to turning prayer into a sort of mechanical cause that is provided with a constant efficacy, and that is irreconcilable with the genuinely spiritual notion of prayer. The spiritual notion always supposes that between human freedom and divine freedom there is a relation exclusive of all mechanical restraint (cf. earlier). But if we adopt the intermediary solution, in what sense are we to understand it? What relation between prayer and the event are we to admit? We already know that the relation cannot be of the physical order (that is, in a word, causal). I take a concrete example. We pray for the cure in a person we love. Suppose that person is cured. We give thanks to God. Does that mean that prayer has acted as a physical cause? Manifestly not, since, as we have already said, the action of prayer is only thinkable for faith (hence it is not objective in the way in which a causal action is objective). But in that case what is the meaning of prayer? How, subsequently, can we regard it as having been efficacious? To answer this question it seems to me that we must first of all try to understand exactly the position of those who deny such efficacy. From the rigorously determinist and naturalist standpoint it could be maintained that we are dealing with a purely blind and absolutely necessary process, which is indifferent to any kind of value and in which it is impossible, save by physical means, to change anything. This, clearly, is the standpoint of physical science. What can we answer? We can say that it is metaphysically false to see in this realism regarding physical conditions the ultimate expression of that which is. We can answer that the value that the cure takes on for us is something in no way less real than any such conditions of fact (that even if we adopt the standpoint of pure fact the value of the cure inasmuch as it is posited as will, seems capable of acting physically). Pure naturalism here only rests on an equivocation. Moreover, naturalism is necessarily transcended by the (Stoical) act of optimism which posits that which is as that which is good; by a free act the mind forever passes beyond the order of blind necessity. In the measure in which Stoicism implies a free act of this nature it transcends all naturalism entirely. Yet from the standpoint of metaphysical optimism of the sort (identification of necessity and the good) it seems that the efficacy of prayer can still be contested and now in a much deeper sense than before. If what happens as necessity is by the same token good, I should abstain from asking for anything. I should limit myself to waiting on events since I can be sure that such events will be in themselves good (however immediately tiresome they may be for me). This is not a question of a pure and simple acceptance of destiny, but of a sort of ideal collaboration by which I affirm—beyond all immediate knowledge—that destiny can only be good, and by which I submit myself in advance to all its decisions. What value has prayer seen from the standpoint of this kind of metaphysical optimism? Prayer can only survive if such optimism can and must be surpassed. Must it be? Can it be?

Notice first of all that this optimism implies a judgment on being (on God) which is identified with the good. On what condition can that judgment be made? It depends entirely on the distinction between the whole and the parts. The parts, if they are considered separately from the whole, may be bad. But inasmuch as they are related to the whole (and as soon as they are really understood, they are necessarily conceived in their organic connection with the whole), they should be regarded as good. I leave aside for the moment the difficult question of the foundation of the statement that posits that the whole is good. If I am myself bad it is inasmuch as I am a part that wishes to treat itself as a whole (as a reality); inasmuch as I participate in the life of all I elevate myself to the good. It is important to ask on what conditions that can be posited. It implies the existence in me not only of the dualism of a rational nature (which conceives the whole) and of a sense nature, but also of the possibility of a progress by which that rational nature becomes more and more actualised in so far as it extends its empire ever further over the sense nature. Here we see an internal difficulty in the doctrine, for on the one hand the good is totally independent of me, it is being, and on the other I realise the good so far as it is in me inasmuch as I become aware of my real relation to the whole. It would be tempting to formulate this last point by saying: I realise the good (the good is realised) inasmuch as I think it as realised (that it thinks itself as realised). This idealist theory of the good which identifies the good with its Idea (or rather with the act that affirms it), cannot, in my opinion, have been that of the Stoics. For them optimism was certainly not a decree of consciousness. But we can see into what contradictions they inevitably fell. If the good *is*, apart from the consciousness I have of it, it appears impossible that awareness of it can contribute to its realisation. Or, more exactly, if consciousness contributes to it, it is not as act but as datum. But in that case we are left with no possible incitement to rationality; if I am myself irrational, the datum of my irrationality should be regarded as an element as much constitutive of reality (in itself perfect) as is the morality and the reasonable activity of my neighbour. And, moreover, if rationality is no more than a datum amongst other data, the ethic of Stoicism collapses—nothing of it can survive.

From this we can derive an important lesson. Metaphysical optimism can only be reconciled with the requirements of a rational ethic if it is posited as a postulate or as the end of rational action, if the good is not thought as being outside the act by which I become aware of it—more precisely, if the good is constituted by the very act that affirms it. But this optimism has nothing in common with the metaphysical optimism that I defined earlier. Instead it appears to me to imply the "logical optimism" (the expression of the neo-Hegelians) that infers perfection from purely formal considerations.

In what way can I push such ethical optimism to its conclusion?

February 25th

I will carry on with that inquiry some other day. To-day all I want is to note down a reflection that came to me this afternoon. The problem of reality as posited by materialism and spiritualism consists really, in the question of knowing *with what* things are made; for example *with what* thought is made. In this field materialism seems necessarily in the right as against spirituality because the question itself only has meaning in the order of material things (we ask ourselves "with what" a given manufactured product has been made). From that point of view the answer of the spiritualists must perforce seem absurd. As they have accepted the materialist way of stating the question, the spiritual nature to which they have recourse to account for the soul becomes a sort of immaterial matter, that is to say something self-contradictory whose existence cannot—by very definition—be established. The superiority of the idealists lies in their absolute refusal to place themselves on this plane and state the question in those terms; for to them, and rightly, the idea of an element out of which thought is made seems entirely meaningless.

March 6th

I have already emphasised the distinction that needs to be established between immanent optimism that binds up the affirmation of value to its realisation by the moral subject—and metaphysical optimism that posits that the good is realised, and that the awareness the subject gains of it is in some way contingent in relation to it. I have noted that metaphysical optimism denies what is specific in moral action in the degree in which it converts it into a pure and simple datum that contributes in some way to the harmony of the whole. There is no obviating this fault by linking moral action up with intellection; for the relation which exists (from the ethical point of view) between the act of intellection and the good—thought as realised—remains unintelligible; either the act of intellection remains absolutely external to its object (this is probably meaningless)—and then it cannot be regarded as participating in that value that it posits as coextensive with itself (with this object)—or else it must be admitted that it introduces into the object a sort of inflation of value, that is to say that, in this act of intellection, at bottom it is the object itself that apprehends itself and hence it looks as if it is in virtue of an illusion that the object can be posited as really independent of the act and so to speak anterior to it. Pure moralism, then, in relation to what I have called immanent optimism, can be defined by its refusal to think the good outside the act that apprehends it, and, (as apprehension here is insufficient), outside the immanent movement by which the moral subject realises it. Nevertheless, as I have pointed out, however elevated such "pure moralism" may be, it is demonstrably insufficient metaphysically. For what in fact is realisation of the good in this instance? Is it not an equivocation? Inasmuch as it is thought as such, does not the good appear as something that is, and has no "requirement" of the subject who realises it? Is not the idea of a creation of values (*Werthschöpfung*) morally unacceptable here? That point must be emphasised.

March 12th

I saw for the first time this morning when talking with A—— in what way our belief transcends all that we know of it. That is why I feel so embarrassed and uneasy when I am asked whether I believe. There is nothing on which one can *interrogate* or *answer*. As soon as my belief descends into knowledge it seems to negate itself—and yet it reaffirms itself beyond the negation of itself.

There is something here that is intimately bound up with the double fact (I perceive it more and more clearly) that divine transcendence only *is* for faith, and that faith can only think divine transcendence as freedom (in relation to the act of faith itself). Divine freedom, doubtless, *is* only for me inasmuch as I have faith in it, but in another and infinitely deeper sense I only have faith in it on condition that I think it as entirely independent of the act by which I think it. The metaphysical solution of this antinomy seems to consist in saying that the act of faith is itself the expression of divine freedom. But we must be careful to remember that this latter statement only has meaning and value for faith.

March 13th

I would like to clear up definitively the notion of the ideality of the finite. I feel I can see there a perpetual source of equivocations and errors.

It must of course be agreed that if the infinite is the negation of the finite this, as the Hegelians saw, is in the sense in which the negation is not a privation or an exclusion, but a reaffirmation or a *Rückkehr in sich*. But in what sense is this reaffirmation possible?

Temporally I distinguish between the finite and the affirmation bearing on the finite. (It is agreed of course that outside the act of affirmation the finite has no more than a purely abstract existence.) In this way it can be said that in that affirmation the finite truly affirms itself. But in what measure does the affirmation embrace its own negation? It seems to me that it is in virtue of the inadequation between the act of affirming on the one hand (which is the expression of the infinite considered positively), and the thing affirmed on the other, which itself only *is* through the exclusion of other things and in consequence does not coincide with the act that posits it. And it is uniquely in the degree to which that disharmony is manifested for consciousness (for the mind, if that be preferred) that the finite appears as transcending itself. Any movement of knowing thought in the strict sense certainly leads to awareness of that discordance and inadequation.

The complementation of the finite thus appears as the effort by which the mind seeks to "bring together" the affirmation and the thing affirmed. This movement can certainly be regarded as the indivisible unity of which the affirmation and the thing affirmed are only the ideal moments.

April 18*th*

In the main I persist in my belief that there is no reason to affirm that the categories cover one another fully. For instance, it in no way follows, from what the personality is at the highest moment that we know, that everything can or should be thought under the category of personality, that a certain neo-critical monadism is true. I feel I have gone a long way from what I would like to call the realism of universality. It will be said that this attitude amounts to admitting the possibility of a juxtaposition of the inferior and the superior, whereas the superior, if it is such, should enfold the inferior and absorb it into itself. But the real question is in what sense the absorption needs to be understood. Inasmuch as it manifests itself as superior doubtless the superior cannot simply be juxtaposed to the known object. The thinking mind, inasmuch as it is mind, is not juxtaposed to the known object. Only I feel tempted to ask myself whether what is superior is not also necessarily on some other plane. The knowing mind realises itself at the same time and on the same plane as the known object (on the same plane as the inferior) inasmuch as it is body. And it can be affirmed that the superiority that consists in knowing could not realise itself without the common foundations which make physical inter-action possible. Now in what sense does the superior really suppress the inferior planes? In what sense does knowing suppress that physical interaction of the perceiving subject (as body) and of the object? It would seem to me false alike to maintain that knowledge is purely and simply juxtaposed to physical inter-action (which obliges us to raise absurd problems) and to say that it suppresses this interaction. The truth is that it implies it and embraces it as its necessary and insufficient condition.

This amounts to saying that we are mistaken if we believe that the predominance of the mind can only be affirmed on the basis of a universal spiritualism, a monism of the psychical. That is a realist and illegitimate 'requirement' that I repudiate. The very categories on which the pretensions of spiritualistic monism are based are amongst those that the correct notion of the mind (as quantity suppressed) obliges us to posit as relative and un-essential. For a veritable metaphysics, that is, for a metaphysics that refuses to be a physics, the question of whether matter is at bottom mind and consciousness at the stage of birth is a question devoid of interest.

Now I am convinced that Bradley's Absolute, an absolute and indivisible unity of all the elements of perfection that our ex-perience discovers, a massive block of reality, implies this uni-versalistic postulate. Real philosophy is beyond monism as it is beyond pluralism, because the categories of the one and of the many both lose all significance in the order of mind.

April 19th

It is worth while going back to these important points. Every-thing leads, it seems to me, to the question of the value of the category of the *also*, or to asking whether connections can be exclusively external. Monism is only intelligible if it denies this radically, that is to say, if it affirms that every external relation has in reality its basis in the absolute interiority of the One. Through fear of having purely and simply to juxtapose the superior to the inferior, monism claims to universalise the cate-gories of the concrete and to affirm that they overlap the abstract categories and are their reality. The idea of suppression thus appears as the fundamental, constituent condition and monism cannot be defined apart from it. It is difficult for me to accept this attitude. I do not accept the idea of the juxtaposition of the superior and the inferior because juxtaposition can only appear to us as the schema of interaction. Two bodies juxtaposed are two bodies capable of reciprocal interaction; it might even perhaps be maintained that juxtaposition already implies reciprocal action. To juxtapose knowing to physical action means trying to reduce one to the other. The standing debate between monism and pluralism turns on the question of whether there is the "also," that is to say the juxtaposed, in the real. The monists, I think, are thoroughly in their rights as long as they limit themselves to stating that the more we elevate ourselves in being, the more the purely juxtaposed tends to be eliminated. In this respect progress in being is progress in interiority. Does it follow that we can realise the pure interiority that the monists desire? Is it necessary to seek to eliminate the ontological value of the "also" (to refuse it all intrinsic reality) so as to deny it? The primary question here is whether such elimination is real or illusory. However hard we may try to deny it there is a plane of thought which is that of the "also." The point is whether, if we deny that this plane is ultimate, we thereby affirm the monist thesis of the reducibility of the external connections to relations of interiority. Once again we want to know whether the monist theory that introduces the intervention of a kind of extension (conceived as totality, as integrality) into the order of the concrete is still legitimate; or whether reality is suppressed extension, that is, that for which the question of extension has ceased to be posited (i.e. that which can realise itself no matter where, but not *everywhere*; for everywhere would once again imply a relation essential to place, place being understood in a sense not necessarily spatial).

The gravest objection that could be made to my view would consist in saying that the concrete should be a power or potency (*puissance*), thus reintroducing the notion of extension. Is that objection valid?

April 20th

Provisionally I leave aside the idea of power or potency so as to note an observation I made yesterday that seems to me important. Independently of all the internal criticisms aroused by the idea of an objective (dialectical) determination of the content of the world, it appears to me clearly that, if the requirements of the spiritual life are to be met, that content should be regarded as objectively non-determinable. Supposing that we could demonstrate objectively, that is to say in a valid way, a way valid for a thought in general, that our universe is governed by a spiritual principle, the demonstration would render impossible the radical freedom that can only manifest itself by faith. Faith (and thence spirituality) is only possible if metaphysical doubt is in some way imposed on the mind by the nature—in itself indeterminable— of the object. Were a science of providence possible, providence would cease to be a religious affirmation, it would be reduced to a sort of perfected mechanism, whereas the postulates of the religious consciousness go beyond all mechanism.

This process of argument presents, in my eyes, an almost absolute value. It is not a question of postulating factual conditions in the name of legitimate requirements (some people mistakenly think this is the basis of the Kantian argument). The argument does not bear on fact. True, it may be objected that what I call the religious consciousness is perhaps only a preparatory moment of the spiritual life, one destined to disappear at the heart of an integral science of reality—I note that the objection can only be made from the standpoint of metaphysical *optimism*—that we can conceive humanity entering into direct and conscious communication with superior powers, demiurges, and those communications taking the place of the mystery of worship and adoration. What about such a hypothesis? I believe it is precisely a hypothesis and that is its weakness; it is essentially something that may, and also may not, be realised. It brings about the intervention in what is actually the religious order, of elements of contingence and potentiality; without previous justification it posits the possibility of communications that would need after all to be founded on laws that are in some way physical. For obviously if such communications are miraculous, we are no longer dealing with the same question.

But then, the argument continues, at the most this proves that religion as such has not to busy itself with such future possibilities. Even so is not reflection capable of envisaging them? But that supposes that it is possible for reflection to transcend the

religious consciousness. Now the value and the supreme significance of religious affirmations reside precisely in this—*that
they transcend all reflection*. To posit as possible a science of what
is actually an object of faith is not to think faith, but to go back to
what faith has left for ever behind it.

When metaphysical optimism posits a science of providence
as possible in the future, it falls short of the religion which, it
claims, can be surpassed.

In consequence, from the moment it has been established that
religious thought transcends reflection, that it is only thinkable
as transcending reflection, the impossibility of an objective or
notional determination of the spiritual content of the world has
been demonstrated. From the standpoint of metaphysical knowledge the world remains the site of uncertainty, the reign of the
possible, it remains contingent in relation to religious thought.
In that sense the notion of progress, conceived in the only metaphysically valid sense of the term, must be radically rejected.

Such an attitude is distinct from agnosticism, it is even
opposed to it in that it implies the radical negation of the science
of the real that agnosticism posits as outside thought and at once
realised and inaccessible. Doubtless we must allow that the
knowing subject, in the measure in which he sets about determining the rational content of the world, posits such a science as
something that must be, so to speak, rediscovered and re-begotten.
Knowledge cannot be defined for itself save as a reproduction,
as a copy. . . . It is only to pure reflection that the object copied
is shown to be engendered by the act that copies it.

Science as science is absolutely incapable of liberating itself
from the idea of the world as realised knowledge that we have to
find anew. It is a legitimate mode of representation and even one
that can be called indispensable. It only becomes vicious when
it is erected into a metaphysical construction. Now that is precisely the mistake common to optimism and pessimism, for both
alike claim to formulate judgments on the content of the real
which is posited as an object of science; that is to say they transpose into the metaphysical order the postulate that consists in
positing the real as science which is exclusively valid in the order
of science. The fundamental contradiction in Schopenhauer's
system consists in formally treating being as science (knowing)

(as it can be determined objectively as possessing certain characteristics) and then assigning to it characteristics of irrationality that are incompatible with the relatively rationalist way in which the problem is tackled. To both optimism and pessimism I answer that: *there is no objectively valid judgment bearing on being*. Here we need to forestall an objection. "You are only re-establishing," I may be told, "the dualism of being and the phenomenon in its most sterile and out-of-date sense, being is no more than the empty and intrinsically unreal 'within' of which Hegel speaks." But the real question is whether the dualism as I conceive it is not entirely different, or rather whether, strictly speaking, there is any dualism between what is within knowledge and what is beyond knowledge (here the problem is stated in terms that are quite different from those involved in the logic of essence, which is itself wholly within knowledge). What I have said elsewhere of the relativity of the dualism of appearance and reality shows how far I am from the attitude attributed to me by this objection.

April 21st

The principal interest of the preceding process of argument consists in establishing the impossibility of any attempt to base atheism on a philosophy of nature. In fact, supposing it were possible to define nature objectively as the realisation of a will or a decree, that definition would have no bearing on anything specifically religious and specifically divine. Faith in providence could not be converted into a science of providence without the collapse of religion. But as soon as it is no longer even conceivable that the philosophy of nature could furnish a basis for apologetics, inversely it can no longer be invoked by the enemies of apologetics; it is entirely indifferent in relation to the religious problem.

It is plain that the idea of an objective refutation of atheism is a contradictory idea. Atheism is by definition that which cannot be objectively refuted; but it is also that which cannot be objectively demonstrated, or rather that of which the objective demonstration should be regarded as essentially void (since the very idea of such a demonstration in some manner embraces its conclusions).

Hence we can see clearly the mediatory rôle of religious thought without which God cannot really be thought. Moreover, we know already that this does not amount to making God dependent on religious thought, but quite the contrary, that the religious act is supremely the act by which thought posits God as transcendent in relation to it, the act in its turn being thought as that which cannot be reflected (that which cannot be treated as a projection). If pure reflection tries to seize on these successive acts and to see in them purely subjective steps, it is reduced to nullity at the outset by the act of faith that goes beyond it and forever denies it.

There we are stating the general critical problem raised by all this endeavour: how is it possible to have a justification of what by definition claims to transcend all reflection? Does not justification mean reflection? Are we not in the realm of the unjustifiable, the arbitrary? And can that pitfall be avoided otherwise than by recourse to a demonstration, that is to say, to something whose impossibility has already been established. I answered this criticism superabundantly when I pointed out that the *I think*, as free act, as condition of certitude, itself also transcends all demonstration because all demonstration is based on it. Yet I recognise that an objection is possible. If, in fact, someone alleges the universality of the *I think* (as opposed to the non-universality of religious thought) and we answer that the *I think*, as self-consciousness, is not universal, by accepting the parallel am I not letting it be understood that religious thought, too, can be regarded as universal in so far as we admit that it cannot not be for itself? And if, alternatively, we refuse to admit this are we not obliged to deny the validity of the comparison and to define religious thought as a subjective and contingent phenomenon? Note, moreover, that to posit the universality of religious thought seems to mean restoring to it that character of objectivity (objective being taken in the sense of *that which is valid for a thought in general*) which appeared to us incompatible with its essence. Recourse to the cogito thus does not seem to help us to elude the dilemma.

By dint of reflecting on the obscure notion of universality I have been led once more to take up the problem of the necessary. It seems to me actually that in the current notion of the necessary we can disentangle three elements: the first is the conjunction or constant succession that appears to be a sign of the necessary, the second is the psychological (or even muscular) experience of constraint which, in my opinion, has not been insisted on enough, the third is rational concatenation such as we see manifested, for instance, in geometry.

What do we mean when we state that between two phenomena given in time there is a necessary relation? Obviously we do not only mean to say that once the first is given the second follows; or rather we admit such a constant sequence, but it appears to us as the sign of something which is necessity. I think we apply to the fact of constant consecutiveness the habit we have of seeking for the cause of phenomena. Necessity (in the vaguest sense) is posited as cause of the constant consecutiveness. And it is here that the two elements I have just been speaking about appear. I am convinced that, in last analysis, we project our experience of constraint into things and that when we affirm that they necessarily follow one another, we limit ourselves to supposing in them a sort of psycho-physiological becoming analogous to our own. But as we reflect, and claim to pass beyond that fiction, we have recourse to the notion of rational concatenation, and for a crude type of constraint we substitute an entirely ideal kind of constraint in virtue of which our ideas link together in certain determined modes. So here we will limit ourselves to postulating ideal relations analogous (though in a more complex order) to those that we recognise amongst the simpler essences that we can study directly.

But this only displaces the issue. The question still remains: How can we confound the relation that unites the constraint in virtue of which our ideas are attracted together or repel one another—with necessity strictly speaking? Is such constraint the sign of necessity, or on the contrary does it create necessity? Are we going to be tempted to say that the ideal constraint is only the interior reproduction of muscular constraint, and so descend once more from the order of ideas to the order of bodies (and see the very idea of the necessary disappear).

April 22nd

I am trying to posit the problem in terms that are simple and lack ambiguity. But first of all, I believe we must distinguish questions that we are in danger of confounding.

As regards what I have called ideal constraint, the problem seems to be as follows. Given the relations the mind discovers between ideas (relations of inclusion or exclusion, of compatibility or incompatibility), how can constraint or ideal necessity be defined in function of those relations? Note that the number of possible solutions here is very limited. Either we see in necessity a characteristic that is constitutive of such relations, or else we posit constraint as exterior in some way to the ideas and the bonds that unite them. The first solution is visibly absurd, for the question regarding the necessity in virtue of which that character is imposed on the mind and received by it remains outstanding. In addition we could show that such a solution would render either error or truth inconceivable (if the action exercised by ideas on the mind were in some way physical, it ought to be infallible—in any case freed from all characteristics of ideality). So we must admit that necessity and constraint come from the mind and not from ideas, though this supposes an unacceptable dualism between the mind and ideas. I will put this first result in a nutshell as follows: Supposing we posit the dualism of the mind and of ideas, it is from the mind and not from ideas that the constraint comes. On a deeper level, if one and the same reality is considered in turn as activity reflecting on ideas and as a whole of ideas reflected, it is as activity that it appears to account for the character of ideal necessity which is attached to the relations that unite ideas to one another. This second proposition, by the fact that it illuminates the fundamental unity of the mind, has the special advantage of excluding any subjectivist interpretation that would imply the reciprocal exteriority of form and matter.

Yet the appearances do not seem to be in favour of this interpretation; for, far from assigning to them a necessity that does not belong to them, the mind appears to itself as finding, between ideas, relations given to it as necessary. How is this impression reconcilable with what I have just said? It is only so, I think, on condition that we insist that the mind recognises itself in its ideas, and that the relations existing between ideas are only imposed on it as necessary because it itself, in them, *is given* to itself, and borrows in some way their disguise. There, doubtless, lies the deepest secret of intelligibility—which realises in itself the union and fusion of necessity (external apparent action of the ideas on the mind) and of freedom (real interior and autonomous action of the mind on itself).

Ideal constraint is only possible and justifiable if it regains possession of the will by which the mind makes itself mind— that is to say the will to be mind.

But, it may be said, the ideal matter with which the mind finds itself confronted is external to it, and so how can it clothe itself in it so as to constitute itself? An objection of this kind refutes itself. For it supposes a mind that is a datum given, is a thing confronted with another thing; a thing (be it a form) to which another thing is external—whereas the mind is nothing save the very negation of such exteriority. The life of the mind, as Hegel has seen profoundly, is the suppression of such exteriority; the mind is the term that suppresses itself as term. So we must not represent to ourselves a realised and ready-made faculty to which ideas are given from without. Were we to set out from such a crude representation it is clear that intelligibility itself would become unintelligible. Instead we must represent to ourselves— outside any spatial scheme—an order that creates itself, but which can only do so by denying exteriority, in such a way that exteriority needs to be given (in the most exact, that is the emptiest sense of the term) at least as appearance for this order to be able to realise itself. In this sense the mind only realises itself as experience for this order which creates itself beyond exteriority and, thanks to it, is experience itself. Necessity appears as the very armature of this experience whereas at bottom it is only the inverse image of freedom.

The Kantian scheme of an understanding informing and ordering from without the matter furnished to it, is in this sense only a transitory and clumsy expression of the fundamental idea that there is only knowledge and intelligibility where exteriority has first of all been affirmed and then denied and reduced. In this way we can clearly see the individual and antinomical link between the empirical and the intelligible.

April 23rd

So I return to the idea of a mind that only realises itself in and beyond exteriority. But there are still equivocations to be dispelled. For do I not seem to be upholding the idea that necessity is in some way a formal creation of the mind? No, I claim that the mind only becomes for itself (that is, only becomes mind) inasmuch as reality seems to it to be directed by a necessity within it. But, it may be said, here we are faced with alternatives. Either it is by an illusion that reality appears to mind as possessing in itself such a character of necessity—and we are back at subjectivism; or else it does effectively possess it and we are once again up against all the difficulties of realism. I believe the answer lies in showing that the two alternatives are equally devoid of meaning. On the one hand we do not escape from realism by realising necessity in a legislative understanding (which, moreover, is defined in terms of a thing exterior to other things); on the other hand, as we already know, when we realise necessity in things, we do not take into account that such necessity is valid for the mind still conceived in a receptive and physical sense. The mind, I said, only becomes mind on condition it recognises a world of necessity. It does not appear to itself as creating this world, and in reality it does not create it; it *discovers* it, and in the measure in which it discovers it, it thinks it necessarily as being independent of the act by which it thinks it. The mind in one sense is precisely this discovery, it can only think itself independently of this discovery by a fiction whose illegitimate character is detected by speculation. But then is it contingent that there may be necessity? Exactly in the measure in which it is contingent that the mind is in being, and no more. Now the reality of the mind ceases to be contingent as soon as a thought arises; the very act by which I interrogate myself on the contingence of mind suppresses the contingence; and as for the act itself, it is only by an illusion that I can try to pass beyond it. The necessity and the intelligibility of nature thus depend on the reality of the mind, though not in the simplicist sense of the Kantian philosophy, but in the deeper sense that the mind cannot be realised save in the degree and measure in which such necessity is constituted—not exactly by it (because it is only for it on condition it is thought as not being by it)—but for it. It is only by an abstraction which the very life of the mind denounces as vicious, that we can dissociate a pure thought subsisting in itself from an undetermined nature that could be the reign of disorder.

It can be seen how these ideas, still only glimpsed confusedly, have begotten the notion of a universal dialectic or deduction—whereas, if better understood, they would have brought with them the certainty that such a dialectic and deduction are impossible. For from the moment at which we have grasped the fundamental rôle of exteriority as moment of spiritual life, the idea of a system constituted by the simple application of an internal principle, merely by the mechanism of a dialectic, is seen to be contradictory. Such a system can never be constituted save as provisional and as within a constructing experience.

Here not unnaturally we come up against the question of the measure in which a spiritual totality of this kind can be regarded as dissociable from the experience in relation to which it is defined. It seems to me that the difficulty is that we always fall into the realism of the intelligible which in reality ends up in the suppression of the intelligible. Intelligibility as I conceive it is a dynamic relation, the relation of tension by which the mind is constituted when it organises its world; it cannot be realised outside that relation. It seems to me that the possible objection here proceeds from what I should call the philosophy of analytics. Is it not intelligible in itself, objectively, that a whole implies its component parts? Have we not there at least one type of intelligibility that does not require the dynamic relation of which I have spoken? But I believe that it is precisely in the simplest analytical relation that it is easiest to recognise the accuracy of what I have said. Doubtless that A is A is posited objectively; but there is nothing in it that imposes itself from outside the mind. Logical thought is constituted by positing that A is A, by the discovery of that internal identity that appears to it as objective and which really is so, provided that by objectivity we do not understand the exteriority of something juxtaposed to thought. I recall once more that such a juxtaposition is in a general way void of meaning (it is a false notion due to the hidden intervention of the notion of the thinking subject as physical agent, as body). Thus thought defines itself in the measure in which the logical relations are defined for it; the dualism which seems to exist between the relations and itself is only the dualism there is between the fact of being in itself and being for itself—a dualism which is resolved in unity; the pure *Fürsichsein* would be a contradictory and empty form; the *I think* is only valid as perception of the unity between the 'in itself' and the 'for itself.'

April 24th

This amounts to saying that intelligibility cannot in any way be conceived as external relation between thought on the one hand and totality of ideas on the other. Any effort to reinforce the notion of intelligibility by trying to show how it is imposed from without ends up in the very negation of the notion; there is only intelligibility where the mind, though not positing its ideas as identical with itself, recognises itself in them. The problem of intelligibility cannot even be stated unless we give up conceiving thought as a term that is either a datum given or a formal condition exterior in some way to what is given to it. From the moment at which we thus stabilise thought and deny it as activity, we condemn ourselves to seeing in intelligibility either a mystery or a purely psychological residue. I take up once again the dilemma that this process of argument seems to bring with it. It can be stated thus: "Either intelligibility is as it were an objective emanation of the intrinsic nature of ideas, which is what you deny—or else it remains a sort of stamp of entirely subjective origin which is attached by the mind to certain relations. And besides being obscure, this last solution is in danger of passing into the first, because it seems that it must be for intrinsic reasons that the mind declares some given relations valid and others not." To this I answer that there is really no dilemma because the two alternatives imply the same postulate (and that is why they come together). This postulate, which I reject, is that there are on the one hand ideas and on the other there is a thought external to them which from outside expresses affirmations bearing on these ideas. Now, I repeat, if we admit such exteriority, if, instead of seeing in exteriority something that thought suppresses as soon as it is realised, we make of it an ultimate relation subsisting between thought and its object, then we necessarily arrive at the very negation of the thought whose exercise we wanted to understand. Thought is only exteriority suppressing itself, exteriority treating itself as provisional moment, and in consequence appearing as a phase which implies it but passes beyond it. If we stabilise this phase we remain in a sort of imaginary space which in no degree symbolises the living, dynamic order which is thought.

But, it will be rejoined, there is still a precise question: How do we make the discrimination between what is and what is not intelligible? First of all, I think, we need to realise that the distinction of what is, and what is not, intelligible cannot in any degree be posited as absolute. There are only absolutely clear-cut distinctions in the elementary field; distinctions appear the more radical inasmuch as thought, as function of harmony, is less completely realised (for example, with the sensations). The value of the distinction between the intelligible and the non-intelligible depends on the value of the norm (made more or less explicit) in function of which this distinction is made; and here we raise a singularly important new question which is that of knowing *what is the value of norms.*

We must notice, I think, that even the meaning of this question is eminently obscure. If interrogating ourselves on the value of a norm means measuring this norm by another norm, we risk being carried away into an infinite regression—unless thought itself can be posited as norm. Can it? If it cannot, either the question of the value of norms is meaningless, or else it ought to be stated in new and different terms which we need to look for.

It is clear that if thought can identify itself as a supreme and unconditional norm the question of the value of a particular norm may have the meaning I have already given to it. But is this so? It is enough to recall what I have said regarding the impossibility of realising thought itself as norm, and regarding the impossibility of treating thought other than as act and as life, to see that only by an abuse could thought treat itself as norm. This is not equivalent to denying that there is a supreme norm of thought, but only to denying that thought can identify itself with the norm and to showing that the question of the value of this norm cannot even be raised, or, at least, cannot be stated in the simple terms that I suggested earlier. (More precisely: suppose this norm to be the principle of identity. We cannot identify thought with that principle, because the intelligibility that makes that principle what it is, that makes it valid, does not belong to it objectively, but is bound to the act by which the mind recognises itself in it, etc.)

To posit (still hypothetically) a supreme norm is thus to limit ourselves to conceiving a first and in some way immediate stage of intelligibility, in which thought must recognise itself before it is able to affirm anything (this, of course, applies to the order of reflection, not to the order of time); and the value of this norm, far from being defined in function of another norm (which would be infinite and contradictory), or through itself (which would be meaningless), remains subordinated to the free movement by which the mind realises itself.

This amounts to saying that however far we go in the objective analysis of the principles and the formal conditions of thought, we will never come to a *primal* condition, if by *primal* we understand a source of intelligibility. Intelligibility itself always transcends all principles and forms of this kind; it cannot be defined other than by an appeal to the very life of thought (which is what Plato saw better than anyone).

Hence we can conclude that in every case there is a sense in which it is illegitimate and even absurd to posit an "eternal axiom" or a unique generating law from which the natural laws derive; it is the objective and realist sense, the sense that Taine uses. Such a law, supposing it exists, is always subordinate to the principle of intelligibility as I have defined it.

Thus we see that discrimination is always subordinated to norms which themselves can only be posited as relative to the realisation of the intelligible, to the constitution of that order that the mind wills when it wills itself.

Here once again I take up the examination of the question of why there is order in nature. My answer is as follows:

The question itself implies the hypothesis of the possibility of a thought which is order and reason and is juxtaposed to an irrational world. But this dualism is suppressed when it is thought; for, I must repeat, thought is not something placed face to face with something else, order is not something external to something else. The order of thought could not be defined for itself if it did not discover the order of things. The progress in rationality which defines thought could not be realised independently of the progress in the knowledge of things which is knowledge itself inasmuch as knowledge is life—this second progress being itself fictitiously realised as system. If someone objects that thought is for itself a mystery and might well be irrational, I reply that irrationality can only be defined in function of an ideally posited reason, and that in consequence the hypothesis is self-destructive.

In short, what we call the rationality of the world is only the fictitious projection of the life of knowledge, a life which consists at one and the same time of finding and constituting. In this sense, far from knowledge being a reflection of the world, the world is the reflection of knowledge; though it must be fully understood—I repeat—that knowledge implies not the idea of a perpetual creation by a pre-existing understanding, but the idea of a thought which is discovered in discovering the world and has its life in that very discovery. The idea of a rational ready-made world that only has to be rediscovered is really no more than an aspect arbitrarily dissociated from the complex movement by which the mind is realised in recognising the world. The idea of a world completed by the mind, through which it becomes conscious of itself, is of greater interest. It is a better safeguard of the indissoluble unity outside of which everything ceases to be intelligible.

But amongst a thousand other problems one special problem arises here. Is not the mind reduced to something which becomes in time, something which, in consequence, is or remains external to itself or dissolves itself, something which flees from itself when it seeks itself? Whereas the mind must be something which finds itself; and that which finds itself, in finding itself, frees itself from time.

The solution I glimpse, though very imperfectly, lies in a relation analogous to the relation I defined earlier for exteriority in general (time, moreover, is only one mode of exteriority, though perhaps it marks a progress in relation to space in the process of self-suppression by which exteriority is realised and completed).

April 25th

This is really nothing more than a specification of my general theory of intelligibility. To realise mind as the site of the intelligible in a non-temporal identity would still mean establishing between the mind and the "something else" that exteriority that it is the mind's function to reabsorb into itself. I repeat that to posit the mind as external to anything whatsoever (even to a world of pure exteriority), is to treat it as a thing that can play its part in an order of juxtaposition, and in consequence is to make it external to itself. In that way there is an explicit basis for what I said previously about the necessity of integrating exteriority as ideal moment.

I would like to throw light on this general theory. Would it be adequately expressed if I said that the intelligible is realised in space and in time? Perhaps, but on condition I specified that the intelligible is not exterior to the realisation, that the realisation is not only the contingent completion of the intelligible, but also a constitutive moment which cannot be set aside without the intelligible destroying itself. Only this in its turn is not acceptable, is not true, unless we add to it an all-important complement, namely that pure intelligibility can only be constituted outside space and time on condition that it has passed through the medium of space and time. (The example that occurs to me, though its validity needs verifying, is the following: geometry, inasmuch as it is a non-temporal and non-spatial whole, is only possible through the mediation of the becoming—at one and the same time temporal and spatial—of a consciousness bound to a physical substratum. I must return to this.) Thought cannot define itself as transcending space and time unless the link between thought and space (or time) is a genuinely constitutive and functional moment of its life; and the intelligibility which belongs to pure thought (that is to say thought transcending space and time) cannot be defined without an appeal to this mediating experience, for it is the experience that makes it possible.

April 27th

All that I have said before leads to the conclusion that intelligibility is nothing which can be defined from without, and in that way certain insoluble questions are set aside. I would say more; strictly speaking intelligibility is not something that can become an object for the mind. It is only by an illusion that thought can believe that it posits the intelligible outside itself, confronting itself. In reality as soon as it confronts intelligibility thought makes intelligibility cease to be itself, for intelligibility can only be defined in thought, and as its very life and soul; it is the moment through which thought constitutes itself as thought, and neither by right nor in fact can thought be separated from intelligibility.

It may be objected that I myself am doing precisely what I seem to condemn. Am I not myself defining what I posited as indefinable? Am I not converting intelligibility into an object?

This obliges me to recapitulate. I set out by saying that intelligibility cannot be considered as an intrinsic property of an idea or of a group of ideas, nor can it be conceived as a relation between an idea (or a group of ideas) and thought itself conceived as external to a given idea or group of ideas. Intelligibility, I said, can only be conceived in function of an immanent movement by which thought grasps itself in a whole of ideas which are only its object in the measure in which it itself can become its own object. A whole of ideas is only intelligible in the measure in which the mind recognises itself in that whole. But here we come to the question that I raised just now. Inasmuch as I think intelligibility in this way, inasmuch as I reflect it, do I not, even when I deny it as an object, or as a property or objective relation, posit it as exterior to the act by which I reflect it? By the very act by which I claim to suppress it, do I not reconstitute the relation of exteriority between thought and the intelligible? We seem to be in the presence of a dilemma. Either all reflection on intelligibility is impossible, or else, if a certain reflection on intelligibility is legitimate, this is because there is at least one sense in which thought can in some way dissociate the intelligible from itself and oppose it to itself. My answer, I think, must be simply this: no doubt intelligibility can be an object of reflection for thought, *but only in the sense in which thought can be such an object for itself*, and provided that we do not make any distinction whatsoever between thought itself and the intelligible. Observe that to deny the possibility would be either to deny that thought can be an object for itself, or else to create once more, though in the opposite sense, the dualistic gulf between thought and intelligibility that we intended to suppress.

I would like to clear up more completely the conclusions that should be drawn from this inquiry.

In the first place we are led to the view that to seek to define intelligibility in function of certain formal conditions (that analysis should discover) is a vain enterprise. Such conditions cannot account for intelligibility itself; they can only appear to do so in virtue of an illusion that can always be detected, and in this sense I see myself obliged to deny all *philosophical* content to the idea of evidence (that is to say of intelligibility *per se*). We can no more dream of realising a principle of intelligibility than we can realise intelligibility itself. So when we think of the forms of order (conditions of intelligibility), we must remember that, from the speculative point of view, these forms should be regarded as posterior to the intelligibility for which at first sight they seem to need to and to be able to account. This not merely because the forms can only be defined *after* and *according to* an experience in which they are already applied or realised, but also, in the infinitely deeper and more *intrinsic* sense, because the strictly formal moment of intelligibility is posterior to and relative to a genuine dynamic and constitutive moment—of which it is only the schematisation and translation into dualistic language.

So intelligibility is not in function of the forms, the forms are in function of intelligibility and, I repeat, it is necessary that this should be so; for to render an account of intelligibility is either to think nothing or else to pre-form the intelligible itself in the formal principle that is destined to give an account of it.

Yet the problem of the possibility itself of this self-recognition seems to be posited in more and more threatening terms. How can we avoid admitting that it is by some pre-existing norm that the mind is guided in the self-research in which I have seen the very condition of intelligibility? And how can we give an account of this norm? (This links up with the problem raised earlier.) If, for example, I say that the mind recognises itself in the identity of A, and that it is for that reason that that identity becomes a norm, does not the question arise of why it recognises itself in that identity?

If I am asked why the principle of identity is intelligible (why the mind recognises itself in it), I can answer by placing myself on several hierarchical planes. On one of those planes I would say: because identity is the very condition of the exercise of thought (this exercise being no longer the formal but the real condition to which I should refer myself). But on a higher plane I would say that intelligibility is not something that permits of a reason; (for, as I said earlier, when we give reasons we only displace the problem, and the question once more comes up of why thought must be capable of being exercised—which cannot be dealt with because the question, as a question, is absurd).

So the answer is always that when thought isolates itself from the identity and separates the identity from itself, it suppresses itself: that thought can only be concretely defined as thought in and through identity; it is *in that* that intelligibility consists though it is not that that accounts for intelligibility (I repeat that intelligibility is not a thing for which reasons can be given). From this point of view the intelligible is defined as that which we cannot genuinely set aside, that which reappears in the negation of itself (this is particularly clear as regards identity).

Hence it seems that every intelligible should be at one with a certain dialectic on which, as such, it is founded—though this dialectic is not necessarily thought as exterior to experience, and, in general, it is experience that functions as dialectic (save concerning the most abstract forms of thought—and is there not even an experience of pure thought? I am convinced there is).

To sum up, intelligibility is to a quite external link between thought on the one hand and ideas on the other what the internal mediation of the judgment is to the unity, considered extrinsically, of the subject and the predicate. That is to say that just as in the judgment the subject must not be isolated from the predicate that is attributed to it (which ought not to be regarded as able to be isolated either), so thought cannot be regarded as really distinct from what it qualifies as intelligible.

Here we are once again up against the problem of the non-intelligible. In what sense can thought reject it and exclude it from itself? If it excludes it does it not convert itself into a term (into a thing)? This links up with several of the oldest and most serious problems of philosophy. On what conditions can a thought be exclusive without becoming external to itself? (Since the *outside of self* coincides with the *inside of self* in the order of thought, cf. above). There is a sense in which, as was to be foreseen, exclusion is impossible; it is for this reason that thought, from the moment it is posited, posits itself as by right comprehensive of everything.

April 28*th*

To-day I would like to ask myself in what measure this general theory allows us to resolve or to suppress certain particular problems.

There is one at least that seems to me to collapse, it is what can be called the general problem of the relations of thought and of the extended, since we have seen that exteriority is not expansion, the manifestation of an internal power, but the condition outside of which thought cannot define itself for itself. If this is so, the problem no longer exists, there can no longer be question of a localisation of thought; but we find ourselves in the presence of this fact, that a thought cannot be defined for itself as thought, unless it has previously appeared to itself as plunged in exteriority. Far from there being incompatibility between one and the other moment, there is thus an internal and necessary link.

Note, moreover, that this relation is still defined in the most general and hence the most undetermined way. We end up less with a precise solution than with the suppression of a pseudo-problem. We are led to say that it is illegitimate to conceive a pure thought defined by purely internal characteristics, so as subsequently to join it up in an entirely external way with a world of exteriority and show how it is impossible that it should enter into communication with it. This links up, moreover, with Hegel: *Das Rein innerliche ist das Rein ausserliche.*[1] Thought cannot really have an internal content unless it gives it to itself, that is to say, unless it mediates that which is given to it as external —it is by this mediation of the given that it mediates itself; because it begins by being also itself immediate; the immediacy of thought is correlative to that of the object. There is nothing which is *already* mediated, which is *given as* mediated. That would be the worst contradiction. And this simple reflection is enough to destroy completely the idea of a thought that is something already. The point has been admirably grasped by the English neo-Hegelians.

[1] Compare the whole *Logic of Essence*.

So it is in virtue of an illusion that I oppose myself as thinking ego to the spatial reality in which I am plunged and to the extended ego that I am. In truth there is an intimate correlation between my intelligible reality and my spatial reality that can in no way be translated into causal language.

May 2nd

But it seems that we are being led to a disastrous dilemma. Either the very notion of thought is abolished so as to make way for the notion of a content which organises itself in virtue of some kind of internal spontaneity; or else the notion of thought survives, but only under the form of a creative disposition, of a sort of specific agent for determining the organisation of the content. But in reality these two solutions are not distinct. They only differ in this: in one instance the mind maintains the duality of what organises and what is organised, whereas in the other it does not. Yet it remains that in one we seem to end with a sort of naturalist mysticism and in the other with an occult formalism. Both these solutions are bound to seem extremely vague and even suspect. Is it possible to elude them?

I must repeat once again what we can regard as already established: intelligibility, as constituent of any thought of whatever kind, and without which that thought is not, cannot be defined apart from some relation to that exteriority (the world of external relations) in the surmounting of which the constitutive function of thought consists. So I ought to take care not to fall into an abstract dualism. Yet it is agreed that a genetic monism, far from suppressing the difficulties I am up against, would fall short of the problems confronting us. The fruitful connection that its intelligibility assures to thought cannot be converted into a logical genesis without making nonsense. There is a particular kind of physics of dialectical relations which is no more than an entirely illegitimate transposition either of real physics or of pure speculation.

Concretely this amounts to saying that we doubtless posit not only the empirical impossibility but even the absolute impossibility of a genetic deduction that claims to reconstitute any individual thought whatsoever from the external data (milieu, heredity, etc.) which are bound up with the thought in question;

and also that we would be falling into absurdity if we set up an absolute and radical dualism between the thought considered in its essence and the external data. The thought is not a thing which can be juxtaposed to other things. Outside these external data it cannot be defined for itself, or for a thought which tries to understand it. Strictly speaking there is no dualism of the synthetic act which realises these external data, by mediating them, and the external data themselves. This is perhaps best expressed by saying that the external data present a character of ideality; that is, they only define themselves from the starting point of thought itself (of the whole) as conditions both necessary and insufficient, that are conditioned in their turn by that very thing that is conditioned by them. They cannot be defined as conditions save for reflection that sets out from what they condition. This amounts to saying that the relation of condition to conditioned tends here to pass into its contrary, and to negate itself so as to posit itself not as logical constitutive expression, but merely as subjective reflection.

An individual thought thus seems to be revealed to us as that which is anterior to its conditions, or, more exactly, that which is beyond the conditional nexus. This amounts to thinking a non-causal unity of individual thought and of the world of exteriority into which it is plunged.

But in this way am I not led to the neo-Hegelian monist idea of an absolute which manifests itself at one and the same time in individual thought and in that which, for such thought, functions as external world—in which the reality of the one and the other resides, in their very unity, and the psuedo-ideas of the ego and of the external world are suppressed in the efficacious and concrete identity of the absolute? This, for me, is the critical point. Does the theory of intelligibility that I am defending oblige me to posit such an identity?

I will not ask yet if such identity and unity are thinkable. The first question that comes up is whether they are required by my notion of the intelligible, and whether they are even compatible with it.

It is clear in the first place that this unity cannot be called intelligible in the sense I have defined. Indeed it is transcendent in relation to the connection that defines intelligibility; if you like, it is not intelligible but supra-intelligible. Yet is this unity anything more than a pure fiction, the product of an act by which the mind realises the dynamic connection in which we have seen the very soul and life of thought? Its aim is once and for all to cement from without two abstract and juxtaposed elements; elements which, as we already know, are only fictitious entities. It will be objected that this is precisely what the monists contend; the elements are abstractions from the concrete and living whole that is reality itself. But that can only be maintained if the whole in question is itself thought as intelligible, as co-extensive with the intelligible; and there we have precisely what I am aiming at. Here the dialectic of the relations of the intelligible and the real can be inserted.

May 4th

It thus seems to me that at this point we find the link between the theory of the intelligible and the theory of faith. Yet there is one point that is not yet clear to me. We have seen on the one hand that pure thought can only be defined concretely by its connection with a world of exteriority, and on the other that such a connection ought not to be realised in a metaphysical or substantial unity. I am going to try to illustrate this concretely so as to make the problem clearer.

Inasmuch as I am intelligible, inasmuch as I am an intellectual centre, I can only define myself in function of the external world extended in space and time to which at first sight I might be tempted to oppose myself. This apparent contingence of the world (of the spatial and temporal data of my experience) in relation to a substantial and non-temporal pseudo-truth of myself, is shown to be purely illusory. I only understand myself when I have discovered that I am only myself by the interiorisation (assimilation) of the so-called contingent data; when I have discovered that it is by a pure fiction that I can think myself as identical in the womb of a radically different empirical content. There we have a first point that is quite clear. But the question of thinking that intimate connection itself still remains. One way of thinking it, which consists in seeing in myself the product of the external data conceived as cause, cannot stand up to reflection. Indeed, when it thinks itself as product my thought ceases to regard itself as an intelligible, it juxtaposes itself ideally to the other things of the world, it sets aside precisely that which obliged it to make the external world enter into its own definition, it negates itself.

(We must recognise that this ends up in a problem, for thought, inasmuch as it is bound to the external world, needs to grasp itself in my body which, in its turn, can only appear to thought as entirely produced, entirely determined from without—which would seem to justify pure mechanism—and as organised inasmuch as it translates thought itself.)

As the dualism is unacceptable for reasons that I have already explained, thought reaches the point of positing a non-causal unity of the world and of itself, and there lies the real meaning and strongest justification of monism conceived as a doctrine of identity. I appear to myself as bound up with the world by the fact that we derive it and me from an identical act by which the absolute begets itself—I have elsewhere developed at length the motives for which I cannot accept this theory, which fails to make the absolute intelligible.

But what then? Would it be a solution to say that this purely ideal connection of thought and of an external world is sufficient for itself, and to treat the need felt by the mind to find a basis for the connection as illusory? I am not sure that there is a real solution there. It would amount to denying the metaphysical unity of thought and the world, of affirming in consequence that that is a problem that cannot be stated in metaphysical terms. But this requires elucidation. What meaning can be ascribed to this denial? It seems to me susceptible of taking on a profound significance. Given the purely ideal connection between what, so as to simplify things, I shall call the centre and the content, a connection in virtue of which the centre is only itself through the content (cf. all I have already said) it is not possible, it is even radically pointless to pretend to ensure an ontological foundation for this connection; the purely ideal connection in question will in no way be reinforced or affirmed because we place below it a sort of substantial or extra-logical basis. But in that case is the problem really suppressed?

What really happens is (this is the nerve of my present thinking and something which I do not think anyone has yet said), that we are in an order in which truth (in the sense of *eindeutige Bestimmung*) is no longer possible. The connection as I have defined it, grasped in its purity, is something that cannot in any way be determined as truth in that it cannot be conceived causally. The very idea of a purely logical causality would vanish when examined, because it would destroy itself for the benefit of monism. And in that way the negative solution of a moment ago is shown to be illusory and even contradictory; for it would still present the character of wanting to be a solution, an answer, a truth, while its merit precisely consists in bringing to light the impossibility of such a truth. When I elevate myself to the level of speculative thought, when at the same time and in consequence I become aware of the fact that I am nothing outside the whole of the external relations that define the content of my experience, I discover that no truth can be disentangled from that intimate connection between the whole in question and myself; it would be as arbitrary on my part to think of myself as creating myself through my experience as to think myself as begotten, as produced by the content. In both cases I fall into a realism that is quite indefensible.

There is no need to explain at length why this attitude cannot be called sceptical. Either scepticism is only confusion, or else it is defined in relation to a truth that is at least ideally posited. Whereas here I see clearly that no truth about myself is possible.

May 5th

I take up once more the point at which the previous process of argument ended. Doubtless I cannot define myself as a centre save posteriorly to my experience and in function of it; but on the other hand no explanation of myself as centre is possible —I transcend any possible explanation of my own reality. It may be tempting to say: "Doubtless you cannot explain yourself to yourself; but for someone else there is no such impossibility. Each of us can think himself, ought to be able to think himself as possible object for an ideal historian." If this were so the historian might well be myself; for historical thought is outside the sphere in which the relations of the self and the other subsist; it is objective thought in general. Yet it is clear that I cannot be my own historian: such a history of myself would be a veritable act of creation by which the historical object (that I wished to be for myself) would destroy itself (by transforming itself). Here there is an instructive and singular point that ought to incite us to reflect. The ego appears to us as that which by essence cannot treat itself as object without transcending that objectivity. But is this a deficiency of the ego in relation to a thought in general? In the sense that thought in general, by applying itself to an individual thought, could find its constitutive law—a law indeterminable for that thought inasmuch as it applies itself to itself? This would amount to admitting a certain exteriority of thought in general in relation to individual thought; and much more: a certain eccentricity of thought in relation to itself, for we know that thought in general is only defined by its connection with an experience, hence as individual thought. But this has no meaning: if thought in general appeared to us previously as eccentric in relation to individual thought, it was inasmuch as it was thought as bound up with *another* individual thought (which in its turn cannot be thought as objective for itself). Inasmuch as thought in general is necessarily bound up with an individual thought, and all individual thought implies the deficiency that I have said, it is clear that thought in general possesses no character, no intrinsic privilege to save it from contradiction. I will never be a historical object save for a thought which in its turn cannot be object for itself.

May 6th

Possibly the foregoing process of argument is not absolutely valid as it stands; I have not sufficiently emphasised the fact that, as centre, as intelligible, I transcend the conditions on which I am trying to make my own reality depend.

But in this there is nothing that is really essential to what concerns us. What matters is this: inasmuch as I elevate myself to the intelligible, inasmuch as I constitute myself as centre (and we know that this, far from being an isolated and so to speak abstract step, implies the act by which I progressively interiorise my experience) I progressively transcend the sphere of begettings and explanations. Just as a work of art cannot in any way explain itself, and has no connection with what there is essential in causal determinations, so individual thought, inasmuch as it is realised more and more as mind, is liberated from the causal order. Supposing it be said that the Idea, that is to say the teleological principle towards which this movement of thought tends, can only be thought as limit? But it is clear that the movement itself implies the positing of the Idea, and the Idea can in no way be treated as the fictitious asymptote of a curve that would not require it.

Thus it seems that it would be idle to try to explain the movement by which the mind makes itself mind; this movement cannot be regarded as *caused* any more than a dialectical process can. And it is in this fundamental sense that to think mind is to think freedom, that to will oneself as mind is to will oneself and posit oneself as freedom. Only, let me repeat it once again, the internal movement by which the mind is created is only made possible through the link to a world of exteriority in which all is explainable, all is caused; and it is in this sense that freedom absolutely implies necessity. This means that the idea of freedom becomes fictitious as soon as it is realised in a world external, so to speak, to the external world.

But there are still many points outstanding. To begin with, as is clear, freedom thus defined is not a property, a character; moreover, and this is still more important, it is not legitimate to look on progress in liberty (or in intelligibility) as progress in being.

A free being is no more possible than a thinking thing. I am free in the measure in which I negate myself as thing; I am only free being, free thing, for external reflection which purely and simply juxtaposes what I am inasmuch as external, to the act by which I make myself mind.

Yet I wonder what the limits are within which this can be stated. Will not freedom end up by being identified with that knowledge by which individual thought in some measure strips all nature so as to plunge itself into the multiple reality of its object?

There we have one of the directions of my thought. If, in fact, far from freedom being excluded by the reality (that is to say, the legality) of the external world, it so to speak requires that reality, and if mind realises itself in the measure in which the world becomes more real for it—i.e. its action on the world is farther extended—am I not tending towards the idea that the sovereign reality of the mind would be fulfilled in its own very dissolution, that is in the fulfilment of the work of knowledge and when all subjectivity vanishes in complete science?

Yet it is against this possible conclusion that my criticism is arrayed. My work ought to tend to show that the theory of intelligibility that I have recently laid down, does not imply scientific realism but excludes it.

Here I must recapitulate the points that have been established. The movement of the mind (a constitutive movement) is orientated towards what I shall call the elimination of the pure causal, that is to say, the assimilation, the interiorisation of what in it remains crude, the basis of external relationships (it is not, as can be seen, a question of the mystical and abstract negation of those relations, but of their teleological utilisation). Here I come back to the Platonic way of stating the problem. But, in consequence, we must raise the question of the relation of the soul to the Ideas (the soul being conventionally defined as subject of that becoming, that creation of self which is mind—according to this the soul is in some way the matter of the mind, is what the mind finds in itself). Thus viewed the soul appears to be the basis of willing, the mind to be the transcendent and fulfilled unity of willing, or again as ideal end which itself wills itself and hence affirms itself as real—And if such were the case the soul would be no more than an abstract moment of the dynamic and autonomous complexus that is mind, an abstract moment, moreover, only thinkable as correlative with the body or with the physical machine.

This leads to the recognition that there is no reason to deny that the soul can have a nature, while the idea of the nature of the mind is contradictory in itself.

It may be objected that the distinction between the soul and the mind is entirely arbitrary, that what we call mind is only the natural efflorescence of the soul. But I reply that this theory cannot be refuted with a genetic description: for the important question here is whether an objective begetting is here thinkable. Now the intelligible, as I pointed out, is defined in relation to the radical elimination of the pure causal: there is no objective derivation of the intelligible (as such). Once again the example of the work of art will help to throw light on what is too abstract in the theory. If we adopt a genetical standpoint, the notion of mind loses all meaning and all content; but the important point lies in asking by what right, and in the name of what metaphysical realism, we are able to affirm the exclusive value of this point of view. From the moment we have grasped what mind is, the problem of the origin of mind becomes, not merely insoluble, but as impossible as that of squaring the circle.

But can we give the soul the benefit of a solution which only has to do with the mind? It seems to me clear that we cannot. We must realise the gravity of the problem raised if we are really to speak of the nature of the soul. It is precisely Plato's problem and Plato resolved it through the idea of the Fall. As an objective (or genetic) solution is impossible, can we have recourse to a dialectical solution? But we have already seen the narrow limits within which such a solution can be regarded as valid. The mind, inasmuch as it speculates or reflects on itself, appears to itself as that which only exists in its relation with exteriority, that which is only able to be isolated from exteriority by an abstraction. From this standpoint the soul appears to the mind as the condition not only of its realisation but also of its reality. Thus the genuine realisation of the mind implies the suppression of the dualism of the mind and the soul. But is this suppression merely ideal? At this point are we going to see the reappearance of the opposition between a purely ideal unification and a real difference? I do not think so. For the mind is defined by the negation of the difference between the ideal and the real (provided that this difference is posited as an object of willing); mind is mind inasmuch as it maintains that negation. This amounts to saying that the mind only *is* on condition that it is realised. Thus the dualism of the soul and the mind only subsists for the mind inasmuch as the mind becomes aware of what is unfinished, unrealised and so to speak potential in itself. There is no truth as regards this dualism in the sense that the mind, inasmuch as it affirms itself as mind, denies it. "But," it may be said, "what value can that affirmation have? Ought not the mind to appear to itself as something in the process of becoming, something that rises painfully out of animal life? Does not the suppression in question belong, for mind, to the order of what is yet to come, what will be but is not yet?" Clearly this interpretation would suppose the denial of all that I have said.

May 7th

From the speculative standpoint I think the notion of progress is one of the least useful that can be found. It implies a realism regarding time that excludes the concrete notion of the mind. All spiritual progress has as principle and as very reality a unity that surpasses it. Because the Bergsonian theory disregards this it conjures spirituality away. But we must recognise that the mind cannot realise itself save as will for itself; the mind is by essence that which cannot be given as a datum to itself, it is its own end (it is what I have called a dynamic autonomous complexus). It only *is* on condition that it wills itself; i.e. that it is not content in itself and is not immobilised. This may oblige us to raise a difficult problem: when the mind seeks itself and tends towards realisation, does it not make for the destruction of that willing which is co-substantial with it? I shall examine this later on.

Spiritual reality thus only *is* on condition it negates itself as existence. Hence the soul appears to the mind as the inert residue of its activity. This is why what can be called activism seems to end up in pure pessimism. For what is this willing that leaves nothing behind it, and tends towards its own suppression? If it is not something deposited and preserved is not value a pure illusion? Or is there a zone outside the consciousness that the mind has of itself (and only has of itself when it wills itself, that is, when it denies what is 'crude' in itself), a zone "in which prayers bear fruit."

Here, I think, we are on one of the roads that lead to religion. Because for mind to be a second condition is necessary. It is that mind should be able to affirm that it has *value*. And here we see the reappearance of the notion of individuality.

I take up once more here the principal points that we can look on as gained.

We saw the soul as the matter, or to use a more precise term, the medium of the mind. But the mind only is (that is to say, only is for itself) inasmuch as it acts, that is, acts on the soul. (Yet here a difficulty arises, to which we will need to return;

is the mind incapable of acting immediately on the external world?) Such action is in a sense immanent, in that the mind is realised by the action itself; but on the other hand the exteriority of the soul in relation to the acting principle (I am sorry to employ such an inadequate terminology) is a necessary condition, for such action should be real. Thus the soul ought to appear to the mind as being a datum given to it (in the sense in which nature is a datum), but also and more profoundly as in some way the material condition under which alone the mind can assume a reality for itself. Or rather, to avoid presenting the mind and the soul as things juxtaposed, the mind is defined by the very act that posits the soul at one and the same time as datum and as material condition of that act. We have to recognise that, however we look on it, we cannot avoid the idea of an act by which the mind posits itself; and it appears, moreover, as if the soul as I have defined it is itself function of this act.

The problem of the relations of the soul and the body is only really raised when thought becomes conscious of itself. Only we must note that for thought that is fully conscious of itself, that problem, by the very fact of assuming all its acuteness, ends up by losing all meaning; at least this happens inasmuch as the mind, which is constructed, as I have said, by overcoming exteriority, far from being capable of maintaining objectively determinable relations with exteriority, in some way absorbs exteriority into itself. This goes to show that a philosophy of mind should be careful to distinguish between the pseudo-problem that I have just disposed of (it collapses as soon as we grasp that the mind could not be in relation with anything else) and the quite different problem that concerns the relations of the body with the soul—the latter being defined as the material of spiritual action. Yet we must recognise that this distinction scarcely seems to bring us any nearer our solution: for either the soul implies consciousness, and we are up against the insoluble problem of the soul; or it does not imply consciousness, and the "insoluble" problem arises in a zone intermediary between the two zones that I have just distinguished. So my elucidation still seems to be very insufficient.

What helps to obscure the problem is, I feel, the fact that the notion of body is *not at all univocal*. We really need to take into account the way in which the notion of body varies correlatively with the notion of the soul. The definition of the body as a mechanical complexus is one of the mind's modes of realisation. Of course this does not mean that the mind begets the body (even ideally); for the mind is only constituted as knowing when it thinks the known as a datum anterior to the act of knowing. But, for all that, the mode of representation of the relations of the soul and the body which depends on the way in which the body itself is thought, also depends indirectly on that very movement by which the mind is realised in knowledge. In other words, (if we only envisage the body) the notion that the mind can form of the relations of the soul and body must be in function of the movement by which the notion of body is constructed. Now this construction of the body is shown to be bound up in an extraordinarily close way with the construction of the external world itself. Can we say, then, that there is a construction of the soul in the sense in which there is a construction of the body (the notion of the relations of the soul and the body would result immediately from bringing these two constructions together)? It seems to me that as soon as we have clearly distinguished the soul and the mind we are obliged to answer this question negatively. It is certainly not possible to define a movement in which the notion of the soul is elaborated in a way parallel to the movement by which the notion of body is defined—and on this point Kantian criticism should be regarded as entirely valid (indeed Kant perhaps did not draw all the conclusions from this that he might have done).

We have to set out from the principle, I think, that, whether we consider it as desiring or as perceiving, the soul is not thinkable, if not definable, outside all relations with the external world.

May 8th

Clearly we are here in full confusion. Only one point seems plain to me; it is, as I have already pointed out, that our conception, our representation of the relations of the body and the soul depends closely on the conception we form of the nature of the body. The parallelist representation, for instance, is in function of the mechanicist conception of the body; which means that parallelism does not remain true at successive stages of the evolution of the notion of body.

In other words there is no ground for positing dogmatically the possibility of a unique relation which would remain valid for modes of representation of the body (or of the soul) that are in themselves absolutely distinct; such a relation is itself function of the modes of representation. Parallelism is only valid from the standpoint of a mechanical representation of the body, and it implies, I think, a representation of the nature of the soul which cannot be regarded as *absolute*.

I insist for the moment on these very general and very indeterminate propositions. We can see immediately the problem they force us to raise: are these multiple representations of the relation of the soul and of the body contingent in relation to a reality to which they "approximate" ever more closely? It is clear that this presupposes another question, namely, what is the reality of the body? (I still leave aside the question of the soul.) If the body has a substantial reality, that amounts to saying that one (and one only) representation of the body exists—a representation which coincides with its object and of which the other representations are only images, inexact transpositions. This real representation would necessarily imply a mode of figuration, also real, of the union of the soul and the body (the figuration being also converted into object). Thus the problem of the reality of the body is shown to be the central problem and upon its solution everything else depends. It is important to state this problem in terms that are as explicit as possible, and I will formulate it thus: under what conditions is it possible to define a reality of the body in relation to which any other representation of the body must be said to function as appearance? When thus stated the problem solves itself. The conditions under which a reality can be defined as such for us can only be of a rational, intelligible order.

Thus the monist theory of the relation of the soul and the body can only have an absolute value if the representation of the body on which it is based can be regarded as real. Here it must be noted that the theory is not univocal; it can either think the body as identical with the soul (on condition that it defines the body as non-extended), or it can think the body as being the extended aspect of one and the same reality which is also soul inasmuch as it perceives itself as non-extended. One of these interpretations can be preferred to the other only if we accept an ontological value superior to the notion of the body.

But if it is true that such an ontological value can never be absolute (in the sense that the transition from the intelligible to the real is always and everywhere critical) it seems to me that we must conclude that no metaphysical judgment bearing on the relations of the soul and the body is valid. This amounts to saying that we cannot even think a real and fixed formula, that of this relation, to which we can "approximate" ever closer indefinitely. I admit that this seems to be in contradiction to experience; it seems, indeed, to amount to saying that the relation of the soul to the body is not objectively determinable; whereas the existence of numerous psycho-physical constants appears to militate in favour of the opposite thesis. Only it is clear that all that I have said so far is entirely applicable to the soul. If the soul is conceived as a substantial unity, as a dynamic centre, it is only too clear that what I could call the parallelistic index is not properly applicable to the relation thought between the soul and the body. Are we able to deny outright that the soul is such a unity or such a centre? In the measure in which it passes beyond pure phenomenalism, voluntarism does not seem to be in a position to dispense entirely with that notion. Thus on the plane on which the soul is so conceived, parallelism is shown to be unthinkable. But what metaphysical value can be accorded to psycho-physical constants? Can we really say that they show a fundamental and definite connection in a univocal way?

END OF PART ONE

PART TWO

It is private life that holds out the mirror to infinity; personal intercourse, and that alone, that ever hints at a personality beyond our daily vision.

E. M. FORSTER, *Howard's End.*

September 15th, 1915

Time has not and cannot have any origin save the present which is the only boundary that can be assigned to it. . . . The illusion that time is *given* before it is *consumed* (as space which *is there* before it is traversed). Would it not be true to say that time is only in act, and space only in potency? Time cannot be compared with a medium into which consciousnesses are inserted, a medium in relation to which such 'insertions' are contingent. It is the *very negation of that.*

Yet time's internal boundary, which is its very reality, appears to the imagination as moving—in the heart of what? It is in this way that the idea of time as medium is born.

September 18th, 1915

Time cannot be thought as object without space; but space can only be a datum given in time.

We symbolise time by movement—and movement is itself symbolised by space traversed. But in that way we are setting aside the essential element which, for lack of a better word, I call *actuality* (corresponding to *hicceity*).

October 15th, 1915

The possibility of divination is bound up with the nature (not the degree) of the interest which attaches thought to its ideal object. But on the other hand, as is plain, an objective dynamic of interest is in itself impossible. Interest needs to be *real*—and this cannot be expressed in the language of quantity. To express it better, the mind needs to participate totally in the interest (mere curiosity remains *isolated* in the midst of pre-occupations that it does not suppress). The essential point is thus the relation of the idea in tension to the mind itself.

April 2nd, 1916

This morning, on a clear and marvellous springtime day, I glimpsed that the notions of so-called 'occult' knowledge, against which 'reason' claims to revolt, are in reality at the root of the commonest day to day experiences which we take for granted: the experiences of feeling, of will or of memory.   Who would be prepared to question that the will 'acts' as suggestion, as magical suggestion? And what are bodies if not apparitions or materialisations? Does not the experience of memory imply the real and effective negation of time? It is all obvious—too obvious for the twilight condition of our psychology.

April 13th

Without question I am inclining to the belief that the central puzzles of psychology, those that our actual knowledge (with its apparent prudence made up principally of laziness and pusil-lanimity) tries to muzzle with conventions and postulates (I am thinking especially of parallelism here) could only be solved from an entirely *extra* or *infra*-psychological standpoint. Thus, far from needing to be conceived as a purely abstract relation between worlds that do not communicate at all, the mysterious relation between the internal and the external is perhaps a centre—an essential fact in relation to which these worlds are only abstrac-tions. This view is certainly to be found in neo-Platonism and, even more plainly, in Bergson. But has Bergson grasped that he has been led towards something which is not psychology—which is beyond psychology? Admittedly he sees the body in terms of materialisation, but has he sufficiently grasped all that this in-volves? There is still something timid about his attitude. The same applies (even more clearly) to his profound and unintel-ligible theory of recollection.

What does 'to conserve' mean? The idea of conservation

implies that of synchronism, or, more exactly, that of parallel durations. Something that is conserved is something that persists at the same time as something else that serves as its datum. By parallel durations I understand that corresponding with the state of one of these objects in presence there is always a synchronised state of the other object, and that the observation brought to bear on this other state does not beget it. When he speaks of the conservation of pure recollections, Bergson postulates that the idea of parallel durations is applicable to the body and to recollection, which amounts to saying that recollection is present (whether it is actualised or not); in other words that the actualisation is as contingent in relation to the memory actualised as the objective observation of an event is contingent in relation to that event. . . .

April 14th

The problem could be formulated this way. Given any plurality of temporal series, are they so related that, for every break made in one of them we can theoretically find a corresponding and synchronised break in all the others?

The solution, it seems to me, is to be found by going into the idea of determination. If these series bear on determinations that are homogeneous in relationship to one another, then it is certain that the synchronism is possible. But the problem loses all meaning if the determinations are not homogeneous. To be examined further.

May 4th

'Realised' this evening with prodigious lucidity:

1. That sensation (immediate consciousness) is infallible, that there is no place in it for error.

2. That in this way faith *ought* to participate in the nature of sensation (the metaphysical problem here lies in rediscovering, by thought and beyond thought, a new infallibility, a new immediacy).

3. That the immediacy of sensation is of necessity a paradise lost. The dialectic and drama of sensation is that it has to be reflected, interpreted—it is thus that error becomes possible. Error makes its entry into the world with reflection. But

non-reflected sensation falls short of the plane of the fallible.

The question is whether intellection on the plane of thought participates in the immediate infallibility of sensation. Fundamentally all reflection is invincibly attracted by that which suppresses it—by that in which it is negated.

May 14th

I realised to-day in an impressive though confused way that the reality of bodies is and only can be a reality of interposition; bodies are mutually interposed or interpose themselves. The function of the body is at one and the same time to bind together and to separate. But *what* does it bind? *What* does it separate? There is a complete mystery here; the data of common sense and of scientific knowledge are clearly insufficient. All that I can see is this: What binds together (or what separates) ought to be in some way homogeneous in relation to what is bound. Hence thought cannot conceive the body, for instance, as binding together the psychic and the spatial. It only binds thought to the world of space inasmuch as thought is *position* (this is extremely obscure), or again inasmuch as the external world escapes from space—which is not clear either. We must go further. If the body binds the spatial in the sense that it is itself spatial, it can only bind the psychic to the psychic inasmuch as it is psychical, inasmuch as it is *charged with meaning*, and itself *is meaning*. . . .

January, 1917

Atheism is theodicy upside down, an apologetics that has gone wrong. . . .

All the judgments made on God by man fall back on to man's own head. 'Thou art not' is man's verdict: but what of the verdict-maker—*is* he?

February, 1917

Notes on immortality.

It seems to me definite that two hypotheses, or rather two attitudes and two only, are possible regarding the problem of immortality (and this, of course, is the inner meaning of the last scene of *Porte-Glaive*[1]). The first is the attitude I still took two

[1] The early version of *L'Iconoclaste*.

years ago, Abel's attitude, to which I may possibly return: viz. that there is no truth of immortality, that by definition immortality falls outside any possible verification. Verification brought to bear on the beyond brings it down to the plane of earth; thus immortality is only *by* and *for* faith: the spiritual order is such that we are bound to think it as transcending the accidents of matter; we only participate in the spiritual order on condition we think in this way . . . belief in immortality like belief in God is involved in the very act of our freedom. Only we must recognise that in this form the statement is ambiguous. Is this spiritual order anything other than the eternity of the Ideas? Whereas the farther I proceed the more I am convinced that the problem of immortality has to be stated in personal terms. The conservation of values of which Höffding speaks does not amount to very much—I am not even really sure that those words have any meaning. *Either* I postulate legitimately, but what I affirm is only an abstract and empty principle—*or else* I affirm something which is a fact in spite of everything; and have I the right to postulate that? This question occurred to me years ago: under what conditions and within what limits is pure thought able to postulate? Clearly the idea of fact here is still very obscure. Can I say that future life is a fact—a fact, moreover, as uncertain as the journey I am to make, or not to make, next summer? How can we escape from this imprudent realism without involving ourselves in a system of statements that have no content? I tried to get beyond this dilemma by having recourse to love and by saying that 'love wishes for the eternity of its object.' But this is perhaps another equivocation; doubtless the lover posits the reality of the beloved as outside and above time but . . . we are up against the problem of the *Palais de Sable*, and it is tragic. It seems to me that there is a sort of mysterious and extremely profound answer in prayer—one that I do not completely grasp. To pray is to postulate that the reality of others, though independent of me, depends in some degree on the act by which I posit it, that the act contributes in some way to the reality. I am convinced that—in the simplest psychological sense—the thought of others contributes to our make-up.

The second attitude, which is much more clear, is that of Lodge, and, paradoxical though this may seem, it appears to me at bottom to coincide with that of Leibnitz. Immortality, understood not in the hyper-idealist sense we were just dealing with, but in the realist sense, can only be absolutely personal. The Aristotelian thesis seems to me absolutely indefensible, with nothing to be said in its favour. I am still a little frightened by Lodge's realism. But I am getting used to it. . . .

February 9th, 1917

A note on telepathy.

In general any communication between consciousnesses seems to imply:

1. A thought formulated for itself, i.e. which becomes conscious of itself and communicates with itself.

2. The conversion of that thought into a material system that functions as sign or symbol and obeys the general laws of matter.

3. A medium or agent of transmission of some kind.

4. The reconversion or retranscription of the initial system (or of a system which reproduces it) into a thought.

5. This thought, more or less identical with the original thought, is revealed to the other consciousness.

From this point of view there is no relevant difference between spontaneous expression, ordinary language, and communication by letter, telephone and radio. In each case a message has to be received by a suitable instrument and retranscribed.

If we admit the existence of telepathy—which we must do for it is beyond discussion—we find ourselves up against something entirely new. The difficulty does not lie in the medium or the transmitting agent as is often thought, but in this: the cypher, the system of conventions that inevitably played its part at the departure or arrival of the message, is now lacking: and so it looks as though we are not dealing with a message but with a vision. This needs to be examined further. It can doubtless be objected that there really is a system of conventions but that it happens to be one that is totally implicit. But in my opinion this is meaningless. Supposing I think something intensely or experience a given state—and determine that the thought or state shall be transmitted to a friend who is in England. If we insist that a message is communicated it must be admitted:

1.   That my thought is endowed with a special 'fluescent' power of emission.

2.   That the emission takes place in all directions but that the waves are only caught by a being tuned in to me.

3.   That this being is precisely the one to whom I wished my message to be transmitted. It would be contrary to the principle set forth at the beginning were I to admit that the receptive condition could be determined by consciousness: it must be already given and must pre-exist the emission of the message.[1]

4.   That this emission, or rather the organic modification produced by it, should itself be retranscribed by the 'receiver' in terms of consciousness—and this though the receiver lacks the cypher (which I also lack), and even has no consciousness whatever of the *effect* produced on his organism by the emission in question.

Who can fail to see that this is a laborious construction, a painful and superfluous effort to conceive telepathy in terms of a form of correspondence, or of a message, whereas it would be infinitely simpler to suppose that the thought of one person is not transmitted to the other person but immediately imposed on him. And are there not psychological experiences, rare doubtless, but undeniable, in which the mind is aware of sharing a thought with another; experiences that I should describe as spiritual contact. After all it may well be that a given idea is not in its origin *my* idea, that it is in no way 'private' and only becomes limited, self-attributed and localised at a secondary stage. This localisation may be due to a sort of internal deficiency of the idea. After all an idea is no more capable of being *situated* than is a consciousness. I was on the point of saying that the less we situate ourselves the more we *are*, but I am not sure that it is true.[2]

July, 23rd, 1918

Perhaps emotion is only suppressed action, action that does not 'emerge'.

---

[1] Nothing would be gained by introducing a mediating consciousness that intervenes between my consciousness and that of my friend; for the same question would come up, namely how I communicate with the mediator, etc. . . .

[2] The above becomes clearer as soon as we compare consciousness with ideas in a consciousness that can be placed in immediate relations with one another in the event of given determining circumstances.

An interesting suggestion: may it not be that between a determined present and certain futures there is the same connection as that established in a creative imagination between ideas that are discovered at the same time and in some way linked together, yet are destined to be exploited only successively (e.g. the scenes of a play for which, at one and the same time, I discover my first act and a scene of the fifth). In other words, between the (Bergsonian) idea of a universe that is pure improvisation and the idea of a world unfolding an eternal content in time, is no intermediary conception possible? Prediction would, strictly speaking, thus be conceivable, though we would not therefore be obliged to believe in complete historical predetermination. From this standpoint there would be situations that implied one another up to a certain point,[1] and yet this implication would permit the subsistence of *blanks* of some sort between them (as there are *blanks* in a story of which we only know the beginning, one or two preliminary episodes, and—perhaps—the end). I do not deny that this hypothesis raises difficulties—notably that of thinking the concrete moments of history as *non-homogeneous* to one another because of their very unequal potential of implication. There is a possible comparison here with the unequal potential of development given to principal themes and secondary themes in a symphony. This, though perhaps difficult for a metaphysician, is plain to a historian or a psychologist. It cannot be contested, for instance, that some dates are critical.

We also need to ask how an initial situation can bring about an ulterior situation—yet *not* the intermediary situations. Yet the psychology of imagination shows us that the thing is possible. And it is even worth asking whether the ulterior situation (which though not yet actual in the historical sense is actual metaphysically) does not itself determine the circumstances which, historically, seem to determine it. I have a clear feeling that, strange though it may seem, this hypothesis may give us a better understanding of what *history* is.

Another difficulty lies in the fact that what I call the *situation* certainly *cannot* be reduced to the consciousness one of the 'actors' has of it, nor to the *sum* of the consciousnesses of the

[1] More exactly, governed one another.

actors; for in this order no 'adding up' or 'integration' is possible. The unity of the situation appears to those 'involved' in it as essentially being a datum given, but at the same time as something that permits of and even calls for their active intervention. Notice that this is true of every act of reflection (of thought) of whatever kind. Here we have something that is inherent in the fundamentally ambiguous notion of 'oneself'. I, for myself, am a situation that surpasses me and excites my activity. ... And the unconscious is no more than the symbol of the transcendence of the situation in relation to the situated. It may be objected that, in spite of everything, the situation becomes an object for reflected consciousness: but on deeper reflection it becomes plain that the situation is not capable of being objectivised entirely. Were it entirely objective for me, it would cease to be mine; it is only mine by what, as regards me, is still—as I have said elsewhere—'attached'. But supposing it is said that for God such attachments are broken? But it is easy to see that, if God is defined in this way, he has nothing to do with me and I have nothing to do with him. This God is only a 'him' who can never become a 'thou'. God interpreted as impersonal truth is the most impoverished of fictions, the improperly realised limit of the process in which I become involved when I take my own context for object. I would be prepared to say dogmatically that every relation of being to being is personal and that the relation between God and me is nothing if it is not a relation of being with being, or, strictly, of being with itself. The bizarre expression that comes to my mind for stating this is that, while an empirical *thou* can be converted into a *him*, God is the absolute 'thou' who can never become a *him*. The meaning of prayer. Scientific knowledge only speaks of the real in the third person.

To sum up, this interpretation of history does not imply an absolute finalism. There are conditions that are only conditions, means that are subordinated to real ends. But, first and foremost, this interpretation depends on the idea of a *dynamism of the situation*, which transcends individual destinies though in one sense it is only the material for them. This living contradictory dualism lies at the very core of the real; all spiritual life is essentially a dialogue.

The scientist sets the relation that binds him to the object entirely aside. Just as, when I speak of someone in the *third person*, I treat him as independent—as absent—as separate; or, more exactly, I define him implicitly as external to a dialogue that is taking place, which may be a dialogue with myself. Religious life begins as soon as this relation is transformed. All this must be examined more profoundly. There seems to be a whole world here that has been but little explored. A judgment in the third person is by essence an instructive judgment, whatever be the teaching or information that it interprets. . . .

Under what conditions am I to employ the second person? This postulate is the opposite of the postulate I have just mentioned. I use the second person only to address that which I regard as susceptible of answering me, whatever form the answer may take—even if only that of an 'intelligent silence'. Where no answer is possible there is only place for the '*him*'.

Thus the key is provided by the idea of answer.

Hence a double relationship of myself with myself.

Every answer, it seems, is made by means of signs or symbols and every sign is an answer to a more or less explicitly formulated question. Between the question and the answer there must be a meeting ground which, if not selected, is at least accepted—it amounts to the same thing—by the question. This implies a certain code from which the person who answers can derive the elements of the answer; otherwise the answer would fall outside the scope of the question and not be an answer.

What is interrogation? It is an effort to correct a state of relative indetermination. Every question implies:

1. A disjunctive judgment.
2. The affirmation that one only of the alternatives is true or valid.
3. The recognition of incapacity to determine which. For example: 'Is it raining?'—either it is or it is not raining, one of the alternatives is true, but which? This (in contrast with what can be called dialectics) allows us to conceive a mode of communication which is not made by means of questions and answers and hence is not accomplished by means of signs. As a communication of this kind has no reference to any cypher or any code, it must necessarily have the appearance of being fortuitous. I would be

tempted to give to this kind of communication the name of revelation.

Analysis of the idea of answer.

Under what conditions is an answer valid?

To begin with the answer must *bear* properly on the question, in other words the question must have been understood; moreover it must bring the specification desired; finally this specification must appear to be founded, not arbitrary—the answerer must be assumed to be in a situation that does not permit there to be any alternative for him (this, of course, must not be due to reflection failing to measure up to the real complexity of the situation).

What does understanding a question mean? First, putting it to oneself, placing oneself in the mental situation of the questioner. I can only give a full and proper answer to my own question. The consciousness of the answerer is the meeting-ground of the question and the answer. . . .

But does not nature answer the questions of the experimental scientist? Yes, but only on condition that the encounter I have referred to *takes place*. The experimental scientist has the task of eliminating all that could make the answer seem fortuitous or accidental, and not in exact relationship to the question as it was asked. Hence the question should be as free from ambiguity as possible, for ambiguity in the question results in the impossibility of interpreting the answer. In properly conducted experiments everything happens as if the question were—could not fail to be—understood.

An answer is only possible in an order in which there are alternatives or margins: what I should call the order of the *either or's*. These alternatives ought to be capable of being indicated; and it is the business of the answer to emphasise the alternative that must be accepted, and in this sense the answer is essentially a sign or symbol. Notice also that it ought to be usable; it constitutes an acquisition—something we can make use of, at least within certain limits, because we have incorporated it. Conversely it could be shown that all knowledge which is not an answer must be sterile.[1]

The world in which *dialectics* is possible is thus a world of

[1] And would it be knowledge?

differentiated experiences that are susceptible of completing one another. In the measure in which I am *attached to* a moment of time and *attached to* a point of space my experience necessarily requires an *Erfüllung*, that is to say, the mediation of a system of questions and answers (in contrast to the order of sentiment for which such words have no meaning, and, more generally, to what I shall call the order of the *manners of being*).

Objectivity is bound up with the existence of a system of questions and answers, but conversely such a system supposes objectivity. And when I say objectivity I mean the continual strengthening of objectivity. For instance, I ask how long it takes to go from Rome to Naples by express. My question implies the affirmation that there is a railway connection between Rome and Naples and that it requires a definite time to make the journey under those conditions. Such a question is given as answered in advance in objective fact (what I call the *him* or *it*), but as only capable of receiving this answer by way of dialectics, through the medium of a *thou*; that is to say by coming into communication with a wider and complementary experience. And this is true for every question that life obliges me to ask. For example: what have I done with my watch? I know this question is answered in objective fact; my watch is somewhere; but I may have the opportunity of interrogating someone (a *thou*) who has seen me place it in an unusual place; (and the *thou* in question may well have been half-forgotten to begin with, and then brusquely resurrected from my own experience). The soliloquy is not a simple imitation of the dialogue. If it is to bear fruit, every dialogue needs at a given moment to become a soliloquy, for unless that happens, the coincidence of question and answer would not take place. This coincidence can only take place in an understanding; indeed it is by the coincidence that the understanding is defined. . . .

This coincidence is in reality a *determination*, a determination of a judgment that was known as undetermined. But does not such awareness of self as indeterminate go beyond the limits of the simple judgment? Is it not already reflection? . . . A question is a reflection in act. But what arouses the reflection? It seems bound up with desire or with intention. I would like to consult my watch—but I cannot find it. The friction of desire as regards the datum obliges me to reflect, or is my reflection in potency: reflection is this friction 'for itself'. Thus every problem implies an 'I should . . . but I cannot.' It is this 'I should', and the action that is first invoked and then immediately inhibited that it sets in motion, which obliges me to observe that 'I cannot', that I have not the necessary means at my disposal.

It seems to me that these very elementary observations have great importance from the metaphysical point of view. No answer is possible unless the question itself is really suppressed as question. Every theoretical affirmation is, if I may so put it, constructed on a totality of questions and answers, whose detail it discards; and, at the same time, it is the point of departure for an infinite questionnaire or an infinity of questionnaires. Moreover, it is only the interest the subject takes in the theoretical affirmation that permits him to choose amongst the questions to which it gives rise.

But obviously we are dealing in abstractions. *Who* asks a question? *Who* answers? . . . It must be noted that the higher we are elevated in the theoretical order, the less the meaning of the question. The dialectic, so to speak, becomes depersonalised (for instance when a metaphysician foresees and discusses an objection it is plain that the question *Who?* is meaningless). But on the lower planes of thought the answer *is attached*, so to speak, to a context that is not made explicit—which it has to set aside. The *meeting ground* is not on the same level (for example when a mountaineer says to a townsman: 'You will be there in five minutes'). It must be repeated that levelling-out is a condition of any real objectivity (the need for a well-established cypher, etc.).

It is important to note that the question *Who?* absolutely ceases in what I have called the soliloquy, on whatever plane it be considered (alike on the plane of the hypochondriac who interrogates himself about how he is feeling and that of the metaphysician who is in dialogue with himself). The *I* corresponds precisely to the refusal to raise the question *Who*, because it would be 'out of place'. It is only a deeper reflection that can cast doubt on the objectivity of this order of answers—which still needs to be defined. But there are evidently fields in which it is impossible not to ask the question *Who?*—those of the order of evidence. Then the question of weight, of guarantee, of *signature* (I repeat, it is only by reflection and by application of this method to myself, that I can interrogate myself on the value of my own signature[1]). The *who* is thus, essentially, a signature, a seal, a mark whose value *should* be, but *is not*, spontaneously called into question. Doubtless the child begins by believing what he or she is told. In this case the dialogue is a soliloquy, it treats the other person's answer as an answer in itself, whereas the adult—the scientist at least—treats the answer in itself as an answer made by another person. The problem of the *who* is thus the problem of credibility, and doubtless in practice it is not originally raised unless there is a discordance between the answer received and the answer expected.

The idea of an absolute *seal* for the answer which would be reality itself (the supreme *seal*, the standard *seal*). What bears this seal is true. The seal will be recognised as conferring truth. But here we must be more exact. An ordinary answer seems to us to express (exactly or not) that which is. We thus suppose a difference between the fact and the answer that bears on the fact, and treat the answer as a mediation between *it* and us. Is this difference ever eliminated? It seems not. In our eyes there is always a mediating action. In the case of experimental science it is the experiment itself that functions as mediator and inter-locutor; for us the fact in question is not a *thou* but *him* or *it*. In other words it seems that for us reality is something that never answers but from which all answers must be derived; even in the simple instance of the man who asks his friend how he is. Hence a new problem. How does this pure reality, this pure *him* or it, nourish or provoke or even permit of, the answer? The most interesting and crucial case arises when the question bears on a private experience. I ask someone 'Are you content?' My question, in objective *fact*, is given as answered; the answer is going to introduce a determination into my disjunction. The 'fact' is thought as pre-existing the answer and the function of the answer seems to consist in liberating it or uttering it. But my question, by the fact that it asks for an answer, supposes itself to be understood; it implies the postulate that itself and the answer will coincide (in this case it implies the identity of the *idea* of

[1] But by so doing I cease to treat myself as myself.

contentedness); thus a question is posited as being exactly reflected in an understanding that confronts the question with the
fact (the *he* or *it*) and utters this in the form of an answer. Clearly
it is important to define this confrontation. My question makes
the other person ask himself: 'Am I content?' But how *will he
answer* himself? How is the *pure him* or *it* liberated, so to speak,
so as to meet the question and answer it? Or, again, how is pure
experience inserted into the dialectic? It appears as though pure
experience must be questioned in its turn, must become a *thou*
and answer. But are we not involving ourselves in an infinite
regression? How can the answer of pure experience (manner of
being) be produced? It seems to me indispensable to note that
in a particular case it may not necessarily be produced at all.
Pure experience may refuse to answer. But whether it refuses or
not it evidently needs, so to speak, to be converted into a person
who *has* or *has not* common ground with the interrogating
consciousness. At least pure experience is sufficiently capable
of reflection to recognise whether the common ground exists
or not. The question, anyway, operates as an appeal, a signal
that may or may not be received. At this point we need to consider the instance in which I cannot answer because I do not know.
The appeal is made, but nothing answers. If on the other hand
the interlocutor knows, his objective knowledge is converted
into '*thou*' who answers. Someone asks me: 'When did Descartes
die?' I answer: 'In 1650'. What does that mean? It is not the fact
that answers (the eternal truth, the pure *him* or *it*): but the truth
as transformed in an interlocutor. We have still to ask whether a
distinction needs to be made between eternal truth and the knowledge of that truth. But this question is not properly stated. All
this needs to be examined. It is worth noticing that a truth such
as 'Descartes died in 1650' or 'Prague is the capital of Bohemia'
cannot be defined *other than* as an answer to a possible question.
To say that I know that Prague is the capital of Bohemia is essentially to say that I am in the position to answer the question:
'What is the capital of Bohemia?' Knowledge, the knowledge of
someone, can thus only be considered as a totality of answers
susceptible of being liberated in this or that given situation.
Real knowledge, of course, is that which can be used in a very
large number of different situations. But it seems at once illegiti-

mate to say that this knowledge is in act, and excessive to maintain that it is only in potency. There is an intermediary notion to be found, that is to say, to construct. It is in this sense that *to know* is *to be able* (I have pointed out that the answer is a sign, that is to say a signal susceptible of being utilised and of orientating action, i.e. in this instance furthering the progress of knowledge).

I note that linked to the foregoing there are other capital questions such as the question of the nature of the effort to recollect. I am searching for a name I have forgotten, that is to say I am questioning; I can look for the name in a dictionary, whose function here is that of mediator between myself and reality. I know that my question is answered in fact—for instance I cannot think of the name of the author of *Rome Sauvée* but I know that the author exists and has a name. But my appeal to myself does not seem to be heard. I only try to recall what I know I once knew (that is to say, what I perhaps know). It seems that to the initial question there must be something that will answer: 'Here' or 'We have got it'. In a word the appeal is addressed to the confused interior multiplicity which is my permanent '*thou*' (the *thou* which cannot be converted into a *him* or *it* unless I call it *me*, or—to use a monstrous phrase—my *me*). It is from this multiplicity, then, that the first answer seems to emanate. And everything happens subsequently as if the interior multiplicity searched on my behalf until the moment when memory arises and says: 'It is I.'[1]

It seems, in a word, that there is an experimental process in which the interrogator ceases to take part as soon as he has made his appeal. Yet the answer may be immediate.[2]

From the dialectical standpoint—which is also the standpoint of experience—that is, in a world in which thought progresses by means of questions and answers, there can be no pure datum, i.e. no datum which does not involve or permit of question and answer. The immediate, which would be the purely insignificant, cannot be inserted anywhere into dialectics, and dialectics—by

[1] Forgotten recollection is mute recollection. Note of 1925. One ought to examine more closely what this search consists in. It is a sort of rearrangement of self in function of the element that needs bringing to the surface.
[2] In this instance rearrangement is superfluous; the interior multiplicity is spontaneously organised so that the element asked for is on the surface plane.

definition—cannot proceed from it. But it goes without saying that we are here dealing with a purely abstract world, a world in which enjoyment would be impossible.

In enjoyment there seems to be an identity of the mediator and of the mediatised (far from only being its expression, the *thou* is confounded with the *him* or *it*); I am in communication[1] with the thing itself and not with a symbol for the thing, but because of that the thing ceases to be the thing in the theoretical sense, it ceases to be translated by a sign. It is in this sense that art, like love, is revelation; it implies a gift. Now in the realm of the pure *him* or *it*[2] there could be no question of a gift. In this way light is thrown on the nature of the act by which we affirm the independence of the object. We do not admit that it is addressed to us, or that we are *for it*; whereas a work of art, to the extent to which it is not a simple thing (a canvas, etc.), is essentially addressed to us. It reveals itself to us; it takes us into account; we are for it. Here we have an interesting transition to the problem of finality.

August 23rd, 1918

In the judgment involving '*I*' the immediacy (absence of the subject, non-relation to a subject, unrelatedness to a subject) functions as subject. This needs to be made more precise. *I am tired*. There is a pure and simple feeling, that is to say an absolute, or something which imitates an absolute, something not related to something else or mediatised. In the judgment of the '*I*' it is precisely the non-relation which functions as the *him* or *it*; on this non-relation the feeling, now become a predicate, depends. So the dialogue proceeds as follows. 'Someone is tired. Who is? I am.' This would have no meaning if the '*I*' were not directed to another interlocutor for whom the '*I*' is someone in particular, a given person. And I only become a given person for myself through the mediating idea of the other for whom I am a given person. In principle and strictly speaking I am absolutely not a given person for myself, I am even the negation of a given person. Hence we clearly see the analogy—it is at least external—that

[1] Note of 1925. As will be seen further on, the term *communication* is absolutely unsuitable.
[2] Note of 1925. More exactly in any order in which a relation with the *he* or *it* subsists, a relation implying the interposition of a *thou*.

exists between *I* and a thought in general (the *Denken überhaupt* of the Kantians) which is certainly not a given (thought) and to which all judgment is referred.

Yet this *I* seems always to be posited as being in confrontation with a *thou*, for whom in turn I myself am a *thou*. And it is in function of this dialogue and in relation to it that a *he* or *it* can be defined, that is, an independent world or at least a world that is—doubtless by a fiction—treated as independent. Here lies the profound importance of Royce's triadism and I think it has never been made sufficiently explicit. In more intelligible language, all independent reality can and must be treated as a *third party*. And if a *third party* supposes a dialogue it is nevertheless true to say that all dialogue is given to itself as a *third party*.

I glimpse a sort of slow transition from pure dialectics to love, in the measure in which the *thou* becomes *thou* more and more profoundly. For it begins so to speak by being essentially a *him* with the form of a *thou*. I meet a stranger in the train. We speak of the heat, of the war news, etc., but even when I address him, he does not cease to be 'somebody', 'that person', in my eyes. He is 'somebody' whose biography I get to know little by little. And inasmuch as he, for me, is 'somebody', I appear to myself as 'somebody else'. (This helps us to a better understanding of the meaning of the English term 'self-consciousness'.)[1] Somebody else communicates himself to me by signs which coincide with signs of mine, and that is all. But it may well happen that I become more and more conscious that I am having a dialogue with myself (which does not in any way mean that the other person and I myself appear to me to be identical); that is he participates more and more in the absolute which is *unrelatedness* and we cease more and more to be 'somebody' and 'somebody else'. We become simply 'us'.[2] In the old philosophical language one would have said he becomes less and less an object for me—but that way of expressing it seems to me ambiguous

---

[1] Note of 1925. Generally speaking the more my interlocutor is exterior to me the more I am by the same token exterior to myself; the more I am conscious not of what I am, but of my qualities and my faults, my 'particular characteristics.'

[2] Note of 1925. This is bound up with the experience of the inexhaustible wealth of a perpetual 'again' which is the very antithesis of boredom. This remark has great importance for our notion of duration.

and not very intelligible. For me, the being I love is a *third person* in the least possible degree. Moreover, that being discovers me to myself, since the efficacy of his or her presence is such that I am less and less *him* for myself—my interior defences fall at the same time as the barriers that separate me from somebody else. The being I love comes more and more into the circle in relation to which and outside which there are third parties, third parties who are 'the others.' But knowledge of the third party does not suppress the third party as third party. And inversely: there are categories, if I can so express it, that do not overlap. Perhaps we ought to make a distinction between knowledge and familiarity, by adopting the latter word in its original meaning, which is not the one we have become used to. Moreover, it is not certain that another distinction ought not to be made—between familiarity and love.[1]

December 8th, 1918

Given the relation of thought to thing which seems to be involved in the act of predication it is worth observing:

1. That the thing can never be regarded as a sum of predicates, for the plus sign only relates to the form of accumulation (the juxtaposition of interests), which is purely mental.

2. That the predicate only symbolises and determines an answer to a determined question, so that when we say A is p we merely mean that in function of the interest, A answers p.

3. That to ask oneself what A is, apart from the predicates a, b, c, d, is either to ask oneself what its other predicates are (which possibly has some meaning, whatever the predicates enumerated, for it may well be that an exhaustive enumeration is unthinkable) or else to ask oneself what A answers to a question which is not one of the thinkable questions, that is, to an absence of question. But we know that the answer is not precisely zero. It is: *this*. A is a predicate (or a grouping of predicates) determined

---

[1] I tend to believe that I can only speak of my soul in the exact and exclusive measure in which the relation of love—whose dialectic is at one and the same time intellectual emergence and in some degree negation—is established between me and myself. But words are deceptive. Here we are not dealing with terms and with a relation between them. There is really an undecomposable whole, namely self-intimacy or interior life.

and affected by the index *this*. And it is only this index that confers on A its apparent substantiality.[1]

Thus we have no right to say that A can be reduced to a grouping of answers; the questions themselves are only possible on the basis of *this*, of immediate presentation.

December 10*th*, 1918

Evidently the thing is that which is not conserved; it is inasmuch as we are things, not inasmuch as we are bodies, that we are mortal.

This obscure phrase refers to a group of undated reflections that I reproduce here in spite of their character being perhaps contradictory in part.

Only that which can be conceived of as dispersed or lost can be thought of as conserved.

Conservation implies the action of a force which is opposed to dispersion, that is to say a concrete unity that is thought as external or internal to the whole; which whole is thus itself a concrete unity in another sense or at least is treated as such.

The idea of conservation implies the ideas of protection and of value; the whole is of value as a whole, either for itself or else for the agent that conserves it (for the moment I am not going deeper into this distinction).

There is a continuity between the act by which I think the whole as whole (not only as aggregate); that by which I assign it a value, a quality; and that by which I conserve it.

Example: the act of conserving a letter instead of throwing it away or tearing it up.

Invariably the emphasis is put on the identity of place, or else, if change of place occurs, we neglect it.

Superficially there seems to be a profound difference between the conservation of a thing by someone and the conservation of self by self; and the first case seems simpler than the second. But deeper reflection shows that this is not so.

I decide to preserve a letter. What does that mean? First I posit that the letter is a concrete unity with a value (what kind of value does not matter here); then that this act negates the

---

[1] Distinguish here between *A* and *an A*. Every judgment bearing on *an A* is at bottom hypothetical; the judgment on *A* is categorical.

forces of dispersion (there is no need to specify further) which are exercised by the very fact that the letter is an aggregate and is not necessarily bound down to a given place (and thus it can be torn up, even by carelessness, or mislaid). In fact I can only preserve the letter because at once I think of it as physical object and because I take into account the way it is given to me and the possible agents of dispersion. Thus at the root of the preservation of *the letter* there is *the idea of the letter*. The latter is not external to the former. They form an autonomous whole. The preservation is bound up with the functioning of this whole. The living centre of it is the value or active quality of the letter. I can never speak of preservation save when by imagination I construct a whole of this type (it is the quality by which an aggregate is negated in some measure as such and in no other sense). From this we can derive a whole series of important consequences. To begin with the idea of preservation can only be applied to the universe considered as a whole on condition that it is not regarded as a sum, as a total of juxtaposed elements.

APPLICATION TO MEMORY

Do recollections conserve themselves, it may be asked, or is there an activity that tends to conserve them? But this distinction has no meaning. Recollections are not external to psychical activity. The idea of preservation implies place in the measure in which only that which is in aggregate *in a certain relation* can be conserved. Recollections can only be preserved in so far as they are elements—that is to say are susceptible of being preserved. But what does this mean? Is there really a sense in which we can treat recollection as an element or as an aggregate susceptible of being dissipated? We seem bound to recognise that in reality the spatial ideas of loss and of dissipation fundamentally imply something spiritual. I say that a whole is dispersed. This means that it ceases to be a datum given as a whole to the psychological activity to which I make reference. . . . To lose is essentially to forget. Mnemonic experience is really the root of the rudimentary experiences to which people claim to reduce it.

It may be pointed out that there is a possibility of absolute loss and total disappearance. But it is plain that this disappearance only *is* for those who survive and remember, who oppose their *now* to a *then* that they imagine or recall—but who at a given moment lost sight of and let escape from the grip of their attention precisely that which they are now endeavouring in vain to recall. . . . Yet can we not conceive of a vigilant and continuous attention being nevertheless impotent to retain what is dispersed? For instance, a mother who cannot save her child who is dangerously ill. Is the power of effective protection the measure of love? We can scarcely think this in view of the radical heterogeneity that seems to exist between the spiritual power that saves and the forces of dispersal it confronts—a heterogeneity that seems bound up with the very nature of the finite. Rightly or wrongly spiritual power seems to us to be capable of triumphing only over spiritual inattention and dispersal. The common belief is that it is only in this indirect way that spiritual power can triumph over material dissolution and anarchic material forces. If spiritual power, and the will for salvation, imposed itself directly on the physical forces of dissolution so as to subjugate them, we would have—and in the technical sense—the miraculous re-creation.[1]

The Problem of the Conservation of the Past

There is a sense in which what we call an event is eternal truth (a totality of judgments that meet); and in this sense it would be absurd to speak of conservation. There is only conservation of that which has duration—of that *on which time gnaws*. The past, it seems, can only be conserved in the measure in which it is transformed by outliving itself (just as in melody the first notes are transformed by those which follow and are given a value they could not have had by themselves). The motionless memory of Bergson is a pure abstraction, it cannot have duration, it cannot conserve itself. It may be contended that the letter that is conserved does not have duration. But it has duration in and through the thought that conserves it, that watches over it. It

[1] Note of 1925. But deep down within us is there not something that protests against the over-strict dissociation of the two types of dispersal, a forefeeling or presentiment of fresh truth that is not yet formulatable?

has duration inasmuch as it is incorporated with a living person, and the same is true of the event which lasts in so far as it is recalled and coloured by the moving present which evokes it and arrays it before itself. We might be tempted to add that the letter has duration materially in that it wears out—the writing becomes effaced, etc. But all this is only the temporal expression of the letter considered as thing, as aggregate, of the letter inasmuch as it is not conserved.

But there are many difficulties. The principle of conservation itself seems subject to duration. Again, duration implies self-conservation, etc. . . . Are we not obliged to convert God into an eternal truth by the fact that we view him as the first principle of all conservation? Whereas an eternal truth is powerless to conserve or—if you will—to save.

Is the eternal the lowest limit of all conservation? *that on which time does not gnaw?* In this sense only an element would be eternal; as indeterminate and non-qualified (for all quality has reference to a totality of other qualities and in consequence is involved in duration). Understood in this sense, the eternal is clearly the infra-temporal, eternity is only a negative value. But can we conceive an upper limit of conservation? That is the real problem of eternity. It is infinitely obscure. For if we conceive as positively eternal the act which apprehends a duration as a whole, as present—it looks as if that act itself must either be an instant, which though perhaps privileged is involved in a duration that stretches beyond it, or else it must be a simple truth, that is to say, something abstract.

In any event it seems to me established that the eternal cannot be defined without reference to value (under pain of being reduced to what I have called the infra-temporal).

I have been reflecting once again on the mysterious relation between conservation and creation. There can only be conservation in the realm of that which is created which is also the realm of that which *has value* (conservation implies the active struggle against dissolution).

We tend to look on what happens to us as scenes in a film that are enacted before us but come from nowhere and lead nowhere. The image is unintelligible. Moreover, it is impossible to conceive the relation between something which happens and the ego to which *this* or *that* happens. It seems to me that this gulf has passed almost unnoticed.

December 11*th*, 1918

On the possibility of prediction (regarding the extraordinary case of T.).

Under what conditions is prediction possible? Prophesying means seeing; hence what is going to happen to us must already *be* —but in what sense? The future cannot be present in the sense in which a veiled object which will shortly be uncovered before me is present. The question *where* has no meaning here (e.g. where is the future?). What will be already *is*, but for somebody else. Does this somebody, in his turn, foresee? Perhaps, but in that case we are making no headway; the same question now arises for this other. Hence this series of consciousnesses that can divine, which is perhaps very long, has for term a consciousness that is master of the future, that is at one and the same time the present and what is yet to come. This can be made clearer with the help of examples. I start telling a story, but not only do I foresee the situation towards which my story is leading, I know where I want to end up; I know what the end will be because I will it to be thus. I cast forward. All prediction seems to me to imply a— perhaps entirely indirect—participation in the life of a consciousness that forecasts. This consciousness does not foresee, it creates in advance. But this applies in innumerable ways. For example, I may well *see* what is not to be. It is conceivable that the consciousness that is master of the future is nevertheless not all-powerful and hence is incapable of realising what it' forecasts'. Hence we are obliged to recognise that effective vision may have taken place even though the prophecy has not been confirmed by the facts. Or, again, inasmuch as this consciousness improvises it may, for its own ends, be led to make use of an empirical material that is provided for it from outside. It may be that we are dealing with something unforeseeable from the standpoint of the beings who participate at its projection, in the measure in which there is something *for itself* and this consciousness does not know how to tackle it. Or it may well be that what is impossible for it, seen from another standpoint, in the centre of another system of references, is an object of potential prediction.

Of course what I fail to grasp clearly is the relation of the consciousness or supra-consciousness in question to my consciousness or yours. It appears to be alike richer and more efficacious; in a word, to be endowed with a superior power of concentration. But is it strictly speaking an 'other'? It would be tempting to say that we are organic in relation to it. But is that intelligible?

December 12th, 1918

This morning I discovered a vital link for my argument. The questions I am able to answer are exclusively questions brought to bear on information that I am capable of providing (even about myself). For example: 'What is the capital of Afghanistan?' 'Do you like French beans?' Whereas the more it becomes a matter of what I am considered as a whole (and not of what I have) the more the answers and even the questions lose their meaning: for instance 'Are you virtuous?' or even 'Are you courageous?'[1]

That is why at bottom it is meaningless to ask: 'Do you believe in God?'[2] when belief in God is understood not as an opinion on the existence of a person but as 'mode of being.' The same possibly applies regarding belief in immortality. Hence it follows:

1. That the belief of somebody else cannot be known by me (it cannot be the object of a questionnaire).

2. A cardinal point. In the measure in which every dialogue with myself (or reflection) is the interiorised reproduction of a dialogue with someone else, my belief can no more become an object for me than can my being. I cannot really question myself about my belief. (This is the deepest meaning of *Le Palais de Sable*—I feel I have never grasped it so clearly.) Hence God can never be a third in relation to the ego-subject ego-object dyad, and this gives their full meaning to my notes of July 23, 1918.

Clarifications. The belief of someone else—I must be clearer about what this means—can only be an object of belief for me, but from the moment that I believe *in* the belief I believe *with* the someone else. The unbeliever does not believe in the belief

---

[1] This links up with the central problem of *Un Homme de Dieu*.
[2] Note of 1924. In the measure in which belief in God is real it is a 'manner of being' and an ontological modification.

of others. By that I do not mean that he judges it to be insincere (though this is often the case) but that he interprets the belief as an existential judgment that is mistaken. When I am asked: 'Do you believe in God?' it is as though I were asked: 'Do you think Mars is inhabited?' or 'Are you impressionable?' In either case we have missed the essential point about belief: namely, that it is a personal way of qualifying the world metaphysically, that is to say, it is experience.[1] It is certain, moreover, that more often than not the attitude of the sceptic consists in looking on belief as a subjective disposition to which a reality may correspond. But this dualism is quite untenable. For to think God is to think him as bound up with the affirmation regarding him (and doubtless as playing a part in it); to think God as real is to affirm that it is important for God that I should believe in him, whereas thinking this table means thinking it as entirely indifferent to the fact that I think it. A God for whom my belief were of no interest would not be God but a mere entity of metaphysics. The sceptic may say: 'I agree. *Either* you believe in God, but your belief only qualifies yourself, *or else* your belief has a metaphysical value, and in that case it does really matter to God.' I want to find out exactly what the first alternative means.

It consists in opposing to the statement: 'I believe in God' —which, it is considered, should properly be changed into a question—this answer: *'Yes, but* God is not.' That is to say it consists in admitting that *reality* (?) speaking through an informed interpreter, gives a negative answer to the question. A person in the know tells you that the *he* or *it* is not divine. But as this can be interiorised by the believer himself it is clear that we reach a point at which we place ourselves absolutely outside the conditions just defined—since we have specified that God cannot function as a *he* or *it* or a *third party* in relation to a dialogue.[2]

[1] Note of 1925. This way of expressing myself no longer seems to me to be either very clear or very adequate. For we are not concerned with a qualification that is itself contingent in relation to the object with which the subject would collate it, but with a relation that is *sui generis* between the real individual who is neither impersonal form nor pure empirical content, and the reality to which he is attached, and grasps himself as being attached, when he makes an invocation.

[2] It is essential to note that all this links up with what I said elsewhere about the unverifiable. All that is of the order of the *he* or *it* is verifiable; that which only allows for a dyadic relation is unverifiable—that is, it transcends all verification. (It must be added that verification supposes the possibility of indefinite numbers of substitutions, which are not conceivable when I am in presence of a *thou*. This is an essential point.)

Here we seem to be saying (to ourselves or to someone else—it amounts to the same thing): 'You affirm that there is a *third party* who is God, but that *third party* is not God; nothing about him is divine.' Now this answer *to a question which was not asked* is meaningless (since we precisely excluded the possibility of a triadic relation between the subject, himself and God). Hence our first alternative has no meaning, or rather it is only a negative confirmation of what we already posited.

Perhaps these reflections throw some light on the appalling problem of the relation between the subject and its predicates. For can we not say that in the measure in which the subject really is (in the sense in which I am) no more than I myself does this subject permit of being determined by means of questions and answers? To the question: 'What am I?' I do not know what to answer, whereas I have no difficulty in answering the question: 'Am I blond?' or 'Am I greedy?', etc. From the moment I think a thing as subject (a way of considering it which may, I think, be illegitimate in certain cases) I think it as susceptible of answering not a global question but detailed questions.[1] This is very clear regarding a person and perhaps even as regards God. But it may be only through confusion and by analogy that I treat a thing as *having* characteristics and as being undefinable considered apart from the characteristics it possesses. Perhaps the idea of thing (subject) needs to be eliminated entirely—that is what I tend to believe. It may be contested that this 'substantialism' is every bit as justifiable if applied to me myself. But when I think myself as myself (and all decision and all action presupposes that I do) I treat myself as a whole; and the same applies when I love or I am loved, etc. Thus we get to an important proposition: in the measure in which a reality is treated as a whole it transcends the course of thought that proceeds by questions and answers; between consciousness and itself it can only establish a dual relation (or more precisely what appears to reflection as such a relation; for when we are only two we are in some way one only— the pseudo-dualism of the epistemologists is in reality a trialism). The dual relation is what in my previous enquiries I have called

[1] That is why substance is unknowable, i.e. surpasses dialectics. And this can easily be understood. How could it answer us save by being given in detail? If it is given all to-gether, the moment of the *he* or *it* and that of the *thou* are identified; we have a dyad (i.e. we are outside knowledge with its bearing on a third reality).

participation. In this way complete unity is achieved between my present reflections and my former ones. We now begin to see how believing in God means having dual relations with the real. But obviously this excessively abstract formula needs to be elucidated and specified.

God is reality in that reality absolutely cannot be treated as a *he* or *it*. Was this not what I meant when I maintained that no judgments on God are possible? But this needs further examination. Are there no judgments in the second person? When, for instance, I say to someone: 'You are good.'

It must be noticed, I think, that all judgments in the second person aim at being heard; they have a finality that does not exist in judgments in the third person. It may be objected that the latter are intended to give information. But this does not apply to judgments in the second person, or at least only secondarily. Every *thou* judgment expresses a relation of myself to the interlocutor and the wish that this relation should be known by him. ('You are good' is equivalent to: 'Know that I find you good.') In short, personal relations could only be between the believer and God, and if one placed oneself outside belief one would be prohibiting oneself from thinking God.

This whole theory is a reflection of belief, but one that implies the non-conversion of belief into a relation of subject to object. To be examined further.

December 14th, 1918

Existence and predication. Only that which can be an object of predication, which can be a datum, exists (to make a judgment of existence one must provide data by predicates). Hence the very clear relation between the fact that there is no meaning in saying that God *exists*, and the impossibility of attributing characteristics to him, of converting him into a *he* or *it*.

But does not this way of thinking God amount to making him entirely dependent on me, since only the object is grasped as independent of the act by which I conceive it? Hence a patently absurd problem that it is hard to avoid stating: What is God inasmuch as I do not think of him?—But (apart from the fact that the words 'think of God' conceal a fundamental ambiguity) it is, clear that when we ask this question we are once more converting

God into a third party. Someone was with me. That person leaves me. I ask myself what happened to him. The question has the same sense as if it were about a thing; it is only possible because the person can in some measure be treated as a thing. But in so far as there is a spiritual relation between that person and me the question changes its aspect. *To be defined more exactly.*

I can now see more clearly the meaning of the judgment in the second person. When it informs it implies that in *thee* there is a *he* or *it* for *thyself*. If my judgment: 'You are (thou art) or you are not (thou art not) this or that; you have or you have not that particular quality' is aimed at informing you, this is because I admit that there is in you something that *is* not *for you*, regarding which you have (at least virtually) questioned me. Whereas if this judgment is not aimed at informing you about yourself, it only has bearing on me (it informs you about me); it is then in *me* that there is *him* or *it* for *thee*. ('You are good: I admire you, etc.') How do these reflections apply to God? The first form is plainly inapplicable here. Because it is, fundamentally, a form of *he* or *it*; I speak to you of someone else who is only verbally confused with me. Now, for God, can there be any *him* or *it* in *me*? The question looks as though it needs modifying if it is to have an intelligible meaning. The second form does not seem to me any more acceptable; for to say that in relation to God there is any *him* or *it* in me is to think of God as a third party; it is to discuss God with oneself. Possibly there we have the real meaning of divine omniscience. In this instance as in others the experience of love puts us on the right road. In me there would be no *he* or *it* for *thee* if *thou* and *I* loved one another absolutely; and this does not mean that you (thou) would have the intuition of myself, but that I would be appropriated by you (thee).

December 18*th*, 1918

What is preoccupying me this morning is how to understand how God can surpass me infinitely without becoming a *he* or *it* for me. To elucidate the meaning of this properly we must take up the fundamental notions once more. In principle and according to current notions the being to whom I address myself is someone of whom I can speak (and consequently on whom I can reflect). This possibility implies a double limitation of both him and me;

it supposes that I can treat him as someone who is not there, that I can set him aside; and also, as far as *I* am concerned, that the bond between us is not absolute (I cannot really discuss the being I love absolutely with a third party). Supposing it be objected that this is merely a contingent sentiment? That objection would be very uninstructive. In reality the being I love has not got qualities for me; I grasp him as a whole, that is why he is refractory to predication. Similarly with a work of art: the more I love it the less I can qualify it, the less any qualification appears adequate for what I experience. But does love involve the affirmation of a closed, exhaustible content? On the contrary—it bears on the infinite. Nothing is more false than to identify the *thou* with a bounded and circumscribed content. Participation in divine life can only be grasped as participation in an infinite. But the infinite cannot be thought apart from the participation; that is what I laboured to express in 1914. Doubtless this participation cannot be separated up into detail, but that does not mean that all is given me at once—to say that would be meaningless. When I talk with someone for whom I experience nothing resembling love, he appears to me as capable of furnishing me with a certain set of answers to questions bearing on himself (what is his name, when and where was he born, etc.). He himself, if you like, is a filled-up questionnaire. The more I love a being and the more I participate in his life the less adequate this way of thinking is shewn to be. The beloved is beyond all these questions; they seem insignificant and absolutely external.

To say that the being I love was born on a certain date at such and such a place, etc. is meaningless. Such determinations in no way enhance the content on which my love is brought to bear. From this we can doubtless conclude that to love someone truly is to love him in God. But there is great need of precision here.

Another difficulty. Are we not obliged to think something which is 'in the third person' in relation to God and the believer (that functions as the *him* or *it* for them)—and that without this something all dialogue would be impossible? In other words do we not end up with a new triad? Plainly this is a major issue. The world would be a third in the unceasing dialogue I pursue with God; but then is it not *it* for both?

Perhaps this may help. The lover finds in things the wherewithal to render homage to the beloved. The lover *offers* the world as well as himself to his mistress: 'All this is yours.' It remains for us to understand how the believer looks on 'all this' as at the same time *created by* God. At this moment I cannot see; yet I know I have understood it. In any case the believer seems to confer a kind of consecration on God. Metaphorically, and departing a long way from the rigorous language I have been using, it could be said that God expects each believer to confer his (God's) divinity on him. This allows us to set aside the insoluble problems of theodicy. It seems to me that on this point the unbeliever could be brought to understand that he cannot speak of God *yet*. . . . Yesterday I found the following formula: when we speak *of* God we should realise that it is not of *God* that we are speaking. We must be careful about this when we treat God as creator. I think that our attitude then is only a degeneration of the 'Yours, O my God,' that is wrung from the religious heart at the sight of a moving spectacle. For this appeal to God has no meaning and value unless it is accompanied by emotion. Otherwise it is only a mechanical formula or the initial stage of idolatry.

And this I think is the meaning of the relation that I referred to earlier. Doubtless I give to God, but what I give already belongs to him. The consecration is at the same time a sort of restitution. All this must be examined more thoroughly. I belong to God, but I ought to give myself to him, to turn myself towards him. Here there is a mystery, but it is involved in the very relation that unites me to God.

Consequences regarding prayer.

All prayer is addressed to a free being (to a being who has mastery over a certain order). Prayer is posited as susceptible of being understood and of influencing the being to whom it is addressed. Notice that when it is addressed to a finite being it may happen that it is not understood, or is not taken into consideration. Does this apply to God? The finite being is able to avoid taking it into consideration because the person who addresses it to him is for him a *third person* with whom he in no way identifies himself. But it may be that I am a *third person* for God. Hence, supposing that what I have prayed for is not fulfilled I cannot say that my prayer has not been heard (or if I do say so, it will be because I have ceased to be aware that it is to God that I address it, because I have fallen into idolatry). By a formula all too human, my resentment will be expressed in terms of *he*. Supposing it be said that in all things I should bow to the divine behests and hence that prayer is useless? That is another idolatry, the idolatry of necessity. The narrow isthmus of religious thought lies between these two idolatries. Here I find *in concreto* what I said earlier. My prayer cannot be thought as not interesting God, not attaining God; to that extent my prayer is certainly efficacious. Supposing it be objected that in spite of this the divine decrees must be considered as being made from all eternity? But I am convinced that if *from all eternity* means 'a time incapable of measurement' we are deep in heresy (and perhaps involved in extreme absurdity). But this must be examined further. To pray is actively to refuse to think God as order, it is to think him as really God, as pure *Thou*.

January 18th, 1919

I can now clearly understand the meaning of *L'Iconoclaste*: it is that mystery has its own peculiar value. And this links up with a whole order of ideas that seem to me essential. The fact that it is known does not change the nature of a thing, but it transforms its value; it gives it a renewed significance and hence a superior efficacity. The same may apply on another plane to mystery. . . . There are certain higher relations which are only defined and elucidated by communion in mystery. There is nothing of banal agnosticism in this—on the contrary, that view maintains that the fact of being known or not known in no way alters the object. Here precisely lies the difference between what is mysterious and what is unknown. Only that which has interest in not being revealed is mysterious. Transition from the idea of mystery to the idea of revelation.

January 21st, 1919

To name a being is to effect a sort of subtle transposition of the *thou* into a *he*. To name is to recall, to *remember* that the being of whom we are speaking can become the object of invocation (I remember how much M. was grieved when I spoke of him in his presence and said *he*).

To return to the idea of mystery. There is only mystery in

the order of *he who knows*. . . . What is unknown and does not
know is merely ignored. What knows and does not wish to be
known, and proceeds in such a way as not to be known, is mysterious (there is also the category of that which is powerless to make
itself known—this, too, belongs to the order of the ignored).
The idea of mystery thus implies the idea of power and it is bound
up with the very idea of God. To think God is to think him as
being in this way mysterious. Supposing it be objected that in
so thinking him I infringe his defences? But we must grasp that
what is not known as mysterious does not participate in mystery
(to realise this we only need to think of what happens in a
mystery novel). But here we need to ask ourselves if I do not
myself become in some degree mysterious for the being who
insists on remaining mysterious for me. And furthermore, up to
what point the mysterious is the object of questions and answers?
This is a cardinal point.

Our world is certainly not a world from which the mysterious
is excluded, a world in which all that has the power of communicating itself communicates itself directly and spontaneously.
Hence there is an intimate relationship between the idea of
mystery and the idea of value. Only that which is capable of
interesting me and presenting a value for me is mysterious. For
why should *the other* refrain from communication to me what is in
no way my concern? There must be a positive reason for this
failure to communicate—not merely the absence of a reason for
communicating. This is very important. Hence there must be an
interest common to both of us. But it seems to me very clear that
when I think myself as existing for the other the other becomes
a *thou* for me. Hence mystery is only possible in the order of the
thou.[1] The agnostics have always overlooked this. . . .

January 22nd, 1919

By its very essence the objective order excludes all mystery. The
object can only be thought as indifferent to the act by which I
think it. There lies the deepest teaching in realism. I can only
think the object as object in realist terms—and as soon as I think
a subject as object exactly the same applies.

(Perhaps it would be better to say that realism is contained

[1] I am no longer (1925) absolutely sure of the validity of this piece of reasoning.

in the definition and the very idea of the object—this point is not only admitted by idealists, it is proclaimed.)

February 11th, 1919

It is evident that the signpost that answers a question does not know that I ask it—and the person who has placed it there does not know either. The signpost is addressed to—and answers—a questioner in general. But this only shows how far we have gone in abstraction. The questions 'Where does this road lead to?' 'Is it prohibited to walk on the grass?', etc. are addressed to 'Anybody'.

We cannot insist too much on the bond between what I have called dialectical thought and the fact of thinking by subject and predicates (in which dialectics are incorporated). The subject as subject is only a filled out questionnaire.

About *What is the Real Julius Caesar?* (Bradley: *Essays on Truth and Reality.*)

It seems to me that my attitude is quite different from Bradley's. For me being is only immanent for thought that loves, not for the judgment bearing on being. P. said to me: "Supposing I am judged to be a mere bookworm, I who, nevertheless . . . " In that case clearly the identity of the subject of the judgment and of the reality on which the judgment bears is only nominal. To judge is to classify. To judge an individual exactly is to classify correctly. What do we mean by that? That there should be a correspondence between the judge's mode of classifying and the mode of his interlocutors (who are supposed to be informed), and that on the other hand the subsequent acts of the individual ought to be such as not to make necessary a continual revision of the initial classification. But it seems to me evident that judgment as such has no ontological value. I cannot see any meaning in saying that the object of classification is (or is not) present. (I would say that all judgment plays on the edge of the real.) This links up with my trialism. Judgment bears essentially on a *he* or *it*, on something which is thought beyond all doubt capable of being put into a category.

February 22nd, 1919

Had an extremely interesting conversation with P.

He wonders whether it is conceivable—even if we admit the 'spiritist' hypothesis—that a 'spirit' can be 'identified'. Let us go so far as to admit that a revelation has been made involving something that only the spirit could have known (the contents of a chest the spirit sealed up when alive). May it not well be that I have entered into sympathetic communication with his state of mind of that time, which, in a deep sense, surely remains actual? The fact that no contemporary knows anything would not be a valid negative proof.

Once again we have contrasted communion (I am looking for an equivalent of *Mitsein*) and transmission. As I pointed out, even pure transmission (by letter, telegram, etc.) in last analysis implies an affectionate solicitude or at least a will to protect the content which is treated as value.

In short, only love—by the recognition of a spiritual continuity—could *identify*; we would have to be in an order in which we said 'It is *thou*' and not 'It is *he*.' We have reflected on the fact that the dead man present in the evocation does not answer; I have pointed out that all that can truly be said is that he does not inform, and we have no grounds for stating that he does not enrich by his real presence (impossibility of etiology in the spiritual order).[1]

To return to the instance of the chest. We set out from the idea (or pseudo-idea) that there is information to be 'extracted' 'somewhere'—and we ask where? But when we say information we mean transmission by symbols; this applies whether I am consulting my guide or another traveller. I treat the traveller's memory (or brain) as the equivalent of a railway guide or notice board. But though in practice his memory is able to fulfil that office for me, it is not in fact a system of symbols. Hence when we speak of 'extracting from a consciousness' what do we mean? If it were a matter of digging out a piece of information there would be need for an operation that is strictly analogous to the operation of reading (deciphering) or listening or interpreting —and that is meaningless. So there must be communication with memory *inasmuch as it is memory* (that is to say inasmuch as it is act or vision and not a system of signs). *The clairvoyant does not*

[1] We even ought to ask whether on a certain plane the term cause still retains any meaning.

read in me he *remembers me in my stead.* He participates in my memory, he informs himself only as much as I inform myself when I recollect my past.

I am fully aware that this is very difficult to take in, and that it is almost immediately travestied by the imagination. Our tendency is to present things in terms of the following points:

1.   That to recall is to make an inventory or to take up a leaf from a diary.

2.   That A, the subject, possesses (?) a collection or aggregate —C—of recollections; B, another subject, possesses another aggregate—Ci—of recollections. It goes without saying that B is able to bring an element—E—from Ci into C if he converts it into an object for A by communicating it (either orally or in writing or in any other way).

3.   Hence that it is impossible for A to find in his collection or aggregate an element that has not been *put* there.

But I repeat we must not identify memory with a collection or aggregate. To recall really means to re-live (in accord with certain modalities) it does not mean to re-read a note. Hence we can grasp why the abstract can only be transmitted or communicated—precisely because it is very feebly lived. In place of the formula I have emphasised above perhaps it would be better to substitute another even though it seems still more paradoxical: namely that *My past becomes that of the clairvoyant.* (It may be said that in any case there could be no question that *all* my past should do so. But fragmentation in itself is meaningless; let us say that the clairvoyant's attention is concentrated on a privileged moment of my past that has become his.) What is *my past?* What relation is there between my past and myself? I notice that I am the less my past the more I treat my past as a collection of events registered or enumerated in time, with my body serving as link. Inversely it becomes more difficult to set up an inventory of what I am when the word being is applied in a deeper way (I am thinking at this moment of my ideas as I adhere to them, of my feelings and beliefs). Thus if by *my past* we understand the past that I *am* as contrasted with the past that I *have*, we must admit that the former past, far from being thought under the form of a collection can only be thought as object of faith or of love; (and my relation with this past remains inevitably precarious and mysterious; it is these elements of myself that are incapable of being forever disposed of that Proust has emphasised so marvellously, though there is need to distinguish between what they are in themselves and the intermittent and lightning apperceptions by which they seem to be given to us at certain privileged moments).

I must admit that what I have just said still far from satisfies me. It still seems as if A is external to the datum of B's past, with the result that we cannot understand how communion can be established. But obviously this is meaningless. B's past cannot be a *datum*. Only that from which we can borrow is *given as datum*, and even here we have two complementary notions; only that which can pass into the state of being information (or which can be treated as potential information) is datum (a railway guide for instance). In this sense to the given I oppose the lived, the lived which can as lived only be trans-lived—*translived* seems an excellent word in contrast to *transmitted*. Inasmuch as my memory can be likened to a diary we can say that my past is given as datum; but from this point of view no communication with it is possible. Thus the more my past is really and intimately mine (the more it is at one with my being) the less it is a datum given. Perhaps it would be more accurate to say that it lives on. But how then can we talk of exteriority? The other person is other for me inasmuch as his collection does not coincide with mine; and hence the one is able to enrich the other. The other person is less other when our collections are less different, and in that the categories of aggregate or questionnaire are less applicable to him—in other words the more he is a *thou* for me. The more I treat him as a *thou*, the more he ceases to be a collection or aggregate for me or, more exactly, the more he ceases to be a person who has a collection—and the less sense there is in saying that he is exterior to me, the less his past is datum for me, the less the expression 'his past' has meaning. If this past becomes once more 'his past' for me, that is to say a collection or accumulation, the possibility of 'transliving' it *should* disappear. It is plain that I have failed to grasp adequately that normal intimacy between two beings does not involve 'transliving'. Yet I feel confusedly that men have done everything to make this experience rarer. (I should doubtless add here that in the case of lovers, this communication has a global character, by which I mean that it cannot be minted in small cash, it cannot be seen in detail and thereby discerned clearly.)

We now need to ask whether these reflections throw any light on psychometry and all that that involves. We can see at the outset that the fact that one of the individuals in contact is not physically present need not disturb us. For we are in a field in which signs play no part. Now, according to the standpoint I have adopted, the body is no more than a mechanism for signalling. We should doubtless distinguish carefully between the sign or signal and the strict appeal.

February 23rd, 1919

It would be vain to deny that in its profounder aspects the question is still very obscure. In the first place we cannot help thinking that where there is no datum there can only be the potential. But that word seems to me dangerous because it is equivocal. I have decided only to apply it to that which is *susceptible* of being strictly given, and hence to say that the past is only potential inasmuch as it is treated as aggregate or collection. It will doubtless be objected that the pure datum is fictitious, that every datum should be in some degree lived, and to this point I willingly agree. But this has not much importance here. Likewise I agree that where nothing is given as datum there is nothing I can re-live. The datum *acts as bait*. And it is for this reason that clairvoyants ask to be brought an object, in preference an object that has been intimately associated with the life of the person about whom they are being consulted. The clairvoyant seems to need the object so as to recall the past that is bound up with it. But at this point our understanding ceases. For in what does the link consist? We tend to represent it materially, to convert the past into a sort of odour in the material, etc., which is absurd. Had the object preserved a material imprint that functioned as a sign, the sign would have to be retranscribed, etc. and we would be up against all the difficulties I pointed out above. The object seems only to act psychically, that is, as representation. So I ask myself without yet knowing whether it is possible, nor even what the question means, whether the recollection of the object in question (this same object as re-called) is not substituted for the initial perception that bears on it; so that, more or less progressively, the recollection brings with it the reconstruction of the surroundings, of the living past to which it belongs. Thus second sight would consist in elevating oneself from the perception of a thing to the recollection of that thing. To common sense this appears at the outset unintelligible, for it does not seem possible to dissociate the memory of the object from the aggregate collection of which it forms a part—*which is not there*. By what mysterious effraction is the clairvoyant introduced into the aggregate or collection in question? But the objection supposes a postulate—namely that we begin by positing an irreducible duality between the 'real' object, (the scarf or glove, etc.) and the recollection of this same object, a memory treated as an article in the collection. Whereas even the idea of any such duality must be submitted to criticism. Notice, moreover, that between the perception of the object by a stranger, by no matter whom—and the memory its possessor has of it— we have to slip in as intermediary term the perception, with its memories, of the person who habitually lives with this object. The recollections bound up with the object are here incorporated with the perception itself, and form with it an entirely indivisible unity. Thus we have a synthesis of the images and movements which form the deepest reality of the object, of the object considered as value and not simply as physical datum. The business of the clairvoyant is to rediscover this complex reality of the object. To achieve this he needs to complete and animate the perceptive schema to which the object is reduced for him. This, in all probability, is the aim of the movements the clairvoyant performs with the object; his movements, which resemble those habitually performed by the object's owner, seem to me, as I see things at this moment, genuine magnetic suggestions exercised by the clairvoyant on this object which are intended to make it yield up its emotive reality, the recollection that is really its reality. It goes without saying that it is only tentatively that the clairvoyant manages to execute precisely those movements and not any others. Thus 'suggestivised', the object transforms itself not into a piece in a collection which it is imagined to be by the realist theory of memory, but into the incarnated thought-habit which it is for its user. It is clear of course that what I call the suggestibility of the object is actually the suggestibility of the clairvoyant. *The clairvoyant has to succeed in making the object an agent of suggestion for him.*

In other words, if I am a clairvoyant and I am brought a glove, that glove has to become a centre of psychical attraction for me, and I must in some way subordinate myself to it so that all that is naturally mine is for a few instants withheld and obliterated. That is why the clairvoyant needs to be in a trance. If he remained wakeful the power of suggestion that ought to emanate from the glove considered as spiritual presence would be annihilated in advance by what emanates from the clairvoyant himself when he imagines and constructs.

February 24th, 1919

Before asking how representation of a scene at a distance is possible (telepathic hallucination), we must question ourselves about the very idea of a scene. The unity of a scene, like that of a picture, is only psychical; hence we must either suppose that I see the scene itself, or else that it is projected in me as an image. As usually there is an interval between the time at which the event occurs and the time at which it is represented telepathically, we are at first tempted to suppose that a projection takes place, and that the scene is capable of being projected either before or after it happened. But I must confess my dissatisfaction with that solution. Ought we not rather to set out from the idea that a scene really takes place where it is lived, in other words that it is not riveted by essence to a certain point of space and of time? At first this appears absurd. For the scene brings into play a certain number of bodies that are situated strictly in space. But ought we not to distinguish carefully between the strictly material phenomenon which is only an abstraction (that we are bound to form) and the concrete scene itself? By very essence the phenomenon cannot be reproduced as such; or rather, were such reproduction realisable, it would be a second phenomenon analogous to the first. The phenomenon is submitted to conditions of space and time which are of necessity unique. Supposing I take as instance a shipwreck. The quality of shipwreck is really superimposed by me on a material phenomenon, on an infinitely complex and non-unifiable totality of *shocks* which in themselves have a rather distant relation to the catastrophe of which I am speaking. The phenomenon as such, by reason of its inhuman and non-psychical characteristics, cannot be an object of telepathy. It is capable of producing psychical effects, but it is also capable of being a snapshot taken mentally by an observer —a snapshot that can be transmitted and converted into notes and that is all. Moreover, telepathy would be reduced to a minimum in a world in which thought proceeded by means of phenomena and in which in practice people themselves could be likened to phenomenal elements. As soon as a scene takes place everything changes. The scene has a real unity, real persons take part in it, and it seems to me that it is through its unity and reality that the scene transcends the contingent conditions of its appearance in space and time. But is it not plain that this also applies to memory? Are not the conditions of possibility of telepathy the same as those of memory?

In a word we need to be careful not to set up a duality between the scene and the appearance, or between the scene and the recollection of it. That the recollection be the feebler need not surprise us, first of all because in recollection the scene, though conserving its unity, tends to be reduced and schematised; but primarily because the recollection of the recollection comes in to obliterate the recollection of the scene, so that a kind of composite and confused image tends to be substituted for the original recollection. As regards the appearance, it is plain *a priori* that this is only possible in the measure in which the psychic status of the person who sees it permits it to occur.[1]

But to return to common-sense objections. Common sense says that the scene cannot be immobilised unless there is an organism to register it, and where there is nothing of the kind it is unable to survive. I answer first of all that if there is really no one there there is no real scene. But we need to go further than that. The scene brings into play the motor apparatus of the person who is present, it thus determines an initial stage of habit, etc. Only these movements can be immobilised—not the scene itself. It may be contested that this amounts to the same thing,

[1] I am inclined to ask myself whether, where the appearance follows after the event and is not contemporaneous with it, it is not in reality a recollection. Without knowing it I was with the dying man at the moment of his death and now I suddenly recall it. But of course this needs further examining and defining.

for strictly speaking the scene is bound up with the achievement of those movements. But that is still far too summary. I am perfectly ready to agree that in the measure in which I recall the scene I tend to reproduce the movements I executed at the time, but I am certain it is not always because I reproduce them that I recall them. But despite this I may be told: 'You were not there to take a snapshot view of the death of your friend, so it is not possible that you should recall it.' But we must notice that the only question we should ask is whether we were *one* at the moment when the scene took place, or if we become *one* subsequently, when the scene is projected in me (this supposes we accept the second interpretation). On reflection it is hard to see by what criterion we could choose between these two theses, since a unity of the kind in question can only be given in experience and is strictly speaking unverifiable. It is only this unity that should receive the philosopher's attention—irrespective of whether or not it is produced at a given and determined moment. For this unity to occur it seems there must first of all be an appeal, an invocation, an 'abide with me' that is more or less clearly enunciated. Secondly, this appeal must be heard, though the subject does not necessarily know that he hears it, and it is on the basis of this mysterious *co-esse* that the vision is built up.

It is enough to reflect on a relation like that expressed by the word *with* (*avec*) to recognise the insufficiency and poverty of our logic. The word is capable of expressing relations of ever-increasing intimacy. I am not really *with* the traveller who is sitting next to me in the railway carriage and never addresses a word to me. The word *with* only has meaning where the unity is felt. A tiny incident on the journey is enough to modify our relationship and give a meaning to the word *with*. It is enough if some harmony, however feeble it be, is manifested between us. It is in these terms that we can achieve the definition of psychical proximity which is rightly, and doubtless also practically, dissociable from spatial proximity; and we may even need to start out from elementary considerations of this type if we are to understand the real meaning of praying for someone. From the religious standpoint God appears as the sole mediator who can permit me to be really *with* the person I am praying for. It is only by positing the necessity of that mediation that we can dissipate the dangers of confusion between the metaphysical order and the order that is strictly religious.

February 25th, 1919

How are we to conceive that invocation can be efficacious? I will proceed as I did with the problems I have already examined and ask about the postulates on which we spontaneously base ourselves if we want to dispute that efficacy. We spontaneously accept the view that if an appeal is to be heard, it should set in play a system of signs. Now, it may be said that the case I considered yesterday consists of nothing but the idea: A thinks of B but it is inconceivable that a real communication can be established between the idea of B which is in A and the being of B himself. For a long time, in agreement with Bradley, I was disposed to deny even that, i.e. the absence of communication between the idea and its object. Now I tend to believe that I was wrong. The idea, when it is only the *idea of*, should doubtless be conceived as isolated and cut off from its object—this is probably enough to bring out the metaphysical inadequacy of the idea as so understood. But our concern is to show that invoking a being is different from, and more than, thinking of him. What exactly do we mean by thinking of a being? We mean concentrating our attention on a particular system of images crystallising either round a special image or else round a name. Thus we mean taking an attitude absolutely analogous to the one we adopt in the presence of the person when that person is, for us, not a *thou* but a *he*. But at the moment of my invocation we must admit that something more than an idea comes into play. Yet the invocation, if I may so put it, must have an ontological foundation. I cannot *really* invoke 'anybody'; I can only 'pretend to' do so. In other words it appears as if invocation can only be efficacious where there is community.

In a deep sense that is difficult to define we must be *already together*. It is possible that from the moment at which we have really been together for a given instant, something of this community remains, but I must admit that this point is excessively obscure. We would need to suppose as with the *scene* (cf. above) that the psychical unity that made us *us*, is not bound up with a moment of time, that it reappears as soon as I put myself in the state of mind which was mine when the unity was formed (this is a very bad way of expressing myself, but I cannot find any other). In consequence, the invocation, now fortified (or, more exactly, nourished) by this real unity would enable me to communicate with the other person, grasped not simply as somebody else but as *thou*. What is obviously very singular is that the other can fail to be immediately aware of the appeal addressed to him. Then in what way is he 'attained'? The current terminology of psychology enables us to say that it is his unconscious that is attained. But this answer, so worded, is absolutely meaningless.

February 26th, 1919

For what is this unconscious? Can it be said to be the person in question inasmuch as he possesses a certain number of predicates that he does not know he possesses? That interpretation seems to me unacceptable. Let us proceed in our usual way. Let us take any type of communication at random. A writes a letter to B. B receives it. What happens? The letter is literally *received* —exactly in the sense in which a telegram or a radio message is *received*, that is to say 'captured'. This letter contains information, it tells B that A has just been ill, that he has recovered and is off on a journey, etc. In what sense is B 'attained' by this message? If he is merely informed and not *moved* by its contents, he only treats A as a piece of paper that he takes out of one drawer in his card-index and puts into another. In this case A is exclusively *him* for B. And, *by that very fact*, B *is* as little as can be for himself; he appears to himself as no more than a 'science', a group of notions associated together. Now suppose this letter to have an immediate emotive value. 'My dear friend, I am done for . . .' Straightway B's attitude is transformed. Now only the word *we* can express the relation of being to being that is set up between B and A (the term relation is itself inexact, for there is nothing here that can be understood discursively). There is compassion, commiseration. This shows itself by an incapacity to judge or predicate. But what is B when he becomes compassionate? He is revealed to himself. In principle nothing takes us more by surprise than our own emotions; it is part of the nature and I would almost like to add part of the duty of a feeling that it should to some extent ignore itself. This unknown element in a being which is revealed in emotion and makes up his value can in no way be treated as *he* or *it*. It is incontestably this that is accessible to invocation. I am fully aware of the contradiction in terms here. But it only goes to shew that we ought to look beyond words.

I quite realise that I may be told that in the case of the letter that arouses emotion, the signs or symbols play an essential and indispensable part; for we agree that they unleash emotion and we find it natural that they should do so because they operate immediately. But here we seem to be content with mere words. What matters is the transition from the *him* to the *us*, that is, to the experience of community. Now I do not think that this transition can be explained in mechanical terms. Emotion makes me come into the scene, it forces the hidden *me* to 'emerge'—the *I* which, as long as we were only concerned with classifying or with the revision of a classification, stayed 'behind the curtain.'

February 27th, 1919

It appears to me obvious that to move with emotion means to 'force to emerge', to mobilise. . . . But in what sense can we speak of emotion as having a strictly ontological value? Of course what is vulgarly called 'imaginary' can be just as efficacious as reality. But what is the value of this distinction?

Emotion only occurs with the 'breaking' or 'loosening of an adaptational bond'. But why does the rupture coincide with the 'emergence' of the I to which I have just referred? This question is obscure. What is the relation between the ego and the bonds of reciprocal adaptation which in emotion are relaxed or broken? It cannot be said that these bonds simply cover up the ego. I take as example the stable sentiment of a man's attachment to his wife. One day he discovers that she is being unfaithful to him. Hence the rupture I have spoken of and the 'emergence' of the ego. A substantialist or phenomenalist type of interpretation is here insufficient and does not even allow us to ask the relevant questions. When it is emotionally attached the ego is lost in its object, or more exactly in the activities that concern its object. By that I mean that the attachment excludes any real division into two. Naturally the subject may become aware of his attachment and know that he experiences it; but between himself and his attachment no living relationship is established—and, in his eyes, the attachment tends to be converted into something inert and inanimate. It is the equivalent of a predicate that applies to me inasmuch as I myself am *him* for myself; inasmuch as I know myself. Here emotion functions as a recall: 'The question concerns me, and I didn't realise it'.[1] The 'Oh but' which is at the root of the emotion sheds a retrospective clarity on what it interrupts or transforms. It recalls to me that it is impossible for me in last analysis to treat myself as *him*; or, more exactly, it is that recall itself.

March 1st, 1919

On the *Essais* of Père Laberthonnière. We need to question ourselves as closely as possible on what we mean by 'affirming being' or even by 'stating the problem of being'. This second phrase consists fundamentally in asking ourselves whether there is being, before we know what being is. But what do we mean when we ask this question? Contemporary writers tend to convert it into a problem of value. But that I think is dangerous. To have—to possess—a value must not be confounded with *being* a value; and now I must ask myself whether this last expression has any meaning. The relations expressed by the verb *to have* seem to me to have been badly defined. It can be argued that the fact of existing constitutes a value; but this would need to be defined exactly. Note that if we state the problem of being in the form: 'Is there being?' we suppose a high level of preliminary reflection. What would be the positive implications of the statement: 'There is no being'? That there are only phenomena. But this is only true in appearance. The phenomenon is only classified as phenomenon in contrast with an idea that is admitted to have no application.

March 2nd, 1919

'To come from myself', 'To come from elsewhere'—what do those expressions mean? (as applied to the ouidja board, dreams, creativeness, etc.).

---

[1] The idea of the ego is ambiguous; the ego is *I* inasmuch as *thee*—as in this particular case—or inasmuch as *him*.

It seems clear that when I gather information this comes from a source distinct from myself, and to that extent comes from elsewhere. Moreover, I may inform someone else, and thus myself function as a 'source of information'. At this moment I am not trying to get to the bottom of this latter activity which is only apparently clear. What is plain is that I am only a 'source of information' for somebody else, that is to say inasmuch as I am— for myself or for another—*somebody else*, that I participate in the nature of *somebody else*. Inasmuch as I am ego I am absolutely unable to give information. The opposition between 'me' and 'elsewhere' is thus in no way comparable to the opposition that would exist between 'a given source' and 'another given source'. To say that something created 'comes from' me is meaningless.[1] But, it may be objected, at least I can legitimately contrast the fact of *inventing* with that of *informing*. But that is not the question. In reality we are setting out from the pseudo-idea according to which each of us possesses a certain fund of information drawn from elsewhere, and from this fund we extract certain combinations. But what *we* (?) extract in this way is as little *curs* as could possibly be.

It seems true to say that the more I am myself the less I contrast myself with others as a source can be contrasted with other sources. The more I treat myself as a guide-book, the less I think of myself as myself.

About some given inspiration we ask: 'Does it come from me or from elsewhere?' But the inspiration cannot be compared to a group of signs or symbols. To say 'This idea comes from me,' means 'It does not come from someone', or 'It is meaningless to ask where it comes from.' We need to disentangle its positive counterpart from this negation.

March 3rd, 1919

I take up again what I tried to point out yesterday. Everything that is communicated by signs strictly emanates from a source. I receive some signals. I am bound to ask myself who sent them, where they come from. All information implies signs. I will not try here to go deeper into the nature of what I call information

[1] It must be understood that 'to come from' is to come from a source, and that at the ego is absolutely not a source, there is no sense in saying that *this comes from me*.

(it could be shown to be something aimed at orientating me, or at augmenting my capacity for action or reaction). I can function as a source of information in that I am a definite someone, a *him*, who has a history, a certain aggregate of experiences at his disposal, each of which can be liberated from its context—that is to say, probably, in that I am not myself or more exactly *I* (because I have shown that *I* am defined by the fact of *not being a given someone*). Hence if anyone asks 'Who has given him this information?'—the name of the best hotel in Paris—I could answer 'I did: that information comes from me'; *me*, only being here equivalent to *a definite so and so*. The more the information concerns something external (this needs further clarification) the more easily I can reply to the question, and the more the distinction between what I know (what I can furnish) and what I do not know (what I cannot furnish) is valid; but *the less* the word *me* is taken in its genuine, essential sense. Now when we are dealing with an appreciation or an idea, this question ceases to have a clear meaning. Why? That about which we can say *it comes from me* belongs to a collection or aggregate, i.e. that which is not me. It could be said that in the spiritual order the question regarding the source of origin can only be asked about that which can be inventoried. What exactly do we mean when we declare that the question regarding the source of origin cannot apply in the case of an experience, an idea or an inspiration?

I note here that the means by which we communicate with ourselves are not really different from the means by which we communicate with others. I may be told that we have a feeling regarding our own life very different from any feeling we can have about the life of others. True enough. But this feeling is not a communication with ourselves, it is what I call a manner of being. The unconscious is that—within us (?) with which we have no dialectical communication. What does 'within us' mean?

We must of course resist the temptation to treat the *I* as a 'container'. There is even an idealist theory that succumbs to it—the theory that the body is in the mind. The body is no more in the mind than the piano is in the music that it plays. Of course, doubtless only 'containers' can communicate. When we look on one another as capable of communication we inevitably treat ourselves as containing contents. It is worth noticing that the spiritualist theory of atomism which isolates the conscious-ness of A from that of B does not avoid this necessity. But it must also be noted that A and B are not isolated inasmuch as they are non-communicating precisely because we cannot legitimately compare them to containers; it is in that we are isolated that we can communicate.

March 5th, 1919

The word 'tabulation' or 'repertory' (*repertoire*) is the best word for describing what the ego is not. I am—I think and I act only because I do not function as a tabulation.[1] To say that the idea as such has no source of origin is to say that it should only be treated as an act, as devoid of any place in a pre-existing tabu-lation. On the other hand every idea, when expressed, appears to be introduced into the tabulation that corresponds to it, it tends by that very fact to imitate itself and reproduce itself.

Tabulation is the *him*.

March 6th, 1919

When we recollect, do we extract from a tabulation? I note first of all that a tabulation only involves answers prepared for someone else, destined for someone else, whoever he may be, even if only myself as someone else. To know is in this sense to be in a state to carry out this or that given operation (here one thinks of the repertory or tabulation of the singer or the surgeon, the repertory or tabulation of a theatre or of guide-books). To say '*I do not know*' in this sense signifies 'This has no place in my tabulation.' I wonder whether even Bergson's pure recollections do not lead to a tabulation. The whole problem of pure memory lies there.

To learn always means to set up a mechanism, and to increase the scope of one's repertory or tabulation.[2] But this in no way ex-hausts the content of the idea of experience. What is deep in the fact of experience cannot be reduced to the act of learning. To learn is always to refer oneself to something further, to put oneself into the state in which one can carry out certain operations when the

[1] Transition to the only intelligible notion of radical freedom.
[2] I leave aside the metaphysical question of how a being is able to learn. At bottom it is Ravaisson's problem of habit.

circumstances require it. In crude spatial imagination this is symbolised by hoarding or gathering in provisions, whereas really it consists in multiplying our active powers. In this sense to learn is not to live in the present, or rather it is to abstract from the lived present. (I am fully aware that I am hovering over the Bergsonian distinction. . . .) It is for that reason that there is such a deep difference between learning and enjoying (*jouir*). It is easy to find concrete illustrations. We may poison our aesthetic enjoyment if we ask: 'Am I profiting from what I see? Would I recognise this work again? How? If later I am asked this or that question would I be able to answer?' Of course there is a counterpart to this in the instance of suffering. Must we say that experience as such (*das Erleben*) survives itself both as pure experience and as mechanical aptitude? But how could it be conserved as pure experience? The idea of conservation here seems meaningless (cf. my earlier reflections on this point). It is better to say that the experience is incorporated in our being, and in consequence transforms it, and that it is in this sense that it continues to live on in us. Yes, it is a living *accretion* (for example, an air that we have heard and that we can reproduce tends at the same time to enrich our being). Ought we to go on to say that it serves to increase our apperceptive 'substance', i.e. that with which we appreciate, that with which we evaluate the universe? I am convinced of it. But how comes it that in our apperceptive 'substance' the experience is still capable of freeing itself for itself, of rebecoming for itself? Inevitably we are tempted to treat it as an element juxtaposed to other elements and as such capable of being rediscovered in the total ($a + b = S$; hence a is still in S). Memory in this sense is certainly a mode of being; I am what I recall in the measure in which I relive it. But can we say that *that* is, in the measure in which I am not *it*? Does recollection survive inasmuch as it is not relived? 'Yes,' it is argued, 'but in the state of potentiality.' But it seems to me here that we are once again adopting the standpoint of the repertory or tabulation. In a word it is tempting to think that I cannot rediscover a state unless this state has lasted as long as me and with me, whether within me or not. But when I reflect that seems to me absurd. '*Then*' remains '*then*'—it does not become '*now*'. What happens is that I rejoin my past—it is not exact to say that my past has followed me and in some way travelled along with me. Recollection does not grow old, it only has one age, which is strictly its own. It is for this reason that a contingent fact (Proust's mouthful of cake) unleashes in us an experience which is in principle identical with the experience we originally underwent, though it cannot be said in any way that this experience has been conserved, because to be conserved is a manner of growing old, of changing.

I must admit that I am not at all satisfied by this explanation and I do not know at what end to tackle this awkward question. Nevertheless, I have a feeling that I am making progress, if only very slowly. When I say that another mind is external in relation to mine, I unquestionably treat us both as repertories or tabulations that do not coincide but are mutually susceptible of completing each other. . . . It seems to me that it is always the body that learns. The mind lends itself to this discipline and that is all.

Being is that which does not frustrate our expectation; there is being from the moment at which our expectation is fulfilled—I mean the expectation in which we wholly participate. The doctrine that denies being can be expressed by the phrase: 'All is vanity', in other words that we must expect nothing, and only the man who expects nothing will avoid being disappointed. I believe that it is only on this basis that the problem can be stated. To say: 'Nothing *is*' is to say 'Nothing matters'. I must make a deeper examination of the meaning of this kind of nihilism. Take care not to confound 'to be' with 'to exist.' Show the bond between the problem of absolute value and that of substance; substantiality considered as the guarantee of value; is there any basis for this impression?

March 17th, 1919

But this is still too vague. I see well enough that being is fullness —but this expression must not be taken to mean a synthesis of intellectual determinations; (or anything resembling the *Ens Realissimum* as it is habitually conceived). We must proceed much more methodically. To ask ourselves if there is being is, I think, to adopt the standpoint of the man who gets—or who would like to get—to the bottom of things, who sees—or who would like to see—through the tissue of phenomena (the veil of happening). The affirmation 'Nothing is' is made to seem the expression of the highest wisdom, of the richest experience, and such superlatives mean that this wisdom or this experience appears to themselves to exhaust the content of life. There is a sense in which life can certainly be compared to a test or to a sifting of this kind. As we progress in life we come to discern better what resists it and what does not resist it, what evaporates and what remains at the bottom of the crucible. The man who says 'All is vanity' can only speak in the name of one experience, whether it be literally his or he has appropriated—of course in idea— that of someone else. That experience, that life is, if you like, also a dialectic in that it implies the reflection of self on self— and it is worth noticing the characteristics of that reflection. Take as example the voluptuary who little by little detaches himself from the objects to which he was attached at the outset of his career. He now appears to himself—as seeing through his previous experience. In other words his present experience, his present manner of appreciation, is not simply juxtaposed to the experiences that have gone before; it lays claim to a sort of onto-logical priority. This is of extreme importance for the problem of being. To be, here, means to survive the test, to survive progressive dissolution. To deny being is to claim that nothing can survive the test. But here we come up against a serious ambiguity; is it in fact or by right that nothing can survive the test? I imagine I may be answered: 'By right,' meaning that the experience of the man who dares to affirm being has been in-complete; that the believer—to take a particular instance—has failed to see through his faith. If this were so the affirmation of being would always be an interpretation of an experience that had been imperfectly reflected. The imperfect reflection might well be explained by the fortuitous and favourable experiences from which the given person had benefited, or, the person himself might be directly responsible for his own blindness. But the meaning of this second alternative would require very close examination. To deny being, then, is to posit deception as universal by right: but does not this involve reference to a singularly formal conception of universality? Indeed it seems as if the intention were to say that when any mind in good faith follows this dialectic to the end it must recognise that nothing is left (cf. the logic of making use of death for this apologetic of nothingness). It would of course be vain to recognise the vital value of illusion and the advantages that may lie in not pushing such reflection to its final limit.

It seems to me essential to agree that such pessimism is by right possible, that the possibility is bound up with the very nature of reflection. Perhaps we must even admit that a world in which such pessimism were not at least abstractly possible would lack religious value. The objection may be made that if there are other worlds in which this world is remembered, some day the pessimist himself may well become aware of his past mistake and *see through it*. To this we may be obliged to answer that we cannot think the other world in that way, i.e. we cannot install ourselves in it by a purely empirical effort of imagination. And so we will be told: 'Thus absolute pessimism is possible. There is a sense in which being can be denied. But who can say that this sense is not final? that such pessimism is not valid?'

Here we must ask the question which is really denied by the man who posits that absolute pessimism is valid: by what in his view is this doctrine or experience opposed? In what instance would he consider himself obliged to bring it back into doubt? Apparently his pessimism seems to him valid if it is in conformity with the facts; and invalid if it is not. But what content has the idea of fact? The ambiguity lies precisely there. To be converted (in the purely rational sense) the pessimist would need a *fact* (which reflection could to some extent support rather than see through in order to lose itself in non-being, a *fact* on which to end up). At bottom we are still dealing with the opposition between the full and the empty—an opposition which is infinitely more essential than that of the single and the multiple.

Hence, in a word, for me being is defined as that which does not allow itself to be dissolved by the dialectics of experience (experience as it reflects itself). Does this mean saying that being can be a content ranged beside other contents? Certainly not. There is not and could not be a privileged content which would be being, or more simply which *would be*, whereas other contents were not. Being, as I have said, stands firm against the test or trial of life. But is this not a sort of ideal limit? There is a need to go deeply into the idea of the resistance opposed by being to the wearing process that criticism imposes on it. It is certain that only life can hold out under this test. And it would be insane to believe that what is lifeless is spared by it. What is the life which holds out under the test of life? That must be discovered. No one must be surprised at my using the word life twice over here; for we are dealing with a criticism of life by life itself. But then is not being the truth? Is being confounded with the true? At first sight it would seem so since it is the true that is established by criticism. But surely the true is only an abstract limit. It remains to be shown that the true does not account for the false, that it lets it subsist without integrating it, and, moreover, that it (the true) is only clearly defined for us in the order of ideal possibilities, not in a universe that permits of detail. We should be able to talk of an act which attains being—whereas truth is only the object set before itself by our will. An ambiguous object, moreover, as often as not.

At this point I should demonstrate that being cannot be a simple limit, that it is something which must be possessed.[1] Yet the true can provide a sort of ontological intimacy; show what is illusory in this. The true certainly cannot be adored, there is nothing adorable about it save the will that pursues it with obstinacy.

March 8th, 1919

Seek out the sense in which the very possibility of a truth is bound up with the particular and contingent nature of our thought. To be examined more deeply.

The *Cogito*. We must grasp that nothing is less instructive than the Cartesian 'I am'. It could be taken to mean 'I am a substance'. All that Descartes shows is that the question of existence—I would like to say of objective correspondence—cannot even be raised (*a fortiori* cannot permit a negative answer) where we are concerned with the ego inasmuch as it is thinking.

It may seem strange that I should identify, as I have done, the problem of being and the problem of salvation. Are not those who deny being also those who refuse to subtend a substantial basis underneath phenomena? But I think that here we have a series

[1] But, of course, not as a predicate.

of confusions. No one can maintain any longer that a phenomenon is a manifestation of being—to be more exact, this formula is far too ambiguous to be informative. It introduces an unintelligible duality between being and the phenomenon. If there is a sense in which being can affirm itself, this is because there is a sense in which the phenomenon can be grasped as being.

A much more interesting question is whether the test or trial in the sense in which I have defined it, is contingent in relation to being. The problem is real and important, but cannot be set out in these terms, I think, because the expression *being* is itself inadequate and meaningless. When we turn being into a noun we seem implicitly to be asking ourselves what predicates it can take. And that is unintelligible. Once more I resume where I left off yesterday: to deny being is to claim that nothing can rightfully hold out against full experience. I am tempted to say to the metaphysical nihilist: 'But *is* this experience *itself* in being?' Is that a legitimate question and how can he answer it? To me it appears evident that he does not even dream of asking it of himself, because he views this inquiry as contingent in relation to the result that he awaits from it. But that result, however negative it may be, is an answer. To say that the universe leaves me dissatisfied, and that in this sense it '*is*' not' is to admit that within me there is an appetite for being. I can conceive, of course, a subjective nihilism which would even go so far as to contest the reality of this appetite, or at least accuse me of misconstruing its real significance. Such nihilism would tend, I suppose, to view this appetite as no more than the expression of a nature that affirms itself. What, then, in my view, is this will for being? Is it a will to find myself or a will to create myself? But this either-or is far from clear. Under what conditions could I myself appear to myself as real? In what sense am I not real? Is it inasmuch as I am dependent? Is 'to will to be' necessarily the same as 'to will to be for oneself'? If we define will in this way do we not condemn ourselves to viewing it as illusory? Clearly all these reflections gravitate round a living centre of thought that I have not managed to attain directly. I have said that the discovery of being would mean the elevation of oneself to a mode of experience or of life over which critical experience no longer had any hold. And that, I think, amounts to admitting that there is no being save in eternity.

March 10th, 1919

To will is to refuse to ask the question of possibility, or at least it is to refuse to treat it as primary. In this sense volition implies the equivalent of a judgment incontestably demonstrated (for when I say 'This or that is necessary' I do not ask myself whether this or that can be). To will means in some way to place ourselves beyond the point at which we can distinguish the possible from the impossible. But is this not the purely logical aspect of faith? The man who asks himself whether he is able, and enumerates the obstacles, does not will in the strict sense of the word. He assures us that 'he would like to, but . . .', whereas will ignores *buts*. I only will from the moment at which I make a *tabula rasa* of all *buts*: though strictly speaking I know them, I know them as suppressed. Now in what measure can it be said that the will sets aside real possibilities that may take their revenge when the opportunity occurs? Or in what measure does it effectively suppress what it denies? That is a difficult question.

To be sure there is a difference between will and faith: indeed will seems to bear on what is to be, faith on what is. But the 'present' (?) of the object of faith certainly cannot be contrasted with the future of an object of willing as a *now* can be contrasted with a *later*. This again is very important.

The question that the will sets aside is that of knowing whether a given action can be accomplished: the question that faith refuses to ask is: 'Is it really possible?' Yet the meaning of this distinction is not as clear as it seems. The *buts* of the man who would like to will and does not will always bear on conditions that are thought as existent and as incompatible with the achievement in question. The man who says: 'I would like to pass this examination but I won't be able to,' places himself in advance at the critical moment and, by his evocation of them, raises the very obstacles that he thinks are bound to paralyse him (nervousness, bad memory, etc.). In a word in each case there is question of not positing what, with Leibnitz, we can call the 'problem of compossibility.' The believer does not ask himself —he refuses to ask himself—whether divine perfection is incompatible with the imperfections of the universe as it is presented to him; the man who wills refuses to ask himself if what he wishes to do is compatible with the 'drawbacks' of every kind that he observes in and around him. In both cases I indicate this 'overcoming' by the expression 'act of transcendence'.

'But,' it can be argued, 'though I may will to set aside these incompatibilities, I do not necessarily succeed.' To this I think we must answer that inasmuch as I will no such dissociation is affected. (The limits of my willing—also, perhaps, of my faith— would be the limits of my power of transcendence.) Doubtless experience of a particular drawback helps to paralyse my will-power; it brings in doubt and tends to substitute an 'I should'— with its nuance of uncertainty—for the 'I must.' Hence a struggle occurs when consciousness recognises the probable inefficacy of such a mitigated statement, and endeavours to react against it; hence tension, determination and powerlessness. Thus there is no will unless there is real detachment, i.e. detachment that is not recognised as such. To will is not to simplify oneself, but to have simplified and even sacrificed oneself to such an extent that the idea of this sacrifice no longer survives. In this way I am able to triumph over the obstacles within me, that is, to negate or suppress them as such; and in this way, doubtless, the will is likewise able to master external obstacles or, to put it more exactly, the external forces that serve as obstacles for what in us does not want to suceed, does not want to act—in a word, does not will. Here it seems to me that the will functions as power, though it is in no way a force; it acts by suppression and so to speak by taking the obstacle in its stride. Hence also we can agree that the will, as Descartes thought, is 'infinite'—there is nothing in it that can be graduated. It has no intensity and, like a pure statement, it does not permit of degrees.

'Yet'—another objection—'I can only will what is within my power.'[1] But this is far from clear; because willing means saying: 'This ought to be, hence this is within my power.' Then the 'this ought to be' is only possible under certain conditions. Between 'that' and 'me' there must be a certain relation. It seems to me that to will is in some way to commit oneself; by

---

[1] This formula would imply the obviously mistaken idea that the will has or is a deter-mined quantum of force—like a lever that is capable of some actions but not of others.

which I mean to commit or bring into play one's own reality; to throw oneself into what one wills. I would be tempted to go so far as to say that to will is to affirm. 'I depend on that (I will only be if that is), hence that depends on me.' But of course this *I* and this *me* are not really identical; between them there is a synthetic and living relation.

Here is an example. I resolve to finish a piece of work. I commit myself with myself to do it. That is to say I bring my own reality in some way into play upon the matter. I will not *be* in my own eyes unless that piece of work is finished. If I fail there would be a sort of collapse of myself. Hence that piece of work must *be able to be* finished. The affirmation that this depends on me is itself an act of will, a decree. Wherever we have to deal with will, I think, we find that to resolve is to commit oneself with oneself. If I fail, I will have deceived my expectations; I will have shown myself not to be up to the level at which I thought I was.

It is hard to see anything of this kind in faith. Yet I can only have faith in what I am or, to be more exact, in that by which I am. I mean that faith could not have bearing on a metaphysical order that was radically foreign to me (any more than I would be able really to will something in which my being was not concerned). And it could be said that we have a sort of symmetry here; whereas will is brought to bear on what cannot *be* save through me, faith is brought to bear on that by which I am. But I have said that faith implies the refusal to ask certain questions or to question oneself about certain possibilities. Which? And in what does our justification of the refusal consist? Here again the foundation can only be positive.

I return once more to the last phrases I wrote the day before yesterday. I said then that critical experience is only unable to gnaw on the eternal. But this is not clear. There must be no question of our understanding by 'eternal' that which is valid for anyone whatsoever at any moment of time whatsoever, that is, the purely indeterminate, the unspecified in itself.

March 11*th*

I come back once again to what I said about will, which seems to me clearer and more positive than what concerns faith. To be able to will, we must first of all have conceived. Volition presupposes a whole round of judgments and a previous intellectual organisation. We must know what we want; there is thus a content—more exactly, a schema which is filled out as the action is accomplished. Fundamentally we cannot know whether we are able until we try; and everything depends on the whole-heartedness of the attempt.

Here is an important and curious problem. Is to feel the same as to communicate? It seems to me it is clearly not the same. A feeling is not a sign or symbol, and though it can be treated as such that is quite a different matter. I think Dewey has made this clear. It is very important for our idea of the nature of knowing.

March 12th, 1919

We have a tendency to look on sensation as produced in us, so to speak, by the object, and as giving us information about it. That interpretation is absurd. I would like to define why it is absurd, and to understand where we get to when we reject it.

To feel is to be affected in a given manner; and we should ask whether the very ambiguity of the word has not a profound and real foundation.

Doubtless we must proceed as in the past and try to define what we spontaneously believe or accept. In sensation we seem to look on the object as delivering to us a part of itself. I mean that we surely do not spontaneously posit the object as distinct from the 'signs' which 'emanate' from it; and it is for that reason that sensation was not originally regarded as a sign. The idea of the propagation of transmissions or commotions originates with science and hence it came late. It is plain that anyone who tries to conciliate the naïve and common-sense realist view of sensation with the mechanist interpretation of science must suppose that between the object and us a communication is established of the same type as that linking two telegraph offices or two wireless stations. But has this any meaning? No, precisely because sensation is affection, not information.

In a word sensation can only be treated as a sign or symbol in function of an object; that is, when it ceases to be an affection and a manner of being and becomes a reference. Now it is of the definition of sensation that it *is not* referred.

All this needs to be taken up again methodically. But here is a preliminary pointer. We say: 'It must be that I am affected *by* something.' But it is here exactly that I see the confusion. Inasmuch as I experience a sensation, the question has no meaning; it only has meaning in the measure in which I cease to experience the initial state so as, however confusedly, to think it—so as to detach myself from it.

March 13*th*, 1919

Had an interesting conversation yesterday with P. Admitting in principle the possibility of a 'mind' (define) utilising the repertory or tabulation of someone living (mine for instance), I suggested the idea that that 'mind' might be sufficiently 'suggestible' to be plunged once again by us, through our will for communication, into the world of signs from which death (?) withdrew it, so that it would make an effort—entirely illusory in its very principle—to recall what we asked of it, and would seek, in our collection or aggregate of 'notes' for the means of satisfying us. . . . I admit that this hypothesis is extremely bold. But at least it partially accounts for the facts. If it is true we can understand why we needed to lend *ourselves*, that is to say to lend our body, to the 'mind'; if we put up a resistance, communication (the word is improper because we are really dealing with a partial substitution) would become impossible.

I would like to take this up more methodically, because it may well be that the hypothesis raises other difficulties that are insurmountable. In the first place, under what conditions would *evocation* in the strict sense be possible? To evoke a being, have we really to *invoke* it? Unquestionably it seems as if some beings are evoked when we are in no way thinking about them. But it must be admitted that this is bound up with questions that are in practice insoluble: we do not know how a body 'in a trance' or 'in the process of going into a trance' can appear to a 'mind' that is animated by the will to communicate. The body needs in some way to be given to it (it makes itself felt). How? The problem would doubtless seem absurd to almost everybody, but my tendency to think that the body must have a sort of psychic reality, and that without it life would be inconceivable, is not of recent growth. Yet even in my eyes this statement is very vague. What I mean is that the body should be capable of being apprehended as psychical, as a psychic unity, with an apprehension that cannot be compared to a mode of perception. This would doubtless be an incipient action and susceptible of being thwarted or even totally 'inhibited' by the subject himself.

As I have already pointed out we should never speak here of communication, but only of substitution or possession. I can only communicate with someone else through signs or symbols. Now no exchange of signs is possible between this 'mind' and me, since this 'mind' is only expressed through me and thanks to what it borrows from me (so that I naturally keep asking myself whether all that occurs does not 'come' from me). But how does the 'mind' preserve its power of selection? How does it manage to make use of the instrument I loan to it? Must we not suppose that when it becomes incarnate it recovers a—very partial— faculty of 're-memoration' that it was incapable of possessing 'beforehand' (has this adverb a meaning?). In a word I would say that it only becomes once more capable of making use of the instrument when it is furnished with it, at which time it becomes a complete living being. The 'mind' is there, it is where my body is, just as I am, and a precarious sort of psychical symbiosis is established between it and me. This allows us to understand the mistakes that are always being detected, as well as the 'mind's' incapacity to give information regarding its new surrounding. The surroundings cease to be its own as soon as it becomes incarnate and it only keeps, doubtless, a confused recollection of them. Moreover, it could only inform us about them by communicating with us; now *it is us* or at least forms with us a whole which for the moment cannot be decomposed.

This hypothesis is the only one that corresponds to my experience. I have certainly had the feeling that beings were making use—very unequally good use—of the instrument I lent them. We can see why a struggle should repeatedly occur between the medium who is insufficiently in a trance, who reacts—and the 'mind' to which the medium does not lend himself without reserve. I would like to call this the struggle for the instrument.

I will make no further insistence on such reflections as these.

Though they are very interesting they do not yet permit of a philosophical elucidation that is entirely satisfying.

And once again I resume with what I have already said about the object. The more I think it as object the less I need to appear to myself as consubstantial with it. As object it appears to me to be in communication with me. But in that measure I too become an object, or more exactly another receiving and transmitting station.

March 17*th*, 1919

Yesterday I was reflecting on the suggestibility of the 'mind.' I tend more and more to believe that it is 'ravished'—which would explain the para-amnesia we observe so often. 'It' has no power of reaction to the suggestion we throw out—no power of rejection, so to speak, such as we possess. To be examined further.

March 21*st*, 1919

Is the memory a mode of communication between the actual *me* and the *me* of the past? I hope no one will object that, for this to be so, the me of the past would need to be still in being. For we are precisely involved in finding out whether it is true that that *me* is no more. Those who see the brain as the essential agent of memory convert memory into a mode of communication . . . whereas I think of memory not as communication but as incomplete possession. At given moments we have all felt ourselves to be invaded by the past. Now I glimpse confusedly that there is no sense in saying: *it is there* or *it is not there* regarding that which is susceptible of invading us and possessing us in this way. These expressions are only applicable to objects which by their essence can be given a site and marked out. Only that which cannot be thought of as being in communication with us is really incapable of being situated in relation to us. Communication means being oneself—while the someone else remains himself. Yet a given communication may affect me (there is possibly a difficulty here).

April 3*rd*, 1919

Working on Bradley recently. Thanks to him and also to conversation with H. I feel I am on the track of entirely new ideas. I accepted the idea that the 'mind' is disincarnate much too easily. Whereas in reality it seems to be 'otherwise incarnate.' Moreover, can my body become its body if it itself lacks a body? In a word what occurs is a very short symbiosis between the organism (?) of the mind and my organism. This idea seems to me more acceptable than that of a pure and simple substitution; and it is only if there are two bodies (of different type) present that we can understand genuine communications and the phenomena of 'materialisation'. What we call materialisation can only be the condensation of another matter, the transition from one material plane to another.

April 6th

Reflected again on the bases of psychometry and the materialist interpretation that can be made of it. I admit that the thing (here distinguished from the object) has been modified by contact—that is certain. I admit that it has kept the imprint (or 'fluid' trace) of the subject A. I furthermore admit, though not so easily, that the believer has a 'sense' that allows him to discern the imprint or alteration. Yet the solid problem remains: How are we to trace back this effect to its cause or to its context? Whatever people may think the fact that the modification in question can only be apprehended by a being endowed with privileged 'faculties' in no way helps to make intelligible the transition by which the thought of the clairvoyant passes from this modification (which is in some way observed) to its cause (it is manifest, moreover, that we have nothing here resembling a causal inference). The transition cannot be understood in principle unless it implies a 're-integration' i.e. unless the unity of the whole which comprehended this modification within itself is re-formed (for example I enter a room and breathe a scent that makes me say immediately, 'So-and-so was here a moment ago'). As Bradley says, this link can only exist between universals. But the whole must have already been apprehended as such by the subject. And this precisely is what could not occur here. . . .

Thus everything supports the impression that, at the beginning of the process is not the thing, but the object represented, the object as linked to a psychical context. . . . A unity is formed and at the heart of it the object operates as an image in a consciousness. (Compare this to instances in which, under some particular influence, I re-become what I was—at least if to recall oneself is to re-become in an imperfect way.)

Bradley is helping me more and more. As soon as we have grasped that we always have to deal with more than the terms and their relations, it becomes clear that there must be modes of concrete unity which are capable of making higher re-integrations possible.

April 8th, 1919

On prediction in the light of Osty's book. The fundamental objection to prediction is that: 'We can only see what *is*, whereas the future *is* not.' But there is a paralogism here. We have no right whatever to say that what is not yet in being is not in being in any way. It may be contended that it is only possible to see what is actual, that the past as such is not capable of being an object of vision, and that memory is only a reconstruction. I feel more and more strongly convinced that this theory is false. I am convinced that the past as past can no more be dissociated from the past as present to the consciousness, than the object seen can be dissociated from the so-called real object. I see the object itself, I remember the past itself. This is only intelligible as regards the past because I *am* my past. Am I also my future? That question is very obscure.

It is generally thought that the problem is resolved if we grant that the future is in some way pre-formed *within* the present and hence can be apprehended by senses (?) more subtle than ours. Is this intelligible? First of all we must eliminate the fictitious idea of the future that *inheres* in the present. The link in this instance can only be qualitative, like that of a melodic concatenation. I refuse to opt between the *and*—pure juxtaposition— and the *in*—implication or enfolding. All that is real (the development of a being, of a story, of an idea) lies outside this pseudo-dilemma. But one question remains outstanding: must not the future that is apprehended by the clairvoyant be a datum given, and does 'given' mean *given to someone*? These questions cause me uneasiness. Of necessity vision appears to be contingent in relation to a situation that it does not beget, a situation which is already in being (the meaning of this must be examined more thoroughly). But is the situation already in being for someone? Last December I was in too much of a hurry to resolve this capital problem. We are bound to treat the situation as already formed. Does that mean it is an object? Here again Bradley helps me by putting me on my guard against a serious confusion. I think, moreover, that when I spoke of a consciousness that is master of the future I meant to say that between such a consciousness and the future there can be no relation of subject to object. (It cannot possibly be maintained that creative activity is thinkable in the language of subject and object.) Thus the future is capable of being formed without being thought by anyone. But am I not allowing myself to be misled by incoherent metaphors? I wrote that in last analysis all vision has reference to an order, to a world at whose centre being and thought coincide (as in creative imagination). I even used the word supraconsciousness to indicate the order that transcends the dualism of subject and object. Can we be more exact? I must admit I am still dissatisfied with this interpretation; it is too schematic.

Inasmuch as I think myself as subject who is at once active and passive, and is affected from outside in manifold ways, it is plain that the situation S seen by the clairvoyant is bound to seem to me to be external, not to be given as datum, to be unforeseeable. But as soon as I elevate myself to the idea of an immanent link (which, by the way, is not thinkable in *relational* language) between me and others (or the universe), the situation ceases to be external, it is the development of an actual situation E which surpasses me so that by essence I am unable to become aware of it. Here is an example. The clairvoyant sees that I will meet a man with dark eyes on a square surrounded by trees. Clearly what is given to him as datum is the situation, the picture. But how does he manage to see *in me* a picture whose elements, at least some of them, are *outside me*?

April 9th, 1919
The broad answer is that on this plane it is meaningless to speak of elements being external to one another. A scene is an indivis-

ible whole and it is only by abstraction that we can cut up its terms or isolate its relationships. 'But,' comes the question, 'in what way is this scene already pre-formed? *Where* is it pre-formed?' To ask this is as meaningless as to ask where the next episode of the story is—the story I am in the process of telling. I know I am running the risk of coming up against the following dilemma, namely: either the episode in question is already an object, that is to say, it is explicitly thought, or else it is about to be improvised, which means that it is not yet in any way in being. I think we must reject this dilemma, and it is a point I did not perceive clearly when I spoke of 'thought which fore-casts' because the forecast is a schema and cannot be an object of vision. Pure improvisation is manifestly the unfolding or reve-lation of a whole (of a qualitative unity); it excludes external deposits that are strictly unforeseeable (unless in their turn they form the interior of a new and more ample unity). But the global unity of the story and the improvisation is not necessarily that of an object apprehended as such—there lies the point that I missed. (We find an illustration of what I mean in everyday ex-perience—e.g. when we start speaking under a sudden impulse and what we say is spontaneously put together in an organised way.) It was in this sense that I said that the unity of the future, of becoming, is *felt* or is a matter *of feeling*; and it is thus only that we can understand the maturing or incubation of the event to which I have alluded.

Only here we are dealing with a story that can in no way be conceived as the contingent, ideal reproduction of a succession that is in other respects real. Becoming and relating, here, are one and the same thing.[1]

This variant on the original hypothesis raises some serious difficulties. If the story is only 'pre-formed' as an indivisible and felt unity, are we to take it that it becomes detailed for the clairvoyant? How is the feeling in question transferred into vision? It would seem more natural to say that it only becomes explicit and is coined in successive scenes in the measure in which it is successively lived and unfolded for the subjects that it concerns. But this is not clear: how are we to conceive of it

[1] There is nothing to justify our stating *a priori* that all comes to maturity at once. That would raise new questions.

being made explicit? If that process necessitates 'contributions from outside' the objection is decisive. But supposing it does not —in what does the 'making explicit' consist?

There is a situation S which is about to arise, that is to say it is felt or fore-felt (i.e. it exists inasmuch as feeling or as fore-feeling). Obviously we cannot help asking: 'For whom? With whom?' Has that question any meaning? And even if it has is it impossible in reason to avoid asking it?

What we can say, I think, is this, that as I am able to look on the feeling as global and as sufficing for itself, there is no meaning in asking who experiences it. Whereas as soon as I begin looking on it as partial I attribute it to 'someone'. It seems to me that here I have once again reached the distinction between the *him* and the *non-him* (the latter not necessarily being treated as an *I* or a *thou*). But is this feeling bound up with knowing? For the time being I am quite unable to see how this question can be answered.

Another method came to my mind this afternoon. It is clear that two people reading the same book or the same notice, may have reached different places in the book or notice in question; that is a question of the position they occupy. It may be objected that the book or notice is not in time. But here we must distinguish a series of possible durations (the duration of elaboration, of publishing, or printing, even the duration of the book in that it gets old and becomes worn out). The contents of the book, it may be argued, are non-temporal—but that is true of any historical content. Supposing it be maintained that, after all, the book survives after it has been read? But that might well not occur. One can conceive a system of signs developed exclusively in time, the equivalent of a discourse or a recitation. . . . Perhaps this hypothesis is fundamentally contradictory after all; I am not sure that the idea of distinct, individualised positions can yet be applied.

July 1st, 1919

Yet again I have come up against the problem of the metaphysical possibility of second sight (the case of Mlle P.). All prophecy is vision bearing on a scene that has become present. In these conditions—they must be defined more exactly—the person who foresees becomes contemporary with another present, with a present which is not that of his body. This seems extremely obscure to us and even contradictory because we take it as axiomatic that at any given moment it is only possible to make one temporal cross-section in the world, an hour of the universe, and that the one and only Present is detailed into an infinity of individual Presents which are those of each consciousness—so that everything occurs as though there were a unique consciousness (though broken into infinite fragments) whose unfolding exactly synchronises with ours and even comprehends it within itself. Obviously if this supposition were imposed on us without redress second sight bearing on the future would have to be regarded as impossible. This idea first occurred to me at Zernetz in 1912 and now I have come back to it, though in a form that is perhaps clarified by my knowledge of Royce. Of course as soon as I take as my datum a world of consciousnesses, I have the right to ask: 'What is happening at this moment?' regarding every element in that world. But this I think only has a meaning if I consider that world as representing a world in space. I must clarify. Let us take a spatial world comprising a whole of elements, E, amongst which figures my body B. I am bound to suppose that corresponding to each state of my body there is in that case a homochronous and synchronised state for every element present in that world. At this very moment something definite must be 'happening' on a certain farm near Perugia that I am evoking. What is happening there? That is an object of knowledge and there are no limits to the *possibility* of informing myself about it, if we allow for a certain lapse of time. Hence for every organic body, or more exactly, for every consciousness expressed by an organic body whose becoming is homochronous in relation to mine, the question *quid nunc?* is legitimate. But when I say it is a question, I am recognising that it can only be answered by signs or symbols. Whereas when I consider planes in consciousness that are set far away from the table of references constituted by the exterior world, the meaning of the problem becomes obscure. Are we still dealing with a matter of correspondences? It would be absurd to imagine planes for each consciousness which were docketed with the same index; or to ask what the consciousness E is experiencing on the plane P on which I am at this moment (and where I experience a certain emotion). The *quid nunc* is meaningless except in relation to a world in which we are active. Given that I know M.R. to be living, I can ask myself: What is he doing at this moment? But that is all. It may be claimed, and rightly, that my question is not only concerned with the position of his body. Nevertheless, it is only inasmuch as I prolong the lines of his action within himself that my question has a meaning. Outside these limits there is no question of representing or figuring, but only of becoming (*Mitsein, sich hineinleben*, etc.). Hence from the fact that transmission by signs or, more simply, knowing, can only be brought to bear on the present, or on the acquired which is the past as incorporated into the present, we are unable to draw conclusions about what surpasses all transmissions of this nature. From the fact that the future as such cannot be the object of a questionnaire, we have no right to infer that it cannot be seen, lived and pre-lived. (These observations are of the greatest importance for the 'spiritist' problem—the problem of the consciousness of the dead.)

July 2nd, 1919

I resume with what I was saying yesterday. All questions asked of the future, all answers from the future, all transmissions of signs between the present and the future are inconceivable. Such questions and answers are only possible in one and the same present (we cannot be informed save about what has been acquired or, as I would be tempted to say, about what belongs to the same layer of reality). But, as is clear, the situation of what we call the future in relation to the present is very difficult to define; and it is not absurd *a priori* to claim that what we call the future is on another level of reality. I would express this by saying that between successive moments there is a difference the nature of which has been far from exhausted when it is called an interval. I recognise that here I am on slippery ground, and that I am tending to convert the successive into the simultaneous. But this, I think, is only in appearance. . . . Yet are we not obliged to admit that what is not yet in being for me may be already in being for someone else who is in some way in advance (metaphysically) of me? I think we are, but we must be careful about the meaning of the words *I* and *he*.

July 4th, 1919

Some new glimpses of light. To begin with it is plain that in immediacy, the pure 'now', a being does not realise the 'fullness of what he is'—I take as instance a feeling that is very deep. The more a *being is*, the less he is reduced to a simple succession of determinations (whether these are events or actions: moreover, the word 'actions' is most unsuitable, because to act in the successive sense is not to act genuinely. An action, as Bergson saw, concentrates a whole past and a whole duration within it). The deep feeling I am considering is not experienced in an instant like a physical pleasure or pain. I wonder whether I will not be led to conceive levels of time in reality and life that are distinct.

(I note that the above links up with what I wrote several months ago on being—considered as that which holds out against the experience of criticism, since criticism dissolves away all that is not immediate.)[1]

July 11th, 1919

Glimpsed several important ideas on the same lines as those of Père Laberthonnière. Perhaps we only have the knowledge we deserve. Perhaps it is what we are that is a measure of what we know, and not conversely. But of course this could only apply to metaphysical knowledge, not to knowledge that bears on simple abstract relations.

July 13th, 1919

Once again I have been asking myself the great question. Can I think myself as being perfectly informed about the universe and yet mistaken? This is at bottom Royce's problem. Only there is another question that precedes this one. Is the universe such that I am able to be perfectly informed about it? Here we are concerned with the—even partial—unknowability of the universe. As long as I treat the universe as a simple object of possible

---

[1] I wonder whether the pessimism of Proust is not exactly on a par with a philosophy of the pure immediate, with an inability to treat the mediate as real.

enquiry, it will never provide me with absolute satisfaction. To be examined more closely.

October 15*th*, 1919

I have been re-reading with lively interest my notes of July 1st and 4th. Yet they turn on a notion that I find very hard to define exactly. As I said then, I can ask myself: 'What is X doing at this moment? What is happening precisely now at P?' And the identity of the plane of X and my plane, between P and the place at which I am at this moment, is precisely defined in function of the possibility I have of informing myself, inquiring or verifying. And, as is clear, even if I conceive of worlds that are placed at indefinitely growing distances from mine, but which lend themselves to my interrogation, what I have said applies to those worlds too. But a dialogue must be possible. Now there is a dialogue as soon as there is perception. To perceive attentively is precisely to be in a state of dialectical tension in relation to a given datum. But, as I have often pointed out, this only applies to what is capable of becoming material for information. Now it seems to me evident that there are manners of being which by their very essence do not lend themselves to this dialectical tension of the mind; and, this said, it seems to me that we have defined in the only valid way what is usually called the unconscious. I am *always and at every moment* more than the totality of predicates that an enquiry made by myself—or by someone else—about myself (cf. my notes of March 2nd, last) would be able to bring to light.

When I review what I have written I am struck by a confusion at least on the surface. Somewhere I say: 'What functions for me as source of information is in this very measure a *thou.*' We must take care to notice that the *thou* appears when I put my emphasis not on the idea of information, but on the idea of answer —which has the implication of community (*us-ness*). I experienced this clearly, I remember, and made the distinction for myself, when I asked the way of someone I did not know. The two aspects that analysis dissociates (the *tabulation—repertoire*—and the *living being*) are in reality indissolubly bound up; we must never forget this, or we will fall into abstraction and absurdity. I think, therefore, that we should inquire more deeply into the meaning of the idea of answer, which is closely bound up with the *thou* and alone can give that idea a content (here my notes of February 25th are useful). Yet in last analysis the *thou* is essentially that which I can invoke rather than that which I judge to be capable of answering me. Perhaps my soul would only be the *ego* of the psychologists, which is really only a *him*, were I not to converse about it with God, were it not involved and vitally interested in this conversation. Of course it can be objected that I am limiting myself to hypostatising simple grammatical categories. This point must be cleared up with the help of concrete examples of warm feeling and deep interior life. If I am asked why my soul can only become *itself* when in relation to God, and when confronted with God, I cannot at present see any means of formulating an abstract answer which will satisfy me. But I can at least say this (though it needs elucidating and sifting): My soul is always a *thou* for God; for God it is always confounded with the subject who invokes him. And this can only occur for a subject in the measure in which the subject, through love, imitates what must be called the divine attitude. The more this *me* is an object of study, something described, something whose development is retraced, the less it is a soul. Between the idea of soul and the idea of prayer, there is thus an intimate relation that cannot be set aside. What I still find very confusing is the proper relation I should establish between all this, which is of the metaphysical and religious order, and the psychological and metapsychological theory that I sketched earlier.

Here there is something missing. I note simply that inasmuch as I am a tabulation (*repertoire*) (that I treat myself as such) I am only in the *third person* for myself. It is only through emotion that I become a *thou* for myself. This involves an interest that in last analysis is love and so far as it concerns oneself is much rarer than is claimed by our terribly conventional psychology. (The whole problem of egotism needs further examination. Most of the time it is merely a way of behaving, a way of taking ourselves into account *without* loving ourselves.)

October 16th, 1919

I would like to take up once more a series of notions on which I worked earlier. That of intimacy is one of the most important (cf. my note on *with* of February 24th). It should be contrasted with the notion of familiarity. Is the relationship between familiarity and intimacy analogous to the relationship that exists between Bergson's two *Reconnaissances?* To be gone into.

I must also reflect on the idea of trial or test. The great difficulty consists in grasping the real relationship between the trial or test and he who imposes the trial on me. When confronted with suffering the religious consciousness tends to see it as a trial. But what are we to understand by that? It seems to me that the idea of a trial can only have an acceptable meaning as functior of the *thou.* Thus we must exclude any idea of competition and perhaps even any idea of selection. In reality selection bears on potentiality; it concerns knowing who is capable of accomplishing this or that given action. In this sense all selection can be said to be natural, whereas the trial bears essentially on that in us which is capable of passing beyond nature. It still remains to be seen whether this is purely verbal; are we not still dealing fundamentally with a potency or power, that is to say a nature? Close analysis is needed. Suppose I take the case of disillusionment or sorrow. Where is the element of risk in this? There is a threat of spiritual annihilation. But what exactly does that mean? The danger I think always lies in obsession, whatever be the aspect of that obsession. The soul runs the risk of having all its attention drawn to a particular object, or, should this object disappear (supposing that this has a meaning), of no longer being really attached to anything, even itself—of being lost and dissolved. That is where the danger lies. The idea of temptation should be analysed in a similar way.

I am sure that this is the right road. The idea of life as a trial. Faith is in essence something which ought to be tried and wants to be tried. Relation to the beyond. We must ask ourselves about the validity of a philosophy of trial and, on a deeper level, what we mean when we ask ourselves this question about validity. Here as elsewhere we set out from the fear of being taken in: 'Perhaps I am being a dupe.' The experience of our fallibility is converted into a sort of active distrust. To see whether that is justifiable by right, I would proceed as I have done for atheism and ask what would be the meaning of saying: 'It is false that life is a trial.' I believe that essentially this negation is as much as to say: 'It is inexact that there exists a being gifted with consciousness who has willed such a trial.' But, unless I am mistaken, a judgment of this type, a judgment in the third person, does not bear on God but on a finite thought conceived by the imagination. Distinguish between an atheistic judgment (which is external to the religious order) and revolt (as in the case of Job) which is in some way bound up with the act of faith. Examine this very closely.

To triumph in the trial is to maintain oneself as soul, to save one's soul. To be examined more deeply.

To begin with I think we must note that the statement 'This is a trial' is meaningless outside a definite spiritual context. It is not one of those statements whose value is independent of the person who utters them. This may at first sight be surprising. And we also need to grasp that we are not dealing here with a proposition giving information such as: 'You are consumptive' for instance, where the value of the proposition depends on the competence of the person who states it. It seems to me, though I am not yet able fully to justify what I am asserting, that only love can provide a real—I do not say a valid—content for an affirmation such as: 'This is a trial.' Between the person who talks to me in this way, and myself, there must be a condition of community. We must be *thou* for one another. The other person must be unable to think as regards me: 'This is a trial for him, it is his affair.' He must *partake* in the trial. In this way we can perceive the link between the trial and charity. But the whole of this process may occur in *my* consciousness between me and myself. Inasmuch as I treat myself as an essence—as 'someone' who is a datum—I am *him* for myself and the idea of trial immediately loses all meaning; it is transformed in some kind of pseudo-biological way. As long as I have triadic relations with myself (and treat myself as an object) I remain on the plane of nature. This is particularly clear with regard to death. It is possible for me to think my death in a way which amounts to saying: 'He will die'; which, at bottom, is like saying. 'The machine will stop'. In this case I am conversing on the subject of death with *somebody else*, whomsoever it be. If I reason in this way about my death or about the death of anybody else I am unable to lift myself to the thought of the beyond. From this standpoint all

GABRIEL MARCEL

there can be is a more and more complete disorganisation of
'the machine'. And nothing else. The idea (?) of a trial is
thus only applicable in the measure in which my unity with
myself is recreated through feeling, through that intimate
life of which dialectical self-consciousness is a more or less complete rupture. If I merely make the statement that 'life is a test'
coldly, that, in my opinion, means I am thinking nothing whatever. We can see here the part that the priest may play. His
mission is to awaken palpitating and indivisible life in us, and
hence to restore its full significance to the idea of trial; but this
is only possible in the measure in which I am a *thou* for him,
when he, so to speak, is the incarnation of charity.

To come back to what I was saying just now. A statement
such as: 'This suffering is a trial' is not instructive, it does not
inform us.[1] But if we continue this way will we not end up in
a poverty-stricken subjectivism? Are we passing beyond the order
of the 'as if'? To consider life as a trial; to qualify our experience
in a way that is personal to us: we are always confronted with
the same dilemma—either objective fact or interior disposition.
Every time I run into it I have the feeling of facing a mountain
that must be moved. Yet I am more than ever convinced that this
'dilemma' misses the essence of religious life and of the deepest
metaphysical thought.

(Does not the problem at the deepest level consist in the effort
to discover how objectivity regarding the purely individual is
possible? In one aspect this is the problem that was brilliantly
stated by Simmel in the last chapter of his *Lebensanschauung*;
though he only stated it on the ethical plane. What causes infinite
complications is the incurable tendency we have all had since Kant
to think of the objective order in terms of legality or *Gesetzmäs-
sigkeit*. Now we cannot even dream of saying: 'Each time someone thinks his life in terms of the category of trial, this particular
thing will happen'.) I am back here at the central theme of my
reflections of 1913-1914, at the fundamental idea that the universal is necessarily the relative; but now this idea is specified
in an infinitely more concrete way. Notice that the question we
are dealing with here is identical with the question that arises

[1] Let us add that it does not attribute a new predicate to a subject previously posited.
This amounts to the same.

203

regarding prayer whose universal efficacy can only be admitted if we treat prayer as a kind of procedure, in other words if we negate prayer.

Perhaps we would not be deceiving ourselves if we said that a statement of the type that I am studying (the word statement is bad, but the term truth cannot be applied) needs to be discovered anew on each occasion. This is also very important. The virtue of this formula is bound up with the way in which it has been engendered and re-engendered by the soul, whereas the scientific formula, in its practical aspect, amounts to saying: 'If you do this particular thing I warn you that such and such will invariably happen. You have no need to ask me how I know it, nor to perform on your account the work that has enabled me to attain this certainty.' Doubtless, even in the spiritual order, once the discovery has been made, it can be universalised, but this can only be thanks to my power of sympathy which enables me to imagine and live through the experience of my neighbour, of my brother, as though it were my own experience. We are never able to transfer a formula or recipe; perhaps all we can do is to awaken in someone else the life in which both of us participate.

I realise that these observations do not take us far along our road. Some critics may say: 'The value of the idea (?) of trial is purely psychological. I will endure a calamity far more easily *if I suppose* that it is a trial imposed on me by a higher will. It is a help.' To this I answer that the word hypothesis does not fit here. 'So be it,' my critics will continue, 'let us say that this way of qualifying your experience does modify it, but only from within; that we are dealing with a purely immanent development.' But does not this take us back again to the standpoint of law, and amount to saying: 'Given a being subject to these or those particular vicissitudes, he has interest in . . . it is a good means of . . . etc.'? Unconsciously we are placing ourselves on the biological level and regarding the use of the 'category of trial' as a condition favourable for self-preservation in the psychological order. But this last idea is singularly obscure. Supposing, for instance, we accept as a trial an incurable malady. What happens to self-preservation in that case? We are reduced, I think, to conceiving in a vague way the maintenance of an *equilibrium*.

And the crowd of mechanical associations and ideas which we immediately unleash will help to reinforce the psuedo-interpretation. But can such an equilibrium be maintained? To take a contrary instance, let us imagine somebody who is incurable and who, with the knowledge that he is doomed, decides to make the best of the time he has left and to live in the most agreeable way possible. Scientific psychology may well comment that this second attitude is irreproachable and is even preferable to its opposite. The religious consciousness denies this and declares that between the two there is no common measure. Psychologists will argue that this judgment of religious value is made in function of a particular personal disposition and hence is purely relative. But on this latter road there is no stopping. The psychologist as such is irresistibly led to posit the relativity of all judgments of value whatsoever. Moreover, analysis shows that this 'pure psychology' in question is an abstraction that cannot survive careful reflection. Are we obliged for that reason to revert to the opposite interpretation and to declare simply that the believer is right? That it is *true* that suffering is a trial that we must learn to accept with resignation? But the words '*to be right*' can no longer be used here. Can I think the faith of someone else in any measure whatsoever if that faith is not mine? In this latter case we could only speak of an adhesion or attachment (however inexplicit).

October 17th, 1919

I need to go further into the idea of trial, making use of my notes of March 6th and 7th, 1919. I wrote that being is something that should be capable of being possessed. I will never admit that this is an ideal limit, as is maintained so it seems by a timid and confused school of neo-Kantian philosophers. I must emphasise again that no problem is harder to state than the problem of being. To speak of *being* as a noun is to imagine some sort of hard core of resistance which survives beneath the perishable bark of the phenomenon. But, as Kant saw, in this way we transpose into the domain of metaphysics, relations that are only thinkable as occurring between phenomena. (As regards the illusion of absolute interiority, cf. Hegel also.) It would be much more intelligible to say, in terms of a restricted but consequent rationalism, that the phenomenon is being as incompletely thought, being as grasped in the least concrete of its determinations. From this standpoint the problem of being amounts to the problem of how a complete system of categories is possible. I am not inquiring whether this way of thinking being is legitimate.[1] I think that it can be shown that the problem is stated in a much more pointed and more concrete way to consciousness than this. Being, as I said before, is expectation fulfilled. There are moments at which life appears to us to be entirely empty. Nothing has any importance, nothing matters. Such experiences are the very negation of the feeling of fullness and profusion that we experience on other occasions. Our attention cannot be fixed and interest is lacking. This danger we run when we live in a world to which we have become too accustomed, a world that answers us mechanically. The same occurs when misfortune lays bare and empties the soul. We have always with us the contrast of the full and the empty which is to me fundamental, and which, speaking generally, has so far only been considered in its physical aspects. Our activity needs to be exercised to the full in a world of fullness. The experiences in function of which the problem of being can be posited in an intelligible way are happiness, love and inspiration. But the problem concerns *being* and not *some being*. It may here be argued that I have reduced the problem of being to the problem of enjoyment. And indeed I am firmly convinced that there is being as soon as there is enjoyment; but it is at this point that the trial —the critical experience—intervenes. But what if it is said that enjoyment as such (and here and now) is absolute, that the judgment that we bring to bear on it after the event is, so to speak, weakened in advance? What of the idea of a fundamental rhythm of activity that we should be able to accept? Of the view that the wise man is the man who is aware of the ineluctable limits of all enjoyment and reproaches us when we claim to pass beyond them? Indeed it is easy to see all the objections that a kind of philosophy can make against retrospective asceticism, against repentance. And we must not reject all of them in our argument. But in spite of that we can nevertheless answer, I think, that many enjoyments do not satisfy the whole of our being, that is

[1] I think we can establish that if we follow this road thought cannot pass beyond the formal, the potential, and hence falls short of its programme.

to say our spiritual nature. They only satisfy us on condition that we have already put a great part of ourselves to sleep. And that part is much the strongest. But here we are in danger of running into a difficult question. By what right can we affirm that the whole of ourselves can ever be satisfied, that harmony between the different kinds of satisfaction is possible? Can we be sure that we are not bound to make certain sacrifices? What can guarantee the possibility of accord? I note in passing that anyone who answered in this way would doubtless refuse to establish a hierarchy between the different modes of satisfaction that he judges to be non-unifiable. As for myself I think the problem is insoluble as long as we state it in terms of the *third person* of abstract analysis. But as soon as it is stated in a living way, that is, for *me* or for *thee*, the situation appears in a new light. I am fully aware of the objection that this answer is no more than a mere expedient. I myself cannot help becoming anxious about the mechanical character of the solution. I must therefore resume the examination in much greater detail.

If in cold blood I divide myself up into 'parts' I am bound to admit that I do not know whether or not these 'parts' can be satisfied when they are taken together. These parts are 'they', they are in the third person, *they are not me*.

October 18*th*, 1919

I am experiencing some difficulty in pursuing this analysis to-day. It seems to me that everything depends on the spiritual *level* on which the problem is not stated but lived. This point seems to me crucial though it is difficult to think if in a precise way, which is explainable, since to think is almost inevitably to convert the *thou* into an abstract *him* or *it*. If we can get beyond this stage, I suppose it is thanks to a sort of intellectual imagination whose nature needs examining—a kind of imagination I must be careful not to call intuition. I note in passing that the problem of freedom, the real problem (I am not speaking of the scholastic problem of freedom) can itself only be stated—as Bergson has brilliantly pointed out—on a certain spiritual level, probably the same spiritual level. It can of course be objected that the state of interior division is not necessarily a superficial state. Yet I think that consent to remain divided is only possible on a certain plane.

All real passion makes us wish to be whole. (This also applies to relations between distinct beings; division is only acceptable for those who do not genuinely love.) But at present I do not want to probe into what this means. Such a formula is certainly not clear. It is one of those formulae that only mean something on the plane of dialectics. We conceive, we posit the ego as coveted by something other than itself, by another *him* but in that way we put ourselves outside the real conditions of interior life.

October 19th, 1919

I revert to the beginning of the preceding discussion. Under what conditions can we legitimately affirm that reality is capable of providing us with absolute satisfactions? I think that at the outset we need to posit the principle that these satisfactions cannot be objects for scientific knowledge or technics. Whatever be asserted by shallow modern 'naturalists' (with their metaphysics for vegetarians) there is no technique for achieving happiness. Or, to be more exact, inasmuch as such a technique is possible, it only applies to 'anybody' and hence to 'nobody'. At this point I suppose we must be ready for the answer: 'It is because it is imperfect that this technique is incapable of being specifically defined. By rights, if we really knew who you were, we would know what you need.' But is it conceivable, even in right, that someone else could ever know who I am well enough to determine what I am in need of? I am *him* for the technician; I am in the *third person*. I am an object, he puts me into a general category, whatever be the specifications that his experience or his diagnosis enables him to attribute to the image he has of me which, in its initial stage, is entirely abstract. But what is it within me that rises up against the pretence of deciding what I need, against such 'moral prescriptions'? Am I merely experiencing an irrational explosion of individualism? Why does it seem to me that my life loses its value if its content is thus provided from outside? Above all why is the case different when we are dealing with a being I love and who loves me? Is it that the beloved is no longer external? For it goes without saying that the intervention of the beloved must not take the form of an order or be condescending.

Why am I enveloped in deep sadness when I consider myself

so as to define myself, so as to recognise the particular sphere that appears to be chosen for my activity? Even the idea that my nature prohibits me from experiencing some particular manner of understanding or of feeling is unacceptable to me. I grapple with my nature and loathe it. Is this merely pride? It would be very superficial to say that. The whole margin of limits that I decide to exclude from the *him* with whom I identify myself seems to rise up and affirm that it is mine.

Absolute satisfactions seem therefore incapable of coming to me, unless it be from a being for whom I am *thou*, a being who turns his efficacious solicitude towards me in an active way. This I take to be certain, but it is still insufficient. The idea of the act of kindness is certainly not a clear idea and here that expression must not be given a realist meaning. The idea of advantages that are sometimes bestowed plentifully on one particular head, and at other times are measured out with parsimony, is an idea that is metaphysically void, as is the idea of any kind of objective valuation or comparison, and for the same reason. Yet I must admit that I cannot see clearly here. Is it enough to distinguish between advantages considered in their material aspect (wealth, honours, etc.) and the internal disposition with which I consider them and even the use I make of them?

October 20th, 1919

Even if we admit that this distinction is valid in itself, we need to elucidate its meaning; and that is not easy because this disposition is likewise a gift. I do not think that it can reasonably be said that it depends on me that I welcome my destiny in this or that given way. At least this raises a problem that is obscure. The more deeply we examine current notions the more we discover the confusions they conceal in greater or less degree. The idea of satisfaction is of the number. Can it be identified with the idea of satiation? Not exactly, I do not think that, considered in itself, the idea of satisfaction entails the idea of 'full measure'. The higher we rise on the spiritual ladder, the less this idea seems to us one of *receiving our portion*.[1] Every moral system

[1] But I am not sure that ethics are not essentially bound up with a particular representation of rights—that is to say of portions—and of the duties that these rights entail as counterpart. In this sense the religious categories infinitely transcend the moral categories (1925).

that is based on the idea of sharing (egalitarianism) is unquestionably vicious even in its very principle. What matters is what is whole in us. And in the first place it is of course of love that I think. My portion; his or her portion—this notion ceases to have any meaning when we are dealing with a *thou*. In the light of this idea, seen in its negative facet, perhaps what I have said above becomes clearer. I cannot conceive God in function of my portion considered as such. When I thank him for the lot he has bestowed on me, I posit myself as a being that excludes other beings, a being who is not busied with knowing the lot of others. And this is the more true the more we take into consideration the external goods that are an object of competition: power, fortune and, if not intelligence, at least the benefits that can be derived from it. Hence we can see fairly clearly the sense in which man is involved in gratitude to God. Beyond certain limits this gratitude changes into idolatry. Actually my gratitude should be less for what I have than for what I am. And of course the more God is for me, the more I *am*; in that way we can see the intimate relation that unites us. My gratitude could only be for the gift that God has made me of himself, and it seems to me that if an advantage can ever be considered as a gift, it is inasmuch as it comes to be regarded as a disguised form of the gift that God makes to me of himself. This is an indivisible gift that has nothing exclusive about it, and has nothing in common with the attribution of a portion. Health, for instance, or perceptiveness can be envisaged in that way. As regards society, the consequences of this are far from clear to me; we should distrust translations of the idea into the practical order when they are too direct: more often than not they depend on misunderstandings. But I can see fairly clearly the intimate bond between interior riches and the need of others (Zarathustra).

October 21*st*, 1919

To revert to the idea I expressed so badly yesterday. There is no doubt that we need to react strongly against the classical idea of the eminent value of αυταρκια or personal self-sufficiency. The perfect is not perfect because it suffices for itself; or at least the perfection of self-sufficiency is that of a system, not that of an individual. Yet we can never be satisfied with the idea of a being whose truth is external to himself. Here there is a subtle nuance that is rather difficult to establish. Under what conditions does the relationship binding a being to what he needs involve a spiritual value? It seems as though here there must be response, reciprocity, awakening. The relationship that can be said to be spiritual is that of being with being; and this is enough to refute and show up the metaphysical nothingness of one form of pantheism.

But seen from this standpoint does not the Kantian idea of the end-in-itself seem artificial and merely juridical? What really matters is spiritual commerce between beings, and that involves not respect but love.

October 22nd, 1919

I am fully aware that I have always judged a being to be worthy of respect by reason of the love that he has inspired (or of which he has been unjustly deprived). Deep down Kantian rationalism is becoming increasingly foreign to me. A being does not interest me inasmuch as he is an embodiment of reason; as such, after all, he is only a *he.* Beyond question Kant over-exaggerated the value of autonomy as the source of values. Of course, as I am fully aware, he concerned himself primarily with discovering that which is capable of being universalised, and he thought that a morality based on feelings is untenable because it rests on a contingent datum, on something which is capable of not being (or which cannot be 'required' in right). To adopt the language I previously made use of I would say that he took a technical point of view. What are the conditions under which someone (no matter who) can act or will in an ethical way? The answer must be universal, that is to say, valid even for the least favourable case. The important question here is whether, if we proceed in this way, we are not in the strict sense cutting ourselves off from the conditions of spiritual life. Fundamentally intention is certainly not as easily grasped as Kant thought (the word 'easily' may seem surprising; Kant certainly worked carefully on the idea of intention and eliminated the contingent element of feeling; yet did he not make use of sleight of hand?).

At this moment I am wondering whether two beings, who are

habitually *thou* for one another, do not tend to be converted each for the other into a *him* if they are in the presence of a third person who is a *thou* for both of them. At first sight this sounds like sheer balderdash. But in reality it is concrete and important. Yet I do not want to say that there is anything inevitable in this, for to do so would doubtless be meaningless.

A difficult question that must be tackled concerns the conditions under which we can think the *thou* without it becoming a *him*. What seems to happen in practice is that I begin by thinking the *thou* as a *him* and then rectify this by a subsequent act. But it is not yet very clear.

I need to recapitulate in a simple way the steps by which I have reached this idea (by means of the notion of *answer* and the notion of *that*). Probably I should also inquire whether to think invariably means to reflect. The answer is certainly that it does not—and love should be able to be thought without being dispelled in an inert relation.

November 25th, 1919

Once again I continue with my diary after a month's interruption. . . . But, no; I am not sure that what I wrote about Kantianism is false. After all Kant gives us a sort of recipe for extracting the best we can from a nature that is badly provided—even as regards morals. If morality is to be possible, this technique must exist. Now morality exists, therefore, etc. . . . But does morality really exist? The question is justified. It does exist in the measure in which I affirm that it does, in the measure in which I have faith in its reality. Possibly—yes, I think I would go so far as to say this—it would be enough for a consciousness to deny morality resolutely and radically, for us to be unable to say that it *is* without a reservation which would be fundamentally destructive. The dialectician can have recourse to trying to establish that I affirm morality by the very act by which I believe I am denying it. This has been the classical method since Plato and it is certainly impressive; but is it really convincing?— that a system of fundamentally ethical statements is involved in any proposition bearing on moral reality—and even involved in any proposition that purported to deny the statement: 'It is *perhaps* true, but is it decisive?' I am aware that this question is in danger of seeming impudent and even absurd. And yet! Is it not possible *to want to contradict it*? 'Not as such', I may be answered. 'From the moment I want A and B at the same time I state, however confusedly, that there is a connection between A and B within a simple unity.' Granted. But may not that unity only be a simple external conjunction, a pure *and*? Though every effort may be made to show me the real incompatibility of A and B, could I not still have recourse to refusing to see this? I may be told that if I do so I am refusing to think. Yes, but supposing I agree not to think? Supposing I opt for a world which is not that of thought? True, there is the recourse of denying what I affirmed a moment ago, and maintaining that morality *exists*, even if I insist on denying it. But such morality would be no more than an abstract order, it would resemble a truth abstractly dissociated from the act that posits it. Now what is the meaning of speaking of a truth that I do not know, that is not for me? Does this mean that I have not been in the situation needed for observing or recognising it? This occurs even in the simplest cases. Yesterday, for the first time, I read the name of a Russian town which is called Slaviansk. This town has always existed, but I was not in a position to know it. There we have a synthesis that I had neither the opportunity nor the means of forming. Can the same be said regarding moral truth which is considered to exist though I deny it? If I could claim this I would absolve myself. I would be no more guilty of being ignorant of such moral truth than of being ignorant of the existence of Slaviansk until yesterday. Moreover, in such a case I cannot be said to be really denying this truth. Because I can only deny what I know. Thus we are obliged to suppose that though I may believe I am denying this moral truth, I am really denying something other than it. I am sinning through ignorance. It seems to me that even in the Kantian type of ethical system there is an enormous and concealed intellectualist element.[1] There is still the further resource of declaring that fundamentally I am not sincere, that something within me recognises the moral truth that I verbally deny. I can deny verbally that two and two make four, I can say that two

---

[1] Yet I must recognise that this does not prevent Kant's formula: *No one ever does evil willingly*, from being radically false.

and two make five. But that is mere words and empty breath. The same, it can be said, applies to the deliberate denial of moral truth. Only in the latter case we must go still further. If this theory is true the immoral act itself is only a meaningless gesture. But in that case it is no longer immoral. According to the other hypothesis it is a lie; but if we admit that hypothesis the whole problem comes up anew. For either the lie is not conscious, and we fall back on the first hypothesis; or else it is conscious, and then it is a pure immoral act in the sense in which I defined it earlier. The first alternative may seem more satisfying, and it amounts to denying radically that immorality can exist as such. If what we customarily call sin is in reality of the same order as the blow I strike when I am asleep, it is plain that any action, in the strongest sense of the word, is always a moral act. Only we then have the problem of whether, in that case, morality itself does not entirely disappear. For to judge morally is essentially to forbid, it is to treat the immoral act as possible and to exclude it. Hence all outlets seem closed. For to deny when we know what we are denying means in reality to *reject*. Morality then ceases to be a system of valid statements and becomes a mode of life that I may or may not accept. Whereas if I am ignorant of what I am denying, my fault dissolves as fault, it is merely error. Supposing it be contended that at least the formula of the law is known to me? Agreed; but why should this formula oblige me to respect it? For we are outside the realm of ethics and in that of arbitrary ritualism. Thus I tend to believe that the first alternative should be accepted: namely that there is no technique for morals, there is no infallible way of inciting me to will the good. Doubtless, to some extent, Kant would have agreed with this. But for all that he does posit as a truth by right universal that I ought to act in a manner that is in conformity with the categorical imperative, and that as I ought to do so I am able to do so; the transition from the *thou shalt* to the *thou canst* is indeed the nerve of the whole Kantian system of ethics. But who affirms to me that this is so? For Kant it is evidently myself, inasmuch as I participate in reason. It is an absolute fact, something which is bound up with my quality of rational being. Kant guarantees to me not only this is so, but also that if I am of good faith I will myself discover that it is so. My essential quarrel is with the legitimacy of that claim.

November 26th, 1919

It goes without saying that the question—it is nowadays far too often discussed—as to whether or not the affirmations of the moral consciousness derive their content from social reality, has from my standpoint, no interest. Society, too, is something which needs to be willed. Moreover, so as to make moral reality coincide with social life, we are led to modify the characteristics of the latter by a series of logical expedients whose details are of no importance here.

A much more interesting point is the question of whether or not morality forms an indivisible whole in the idealist sense. Whether, when I commit a particular immoral act, I really deny morality as a whole. All that we can say about this, I think, is that inasmuch as I act in an immoral way, I exclude myself from a certain life, I refuse to participate in it. And in that way I make my future participation in it more difficult, because my act contributes to determining me myself.

Here we must foresee at least one question. I have spoken of that life from which I exclude myself by my act. But is this realised in practice, in act? The problem is serious because, unless I am mistaken, there can be no question of a formal totality of rules that are in the strict sense valid; or, rather, these rules are *offered* to me, *presented* to me. When I reject them I deny that they have the character of rules, and say 'Let there be rules for others but not for me.' But in that way do we not convert them into 'manners of living' that are purely contingent? Or more exactly are we not admitting that for the agent himself these 'rules' are nothing more than that? But this agent cannot be judged guilty unless in our estimate of his act we adopt the very criterion that he himself refuses to accept, that is to say unless we attribute to these rules the value of universal law. One man calls guilt that which for another is only non-conformity. Who is to disentangle them? And here the previous argument comes in, with all its weight; I must entertain no hope of demonstrating to the agent in question that it is I who am right, and that he is *really* guilty. But what follows? We have reached a point that could be called pure ethical monadism. The 'guilty' man and myself are shut up in the enclosures of our different ways of estimating. As soon as I admit that the 'guilty' man denies with knowledge of what he is saying, I prohibit myself from speaking of moral truth. It is not a question of something that I know and that he does not know. I have no more elements at my disposal than he has, I am in no better condition than he is. To say that I am favoured by my nature would again amount to denying morality as such. So what follows?

When I act in conformity with certain norms, I believe that my action has a value. Yet this formula is not enough to set us on our way to a really positive solution. I accept what he refuses. I accept what he rejects. That is all we can say so far, and it must be admitted that it is not very informative. I do not only accept, I affirm that I have reason to accept. If I limited myself to accepting, it would be said that we have each our different ways of seeing, of feeling or of being. But I say that I am right. And this is not clear because I have not, at least in right, a valid motive for affirming that the 'guilty' man can be put into a condition of self-contradiction and thus can be obliged to withdraw. But then what? The problem does not consist in changing the conditions in which he is placed, but in transferring his *being* itself, in converting him. It may be objected that this distinction between the conditions in which he is placed and his total being is arbitrary and, above all, that as soon as I begin considering the individual being I fall back into the field of pure empiricism: I *am* in a given way, he *is* otherwise than me. What is the meaning of my saying that I am right? This objection is important in that it brings to light the danger that lies in this way of expressing oneself. Yet it is only a question of terminology. May I not lay claim to a certain type of superiority in relation to the other man whom I persist in declaring guilty? Meanwhile is the other man able to place himself in my situation? It must be repeated that I am not really better placed than he, that I possess no lights refused to him. Nevertheless, the question still seems to me very obscure. For if to say 'he is guilty' really means 'he is taking the wrong path and is mistaken whereas I am on the right path,' then we are involving ourselves in phariseeism and are a thousand leagues from genuine moral life—and in addition we are entangled in a labyrinth of contradictions. To claim on the other hand that to say 'he is guilty' is to posit between him and me a difference in being, is really very equivocal; can I proclaim that he is outside the life in which I participate without thereby absolving him?

November 27th, 1919

I return to what I was at great pains to express yesterday. First of all it must, of course, be admitted that what I am concerned with here is only the attitude of the man who wholly refuses to recognise moral values as such. If my argument is exact, to say of that man that 'he is guilty' is to recognise that he nevertheless in some way participates in the life from which I declare him to be excluded. But how is that possible? It does not mean, of course, that he affirms what he believes he is denying, but that metaphysically he is all the same a member of the society from which he excludes himself. I am fully aware that he will have little inclination to subscribe to this interpretation, and will absolve himself from doing so, either by saying that in fact a case resembling the one in question does not arise, or else, that if it does, all we need to see in it is an anomaly of a pathological type. I will consider these two ways in turn.

To begin with, can it be stated as a fact that there is no one who deliberately excludes himself from what we commonly call morality? I maintain that any such statement is inexact, and in any case that it is *possible*. I will go further. There is reason to think that in all of us there is to be found at least a little of that kind of immoralism. Moreover, it would be easy to show that to introduce here the idea of health or of norm is either to fall back into intellectualism, or else to treat morality simply as a contingent 'manner of being.'

I am thus bound to think the guilty man in one respect as belonging to a world from which in another respect he is excluded. And to say that this dualism has a metaphysical character is to affirm the absolute irreducibility of these two aspects or of these two natures; the impossibility of bringing them to unity by a reasoning of the platonic type; and the necessity of conversion—that is to say of a strictly supernatural action that can alone achieve their unification.

Moreover, for the sake of clarity it would doubtless be best not to make use of the word 'guilty' here, but to reserve it for cases where there is responsibility in the strictest sense, that is, for cases of an infraction of a known and recognised law. Nor can it be said that by refusing to speak of guilt I have placed myself once more on the plane that I claimed I had passed beyond. The only difference in this is that the condemnation is directed against a mode of life rather than against the agent himself.

I may be asked yet a further question. By what right do I posit a condition in the supra-empirical or metaphysical order where there is no difference in the empirical conditions? 'In reality,' it can be said, 'you are looking for a means of justifying the over-bold step by which you, judging from your point of view, condemn someone who places himself on grounds other than yours. The difficulty arises from the fact that you refused to admit that your point of view and that of the agent we are discussing are absolutely different. But in this way you may be creating artificial and insurmountable obstacles for yourself. I who have accepted the fundamental conditions of all social life claim the right to judge the man who withdraws himself from them.' But this is very questionable; for what do we mean by judging somebody? A judgment by its very essence should be recognised as just by the man who is judged. And that is precisely what is impossible in this case.

And if I be told that one can judge a being without preoccupying oneself about his eventual reactions, just as we verify an operation of logic? But can a human being be compared to a logical complexity?

November 29th, 1919

Yet I think the argument can still be maintained: 'The erring person whom you are discussing is, for reasons which vary in each particular case, in no condition to recognise the order whose reality you for your own part affirm. Nothing justifies your seeing in his incapacity anything save an infirmity, a sort of blindness. Are there not intellectual forms of blindness (in mathematics, for instance)?' Thus stated the objection is not lacking in force. But I do not think it is decisive, because there is nothing positive about the fact of being unable to understand a demonstration. It is only a limitation—and should we not add that the man who does not understand at least *knows* that he does not understand. But it is not enough to say that if this difference which is judged to be fundamental bears on conditions that we have no power to modify; we are still led to posit an election, a choice, though this is a natural choice which destroys the very notion of morality. Strictly speaking, that too can be contested. Aesthetic enjoyment also depends on natural conditions. Is that a reason for denying that there are aesthetic values? May there not be moral values in an analogous way, although the empirical recognition of those values is bound up with the contingent achievement of a particular state of fact? But this formula is only clear in appearance. Who affirms that these values 'exist'? It is the man who acknowledges them. He goes so far as to denounce *a priori* as null and void the affirmations of the 'unhealthy' people who do not recognise them.

This conception resembles an infinitely degraded Platonism, a Platonism in which no discussion can take place between the opposite parties. The affirmation of the moralist amounts to saying: 'They must undergo treatment' (supposing treatment can be attempted). The idea of 'operation' tends to substitute itself for that of conversion or persuasion. And now we need to discover the conditions under which an *operation* is possible or conceivable. . . .

December 1st, 1919

A treatment or operation aims at permitting an apparatus to function 'freely' 'normally,' etc. But can 'normal' life be compared to the functioning of an apparatus? What makes me uneasy here is the example of aesthetics. . . .

As a result of reading my notes to P. I am reverting to the *thou* to define still more precisely this important and difficult notion. The *thou* is not only the person interrogated as such, it is that which is questioned inasmuch as this is not itself treated as the object of an interrogation. I approach someone with the intention of asking him a question, but at the same time I ask myself whether he will be able to answer, whether he has the wherewithal for informing me. He is not *thou* for me, but *he*, a collection or accumulation of data. Even on the most elementary plane the *thou* is only capable of being defined in function of faith, of the spontaneous refusal to ask questions. Only when I am dealing with a person who is given to me empirically, I cannot prevent myself from thinking objectively, *that is to say doubting*. I will be told that my doubt bears on the predicates, not on the existence of the subject himself. But here it is possible to bring in the old Hegelian argument according to which it is only the predicates that matter. What assumes tragic importance in the history of our relations with others is not existential doubt, but doubt as regards being, or more exactly doubt as regards 'value'. We may wonder whether this doubt is doubt of the predicates. We only need to reflect on the deep meaning of one simple question: 'Is he worthy of my love for him?' to feel with unbelievable intensity the insufficiency of our categories. On what does the question really bear?

At this point we must ask ourselves once more about the sense in which I have predicates. Of course I am able to give a description of myself—but, leaving aside the difficulty of understanding how this description is metaphysically possible, ought we not to say that my deepest reality extends infinitely beyond any such description? Here there is a whole group of questions that are so tangled that I cannot really see how to disentangle them. I can attribute to myself a series of predicates as though somebody else were attributing them to me; in this measure I am 'somebody else' for myself; I speak of myself as I would speak of anybody else. But all that is deepest in me falls outside this mode of thinking. Freedom, for example, is only conceivable in the measure in which I have in me the means whereby I can transcend the order of the *him*. I am unable to set down my intuition in detail in a discursive way, though I am sure I shall succeed in the end—but I feel strongly that to will is to cease to treat oneself as *him*. My notes of March 1919 must be interpreted in this way. Not to will is to say: 'I shall not be able to, given what I am it cannot happen that . . . ' In that instance I am treating myself as a third party, I am speaking about myself as a third party. But to will is to cancel oneself out as *him*, and to rediscover the fertile indivision that was abolished by dialectics. So it is a serious error to see an interior tension in the will, and on this point nothing is more deceptive than the dramas of Corneille. I maintain on the contrary that to will is not to stiffen

oneself but to relax. In a word the person who fails to will hypno-
tises himself with a calculation of possibilities, and it is here that
the *buts* intervene: on the one hand there is what I might call my
desire, my preferences, etc., on the other there are particular
obstacles and difficulties. Either literally I get lost in this calculation, that is to say I set myself aside; or else I treat myself
as a datum amongst other data, and to will is precisely to refuse
to treat oneself in that way. In this sense the comparison with
faith is essentially correct, for to believe is to refuse to throw
into the balance. At the root of faith there is the will not to compare. In this way I come back to my difficult and abstract arguments of long ago, but it seems to me that I now have the equip-
ment for stating them more solidly. "Within me," I said at one
time, "there is the wherewithal to transcend all true judgment
brought to bear on myself." What exactly did I mean by that?
That all judgment brought to bear on me is brought to bear on a
third person who, by definition, cannot be one and the same as
myself. The man for whom I am a *thou* goes infinitely beyond
these judgments even if he accepts them. When he loves me
he as it were opens a credit account for me. Royce has probed
deeply into the fact that love individualises. But does the principle of individualisation, as he believed, reside in the unique end
that this given being alone is in the position to realise? Note
that this end is not capable of being grasped either by the man who
is thought to realise it, nor by other empirical subjects. Must
we say that God alone can grasp it? That would be recognising,
it seems to me, that the person in question is a *him* and not a *thou*
for God. In any case it would not account for what is distinc-
tive in proper human love and the human bond. At this point I
am persuaded of the need to appeal to an order of ideas or of
experiences that infinitely surpass the teleological plane, and this
research is the more difficult in that it would be vain to appeal to
the idea of a quality proper to one individual, that only a given
other individual would be able to discern. To love is not 'to
know adequately.' It may be that love dispenses a privileged
knowledge, but it precedes it as it also precedes evaluation. I
perceive yet another point, which is that love is bound up with
the emergence of the '*I*' which, far from positing itself as essence,
springs forth as lover. Love rises up like an invocation, like an

appeal of the *I* to the *I*, and what I said formerly of the opposition between invocation and indication applies here perfectly. But we must take care. From the fact that the invocation is not addressed to what I have called the ego-source of information, are we to conclude that it is addressed to a *me* destitute of predicates? I do not love him because of what he is, I love what he is because he is he, I thus boldly anticipate all experience; I anticipate all the predicates in which experience will be deposited. True, it may be contended that at the origin of this anticipation there must already be the recognition of a predicate, but I think that that is false. There is an act, a state, a manner of being, as you will, which the descriptive consciousness compares with the recognition of a predicate, but in reality it is an unforeseen enrichment of my being.

December 2nd, 1919

There is love only where there is absolute renewal and even rebirth. Love is life which decentralises itself, which changes its centre. But this raises a formidable metaphysical problem. From the fact that love does not bear on an object, on a *third person*, am I to conclude that it directly attains what I might call the *non-him* in the other? Common sense says that I must not. Common sense does not admit that the person I love can be effectively reached by my love, unless my love be communicated (by signs). Even in that case it is not my love that attains him. But it is not at all certain that common sense is right. And here we have the whole subjectivist conception of love whose principles need to be revised. We commonly reason as follows: 'The being that you love is different from the real being, hence your love does not bear on being itself, there is nothing ontological in it. But all that we have the right to say is that on love, which is never a judgment, we build an intellectual construction which may be entirely false. But this only puts off the difficulty. It will be agreed that the transvaluation which is at the basis of love corresponds to a real transformation of the lover, but has this necessarily for correlative a modification of the 'beloved object'? I must note immediately that in a system of triads the question is probably meaningless; I posit myself as external to the lover and the beloved; I consider their relation from outside.

They appear to me as radically separated; but is not this due to the fact that I can only really think this love if I participate in it? It is not for me unless it becomes in some way my love. This is tantamount to saying that the question asked only really has a meaning from the standpoint of the lover himself. 'Does my love', I ask, 'really reach or qualify the being of the person I love?' Two remarks are necessary. The first is that, doubtless, the beloved cannot be modified empirically by the love he inspires. The second is that the reality of each of us, that is to say, if you will, the complete notion of each of us, comprehends the feelings which we inspire in others. But is not this complete notion a sort of ideal fiction? In sum our concern is to know whether there is anything in the world that I am trying to explore that corresponds to the enrichment of the notion considered in itself. Metaphysically the problem divides up as follows: (1) Does love bear not simply on the idea of being but on being itself?[1] and (2) can it bear on being without affecting being? As regards the first question there can be no doubt whatsoever. But the second question seems to me very doubtful. I can certainly think my own love as *not attaining* the being that I love, but perhaps that is a delusion of the mind due to the fact that I posit myself as a third in relation to both of us, and hence treat us as distinct and separate. This is a love that excludes faith. In a word, I seem unable to ask the question without depriving it of meaning. On closer examination it will be seen that if my love can exercise an action on the beloved, it is only inasmuch as this love is not desire; for in desire I tend to subordinate the beloved to my own ends, to convert the beloved into an object. Thus it is perhaps only absolutely disinterested love that is susceptible of affecting the *thou*. And this remark should throw some light on the practical function of sanctity.

December 3rd, 1919

Ever since yesterday I have been busy with the problem of understanding what constitutes praying for a person. At first glance it seems as if the person for whom I pray is a third person

---

[1] Should we also ask whether this same question arises regarding hate, for example, or envy? I have a feeling, though I am as yet absolutely unable to justify it, that it only has a meaning for love.

in relation to God and myself, while on the other hand it is manifest that he is not simply *him* for me. To pray for a being is to have faith in the potential efficacy of the prayer in question; it is even, it seems to me, to be convinced that the prayer made is not in vain, even if it is not heard in a material way. Here the path becomes wide. It seems to me obvious that there is a type of prayer for oneself which is legitimate, and a type of prayer for others which is not. Prayer for myself seems only able to bear on what is susceptible of being regarded as a divine gift, or to put it more exactly, I can pray to *be* more, but not to *have* more. Every day this distinction seems to me more important. We are not in any way dealing with what can be possessed, but only the use that can be made of the possession. What I have can scarcely appear to me as coming from God. In any case I cannot pray so that my portion in this world should be increased (see the notes of October 19th and 20th last). In *La Grâce* I spoke of those goods which increase when we communicate them. In so far as my prayer for someone else is dictated to me by the consideration of what is useful to me, it is vicious in its principle. I am only allowed to pray for the recovery of my servant inasmuch as my servant is my friend. In a word it is only legitimate to pray for a *thou*, and hence a new triad of relations arises, which in reality conceals a dual relation. In last analysis I pray God for *us*. In other words I can only pray for someone else when between that someone else and myself there is a spiritual community whose essential character I tried to express earlier. To pray for my own soul and to pray for the person I love is doubtless one and the same act. In this way, it seems to me, we get back to what I was trying to say yesterday when I spoke of disinterested love. Yet I am fully aware that the distinction I am trying to establish between what we are and what we possess is far from clear. Where, for instance, should we place intelligence? Can we pray to become more intelligent? Perhaps, if this does not involve praying to be more powerful in order to have more mastery over the natural order, but in order that we may participate more completely in being. As regards the efficacy of prayer, it seems to me that we should be able to find confirmation in what I have said about the will. To pray is to refuse to admit that all is given. It is to invoke reality considered as will. But are we obliged to say that when I pray I set up being as will, that I create it as will?

December 4th, 1919

To begin with I think that we should go deeper into the difference between praying and requesting. Every request involves an appeal to sympathy. If I ask a stranger the way I expect him to 'put himself in my place', to realise my embarrassment and provide me with the information he possesses; and I count on his sympathy prompting him to pronounce a word (or make a gesture) that he would not have pronounced (or would not have made) had I not addressed him. Thus my request is taken as being bound to modify my interlocutor's behaviour. In the case of prayer this obviously cannot apply. The more my prayer resembles a request, the more it bears on something that can be likened to a means of increasing my power (a piece of information, any object whatever), and the less it is in the strict sense a prayer. Whereas in the measure in which it tends to enrich my being itself, it is obviously not addressed to a finite individual. In short it seems to me that prayer is always of the type of 'Abide with me, help me.' Not in the abstract, but in a given and determined situation. It would be tempting to say that all sincere prayer is prayer that is answered, but this formula is dangerous; for it runs the risk of being interpreted as: 'If you pray with sufficient intensity, you will believe that your prayer, if not granted, is at least heard.' Now I believe we must formally oppose any such interpretation with all our strength because for the living reality of prayer it substitutes a mechanical schema. Moreover, what matters is not the intensity of the prayer, but its quality. Of course I must admit that this is by no means enough to refute the views of the psychologist. We could only achieve that, I think, if we showed that psychology always supposes a dualism between what is only an individual 'manner of being and what is really an object; whereas this dualism is untenable in metaphysics, and sociology, when summoned to the rescue, is incapable of upholding it.

In any case the problem has to do with what I shall call the ontological value of prayer: is prayer anything other than a contingent interpretation of the real in the phraseology of will? I think this question can be resolved by use of the method I have already employed so often. To begin with we must ask ourselves what we mean when we say that prayer is only a mode of representation or interpretation. The question is the clearer in that manifestly this interpretation transforms the being of the person who accepts it. The believer feels he is being helped, and derives strength from this feeling. Are we merely to say that he is helped because he believes he is being helped? And in what circumstances could the opposite happen? Real assistance manifestly needs to be distinguished from faith in it. If I call on someone to help me to open a door, I must have confidence in him, it may even be that my confidence in him helps to give him the strength to open it; but for all that it is he who opens the door, it is not opened by my confidence in him. The unbeliever wants us to maintain that the divine answer is objective in an exactly analogous way. But it seems to me that we have the right to point out to him that were assistance recognisable objectively it could not be of divine origin.[1] The act by which I have recourse to someone else is of the same type as the acts that I can accomplish myself. At the least it is a prolongation of them. But this certainly cannot be said of the help that I implore through prayer. Doubtless it will be answered either that this help is not really given to me, or else that it emanates from unconscious parts of myself. Reflection on this second alternative is badly needed. At present I tend to believe in a general way that the very idea of applying an etiology to such assistance is meaningless, that divine action can no more be understood causally than can will itself. But I am not sure that I am yet capable of establishing it for certain, or, rather, I am not sure that I can furnish a positive counterpart for the above negation.

December 7th, 1919

All the foregoing considerations bring me back to my notes on atheism. The unbeliever, as I pointed out, reasons as follows: 'I am within the normal conditions of experience, and yet I have not the experience of God. But this experience, if it is real, ought to be objective, that is to say it ought to belong to every normal being. Hence it is not a real experience.' Dogmatic atheism, in

---

[1] Or more exactly that this objectivity can only be recognised by faith, it cannot be demonstrated by an observer in general. (Note of 1927.)

short, asserts that what *is* not for one person cannot *be* for
another person. But as I said at the time, the idea of 'normal
conditions of experience' may well be meaningless in this context. Such conditions must necessarily refer to the competence
of whoever states and defines them. M.D. considers, after enquiry,
that he is within the normal conditions of experience, that is
to say that the totality of the (physical and logical) apparatus
he has at his disposal is in good condition. We are dealing here
with the order of the potentiality of 'having'. Were I an ophthal-
mologist it is probable that after proper examination I should
have the right to tell someone who sees red when I see green
that he is making a mistake, in other words that he is not within
the normal conditions of experience. But can this have any
application here? I think that were M.D. a psychologist he would
tell me that though he does not judge his own experience to be
more normal than a believer's, he can at least deny to the believer
any right to objectivise himself, to establish that he is in relation
with a reality. Only we must be careful to note that it is essential
to the experience of the believer that he should *set himself in such
a relation.* To deny him this right is not to leave his experience
intact and merely deprive him of a complement which is arbitrary
and exterior; it is to mutilate his experience. Of course if the
believer thinks this reality as an object, as a force of nature, the
psychologist's attitude is thereby justified. For in that measure
the believer straightway gives him the right to verify. But this
ceases to be the case as soon as the believer reflects his belief and
prohibits himself from making such an affirmation. Moreover, as
soon as the psychologist recognises that this faith is real (instead
of treating it as a simple subjective phenomenon) he associates
himself with it. I cannot say: 'God *is* really for you' without
conceding that in a sense he *is* likewise for me. I said 'for you.'
If indeed I limit myself to saying 'God is really *for him*' it is clear
that I have not got away from the domain of the objective and
that I am distorting the relation in question between *him* and God.
But the psychologist cannot make a judgment in the *second person*
without descending from the psychological plane to the human
plane; he is henceforward only a man amongst men.

I would like to discover the degree to which this process of
argument can also be applied to the problem of divine assistance.

Some given person says to me: 'I prayed, and as a result of praying I suddenly felt stronger.' In so far as I proceed as a psychologist I must treat *a given person* as an object, that is to say, as a certain kind of system that behaves in such and such a way. Prayer appears to me as a process capable of definition that has taken place in the centre of this system. Even if I deny it all efficacy, I at least declare that it is only the belief in its efficacy that has had a causal value in this case. I thus admit that 'in a subject with this particular character the belief in the efficacy of this given step can bring with it this given result.' I make a universal proposition regarding 'suggestion.' The psychologist thus does not address the believer, he speaks of him as of someone who has been the *site* of a given phenomenon. He is a theme for discussions and investigations. And in this way the believer's story is branded as null and void. Thus the psychologist proceeds in a purely dogmatic way; he treats himself as a norm. Of course he will defend himself by saying that he is translating into a universal language an affirmation stated in terms that cannot be made universal. But the whole point lies in whether this translation is legitimate. If I am a believer I will say to the psychologist: 'Are you qualified to translate this experience through which you have not lived? Your translation is only possible because you have not lived through it.'

From this I tend to conclude that when prayer is entirely sincere and appears in the eyes of the person praying to be answered, we are in a realm that is beyond all valid criticism.

December 15th, 1919

Two important reflections:

1. Why is it absurd to imagine that a given individual[1] can demonstrate the existence of God (whereas everything in nature can be conceived as capable of being detected by some particular person)? That of which the existence was capable of demonstration would not be, and could not be, God. The impossibility of an objective proof of the existence of God, the absurdity of this way of stating the religious problem—there we have something *beyond doubt*. Show, notably, that to establish

[1] Imagine a news-agency report announcing that Mr. X has discovered the existence of God. Why is it radically absurd?

that something exists is to identify it and detect it—unless it means discovering a relation that is purely ideal. . . .

2.   To think the object is, it seems, to think something for which I do not matter (with a reserve to which I shall return).   Naturalism treats the whole world, the universe, as an object for which I do not matter. But is there any meaning in saying that within this totality for which I do not matter, there are parts for which I do matter? It seems to me evident that in the measure in which I matter for them, they are not parts. This needs to be examined.

Moreover, in what degree have we the right to say that I do not matter for the object? On the contrary at least physically it takes me into account. But this relation of object to object is not the one we are concerned with here.

December 17*th*, 1919

I was reflecting just now on the relation that can be established between God and me, in the measure in which God is in the *second person* and the world is in the *third person* for us. But is the world really able to be in the *third person* for us? This is uncertain. To be able to be in the *third person* it would have to be able to be thought of as foreign to God. I discuss a question (politics for instance) with a friend. This question is *it* for him as it is for me. But does the same apply when we are concerned with something that touches him more intimately—a secret for instance? I tend to believe that to think that the world can be an object for God is to *deny God* as God. But as yet I am unable to explain my feeling clearly. Yet certain remarks I made the day before yesterday may help to explain it. To think an object, I said, is to think that for which I do not matter . . . 'But,' I may be asked, 'are we not able to think the world in that way?' Do I not lift myself to the idea of the living God for whom I am *thou* from the idea of a world for which I do not matter? The dialectic here is perfectly easy to grasp. But, for this relation between me and God to be living and enriching, we are concerned with whether we must not renounce grasping God as being in some way above the universe: in a word, must we not pass beyond what is dangerously abstract in such a relation. I tend to think that this elevation of the soul to God *above* all that happens is transitory and is only a preliminary step and a preamble so to speak of religious life. Inasmuch as I only *am* in the measure in which there are things, or beings, let us say, that matter for me, can we believe that these things or beings only matter for God in the measure in which I place myself between them—and him? That would be pure egotism. I only really lift myself up to God from the moment at which I think that an infinity of other beings also matter for him, or at which I wish they should so matter with all my strength.

I want to probe further into the question as to whether anything in the world can be exclusively in the *third person* for God. To answer this question in the affirmative would amount to recognising that in the world there is something which is absolutely unable to be loved or saved; but what kind of reality would *that* possess? Would it be an empirical reality? We would need first of all to ask whether the empirical order can *be* for God. This is a major problem.

December 18*th*, 1919

In F. de Curel's *Fille Sauvage* we read: "Here you are, speaking as though you admitted the existence of God . . . I speak in respect of the most venerable of hypotheses." And a little further on: "God and the immortality of the soul, which are the most grandiose conceptions of the human mind, are only *illustrious hypotheses*." It is against this way of thinking that all my work is directed. God is that which absolutely cannot be thought as hypothesis. For a hypothesis is a certain method of representing the way in which things happen in a case in which observation, for some reason, is impossible. It is a mode of figuration. But this cannot be brought to bear on a being. To love God, to pray to God . . . could that have any meaning if God could really be treated as a hypothesis? And if it be said that the hypothesis consists in admitting that these actions have bearing on a real object? In that case I would answer that this word 'real' is ambiguous here, and its meaning is so far from the meaning of 'genuine' that any attempt at certification would end up by suppressing the divine as such.

January 28*th*, 1920

Saw clearly this morning—perhaps partly under the influence

of Richardson—the following connection: there is surely a link between the fact that the body cannot be treated purely and simply as an instrument for the soul, and the fact that the metaphysical object (the *noumenon* if you like) cannot be regarded as being in communication with me. A sensation is not a message, and the body is not a machine. I still do not see where this leads but it is surely very important. In any case there is enough in it to refute the theory of Ward and Richardson according to which the object is only a subject as it appears to another subject. For this amounts to admitting that the object is interposed between subjects. I may be told that there are communications of this kind; words, gestures, etc. But everything leads us to think that for subjects there can be a communication which is not a communication. Might not sensation be of that order? We admit in general that sensation is a communication because it implies the transmission of something. But can it be compared with the reception of a message? (There are a lot of equivocations here that need dissipating, because the reception of a message only occurs if there is a communication.) When I smell an odour do I capture a message? Does to feel mean to decipher? Under what conditions can I treat something as a message?

February 22nd, 1920

When I wrote on December 2nd that love seemed to me to bear on being and not on the idea of being, what did I mean? On the contrary, if we listen to common sense, it looks as though I love the idea of a being that I form for myself, not this being as it is in itself. But what does this mean? That my idea may be *inexact*? This is singularly obscure. Can it really be said that I ascribe to this being in question characteristics that he does not possess?

February 23rd, 1920

All this is terribly confused. When I say 'I was deceived about him,' that means 'I construed him inexactly.' (Just as we can construct a curve badly by wrong interpolation or exterpolation even when we set out from exact points of reference.) Thus when I recognise my mistake I affirm that there is a truth regarding this being, that there is a correct construction. But does to love mean precisely to refuse to treat a being in this way?

It would doubtless be absurd to say that love is brought to bear on that which is unknowable. What is mysterious is not the object of love as such, but the type of relationship that love involves. It is vain for the lover to enumerate the characteristics and the merits of the beloved. He is certain *a priori* that any such inventory will not give him his love, which is transparent in itself. Even if he managed to pick out a special characteristic, this special characteristic would still be unexplainable to him: it is inasmuch as this characteristic is not treated as such that it is active. (One could say that it casts a spell.) Hence the question of *why* has no more meaning in this case than it has when asked about what I am. 'Why am I what I am?' The answer will of course be that this question is not absolutely meaningless: there is an etiology about myself. I am infinitely 'dependent': yet is it this dependence that makes me be what I am? I do not think so. This needs further examination.

I notice in another realm of ideas and as regards the real efficacy of love, that if it be true that love only *acts* on the beloved when it is manifested, we are not therefore obliged inevitably to conclude from this that love does not act through itself, but rather that it only becomes completely itself on condition that it is manifested.

I need to reflect on the *unsayable*. It is not that which we have failed to express in words, but that for which no words can be found: it is that which cannot be conceived. But how can we speak of *what cannot be conceived*? We must realise that all we can do is allude to it. Yet this is not clear. Is not the word that is used to indicate or point out also an allusion? We must distinguish. Each time that a particular objective whole is presented, the proper word appears as applying to it and indicating it. Hence we should expect the unsayable to be that which cannot be pointed out or indicated. But what are we to understand by that? Do we mean that which can in no circumstances be recognised, i.e. the pure 'new'? But even this pure 'new' may reappear in another context, and hence enable me to give it a name. Or are we to suppose that the unsayable is precisely that which needs to be treated as incapable of reappearing in this way, as absolutely not a content? That idea is more important but we must express it in another way, I think, and say that if we are to be able to speak of the unsayable we must precisely avoid this distinction between the person who experiences and what is experienced. Anything that can be treated as a content is by that very fact *sayable*.

Do these remarks help us to a better understanding of love? Is an *explanation* of love rightfully impossible? As soon as we treat love as a phenomenon we are obliged to account for it in terms of attraction, or affinity—that is to say in terms of a relation between universals that fail to become explicit as universals. But what do we mean by not treating love as a phenomenon? Quite simply we mean *to love*, to love oneself. If I put my emphasis on the fact that someone loves someone else (even myself) it becomes impossible to avoid treating this love as a phenomenon, a feeling. Whereas if I participate in the love I cease all efforts to fit it into my logical index; on the contrary I recast my whole being so as to be able to penetrate that love. I do not subordinate the love to me; I subordinate myself to the love. It will be said that objective understanding involves the use of categories that belong to no one. But this may be an illusion. In reality these categories are common, they are mine in spite of everything—they are instruments at my disposal. It is certainly I who understands or think I understand; we should distrust the *Denkenüberhaupt* which is only an abstraction and an abstraction that has been singularly misused. Here there is a distinction analogous to the distinction between the works that only give us the opportunity of bringing our categories into play and the works that enrich them. It has been my experience, especially in music, to contrast the work that I appreciate immediately because it fits into special frameworks or schemas that are already there (reminiscences) and the work that I only come to love later but much more deeply because it obliges me to invent new categories for it; it exercises its authority on me, it becomes a centre which imposes on me a regrouping of myself. Here lies the whole mystery of conversion.[1] There is an analogous experience at the origin of love. An unknown element (X) that I make no attempt for the moment to qualify imposes on me a sort of preliminary dis-

[1] It would be worth while asking whether there is a sort of secret polarity between this 'centre' and . . . what might be called the depths of the ego. But this is not clear.

articulation of myself and it is for that reason that to love is in a sense inevitably to suffer.

But can this initial act be understood? I answer with another question: understood by whom? For the lover love is logically anterior to any possible reduction. When I love it seems to me 'perfectly natural' to love as I do; I am what I am. Supposing it be maintained that this act should be comprehensible or foreseeable for someone else? On what does the privilege of this other, absent, person depend? Doubtless at first sight there is something intolerable in declaring that love is fundamentally unintelligible. But this comes from the fact that people insist on treating *me* as *him*, as a datum. Relate this to what I said about the will (December 1st, last). The basis of will seems to coincide with the basis of love.

February 24th, 1920

At first this may seem surprising, but does not freedom mean choice? When we love do we choose to love? But doubtless we must dissociate radically the ideas of choice and freedom. In what measure can I say *me*? That is the real problem.

February 25th, 1920

Faith seen as power of attachment to being. Look into the implications of that. Return to the idea of trial or test and the close bond between it and the very idea of faith. Faith needs to be *tested*. To test means to try out an instrument so as to recognise the use to which we can put it. But generally speaking such tests do not transform the instrument. For there to be testing there must be *judgment on self*. I do not know my capacity of resistance to temptation. If temptation arises it will constitute a test for me, but only on condition that the judgment on myself for which it affords the occasion is efficacious and has a transforming value. Can this be? In this judgment on myself a certain real myself is at work—a reality which cannot be given as datum and is even the antithesis of a datum. A test can only happen if the situation in which I am involved brings to birth within me a genuine duality between what I am as datum and what I am as a person who (ideally) reacts. This duality is obviously relative to an identity, which is less thought than felt, between the me that is revealed and the me who judges. The zone of the test is the zone of freedom itself. But supposing it be said that all I can ever attain is the discovery of what I am already? Here we must distinguish between two sorts of reality. Obviously the test obliges me to measure myself with myself. Will I come up to my own proper level? There lies the whole problem and it can only be resolved by my action. The philosophical difficulty is aggravated by the fact that the test appears to us not only as implying a finality, but also as being inflicted by one being on another being. How are we to avoid being obliged to declare that this is a mere subjective interpretation, a way of treating temptation, for instance, *as if* it had been *sent*? But here we have once more the old issue. If we state the question in this way we take our stand outside the real conditions of religious life. If I treat myself as object, if I think God as an agent external to myself, in a word if I remain in the order of causality, the test loses its spiritual character and becomes a competition. I can only appear to myself as willed by *thee*. When I treat myself as an effect I transform myself in my own eyes into *him*. In the residue to which scientific knowledge purports to reduce me, I cease to recognise myself. The metaphysical problem of the test or trial can only be solved by going more deeply into the *willed by thee*. The relation of filiation is purely actual; it is meaningless to throw back into the past the act by which I have been willed. To think religiously is to think in the actual in the same species as the divine will. Yet even in the actual order what type of relation can be established between the infinite totality of conditions which determine the present situation and make it to be what it is—and the divine will? May not the divine will be only a *fiction that masks the causes*? Or is it a power? And in the latter case are we not still confined to the realm of causality? Beyond the classical dilemma of a God who is responsible and a God who is powerless, we must succeed in finding a solution that is surer and less precarious than Royce's. . . .

February 27th, 1920

Re-read my notes on the unjustifiable. What does to justify mean? In last analysis it means to justify in relation to oneself, to say 'in such and such circumstances I would have behaved as you did and both of us would have been right.' I take the instance of the man who justifies himself before me. He undertakes to establish that the norms to which he has conformed his conduct are the very ones to which I claim to conform my own conduct—it being of course understood that any gap between what I do and what I ought to do is here suppressed. In these conditions what happens to the metaphysical problem of the unjustifiable? The universe can only be justified personally and in function of a divine personality. There is no justification possible save for what can be regarded as a way of acting or of behaving. Sentimental atheism can be expressed in this way: 'If the events that happen in the world are the acts of a God, they ought to be capable of justification. Now there are some events that are not justifiable; hence those events cannot be produced by divine causality. But a powerless God *is not* in being.' Are we obliged to establish such a strict connection between the idea of divine reality and that of a global justification of what *happens*? I cannot believe it.

February 28th, 1920

As soon as we attempt to compare the universe with a work of art one difficulty becomes obvious. How am I to place myself in front of this work of art so as to judge it? I am part of it but in what sense? This also needs to be gone into. At least it should be possible for me to identify myself with the Idea of this work of art—and that is absurd.

February 29th, 1920

This morning I had the clear intuition that joy is not the mark of being but its very upsurge. Joy—fullness. All that is done in joy has a religious value; done in joy means done with the totality of one's being. Whereas any separation of the soul from itself alienates it from God. This lesson I learnt, and lastingly, from Hocking. Hence nothing is more dangerous for spiritual development than *boredom*. When we are bored we feel that we are not attached to what we are doing or even to what we *are*. We can bore ourselves and be bored at living with ourselves; with living in a state of pure distraction, i.e. a state which is *not compensated*. But cannot one do evil with the whole of oneself? May one not throw one's whole self into an evil action? That also needs to be examined more deeply.

There is a close connection between the problem of boredom and that of time and eternity. To be bored means to lack the wherewithal for filling in time, it is to let oneself down. Boredom as consciousness of empty time. Eternity as act of unique attention to the universe.

Disquiet. On the one hand the privilege of the religious soul seems to be the state of perfect confidence, the state of faith. On the other hand we doubt the value of a belief that knows no disquiet. This is because religious joy is the antithesis of self-satisfaction, but it runs the risk of being confounded with self-satisfaction if there is no disquiet. Religious life makes the paradoxical claim of conciliating the sentiment of unworthiness which is bound up with the very nature of the finite being who knows himself as finite, with unwavering faith or what elswhere I referred to as the experience of fullness. Hence the complex drama with many involutions which makes up the life of the believing soul. It is here that we can find the deep meaning of the idea of test or trial. Faith needs to triumph over the state of self-division which is bound up with the conditions of existence of a finite being.

All this must be examined more deeply. Fullness is perhaps in essence the feeling of *resource*. As regards others, the death of others for instance, we must not purely and simply detach ourselves from them (purely formal transcendence); we must hand them over, confide them. Here too there is a danger; that of facile or fatalistic resignation.

One's centre must be not in oneself but in God—outside of that there is no religion.

March 1st, 1920

Yesterday I had a conversation with J. about the death of his father and its strange beauty could not have been more striking.[1] That kind of death obviously looks as though it were willed. And side by side with it there are innumerable deaths that are meaningless, long agonies whose useless cruelty disconcerts our reason. Must we take it that there is always a justification—or that there never is? It seems hard to conceive a middle term. To say that

[1] M.B. . . . died in the pulpit immediately after a particularly fervent sermon.

there is never a justification is to take one's stand in the realm of objectivity. I am still convinced that an event is only significant for the man who lives it or for those who are in a state of communion with him and form with him a Church—however we interpret that word. But are they right, I may be asked, in attaching this particular *meaning* to this particular experience? But the question still is whether we have the right to take into consideration a reality in relation to which the interpretations we make of it must be judged to be 'purely contingent.' Here I come back to the central theme of my reflections in 1919. I already held then that from the standpoint of a thought 'in general' the question cannot even be asked; that it only arises for the individuality that has been re-created in and through faith.

March 17*th,* 1920

It seems to me obvious now that earlier in my effort to determine the real content of religious life I failed to attribute a big enough part to realism. For to believe means in some way to say: 'You will see that I was right; one day you will recognise that you are wrong.' In short, for the believer a certain type of verification is possible or at least is postulated. Otherwise we would end up with the *Palais de Sable*. We must simply say that this verification is certainly not within the reach of all indiscriminately. In this religious context it is probably absurd to speak of *normal conditions of experience*. It is here that we attain the deepest meaning of the idea of grace. These conditions of experience cannot be posited by us but only by God alone. Yes . . . but is this really clear?

May ɪst, 1920

My evolution in the direction of realism has obviously been much accentuated in the course of the last month though I cannot see exactly where it is leading. For I still feel that this realism is ambiguous. Yet I glimpse ahead the whole difficult and new work of re-thinking, beyond idealism, notions that we too easily took to be over and done with. A state of interior anarchy. I am no longer even capable of stating the problems.

July 3*rd,* 1920

. . . To judge God, as I have already said, is to judge my portion, my lot. What I would like to examine is the relation between the judgment on God and the judgment on self. They seem in no way to be the same. So little do I seem to be my lot or portion that I would not hesitate to declare in this or that given case that I *deserve better*. But reflection shows that this distinction between me and my lot is precarious as I have no quality which cannot be regarded as having fallen to me as my lot. For instance it is only in a merely empirical sense that I can distinguish between a datum and the use I make of it. What further complicates the question is that I am able to declare myself 'personally satisfied' and yet judge the universe to be in itself defective.

July 4th, 1920

Temptation and the impossibility of judging for others.

July 5th, 1920

I mean that when we ask ourselves questions about the *value* of the world we live in we inevitably think ourselves obliged to put ourselves in the position of other people and ask ourselves whether their world is acceptable to them. But I am only able to judge my own universe, if that. The universe of others is not given to me as datum and hence cannot be an object of my appreciation. Of course I am almost inevitably driven to put aside this difference between *their* world and *mine*. By and large I admit that, strictly speaking, we have the world in common; but all that I have the right to say is that under these or those given conditions life would not be tolerable for me. We can go on to ask whether under such different conditions I would still be myself, whether they would not be the source of new springs within me.

In short, every judgment expresses a particular selection; and yet it claims *to have value*. That is Bradley's paradox. But then . . .

July 9th, 1920

Perhaps the question of what I am *worth* is only legitimate when it is asked in detail and not globally—and the metaphysician when he asks it outside the sphere of the particular in which it has a meaning, is playing with words. For instance I may ask myself what services I am able to render in this or that domain —the value of my services being priced on a given market.

I can ask myself what is my possible output. But this question is not to be confounded with the question of *value* strictly speaking; no religion is possible save on condition that they are dissociated.[1]

October 21st, 1920

About the article on *Metaphysics and Psychism* on which I am working at this moment. I have reached the cardinal point: is *identification* in the 'spiritist' sense of the word possible? P. maintains that in any case it will always be possible to suppose that we are limited to reading into a determined past. But am I really able to attain an experience that is not contemporaneous with my own experience? The past of a contemporary, if I may so express it, is really 'attached' to his present—and his present can be 'translived' by me; but what if this experience is interrupted by death? I am fully aware that there is bound to be a contradiction even in my way of stating the question; but in what does it consist? Supposing that death is really the cessation of a determined experience; is that experience nevertheless still *accessible*? Can I still participate in it? Or recapitulate it in memory? It looks as though we can only recapitulate in memory what is *there*—and this part precisely is there no longer. Supposing it be maintained that it is only the instrument of normal actualisation, i.e. the body, that is no longer there? I am sure that this is meaningless. It cannot be maintained that this past survives its subject in the way in which a collection survives its proprietor. I *am* my past. If the subject is no longer there, the past as experience is no longer there either. Hence I think we are obliged to say that the clairvoyant or medium *really reascends the stream of time*. Here is an example: a medium begins talking to me about a departed friend and communicates to me, as coming from that friend, things I did not not know and which later I recognise to be accurate. According to the anti-spiritist interpretation the medium recalls with me (or in my place) the scene in which my friend and myself played a part; the medium *gets back to* the experience of my friend (at its point of junction with mine)

[1] I am fully aware that there is something at least apparently contradictory in these remarks. But I maintain that no religion is possible unless the global value of a being can be stated in a distinct way, and after all it is not certain that it can.

and then reascends it like a water-course. The scene which I recapitulate in memory is one and the same as the scene lived by him; the scene in my life, the scene in the life of the other person, are not incommunicable as the monadists claim; they are a unique scene which forms a knot of experiences and we can plunge into one as into the other. The past of my friend continues still to be attached to the actuality of my experience and this actuality is enough to enable his past to be recaptured.

October 23rd, 1920

I would like to achieve an exact statement of my metaphysical ideas on death, not because they are clear, but at least so as to establish the limits of my uncertainty.

Can we believe that death is the real cessation of personal life without implicitly recognising the truth of materialism?[1] It is a gross question and in certain aspects shocking and it is rarely stated frankly. To admit that this is the meaning of death is to suppose that the *normal* conditions in which a consciousness can communicate with other consciousnesses are the same as the conditions that permit it to communicate with itself; or again, that a consciousness only *exists* if it can communicate by means of messages with other consciousnesses. To say that a consciousness survives death is to suppose that these conditions are not the same. Yet the idea of a solitary after-life may well be unintelligible. For a consciousness to exist it is perhaps necessary that it should be in relation with others than itself. To be examined.

The problem of personal survival would thus seem bound up with the question of the possibility of communications which are distinct from those effected by way of messages.[2] But this condition though necessary would be *insufficient* to account for survival; for it would still remain to be seen whether X, this new mode of communication, were not *bound up* in some way with the normal modes of communication; in such a way that when they were abolished it would disappear in its turn. But stated in these terms the problem seems insoluble. For we would have to establish empirically that this mode of communication, X, subsists

[1] In practice there is a kind of idealism that is at one with dogmatic materialism; this is a disagreeable truth to which people prefer to shut their eyes.
[2] Thanks, I mean, to the transmission of a material element, whatsoever it be.

even when the habitual mode has been suppressed. But that is impossible. Whether or not I have recourse to an intermediary that is distinct from myself, the new communication which is established cannot be demonstrated to be independent of the existence of my organism (for instance, in the case of automatic writing, the apparent communication X which is established between me and an entity (?) may really be the result of the fact that I am in a certain relationship to myself which is conditioned by my organism.

It must be added that the value that we accord to communications which are effected by messages is bound up with the fact that we can verify their exactness through the normal means of information that we have at our disposal. Supposing we could conceive a world, a beyond, in which the relations of consciousness to consciousness were reduced to processes of partial identification and participation, that world would be the kingdom of the unverifiable. In last analysis even the distinction between beings would be abolished like the distinction between experiences; and the very notion of truth would lose its content. Thus if a beyond in this sense exists, we must either presume that communications by way of messages are still possible in it, or else that the beings who people it depend on 'mediums' to whom they must needs have recourse so as to actualise themselves and that they only become self-conscious in the measure in which they make use of this kind of 'mediation'. Is this second alternative thinkable? In practice it merges with the anti-spiritist's hypothesis. Thus, contrary to appearances, it seems indeed as if a real survival of consciousness is only conceivable if in the beyond communications by means of messages are still possible; in a word *if death does not involve disincarnation*.

But can it not be maintained that death, i.e. the destruction of the instrument which allows us to send and to receive messages, involves the pure and simple negation of a life that is only maintained thanks to that interchange of messages? To see whether this is really so we must re-examine with the greatest care the idea of the message itself. What is the relation between myself and the instrument that I make use of—i.e. my body? Obviously I do not restrict myself to *making use of* my body. There is a sense in which I *am* my body, whatever that may mean.

Note that communication by signs or symbols can only be effected on the basis of sensation and that sensation can in no way be compared with a message. Beings who did not feel one another, that is to say, did not grasp one another as affected, could not communicate in that way. And in consequence if death is not an absolute cessation it cannot be the pure and simple suppression of feeling itself; it can only mean a transformation in the *way* of feeling. If we admit this positive reality of death it becomes perfectly obvious that *death* can be compared to someone of whom we have ceased to know anything, someone who can give us no information about himself.

For an inquiry such as the one I am tackling here, it is essential to disentangle the exact meaning of the ambiguous formula: 'I am my body'. It can be seen straight away that *my* body is only *mine* inasmuch as, however confusedly, it is felt. The radical abolition of coenesthesia, supposing it were possible, would mean the destruction of my body in so far as it is mine. If I am my body this is in so far as I am a being that feels. It seems to me that we can be even more exact and say that I am my body in the measure in which my attention is brought to bear on my body *first of all*, that is to say before my attention can be fixed on any other object whatsoever. Thus the body would benefit from what I may be allowed to call an absolute priority.

I only *am* my body more absolutely than I am anything else because to be anything else whatsoever I need first of all to make use of my body (here we come back to the idea of the body being *interposed*).

From this standpoint the problem of death becomes clearer. Is it *absolute distraction* or does some mode of paying attention to the real still remain possible after the destruction of what I call my body? Yet does not this attention in question imply a centre —a point of application—in a word, a body?

I am jotting down the chance thoughts that occur to me. Perhaps at some given moment a way will open up. Is it not only inasmuch as it is not an idea, inasmuch as it is not thought as object that my body can function as instrument for me? My incapacity to carry out a habitual movement if I concentrate my attention on it would seem to bear out this remark.

All that we have so far gathered—and even that is not certain

—could be formulated as follows: I am my body (in the sense in which I *am* my ideas or my work) only in the measure in which I do not treat my body as an instrument. There seems to be room for a double relation between my body and myself, granting that the term relation fits here. But then a singular problem arises. If I can only exercise my attention through the medium of my body, it follows that my body is in some way unthinkable for me; for in last analysis the attention which is concentrated on my body presupposes it. Supposing it be maintained that what is true for my body is not true for the body of others. But it is obvious that I can treat myself as *him*, as someone else, and inversely.

The argument would thus amount to proving that my body is unthinkable, and that when I imagine I am thinking its destruction I am really thinking of the destruction of something else which is not my body, something that I substitute for my body. To posit the absolute priority of the body is to say that the mediation of the body is necessary for paying attention to anything whatever, hence for knowing it itself. But under such conditions how could the nature of this mediating function come within the grasp of attention and so be known?

Hence it follows that as soon as we posit the absolute priority of the body we make it unknowable, by withdrawing it from the world of objects. I return once more to this cardinal point. At bottom only three hypotheses are possible:

1. Either we deny the absolute priority of the body which amounts to saying that the attention can be exercised on any object without mediation.

2. Or else this priority is recognised, but then either (a) we admit that each time the attention is exercised something enters into play which cannot be conceived as object and which, in consequence, is not identical with what I habitually call my body; or (b) we posit that in principle this X and my body must be identical.

The first hypothesis, I think, must be immediately rejected as being incompatible with the structure of our universe. The alternative that I have just pointed out, stands.

October 24th, 1920

I am not at all sure about the soundness of the observations I made yesterday. This is the point I thought I had reached: if *I am my body* only means 'my body is an object of actual interest for me' we have nothing that can confer on my body a real priority in relation to other objects. This is not so if 'my body' is regarded as the necessary condition for an object to become a datum for my attention. But in that case the attention which is brought to bear on my body presupposes the exercise of this mediating element which itself falls outside the realm of the knowable. Only by an arbitrary step of the mind as in (b) can I identify the body-as-object with the body-as-mediator.

But what are we to think of the idea of a primary instrument of the attention (whether or not it coincides with what I habitually call my body)? From what I pointed out yesterday it emerges that no idea of a mediating principle by which the attention can be exercised is possible for me. But is that which can in no way be an object for me by that very fact incapable of being an object for anyone? Can we not conceive a type of organic structure and optics of the intellect that are different from ours so that from their standpoint the problem would collapse?

We must first of all delve deeper into the nature of the instrumental relation. Fundamentally it seems to me that every instrument is a means of extending or of strengthening a 'power' that we possess. This is just as true as regards a spade as regards a microphone. To say that these powers themselves are instruments would be merely playing with words; for we would need to determine what these powers themselves really prolong. There must always be some community of nature between the instrument and the instrumentalist. But if I look on my body as my instrument am I not yielding to a sort of unconscious illusion by which I give back to the soul the very powers which are merely prolonged by the mechanical dispositions to which I have reduced my body? It must be noted, moreover, that if I deny that the body is entirely thinkable, I am contesting that it can be treated as an instrument, since an instrument is essentially that of which an idea is possible, indeed that which is only possible through this idea of it.

Under such conditions the initial question changes its appearance. When I insisted on the necessity of a mediation for the attention to be concentrated on any object, had I not the impression that I was speaking of an instrument? And on the other hand when I said that, strictly speaking, I could not form an idea of that mediation, was I not implicitly denying that it was an instrument? I appear to be involved in a whole network of contradictions. All this should be taken up in detail.

If I think of my body as instrument I thereby attribute to the soul, whose tool it is, the potentialities which are actualised by means of this instrument. Nor is that all. I furthermore convert the soul into a body and in that way become involved in regression without end. To suppose on the other hand that I can become anything whatever, that is to say, that I can identify myself with anything whatever, by the minimum act of attention implied by an elementary sensation without the intervention of *any mediation whatsoever*, is to undermine the very foundations of spiritual life and pulverise the mind into purely successive acts. But I can no longer conceive this mediation as being of an instrumental order. I will therefore call it 'sympathetic mediation.' Is the idea of such mediation possible for an intelligence that is different from ours? Once again we need to make a roundabout approach. Instrumental mediation and sympathetic mediation seem to be bound up together and even unthinkable apart. But what exactly does their bond imply?

All that I can say from the standpoint which I have so far attained is that telepathy, for example, is doubtless only a particular case of a general mode of mediation which is alone capable of making instrumental mediation possible. But obviously we will not get an inch nearer the solution of the problem I have stated by interposing an unknown occult body between spiritual activity and the visible body. Moreover, the expression 'spiritual activity' does not satify me. Things must be considered on a higher level. To say that the attention cannot be exercised directly on an object is to refuse to regard the attention as an independent reality. Could we not say that attention is always attention to self and inversely that there is only self where there is attention? Besides it is quite clear that to pay attention to something is always to pay attention to oneself as a feeling being. Yet we need to grasp that this *self* still *falls short* of all objectivity. Here we come back to the criticism that I made earlier of formalistic doctrine of the ego (as object that has nothing objective about it, that is neither a *what* nor a *who*).

I am unable to appear to myself otherwise than as an attentive activity bound up with a certain '*this*' on which it is exercised and without which it would not be itself. But have I not said that no idea of this '*this*' is possible? Whereas must it not at every moment be a given *such*, that is to say, must it not be determined? (I would not like to insist here on the problem regarding time that we will come up against soon enough.) The *this* of which I am speaking is not an object, but the absolute condition for any object whatever to be given to me as datum. I wonder whether I would be betraying the thought I am trying to 'bring to birth' at this moment if I said that there is no attention save where there is at the same time a certain fundamental way of feeling that cannot in any way be converted into an object, that is in no way reduced to the Kantian *I think* (since this is not a universal form) and without which the personality is annihilated. To sum up, this fundamental sensation is confounded with attention to self (the self being no more than absolute immediacy treated as mediation).

But we must grasp clearly that this *Urgefühl* can in no way be felt, precisely because it is fundamental. For it could only be so in function of other sensations—but by that very fact it would lose its priority.[1] But is it not conceivable that for other beings placed on another plane, this fundamental quality can on the contrary be felt? . . .

When I re-read the bulk of the foregoing reflections I think I can see a 'hole' in my argument. Can I not be reproached for having taken as a sort of self-evident postulate that this fundamental quality cannot be identified with my body? Whereas I am really unable to identify the object and the condition of objectivisation.

Nor are we at the end of our difficulties. If my body is not to be indentified with this mediating quality, how does it happen that my body appears to me as being *more* than an object amongst other objects? I think the answer is that for sympathetic mediation to take place, there must also be instrumental mediation. Hence, for there to be a medium there must also be a knowable instrument—i.e. a body.

The kind of antinomy involved in all this is essentially bound

---

[1] The idea of an individual *a priori* of pure sensibility still seems to me to be a fundamental discovery (1925).

up with the very nature of personal life, because were all instrumental mediation lacking, we would be in the realm of pure
diversity, of that which cannot be grasped.

October 25th, 1920

Actually would I not be back at that immediate that cannot
be mediatised which I emphasised so much in my enquiries before
the war? But that immediate would at one and the same time be
absolute mediation and would only be non-mediatisable for
itself. I must admit that this is extremely obscure.

I feel more and more clearly the impossibility of making a
pronouncement on the nature of this mediation. And this is bound
to be the case, because strictly speaking we are unable to form
an *idea* of it. This morning I glimpsed that this *unfelt quality* or
fundamental feeling is capable of not being an absolute constant,
of being enriched and of growing in the course of experience. This
is very important but difficult to examine.

If I am asked what interpretation of the relations between
the soul and the body I have now reached, I must answer approxi-
mately as follows:

To begin with we must resolutely take our stand outside
dualism. There are two senses in which my body appears to me
myself as in a situation of privilege as regards other objects. On
the one hand it is presented to me as absolute instrument, on
the other as endowed with priority as regards feeling. The modi-
fications of which it is the site (or at least certain given modi-
fications) are the only ones that are experienced immediately.
But the instrumentalist interpretation is obviously incoherent.
And it still remains to be seen in what that of which I have
spoken consists. Can I maintain, as I have just said, that my body
is immediately imposed on my attention? Viewed in this light
the body could no longer be looked on as a universal instrument;
moreover, it becomes impossible to see how the attention could
be applied directly to any object whatsoever and why to one
given object rather than to another. Let us note that it can never
be the object as such that invites our attention, but only a defined
manner of feeling. But if someone says that the attention is
aroused by certain felt sensations? But what is this attention?
What gives it its unity? It is an abstraction. There could only be

spiritual life where a principle of real unity opposes the dispersal of particular 'states'. To posit this attention as being in itself *one* is to say nothing at all. So that we would be led to affirm that the attention is only exercised in an intermediary way by means of a definite intermediary quality which makes it be for itself and is incapable of being objective.

If at this point I am asked where consciousness in the strict sense is inserted, I answer that it goes without saying that I in no way claim that it comes into being. In reality we never at any moment lack consciousness. All that can be said here is that I cannot be conscious, save of something which is determined, and that *attention to oneself* can only be viewed as the condition of this consciousness.

Yet all this seems to be still insufficiently elucidated. It may be that a renewed analysis of the meaning that we should attribute to the question *what am I?* will enable us to make progress.

It is plain that there are no judgments of predication whose sum could constitute an answer to this question (moreover, the idea of sum here is meaningless). And there I think lies the justification (which, by the way, is entirely negative) of substantialist theories. I am still convinced that the nearer a being is to me spiritually (the less a being is a pure object for me) the less it can be *characterised*. The same applies to me inasmuch as I engage in spiritual commerce with myself. When this commerce is interrupted I become 'someone' for myself. Hence the existence of the self seems to be bound up with the impossibility of integral self-knowledge. But then *what am I*? Or rather, what exactly do I mean when I ask myself that question? I have said that *I am* the more my past the less I treat my past as a collection of events jotted in a notebook as possible answers to eventual questions. I *am* the more the less I look on myself as a tabulation or 'repertory'. But my recent reflections complicate the data of this problem in a singular way.

I am my past. Does not that mean that between my past experiences and my actual experience there is a relation of sympathy, but that this relation is closely bound up with the instrumental function of my body? (This is almost orthodox Bergsonism.) Is not this global experience which is me, but which far from being capable of being objectified is the condition of any possible objectivisation, the mediating element which alone allows the attention to bear on itself, that is to say, which alone allows it to be? And the impossibility of defining this *past-as-subject* which makes memory possible is only another way of expressing the impossibility of treating the mediating element as an object and of forming an idea of it.

It seems to me that I have made a considerable step by collating the very abstract results that I reached in these last few days with the concrete conclusions I came to previously. What I need to get clearer now is whether, as I have suggested, this immediate that is not mediatisable for me, can be a datum for somebody else. It is plain that if we take the expression *somebody else* literally this is an impossibility. Inasmuch as the somebody else is really somebody else he is only an object. As I have already pointed out, 'to see' into another is to recollect the other, even to become the other. Thus this past-as-subject which, as it is not an object, is nowhere, needs to be partially liberated and 'detailed.' But how can it be detailed for someone else? I visit a clairvoyant. She describes to me people about whom I was not thinking but who really played a part in my life. What happens? These people really form part of my past-as-subject and in some manner they are *me;* moreover, a kind of will-to-identification comes into play under different forms both in the clairvoyant and in me; were there no such harmony of wills doubtless nothing would happen. This past-as-subject does not change place nor does it pass into the clairvoyant—the clairvoyant allows herself to be made to participate in it or to be penetrated by it. It appears as though this past-as-subject sets itself free by the ways that are open to it—the clairvoyant's temporary 'disactualisation' puts her at its disposal. If this be the case there is no absolutely strict relation between the past-as-subject on the one hand and my body on the other. My body is only a possible instrument. . . . But we have no right to conclude from this that the complex attention-experience is independent of all material factors. On the contrary I incline to believe that where second sight occurs we must suppose the presence of a physical phenomenon which is not thinkable for us because it belongs to a type of organism which does not come within the scope of our mode of perception; a phenomenon which could nevertheless be perceived by beings endowed with sense-organs different from ours.

Can this be applied to the apparitions that sometimes occur at the moment of death? For the moment I leave aside the question of synchronism. It is important to note that, as any real transmission is impossible, there is no reason why the imposed image should *reflect* (?) the real scene. As I view things at present I am tempted to attach an extreme importance, for the explanation of the phenomenon of telepathy, to the fact that certain clairvoyants perceive around the consultant those 'beings' who are close to him. *A spiritual aura.* But supposing it be said that the 'beings' discerned by the clairvoyant are only 'ideas' drawn from the consciousness of the consultant? I answer that it is impossible that any extraction of an element from a collection can occur in this instance. The past-as-subject is the condition which makes the ideas possible. I admit that here I am on slippery ground. Broadly speaking I can still only see one capital fact. Those beings with whom life has associated me have a reality which is not objective in the strict sense of the term but which is not purely mental either—if by mental we understand *private*. And this X round which all my reflections since the day before yesterday have gravitated must needs be in close and indissoluble connection with these beings. But if I choose this path, will I not end up with the ideo-plastic theory? I still decline to subscribe to it. All that I can see is that X can only be grasped in correlation with felt presences which subsequently are converted into images. This complicates the 'spiritist' problem infinitely. For what are these 'presences'?

What I mean is that telepathy needs to be explained by the existence of connections which are analogous to the connections which allow the clairvoyant to see around me beings who have played a part in my life. This seems to me certain. Yet it is extremely difficult to define exactly. What is this relation?

To begin with, are these 'presences' the beings themselves? In time gone by I used to think that there was an ontological bond between a being and its idea. I am now sure that I was mistaken. But this *is not an* idea. So what then?

(Is the idea of a spiritual aura capable of more exact statement?)

Unless I am mistaken everything happens as though in particular circumstances I were capable of becoming conscious of the presence that is detected by the clairvoyant.

I think that in the past I was right to attach great importance to the rôle of invocation. But we must understand that invocation is a means of making ourselves present to him whom we invoke. The word 'means', moreover, is quite unsuitable. I must reflect further on this. At all events the invocation goes beyond the idea. It looks as though the appeal 'Abide with me' were converted into a *fiat*, into 'I will appear to you.' But what part does the approach of death play here?

Death, unless I am mistaken, is the abolition of the usual type of instrumental mediation, and also perhaps the priming of a new type of instrumental mediation. It seems certain that there is a link between the weakening of the instrumental function and the possibility given to the subject of manifesting himself elsewhere, or, in other words, *appearing*. Yet the metaphysical problem still stands. Of what order are these 'presences'? I think that the alternatives object *or* image (simple image) must be set aside. Perhaps these 'presences' are the projections of a reality analogous to the reality that I possess inasmuch as I am subject, and perhaps in consequence they must be posited on a metaphysical plane which is anterior to images. To 'see' would be to set oneself on this pre-objective plane on which I am in a real relationship with my spiritual aura or surrounding. Perhaps the latter is inevitably imagined in terms of my own personal system or images.

Is it not, perhaps, legitimate to symbolise these 'presences' or 'fundamental qualities' under the form of fluids? Does not this way of symbolising them answer to the instrumental aspect of pure sympathetic mediation?

October 26th, 1920

As I now see more and more clearly, the dilemma of 'real object or simple image' is unacceptable because my past inasmuch as it is object is neither the one nor the other. Suppose for an instant that a subject can be given as subject. In that event it is neither an object nor an image; moreover, we may mistake it, because it can only be given as datum seen through a layer of images, images that are doubtless familiar to the consultant.

Were this vesture and interposition lacking, how could it be recognisable or identifiable? It would be a merely abstract entity or a felt quality. It is, of course, possible that all feeling implies a presence that cannot be actualised, or at least a presence that is not actualised in practice. By this path we get back to the idea of feeling as real conjunction, feeling as extending beyond the private domain, beyond the *se ipsum*.

The reality of the beings that constitute the spiritual aura or surrounding would thus be of the type that belongs to the subjects as such—the subject coinciding with what I have called the mediating quality.

Nevertheless, I am in no way unaware of the deep obscurity of this hypothesis. In what sense can we say that these subjects actually exist? The clairvoyant discerns a given presence near me. But is this departed person now living? I wonder whether at this point I ought not to introduce conceptions whose origin goes back to my stay at Zernetz (1912). It is in no way certain, if I may so express it, that the coincidence, layer by layer, of the becoming of these subjects with my becoming is possible (cf. my notes of July 1st, 1919). In a word, it is manifest that I cannot conduct an interrogation about these subjects. The metaphysical separation that exists between them and me is as it were the counterpart or price paid for the intimacy of the bond that unites me with them. A person who gathers information takes his stand on the plane of objects; and *hence in this domain error must be the rule*.

I must admit that I myself have great difficulty in accepting such a complicated notion. Instead of admitting that the clairvoyant *reaches* (?) this order of subjects so as to convert the subjects into snapshot images, why not simply suppose that he evokes recollections that are familiar to the consultant? But it is important to grasp that a minimum hypothesis of this kind does not help to throw any light on premonition. Furthermore, I feel that the intelligence is forced to accept the idea that there is a connection between the type of unity involved in the telepathic relation and the type which is manifested by the 'spiritual aura'. We have here a group of views whose systematic value these days seems to me striking.

We need to ask whether prophetic vision does not imply the mediation of a subject who, because he is not placed on the same plane of time as we are, grasps as a whole what we can only grasp as detail. But is not this 'detailing' process necessary for action? Bergson.

To sum up. What attitude must I now adopt towards the 'spiritist' hypothesis? The problem takes on a new form if we suppose that the beyond is a world in which messages (instrumental mediations) are still possible; now I thought I saw that on the one hand no spiritual life is conceivable without attention, and on the other that attention invariably supposes a *this* which can only appear 'externally' as body. Yet this does not suppress the difficulties raised by the spiritist hypothesis—far from it. Nothing allows us to affirm outright that harmony—a communication—can be established between 'transmitting centres' of different orders. Here there is a *physical* problem which may be insoluble. On the other hand the durations do not seem to coincide; the presents are not *homochronous*; so that *a priori* we can conceive the need of a mediating organ (which would actually be the 'control' and would be placed at the intersection of the two durations). Nor is that all. It is impossible for us to make a pronouncement on the possibilities of the actualisation of memory of these hypothetical subjects. Doubtless the past cannot be detailed or tabulated for them as it can for us. Probably it is we who lend them an organ of actualisation which they can only use in a very fumbling and uncertain way. Under such conditions we can appreciate that the possibilities of error go beyond any assignable limit. . . .

The problem of criteria. It seems to me clear that in no given case can we be objectively certain that we are in the presence of a definite and determined personality; such certainty must always be subjective and uncommunicable. The idea of an objective certainty in a field like this is absurd, and is excluded by the very nature of the facts. Objective knowledge perforce endows either the medium or the consultant, or both, with mysterious potentialities in indefinite number. This is one of the penalties of knowledge, of the idea of objective knowledge. Rigorously speaking I do not think that there can be a technique of second sight, of prophecy or of necromancy. And about that for which there is no technique, *a fortiori* there can be no scientific knowledge.

How, in these circumstances, are we to define 'being a medium'? I think there is a sense in which each of us is a medium. Could not pure sensation itself be a form of 'being a medium'?

Late. I have glimpsed new ideas. Could not dreams and artistic creativeness be a sort of rehearsal for this *internal transmigration* to which I have reduced death? Moreover, does not the dream spontaneously become prophetical at a certain depth, when the sleeper sees or passes into a consciousness of another type, on another scale, and participates in its life, without entering into communication with it, without knowing *who it is,* and without even suspecting that it is outside the self?

October 27th, 1920

Several points to examine. To begin with, are the beings that make up what I have called my spiritual surrounding or aura conscious? Look into the meaning of this question.

This morning during the elementary explanations that I was giving to my pupils on the relations of the soul and the body, the problem of the instrument occurred to me again with renewed force. I am obliged to compare my brain with a keyboard on which an unlimited number of combinations can be carried out. Yet it would be absurd to say that it is no more than that. I must *be* the instrument. What are we to understand by that, if not that the instrument is given to me as datum in sensation? But what is immediately given to me falls short as it were of the instrumental relationship. Now if to perceive or to imagine anything whatever this instrumental action has to be exercised, then this immediate datum *cannot* become object, it must instead be the condition of all objectivisation.

I think that now I can see the meaning and bearing of the foregoing inquiries. We are concerned essentially with determining the metaphysical conditions of personal existence. As regards this, my remarks of the 23rd are of capital importance. A world of spirit in which the identification of beings were no longer possible, would be in itself contradiction.[1] It is essential for personalities to be able to identify one another. Without that they cease to exist for themselves. Hence, between them, messages or instrumental mediations must be possible, and this

[1] Unless this world were a unique consciousness.

excludes disincarnation in the strict sense. Yet the idea of instrumental mediation seems itself to involve contradictions, since the being is and is not its instrument, which goes to show that here we have a relative category and nothing more.

Now to ask oneself what are the conditions of personal life inevitably involves adopting both an ontological and a phenomenological standpoint. But it is first and foremost the phenomenological standpoint that I am adopting here. A being will never be able to appear to itself as a personality unless it appears as bound up with a body which it can regard as endowed with an absolute priority as regards all other objects, yet which it cannot therefore treat merely as instrument. The obscurity that surrounds the idea of 'relation to an organism' is thus involved in the very idea of absolute instrument. Now what am I to say from the purely metaphysical point of view regarding the conditions under which personal life is able to be realised? If the phenomenal unity of the person is bound up with the existence of a body, the real unity of the person only seems possible if we suppose an immediate that is not self-mediatisable, which I will call sensation or fundamental experience. It is obviously impossible to deduce the phenomenological conditions from the ontological conditions, since an object cannot be explained by speaking of something which by definition cannot be an object for us. To what extent should we emphasise the words: *'for us'*? This is the vital question. But we must clearly grasp that this immediate can only be apprehended as object where it is not at the same time the condition of objectivisation, that is to say, by beings whose power of apperception it does not mediatise. Yet I admit that this still seems to me rather obscure.

Perhaps there is something here analogous to what happens in the instance of any sensation. According to all appearances a colour in itself is a determined immediate which appears to me as object in virtue of the (unobjectifiable) power of mediation which allows me to apprehend anything whatever. But to other minds, even this power itself would appear as a quality, just as the 'fundamental distillation' of the flower is presented to me as a colour or a perfume. In this sense the metaphysical conditions of the possibility of the body would lie *in another world*.

Hence 'materialisation' in the technical sense of the word

appears to be theoretically possible, but the objective conditions on which it depends are of necessity indeterminable for us, just as are the conditions that govern the apparition of organised bodies. Why are we irresistibly inclined to believe that the personality depends on conditions that can be determined objectively? Is it not because objectivity as such excludes limits (space, time, causality: *unlimited*)?

I may be asked whether I am really doing anything more than resurrecting the idea of spiritual substance. But for me veritable substance consists in the object conceived as relation between diverse predicates. Now the *this* of which I have spoken (the non-mediatisable immediate) is nothing of the kind and can only function as object in a spiritual context that is foreign to our world.

I am perfectly willing to admit that this metaphysical argument gives me a feeling of uneasiness. Am I not running the risk of confounding what is thought and what is felt? Even if I admit that beings belonging to a world different from mine see me otherwise than as I see myself, does their sight permit them to explore my thought? Am I not becoming a victim of materialistic paralogisms?

Perhaps we must admit that to experience a sensation is really to become in some manner the thing sensed, and that a sort of temporary coalescence is established between beings situated on different planes of reality, and in consequence belonging to distinct worlds?

October 28*th*, 1920

From this standpoint what becomes of the general problem of sensation? I leave aside the epistemological question, that of knowing how sensation can be interpreted objectively. My concern is to examine whether sensation itself can be regarded as a message. It seems to me that the question is of the same order as that regarding the instrumental value of the body. Every message supposes a sensation. Sensation can no more be treated as a message than the body can be treated *simply* as an instrument.

That is, it would be meaningless to suppose that at the outset a certain quality is transcribed into movement—is transmitted, and then retranscribed. To feel is not to communicate, since all communication supposes a mode of feeling. But then if this initial act of feeling is really immediate, how comes it to look as if it were conditioned by mediations? And furthermore, how avoid comparing blindness to the interruption of a current or of a circuit? Sensation appears as though bound up with the normal functioning of an instrument.

Inasmuch as the body is an absolute instrument (or appears to be such) it must needs appear to be interposed between us and objects, and we are therefore convinced that it mediatises our apprehension of the objects; whereas in the only sense that is metaphysically valid, treating the body in this way involves a contradiction. Examine the consequences of this as regards sensation.

From the point of view of the mechanical world which is the world in which we act, the world in relation to which the body functions as instrument, sensation is bound inevitably to seem *emitted* and *transmitted*. Only, as I have long realised, this interposition is in some way illusory. Hence there is a sense in which sensation differs radically from any conceivable message. But from this new point of view sensation ceases to be defined in function of an object. To feel is not to receive but to participate in an immediate way. But personal life involves the impossibility of dissociating this immediate participation from the inevitable appearance of mediation and of communication. Hence the metaphysically unintelligible element in sensation.

We need to inquire whether these remarks throw a new light on volition and action. To act, it seems to me, is to emit a certain quantity of force, it is first and foremost to *exteriorise*. Such a definition is bound up with the instrumentalist view and involves the same contradictions. But it has its roots in the very nature of personal life. Hence its element of inevitability. If we went deeper into this we would get back to the idea of will as relaxation that I tried to extricate some time ago.

Possible transition to the theory of the *thou*. From the instrumentalist standpoint, other consciousnesses are bound to appear to be sources of information. Other consciousnesses are confounded—yet are not confounded—with their bodies. Show here how the *him* can become a *thou*. By a real association without which the spiritual aura or surrounding could not be made real.

Could not this association comprehend *even* things? Thus we would find the basis for psychometry; and the possibility of this association would depend on the double nature of sensation.

November 6th, 1920

I *am* my body; but I *am* also my habitual surrounding. This is demonstrated by the laceration, the division with myself that accompanies exile from my home (this is an order of experience that Proust has expressed incomparably). Am I my body in a more essential way than I am my habitual surrounding? If this question is answered in the negative, then death can only be a supreme exile, not an annihilation. This way of stating the problem may at first sight seem childish. But that, I think, is mistaken. We must take in their strictest interpretation words such as *belong to* (a town, a house, etc.): and the word *laceration*. It is as though *adhesions* are broken.

Can all this be defined more exactly? I can see clearly that the value of the copula (in I *am* my body) is uncertain. It has not the value here that it has in the judgment of predication (cf. my notes of January 23rd, 1919).

November 8th, 1920

There is a close relationship between *I am my body* and *I am my past*, for my body has registered all my former experiences. Of course here a distinction is obligatory.

November 9th, 1920

When I say that I am my body I mean that no relation of thing to thing (or even of being to being) can here be considered. I am not the master or the proprietor of the content of my body, etc. It follows that as soon as I treat my body as a thing, I exile myself in infinite degree: the negative justification of materialism; we end up with the following formula: 'My body is (an object), I am nothing'. The idealists can seek a refuge by saying that I am at least the act that posits the objective reality of my body. But is this more than a piece of sleight of hand? I am afraid not. Between any such idealism and materialism the difference is, so to speak, evanescent. Everything happens as though materialism were true—and the privilege of the act of feeling which is at the root of the affirmation *I am my body* and is its necessary foundation, is left aside. I am only my body in virtue of mysterious reasons which account for my continually feeling my body and because this feeling conditions for me all other feeling. But am I this feeling itself? This feeling seems bound up with real fluctuations that scarcely seem to me to be capable of bearing on anything save on the body's potential action, its instrumental value at a given moment. But if this is so my body is only felt inasmuch as it is me-as-acting: feeling is a function of acting. But in that case would not *I am my body* signify: 'I am a determined power of acting which apprehends itself as instrument, and at the same time grasps itself as alternately inhibited and favoured in its exercise by external conditions'? An 'energetic' interpretation of the body. Unfortunately nothing could be more ambiguous. For what is this power of acting? Nothing in this notion or pseudonotion accounts for the real unity implied in feeling (unity sometimes compromised and as often restored). And if we decide to say that I am a being to whom this power 'belongs', all the difficulties reappear.

Thus I believe that the formula can only be given a negative meaning: i.e., *it is not true to say* that I am not my body, that my body is exterior to a certain central reality of myself, for no truth regarding the relation binding this pseudo-reality with my body is possible.

November 18*th*, 1920

There is no problem of the relations between the soul and the body. I cannot confront myself with my body (as I must do when I think an object), and ask what it is in relation to me. If it is thought my body ceases to be mine.

In short I wonder whether, whereas a body is in itself an object, the body of *someone* does not become—for me who am trying to think it—my own body, and straightway therefore ceases to be thought.

Fundamentally what does to think 'someone else' mean? It means to set recollections and images in motion round a particular centre; but this may take the form of a rudimentary sketch, or it may, on the contrary, be a concrete evocation which extends beyond available information, and arouses an original flow of recollection and of the imagination: I set myself in a particular current and recollections begin to flow. This is only possible regarding beings that I have known. The more real my experience has been, the less the dissociation between soul and body is possible. What I have been given as datum is neither one nor the other (the importance of the evocation of a gesture, of an inflection in the voice, etc.). Whereas as soon as I am dealing not with the undivided experience of a *thou*, but with a total collection of information that I have gathered, I tend to think as a dualist.

November 30th, 1920

Yesterday I re-read part of my pre-war journal. I clearly see the problem that I set before myself at that time. An object as such, I said, is given as datum to a thought which sets aside the individual element in it. The object as such is defined as being independent of the characteristics that make me be this particular person and not another person. Thus *it is essential to the very nature of the object not to take* 'me' *into account*; if I think it as having regard to me, in that measure I cease to treat it as an object. The cogito is the affirmation of self as universal power of intellectual determination. Is God an object in the sense that I have just indicated? The dilemma that I rejected is, in last analysis, that we commonly suppose that if God is not an object, he is simply the conceptualised expression of a particular manner of being or of feeling which is properly *mine*. I endeavoured to show that this either-or ought to be rejected and that faith, though not an objective mode of apprehension, cannot therefore be reduced to a more personal disposition. Thus the question amounts to asking what is the nature of the subject in the *I believe*. Moreover, it must be clearly grasped that this impersonal thought which is the only foundation for objects cannot be constituted other than on the basis of *personal* consciousness. The inexpressible quality of immediate experience vanishes in the course of the dialectic by which the object is constituted. Is a dialectic of this kind possible here? To answer this question in the affirmative is to affirm that real judgments on God are possible. (We must never forget that true and false are qualifications which are essentially applied to an answer according to whether that answer is or is not usually accepted by judges who are taken to be perfectly competent.) To answer in the negative is not inevitably to say that God *is not*. All we need to do is to find out in what manner God can still be affirmed at this new stage.

I said that the object as such does not take me into account. And there we have the real answer to Bishop Berkeley's question: "What becomes of it in my absence?" It follows that invocation is made to someone who is in no measure thought of as an object. Invocation is made to *thee* and there the opposition between the *thou* and the object comes into full light.

If God is treated as a metaphysical *that* on which we make judgments that we expect to be in harmony with one another, the result is chaos. But is there any need for God to be either *that* or to be nothing? When formerly I wrote "No truth concerning God is possible," I really meant that he cannot be thought as *that*. But if this is so are we not thrown back into pure subjectivity? We can at least conceive that the mind is not obliged to accept this conclusion, for subjective means 'contingent in relation to object already posited;' and there we are concerned with thinking an order which transcends objectivity. If God is essentially a *thou*, for whom I exist, for whom I matter and who perhaps is only for me inasmuch as he wills to be, it is easy to understand that he is capable of not being for my neighbour.[1]

Hence we see why no demonstration of the existence of God is possible. There is no logical transition by which we can mount up to God from a starting point which is not God. If the ontological proof still stands it is because it is established in God at the outset—and in that measure it is suppressed as proof.

Formerly I tried to go much further and disentangle existence from a connection between the *I think* and the *God is*. But the whole of the terminology that I employed at that time must be modified.

December 1st, 1920

The idea of an absolute appeal or an absolute witness.

I cannot think God without thinking him as absolute appeal; and in saying this I emphasise the personal relationship between

---

[1] The ideal substitutions of subject for subject which make objective knowledge possible are strictly impossible here.

God and me to which Royce, for example, with his theory of the All-Knower, pays far too little attention. We can easily grasp why the idea of God (the term idea is inadequate) arises with such force in the tragic instance of the individual who cannot accept his solitude; whereas social life tends to obliterate it (it reappears once more as soon as the compact group to which the individual belongs seems to him to be threatened).

But how can this absolute appeal be declared between beings of whom either can legitimately say: 'I have only thee'? There is no reason here to bring in the intervention of divine impartiality (indeed, if I may so express it, God seems to me to be universally partial). For to judge impartially is to determine whethe a given predicate fits a given subject; it is the practical form of objectivity. In the eyes of the impartial judge I am a *him* and vice versa he is *him* for me. Now prayer precisely involves a refusal to think God as *him*. And in that way we can see the completeness of my dependence in relation to God; whereas when I am confronted by a *him* I posit myself to be relatively independent and detached. The divine judgment cannot be a subsumption; I am for God inasmuch as I am unique.[1]

Under these circumstances what becomes of the traditional opposition between the pure ego and the empirical ego? As I conceive things the thinking ego is not to be confounded with the idea of an intelligible order in general; it is an act, it is the central affirmation involved in every affirmation whatsoever. But it must be clearly grasped that we must not establish a difference of being *and* being, between on the one hand the pure ego and on the other the individuality defined in time and space that that ego apprehends itself as being. In no way can I be regarded as contingent in relation to myself. And, in the practical order, we cannot say that I have been unjustly treated nor can we make a distinction between me and the lot or portion life has brought to me. Of course I cannot help comparing my portion with that of other men and noticing that I am healthier than so-and-so, or poorer, and so on. But from the metaphysical point of view I need to elevate myself to a global view of myself, and there is no question of adding up and making an algebraic sum of my advantages and misfortunes. Self-disgust and boredom can poison a life that

[1] God only acts through particular wills.

seems to be of the happiest, or faith may illuminate the most wretched of destinies. I do not wish to say that for God who sees everything a balance is necessarily established between individual destinies—that would be to convert God into an equation. What I insist on emphasising here is that I cannot compare myself with anyone else. And for that reason I am in no condition to make any real appreciation of what I am or what I am worth. An evaluation bears only on abstractions.

But can we ascend from this criticism of the idea of lot or portion to the affirmation of God? In 1914 I tried to establish that as soon as I cease to treat my empirical destiny as a lot or portion attributed more or less arbitrarily to someone, I am led to recognise that I am willed by God. At first this seems a paradox—because it is the attribution itself that appears at first sight to imply the act of a higher will; but, as we see, that will would only be a law-maker's will, it would not be a creator's will. The real difficulty lies elsewhere. Are we not in danger of falling into a crude naturalistic theory whereby the ego that is not distinct from its lot or portion can only be an object and the outcome of the inevitable course of things? The hill that is worn away by the waters is confounded with its destiny; do I resemble it? It must be answered that I can only think this if I treat all reality as being in the *third person* in relation to the kind of community that I form with myself. But in this measure I am incapable of avoiding judging reality—and of avoiding judging it in relation to me myself. The appeal here is to myself (a certain idea of my due, of my rights). Naturalism is possible, it is a perpetual temptation of the mind; but when I think as a naturalist I destroy myself as individuality.

I also need to show that the idea of an absolute appeal or recourse is in function of faith, for faith is rigorously opposed to criticism as such.

In what way can God answer prayer? Nothing is more foreign to genuine religious life than the additions and *maximal* problems that Leibnitz makes his calculating God invent and resolve.

For a long time I have seen clearly that the 'action' of prayer cannot be objective—that is to say verifiable. It would be contradictory to allow that a mind placed in so-called normal conditions of observation would be able to recognise the effect of prayer. Yet we need to safeguard the reality of the action of prayer and of its effect unless we are prepared to see religious life reduced to a game of subjective appearances.

It will be agreed without too much difficulty that prayer can transform 'the state of soul' of the person who prays; what will be contested is that prayer can have any action on an external reality. This at first sight appears logical. But I am convinced that after complete examination such a position is not tenable. To begin with what does the word external mean here? Any such exteriority is expressly denied in prayer—prayer is precisely a refusal to recognise it. Will it be objected that this *exteriority* is *real*? But, as can easily be seen, the meaning of these words is very obscure. They unquestionably conceal a very confused theory of realism. I would like to establish that if prayer can be efficacious for me it can also be efficacious for others, because I cannot pray for somebody else unless I am in the same relation with him as I am in with myself.

What if it be objected that prayer unleashes a definite force but that it is a force that can only operate . . . on the spot? But if it is a real force, how can I know the limits within which its action will be felt? Supposing it is argued that this force is one and the same as the act that unleashes it (auto-suggestion)? Even in this case it is impossible to determine in advance the sphere in which it will be manifested. In practice, as is obvious, auto-suggestion can be converted into a power of external suggestion. It seems that my previous reflections on the metaphysical foundations of telepathy allow me to set aside the realist objection that I have just mentioned. At the basis of prayer there is a will to union with my fellows—without that, prayer would lack all religious value.

December 2nd, 1920

But the principal difficulty still stands. As soon as I begin interpreting the outcome I seem to move into the sphere of the arbitrary; it is difficult for us not to believe in the possibility of truth regarding whether or not my prayer has been heard. I have always maintained that we must be careful not to treat interpretation in this field as contingent in relation to facts, to truths that can be stated. . . .

If I ask myself what in practice is God's attitude regarding my prayer I convert my prayer into an object and I set myself outside the sphere of invocation. If I ask myself whether my prayer has in fact been heard it is no longer of a *prayer* that I am thinking—I am only thinking of a step I have taken with regard to some kind of power. As I expressed it before, when we speak of God it is not of God that we are speaking. To suppose that it could be otherwise is to come down to the crude idea that it is possible to keep accounts with God. In a word, under no circumstances can prayer be treated as a means about which we can interrogate ourselves retrospectively or whose efficacy we can question. Pragmatism in this field is the very negation of religion. This consideration involves other consequences that are very important. To pray implies a refusal to treat the present situation as a case that is capable of occurring a second time, for which we can once more use the same means if they have already proved their efficacy. Religious thought is only exercised on the present. For religious thought the present moment can never be resumed in a law of which it is merely one example. So prayer is renewal, it is so to speak an active negation of experience. Moreover, the religious soul *knows no precedents*. The religious soul is forever calling everything back into question; there is no such thing as an established possession—and this is only an indirect way of defining hope.[1]

But if we adopt this standpoint how can we safeguard the unity and continuity of religious life? And first and foremost how can we still speak of the divine will and of God's plan? The difficulty lies in this, that I cannot treat the divine will either as a *given* determined will (which would be in the *third person* for me) nor as an abstract order. It is *thy* will and in consequence it is not imposed; I can only submit myself to it freely, 'Thy will be done.' Yet it is obvious that if this will cannot appear to me as *determined*, as not necessarily coinciding with mine, it is no more than a seal that my fantasy affixes either to my own whim or to the event in question. Hence a criteriology of divine will would have to be possible. But this implies a contradiction: for

---

[1] It goes without saying that this is only a marginal attitude and that in practice prayer tends inevitably to be treated as a means. Between a certain kind of religion and a certain kind of sorcery, no rigid line of demarcation is possible.

there is only a criterion in the abstract; if we are given a particular category the question is whether a given case can enter into it. We set out from an abstract notion such as that of justice and we ask ourselves whether a particular case can be brought under this general heading, if a given way of willing can be called 'just'. Now any such interpretation is the very negation of God—indeed in practice it is implied by every atheistic theory. This is the real meaning of statements such as that 'the will of God cannot be sounded'. I admit that I am not sure that the problem I have just stated can be solved; because after the event I can neither hope to recognise what God willed nor—which amounts to the same thing—can I affirm globally that everything that happens is willed by him. Moreover, there is another problem here—the problem of quietism. How am I to avoid the temptation of pure abandonment to the divine will? Yet I feel confusedly that if I abandon myself entirely to God it is not to God that I am abandoning myself.

Hence there is still a great deal of obscurity. I feel inclined to think that we must not look on the idea of the divine will as a principle that is susceptible of determining our conduct. By this I mean that if I am confronted with a situation which forces me to choose between different possible paths it is meaningless to ask: 'Which is the way that God wishes me to take?' For that would imply the criteriology of which I have already spoken; a criteriology which is essential to ethics, but which is completely foreign to religion, because religion bears on being, on concrete and total individuality. This criteriology is as foreign to religion as it is to love. Prayer, which is at bottom the act by which I affirm myself to be dependent, is as essential to religion as autonomy is to morals. The idea of a moral objectivity is more or less modelled on the objectivity of knowing.[1]

I think I can see what we mean when we speak of 'praying to be enlightened'. Doubtless the enlightenment for which prayer appeals has no resemblance to the enlightenment which is derived from an enquiry or even from a chain of reflections. The condition of the heart from which prayer flows forth is unique for the

[1] Nowadays all this seems to me very obscure and questionable. In practice is not the believer constantly obliged to refer back to the idea that he forms of the divine will as considered in relation to himself and to his own individuality? What I wanted to say, I think, is that here we should substitute prayer for reflection. (Note of 1925.)

subject and unique for God: thus it calls for *inspiration*. At this point we see the full contrast between the moral order and the religious order.

What I have just said can be illustrated by the example of a conversion. I could add, moreover, that we can regard every predicament as a trial or test; for in practice it involves a temptation and a wager. Religious life is only for souls that know themselves to be threatened. To pray that I shall be enlightened is to pray to be so placed as to be able to see how the spiritual wager can be won.

December 3rd, 1920

. . . I do not think that Royce was right when he maintained that the idea of an omniscient and really existing thought is involved in every search after truth. It seems to me that he has not made sufficiently explicit the sense in which it is true to say that every question that is properly asked presupposes that an answer is, in actuality, already given. The nerve of his argument lies in the criticism of the idea of bare possibility. According to Royce it is not possible that the answer to our questions should only exist in the state of potentiality—because the potential supposes the actual. But my question is whether the very notion of answer inasmuch as it is answer must not be referred to a dialectical attitude of the mind. If that is so we only have the right to state that there really is something which is susceptible of being converted into an answer under particular conditions; we cannot say that the whole of this answer already exists as *such* for an omni-comprehensive prayer. (I believe furthermore that if an omni-comprehensive thought is conceivable it is on condition that it is situated, if I may so express it, on a plane on which dialectics disappear and there are no more questions and answers, either actual or potential. And I am not sure that this does not lead us back to the Kantian and post-Kantian notion of the intuitive understanding.)

An idea occurred to me this afternoon that may be important. Could we not say that any judgment of existence implies a deviation of the mind from the dialectical attitude that makes the affirmation of any object possible? This would enable us to see immediately why any existence is not a predicate;

because a predicate is always an answer, a dialectical element. We would also be able to appreciate that dialectics operate in the realm of pure hypothesis and fall short of the existential realm.

Long ago I realised that every existant must appear to me as prolonging my body in some direction or other—*my* body inasmuch as it is *mine*, that is to say, inasmuch as it is non-objective. In this sense my body is at one and the same time the prototype of an existant and in a still deeper sense a landmark for existants. The world *exists* in the measure in which I have relations with it which are of the same type as my relations with my own body— that is to say inasmuch as I am *incarnate*. I have already noted that it is incarnation that makes the dialectical standpoint possible. Dialectics which were not based on an experience which is not completely mediatisable would not even be dialectics. This brings me back to my reflections of last October. The non-instrumental mediation that I tried to define as being the condition of any sort of objectivity would thus be the secret spring of the existential judgment.

December 4th, 1920

Unless I am mistaken existence can only be sensed, as sensation is the mode in which the continuity of anything whatever with my body can be given to me as datum. This would give us a meta-physical foundation for 'sensism' which, within limits, is fully legitimate. Of course I would need to show why I cannot avoid thinking the world of existences as infinitely surpassing what is either felt actually or is susceptible of being felt by me. Do not dialectics introduce this infinity into our existential judgment? [Dialectics—Infinite—Relativity.]

December 7th, 1920

Glimpsed confusedly that—on the plane on which there are souls—events may possibly be ordered for souls inasmuch as they are souls. That would amount to saying that a soul would only be possible in the measure in which an order, defined up to a certain point in relation to that soul, were able to be mani-fested in events; furthermore the soul and the order would not be two separate things but one only. This would give us an explanation of the strange conformity between what we are and what happens to us.

December 9th, 1920

I am inclined to think that there can only be a body where there is the act of feeling, and for there to be this feeling the distinction between the *here* and *there* needs to cease to be rigid. The distinction is only valid on the instrumental plane. Now the body-as-instrument supposes a metaphysical body (the real kernel of the doubtless mythical notion of the 'fluid body'). Am I in process of discovering the ontological foundations of invocation? This must be looked into very carefully. (Because this particular road might in the end lead me to fetishism.)

These days I am very preoccupied with the phenomena of vision through solids yet I cannot manage to state the problem in satisfactory terms. I am convinced that the idea of sensation is still the key.

I must admit that what I can see at present is rather vague. In front of me I have a gummed-up letter. Normally I can only get to know its contents if I go through certain movements. In that case the 'sensation' is clearly in function of a determined instrumental activity. And even the idea of the *closed book* has reference to steps that it is possible for me to take. In a word, the order in accord with which objects are set out for us is relative to the activity of the body-as-instrument, but as soon as I cease to treat my body as an instrument the correlative order of objects is likewise transformed.

As example I take the clairvoyant who from a distance describes to me what is happening in my flat. Inasmuch as his vision is ordered in relation to his instrumental activity, it does not really differ from mine and it is subject to the same limitations. But here our task is on another plane and we need to understand how a *re-grouping* of the real is possible. We usually suppose that this re-grouping implies an objective change. To see what is happening in some particular place we imagine that we must go there, that is to say that we must put our instruments or registering apparatus *within reach*. In this way many occultists suppose that I have at my disposal a second body that I can send to represent me, a sort of messenger who makes the trip on my behalf and brings me the relevant information. But this seems to me absurd; and there is no reason why we should envisage such a hypothesis if we set out by recognising the relativity of the instrumental point of view.

At this point it would be worth while to re-examine Mill's definition so as to see what exactly it means. To say that matter is a permanent possibility of sensation is surely to suppose that it is a possibility of actions made by the body to which determined sensations normally correspond. The 'phenomenist' theory of knowledge is entirely dependent on the idea of this connection.

But this definition is obviously unsatisfactory. We cannot admit that existence should be defined as a mere possibility; moreover, the clairvoyant's vision seems bound up with the fact that there is a margin between existence and possibility—a margin that is deliberately ignored in rational foresight. Thus a re-grouping, which implies no change in the disposition of the 'elements', must somehow be possible. The clairvoyant has no need to act in order to see—on the contrary his vision is in function of his passivity just as much as my normal perception is in function of my activity. But on the other hand, unless I am mistaken, the structure of an acting being of necessity implies at least the ideal possibility of this kind of vision. Under what conditions can it occur? I can now see clearly that the future is the more apparent to a being the less that being is prisoner of his own activity and of his own value as instrument.[1] The world of time is no less completely disposed in relation to my instrumental activity than the world of space.

December 10th, 1920

In other words the 'disactualisation' of the clairvoyant is a partial 'disincarnation.' But to leave one's body means to cease *to make use of it*. I do not deceive myself about the obscurity of all

[1] I note in passing that in the field of psychology this also applies to the totality of the means, of the ideas, that I bring into operation so as to face up to a situation. There is a vigilant, active and tense attention which is the very antithesis of vision. The man who is on the watch sees nothing. I think that this is the only way to explain the mysterious gifts of certain naïve people (for instance of Dostoevsky).

this. Does the body nevertheless still condition vision? In that case it is still an instrument. If it does not condition vision, then the 'disincarnation' is defective—which is very mysterious if not unintelligible.

It may well be that the problem can be stated more clearly in terms of time. Simultaneity can only be thought in function of potential perception. What is happening at this moment in Pekin is what I would be able to perceive were I there; in this sense the idea of the present is in function of an instrumentalist representation of the self. When I say that vision is not perception I am saying precisely that it implies nothing of this kind.

December 15th, 1920

I come back to the notion of the divine will. I cannot think the divine will as a historical factor, but only as in relation with my *task*. I can conceive of a man like Paderewski being anxious to know whether it is God's will that Poland should survive. But it would be absurd for a foreign journalist to ask himself such a question because his attitude is purely critical and for him Poland is not 'my Poland.' I felt this before when I said that God can only be defined for real individuality and never for thought in general. The critic is only someone who claims to see clearly; he has no cause to defend. This links up, on a deeper level, with Royce's idea of loyalism. But though the notion of universal loyalism has an ethical value that is incontestable, I think it is foreign to religion.

We are still confronted with the same question. Am I able to discern whether God loves the cause I am serving? If an experience of divine adhesion or approval is possible, this must either be within the order of feeling—which is very fleeting and unsure —or else it must be reflected, and must presuppose a criteriology which seems to me illegitimate even in principle. To ask oneself 'what God thinks' is either to interrogate oneself about truth which is conceived impersonally, or else to convert God into *somebody* with whom I cannot see why I should necessarily agree. This only goes to prove that I am stating the problem badly, that the question is contradictory, and that prayer is not of this order. It can be shown that it is fundamentally absurd to 'try to put oneself in God's place', and yet that is just what the question 'What is God thinking?' implies.

December 17th, 1920

I return to the problem of the relations of time and action. I appear in my own eyes as contemporary with the things on which my action has a grip. At first sight this seems paradoxical. Is not my action conditioned by the mode in which I am inserted into time? Is not the fundamental datum—*my date?* But what do we mean by that?

The idea of *date* seems to me correlative with the idea of event. A date is a number attached to an event within a particular series. I have a date inasmuch as I treat myself as an event. But an event is not the same as a predicate; in principle an event is an external circumstance which plays its part in modifying the content of the life of a mind. Moreover, it needs to be represented by the person whose development it is to influence. A subject is not an event. I am tempted to anticipate a process of argument that I feel lies ahead and say: 'The event as such cannot be a datum given to a *vision.*'

January 30th, 1921

During the last few days I have been feeling strongly the need to define exactly what I mean by the notion of the absolute *thou.* I need to be on my guard against a possible mistake, that of attempting to enclose God within the circle of his relations with me. In reality to think God is also to think that it is not only I who count for him. But then there is the problem of how to avoid treating oneself as an element which God 'takes into account.' Fundamentally I am always up against the same problem.

April 11th, 1921

I have been re-reading my notes of December last on the question of existence. I think they suggest a whole world that needs exploring. Here are the essential points:

1. For me all existence is constructed on the model of and in prolongation of the existence of my body.

2. Unawares I insert into my notion of existing object that

which in my body (inasmuch as it is mine) transcends objectivity, that which does not derive from any dialectical process but itself makes dialectics possible.

3.   Thus between me and all that exists there is a relation (the word is quite inadequate) of the same type as the relation that unites me to my body; instrumental or objective mediation is completed by what I have called a non-instrumental mediation. This amounts to saying that my body *is in sympathy with things*.

4.   And in this way a certain mode of *vision* becomes possible.

In other words, I want to show that I am really *attached* to and really adhere to all that exists—to the universe which is my universe and whose centre is my body.

May 23rd, 1921

When I re-read my notes I observe that one of my usual methods of research consists in reasoning somewhat as follows: Admitting the hypothesis that this given phenomenon is real, what are the conditions under which it is able to be real? When I have determined those conditions by analysis do they not allow me to understand that which in practice is unintelligible in normal experience?

May 26th, 1921

At bottom my attitude to existence consists in maintaining that Berkeley's *esse est percipi* is only true on condition that by perception we understand not representation but a prolongation of the act by which I apprehend my body as mine. If *per impossibile* a radical discontinuity between my body and any part of the world whatsoever were conceivable, I cannot see by what right I could still maintain that that part exists. Is it possible to object that it is arbitrary to identify existence in general and existence that can be grasped by the senses? But this is a question —though a major one—of pure terminology. To say of an idea that it exists seems to me meaningless. Yet I cannot avoid thinking that what is mental exists. But perhaps this is the point at which we need to bring in the quasi-occult notions to which I had recourse earlier. I must suppose that what is mental for me is capable of being sensed by others. The necessity of making a criticism of the notion of the *senses*.

Is it not after all conceivable that an idea should exist as a perfume exists? But what if it be said that a perfume is material? That is nonsense. The whole Cartesian criticism of the secondary qualities needs to be taken up anew.

June 3rd, 1921

I now seem to be in a position to formulate my process of argument of last October in the following way: I can only pay attention to an object in the measure in which the object affects me in some way. This 'affection' that I feel is as it were the middle term, and if it be lacking I cannot even conceive the possibility of exercising attention. But this affection cannot be an object, otherwise we would get involved in an infinite regression. What follows from this regarding the body itself is obvious. The body appears at first sight as the supreme object of actual interest or as the privileged object which is interposed between me and all other objects. Yet if the body *is only an object* we need to re-establish between my attention and the body the modification of feeling, otherwise the body would not even be an object. But it may be said: This proves that the body must be sensed before it is an object. But what do we mean when we declare that the body must be sensed? It is here that the difficulties begin. For we want to know whether this sensation supposes that an instrument comes into action. Ought the body to be regarded as an instrument of which I am bound to *make use* so as to experience sensations, as I am bound to make use of a telephone if I want to 'ring someone up'? That is obviously absurd. I can only think my body as instrument on condition that I take for granted the —logically anterior—existence of a body that is not an instrument. So that from every point of view we are led to conceive a sensation which is not a message, an immediate that is presupposed by all mediation because this immediate, if I may so put it, is absolute mediation (that is to say, presence of the universe for everything that exists).

I admit that this interpretation involves a partial rehabilitation of substantialism; but its distinguishing feature is that it implies that we are not permitted to objectivise the fundamental quality. I only *am* inasmuch as this quality is not an object for me. Possible transition to the theory of love.

There is no denying the uneasiness I feel when I review this thesis. Does it not amount to attributing to myself an unspecifiable, that is to say contradictory, predicate? But this, I think, is only in appearance. For we must take care to notice that even the form of predication has no application here. We are really dealing with a particular kind of being that is given to itself as datum though it is nevertheless incapable of treating itself absolutely as object. There is thus nothing in it to be indicated.

This point becomes clear when we realise that the question *What am I?* cannot be converted into the question *What is he?* without becoming meaningless. This would not be so in an instance in which the question was about a predicate. In a word, it is of the essence of a being who acts and who apprehends himself as acting that he should be given to himself as datum in a special and immediate way, a way which mediatises everything in his experience that can assume the figuration of object.

Add to this that if we take the word history in its strictest sense it is not true to say that I am my history, that I can be reduced to the totality of the determinations that an all-knowing historian might attribute to me. This amounts to saying that the historian's point of view, if I may so express it, is eccentric as regards the real.

This obscure doctrine becomes a little clearer if we remember that my body is my present and that I cannot identify myself with this present without denying everything in me which makes me myself. But I do not transcend my present merely by thinking myself as a succession of presents, as history. Recently in a conference on music I said that there is a point at which all our past becomes feeling, and it is at that point that music takes its rise. To understand what this means we must refer to the idea of the past as it is felt. Considered globally that past is myself; it is my history as turned into feeling, (as interiorised in feeling—which is only possible beyond historical thought). Here there lies a field which is intermediate between the duration of the body and eternity and it may serve as a basis for a theory of prophecy.

I have been re-reading my notes on the spiritual aura or surrounding. There is no reason why we should accept the monadist theory that this substance-quality which conditions and centres my experience must essentially be isolated. Indeed there may well be reason to think that it is bound up with other substance-qualities, that it is pledged in a personal context which the normal conditions of experience do not allow to become explicit. Possible transposition of the communion of saints. The spiritual solitude to which the monadists refer is created for himself by the knowing subject.

December 8th, 1921

I would like to make an effort to clear up once and for all the ideas that I have been developing during the last year regarding the body and sensation. I am more and more convinced that the key to all problems lies here. To admit that the 'problem of sensation, or of the relations between the soul and the body' is unintelligible, would be purely and simply to throw up the sponge.

Usually we suppose:

(a) Either that sensation makes use of a personal code so as to translate something which in itself is a kind of commotion or vibration transmitted from one point in space to another,

(b) Or else that sensation is a real message which had to travel under a disguise so as to reach us and be deciphered by us.

Strictly speaking we cannot describe the first alternative as a message. What is given to me as a scent or as a colour is not a scent or a colour at the outset. With the second alternative it is otherwise. In view of the fact that verification is totally impossible many scientists and philosophers refuse to choose between these two alternatives. How can I 'leap out of what I am' so as to explore whether the *ignotum quid* which in me becomes sensation was already sensation before it penetrated into my universe? An idealist would go so far as to say that the question is meaningless. He would declare that 'as this universe is mental it cannot be compared to a region in space into which something can enter,' and so dispose of the question. But is this possible? I am afraid the argument is no more than a piece of logical conjuring. I breathe a scent and verify that it derives from the nearby flower-bed. Of course I agree that it is meaningless to say that the flower-bed is external to my consciousness. It is no more external than my body itself. But what are we to conclude from that? A physicist would say that a transmission of a wave of particular effluvia has taken place and that that transmission can be given a physical definition. Something has travelled between the flower-bed F and my body, B. I am perfectly capable of conceiving that some obstacle may be interposed between F and B which makes this journey impossible. It is usually supposed (a) that what is in itself only a physical event (the fact that certain particles emitted by F impinge on the olfactory nerve—or some analogous fact) is translated by me into terms of sensation. But some people (b) presume that at the origin of the transmission there is something analogous to that which is presented to my consciousness, so that we are really dealing with a sort of message that was first transcribed and then re-transcribed. But we must observe that the hypothesis that a first transcription occurred at the outset does nothing to render intelligible the re-transcription which, both in cases (a) and (b), I am admittedly obliged to perform myself. And it is very difficult to see why we are bound to think that the transcription and the re-transcription in question should be in exact correspondence with one another, as nothing obliges us to suppose that there are two instruments that at one and the same time function in an analogous and an inverse way. So let us leave (b) aside and set about examining whether the translation implied by (a) is really thinkable. What happens when I translate? To put it briefly I substitute one group of objective data for another group of objective data. Here, instead of objects we can speak of *instruments*. I make use of a certain instrument *in place* of another instrument (this can also be applied to a translation from one language into another or to a transposition of a piece of music for some other instrument). In other words I must substitute something which is given to me as datum or that I give to myself in some particular way for something which was given me in another way. But, as is obvious, nothing of this kind happens in the instance that concerns us here. For it is of the character of the physical event that it is not given to me as datum. It occurs on a plane that could be called infra-sensorial. Moreover, even if it were given to me as datum that could only be thanks to sensations for which the problem would arise anew. Hence, if my reasoning is correct, to treat sensation as translation is meaningless. Sensation is strictly immediate and can in no way be regarded as the interpretation of something which is other than itself. It is the basis of all interpretation and communication and thus it itself cannot be an interpretation or a communication. But it is obvious that I cannot speak of immediate sensation and of an object at one and the same time. The moment I refer the sensation to the object or treat it as a kind of emanation of the object I am no longer speaking strictly of sensation: I am outside the realm of the immediate. But action is only possible inasmuch as I succeed in defining objects, inasmuch, therefore, as I treat sensations as messages and do not trouble about the fact that it is radically absurd to consider them in that way. Thus I am inevitably led to look on sensation from two contradictory and incompatible points of view. In one way it is true to say that sensation is immediate, in another I am obliged to view it as a message that has been sent out and transmitted and is capable of being *received*. Yet it must be admitted that there is something disturbing about this antinomy. If visual sensations are immediate, how is blindness possible? Why does everything that happens suggest that messages are received if in reality they are not? If I block my ears, I do not hear what is said to me; how is that possible? In practice does not everything combine to suggest that the interpretation I am rejecting is the true one? Why then say that it is false?

I note to begin with that facts such as those that I have just mentioned are in no way unintelligible granted we interpret them correctly. There is no doubting that something ceases to be transmitted, that something is received. But the whole question is whether this something is sensation. 'That is of no importance,' I may be told. 'The failure of a particular physical event to take place is enough in its turn to prevent the sensation from taking place. This is enough to justify our affirming that sensation is in function of the physical event.' But I would like to observe that this kind of statement is very vague. From the fact that this particular sensation can only be experienced when the body adopts a given attitude or has a given disposition, can we conclude that sensation is really the translation of a physical event? Surely not. May we not maintain that a certain attitude of the body is necessary for the evocation of a given recollection without thereby affirming that the recollection is no more than a translation of a momentary arrangement of cells? Considered in themselves, sensations that are never actualised (or rather, *pure feelings*) cannot validly be referred to the body or treated as function of the body. Here we come back to what I said about the ambiguities concealed under the idea of *my body*. As I pointed out we have to choose between either treating the body as an object amongst other objects or else treating it as the mysterious condition of objectivity in general. Inasmuch as I treat my body as an object I am forced to deny it any privilege in relation to other objects. Only on this condition is it a datum.

February 1st, 1922

It seems to me clear that we cannot admit the radical pessimist's claim to penetrate an experience that is not his. We cannot agree that his opponent's resistance to his denials has nothing positive about it. Supposing he maintains that he is only being opposed by ignorance and half-voluntary lying—systematic blindness about the wretchedness that is universal? What does this mean save that he is contrasting the state of illusion in which his adversary lives with what he views as the veritable state of the universe; and that he considers this real state can be recognised by impartial inquiry? This is the heart of the question. What we need to know is whether the exact value of the world can be the object of an enquiry. I note, here, that the idea of 'exact value' must have reference to the idea of hierarchy and thus of an objective scale. The childishness of measuring out doses of pleasure and pain as Schopenhauer, Hartmann and their followers did is generally recognised. In last analysis pessimism can only be a philosophy of deception. It is thus essentially a polemical doctrine (whether the pessimist is fighting against himself or against X). It might be described as the philosophy of 'Well, after all, no!' In the measure in which systematic pessimism is confounded with radical atheism, as I do not hesitate to think it must be (that is, with the doctrine that the soul has no possible recourse or appeal), it can be viewed as a refutation of objective or empirical theism which teaches that the divine *is*. Indeed we can conceive of an ascending dialectic in which systematic pessimism prepares the way for immediate transition to a higher plane.

I note that I have just expressed myself in terms which fail to correspond to my thought. For does it not look as though I am saying that in reality *there is* appeal (thereby exposing myself to being asked 'Produce it!' and thence falling back anew into the radical atheist position)?

This fundamental question needs to be examined again.

February 2nd, 1922

Every time I find myself up against the impossibility of affirming the *existence* of the absolute recourse or appeal, I feel the same uneasiness. I cannot help asking myself whether I am merely dealing with an idea that *falls short* of existence. The basic question remains: how it is possible to conceive a *thou* which is not at the same time a *him*. It is very tempting to view this pure *thou* as a sort of illusory projection which—if I may so express it—has nothing to live on. On this point it is indispensable that I manage to explain myself; and for that purpose it would be impossible to overestimate the importance of what I wrote last April. There must be no question of enclosing God within the circle of his relations with me. God is such that, taken alone, I do not count for him. But here there are difficulties. Am I not in practice indirectly restoring to God that very objectivity that I considered could never be attributed to him? I have a confused feeling that the whole of my philosophy of invocation needs widening—that we must break out of the narrow framework in which I conceived it at the outset. Yet does not that involve a risk that I may deprive myself of the precious advantages that I owe to my strict way of stating the initial questions? All this needs a thorough examination and must be considered in close association with the ideas of object and of existence.

For more than a year (and in a confused way doubtless for much longer) I have been inclined to effect a radical dissociation between the ideas of existence and of objectivity. And it may well be that it is above all in the light of this that my former reflections on the body get their importance. Things exist for me in the measure in which I look upon them as prolongations of my body. But I only think them as objects in the measure in which I adopt the viewpoint of 'other people', of 'somebody or other,' and finally of 'nobody'. If now I lay claim to eliminate from this objective world all that 'comes from me' (and the expression is as equivocal as it could be) the upshot of it is that there only remains a network of abstractions to which, by reason of a singular illusion, I persist in attributing that existence which is *exclusive* of pure objectivity.

In short, it is necessary to tackle much more vigorously than heretofore the idea of a dummy-reality clothed in appearances by the subject—who himself is not aware that he is so clothing it. It seems to me that there must be a means of confuting once and for all the idea of a subject who in some way projects appearances on to a colourless and naked reality.

Thus it seems to me that in the measure in which we define objectivity by the universality of certain characteristics that can be recognised by any mind in good faith, we are tending to dissociate objectivity from existence as much as we possibly can or we are tending to *minimise* existence. It is not a question of cutting the roots that link objectivity with the basis of pure sensation on which it is constituted. Knowledge minimises its object. It tends increasingly to reduce it to a totality of formal arrangements bearing on pure symbols to which it is only possible to restore a content if contact is re-established with an experience which, inasmuch as it is experience, escapes from the very conditions of intelligibility that knowledge holds to be the only ones that are valid.

But it is obviously here that we should try to elucidate once and for all the obscure question of the relations between existence and invocation. Here my former reflections ease my task considerably. To invoke can never be reduced to 'to think of'. Something more or something other than an idea is needed here. Invocation is only possible if it presupposes the sentiment of 'community' (which is what I should call the ontological foundation of invocation); yet here there is a difficulty that perhaps I have not yet faced up to adequately. 'It is agreed', it may be argued, 'that invocation supposes this sentiment of community—but this sentiment may be an illusion. Your interpretation only has a phenomenological value. Nothing guarantees to us that there is a real community between the being who invokes and the being who is invoked.' Obviously the objection is worth examining closely.

It seems to me that it could be developed in the following way. Either the sentiment of community is fundamentally a belief which has an object distinct from itself, an object which is capable of being verified or rejected on empirical grounds; but then we ask whether this belief is verified in practice. Or else it suffices for itself and does not involve any verification; in which case it is an attitude of soul, an interior disposition and hence no ontological bearing can be ascribed to it.

A.   How could we conceive a way of verifying this community which would enable us to establish that it is real? We must not overlook the fact that verification always implies the idea of a *third party* (X: it is of the essence of the *third party* to be *no matter who*) and bears on an object. But here the intervention of a third party, of someone who verifies, is unthinkable. At this point I come back to the important and profound idea of the metaphysical value of the *secret* (the *secret* is only conceivable in a field in which a fact is modified as soon as it is known—in contradistinction to the world of objects where being known makes no difference).

But the difficulty still remains. For I seem perfectly capable of being mistaken about the degree of intimacy with another being which I have managed to attain. This needs elucidating, but it goes to prove that we are dealing here with more than a simple impression that is susceptible of being strongly felt (yet which falls short of the true and the false). This faith, this expectation may be mistaken—but only in the measure in which the *thou* remains a *him* about whom I reserve for myself the possibility of saying: 'Wretched fellow, he deceived me, he abused my confidence'. The possibility of doubt and, as I should express it, of future denunciation is directly bound up with the ambiguity of a relation of this kind. Now suppose we imagine that this ambiguity disappears, that the *thou* is only a *thou*: in that measure, doubt and denial become impossible, credit is no longer accorded with reservations about verification, it is open and unconditional. At this point we can see the indissoluble connection between faith and charity.

B.   Hence we seem obliged to conclude that acceptance of the second alternative is not bound up with rejection of the first.

It seems to me that these reflections throw a great deal of light on the veritable relation (the word *veritable*, by the way, is as inadequate as it could be) which unites the believer with God; yet there is still a danger of viewing this absolute *thou* as no more than a sort of ideal limit towards which all love tends inasmuch as it is purified and filtered, and all elements of egoism and disquiet are eliminated from it.[1]

This links up, moreover, with what I said about the object being a *third party* in relation to the conversation that I pursue with myself. And, strange to observe, I myself become this third party whenever I refuse to will, whenever I shrink into a sort of fatalism and pessimism regarding myself. ('I will never be able to —*he* will never be able to, I assure you.') I (A) hold a conversation with myself (B) about myself (C).

But now a new dilemma appears. Either this absolute *thou* is implied in some way analytically in the finite *thou*, or else it is empirical, but in that case it must be given as a datum: and what value can we attribute to a fact of that kind?

I know that I have come across this dilemma more than once already, but I should like to dispose of it once and for all.

It seems that we must reject at the outset the 'either-or' of the given and the conceived. This becomes quite clear if we consider the instance of love, which has no bearing on an idea, but even less on an empirical datum.

The absolute *thou* cannot be implied in an empirical *thou* because we can only speak of implication as regards characteristics, groups of characteristics or universals, and the absolute *thou* is nothing of this kind. As for the second alternative, what strikes me as outstanding about it is its extraordinary vagueness. Supposing I have met someone who has had a considerable influence on me and on my spiritual development. I imagine a rationalist would say to me: 'You cannot base yourself on the happy chance from which you have profited. There is nothing there that can be made universal because your neighbour has not had the same privilege.' And he will go on to ask: 'Is the discovery of God a chance benefit of this kind?' In a word the rationalist would like to see all minds in good faith attaining to religious certainty by following a prescribed method—while at the same time he considers that this is impossible. Thus he sets

[1] More emphasis than this should be put on the fact that the *he* is in some way in tension with the *me*. This is illustrated in familiar experience. For instance the experience of a traveller who has to wait at the ticket office while someone else counts endless change: 'But is that man there never going to finish!'

out from the postulate that God should be a truth (i.e. a truth as defined for X, for no matter what reflective *third person*). But the answer to this is that we are not concerned with a God of that kind. As for my reference to the discovery of God, there is need for clarification. We are told: 'It is immaterial whether or not this discovery of God has this or that value for the particular individual; the value does not belong to the individual in himself, it derives exclusively from the fact that he had such and such dispositions, it is due to a fortuitous conjunction. He does not look on it as fortuitous, but he is mistaken and it is I who am right.' This is a claim to see through a particular experience which the subject who has experienced it is incapable of interpreting correctly.

February 3rd, 1922

Put shortly, the rationalist argument seems to be as follows:

'You believe that this experience has been "sent" you by God; but that is a mistake.'

In other words the mystic is like the man who believes that a favour from which he has benefited was bestowed on him by a particular person whom he mistakes. But we must be careful here. When I imagine that a present has been given to me by a particular person, whereas really that is not the case, my mistake can be shown up (either by asking the person in question or by making some other inquiry). This obviously cannot happen here, for the reason I have already emphasised so often, i.e. that God cannot be *him* for me, and no inquiry on his way of behaving is possible. But will not my adversary conclude that if inquiry or verification is impossible, it is meaningless to say that it is *true* that God has revealed himself to the mystic? And hence are we not obliged to confess that we are dealing in mere appearances which fall short of the true and the false? I note immediately that the word 'appearances' is inadequate, because appearances only occur where there is reality, they only occur in relation to a possible truth. As for this *'falling short of the true and the false'*—why not say *'beyond the true and the false'*? What meaning can be attached to such pejorative expressions as these?

285

The serious objection that I examined at length in 1914 is that from this standpoint all experience runs the risk of being viewed as transcending the judgments that we claim to bring to bear on it. But I feel that I am better equipped than I was to face up to this objection. This transcendence can only be stated regarding an 'experience' which is legitimately reflected. Does not superstition inevitably convert God into a *him*, so that we are obliged to deal with false causal relations? I am inclined to think that all mystical 'experience' (I dislike this word) is beyond criticism— by its very essence it evades the grasp of the person who reflects it and thereby falsifies it; and I cannot see how my attitude can be condemned.

July 8th, 1922

Does the *thou* exist? It seems to me that the more I establish myself on the plane of the *thou*, the less the question of existence arises; yet is it not possible to *fall short of* the *him*, and be in a condition of pure infra-existential subjectivity? Actually I cannot help treating the 'fact of being *thou*' as the predicate of a *him*. But this could only be so if we needed to accept the Leibnizian either-or of subject or predicate; perhaps substantialism is merely the metaphysics of the *him*. Whereas the *thou* is to invocation what the object is to judgment, it cannot be disentangled from what must be considered to be its function without ceasing to be *thou*.

Inasmuch as I regard the *thou* as a *him* which is only accidentally *thou*, I postulate that the conditions that make invocation possible reside at one and the same time in *him* and in *me*. But humility consists in concentrating in *thee* all the reasons (improper term) for which *thou* art *thou* for me. In this way we exclude belief in my merits, or, if I may so express it, in their uplifting value, in the part they could play in the success that I am hoping to achieve. *Thou* wilt become more essentially *thou* for me, inasmuch as this idea of *success* appears less applicable and is less dependent on conditions that I have the 'good fortune' to attain. In this way we can define the possibility of progress in the realm of the *thou*; but is the absolute *thou* which transcends all existential questions anything more than an ideal limit? I must delve deeper into the meaning of the distinction between a *thou* which would *only* be a limit and a *thou* which would be *more than* a limit. I cannot say that the *thou* is *only* a limit without contrasting it with a real *thou* which is thought as *imaginary*; but to admit that this *thou* is not real, is to transform it into *him*. These abstract reflections seem to me extremely important. They cast a sidelight on the whole problem of atheism.

September 29th, 1922

As I have often said, the object is that which is thought as not taking me into account (even idealists recognise that everything occurs *as though* the realists were right). But the word *me* here does not mean my body; it is my desire (there is a fundamental agreement between scientific knowledge and an ethical system which is essentially stoical). Yet I can constrain things to take me into account in the measure in which I function as physical agent. My body is the indispensable mediator by which I can act on things, because it itself is homogeneous in relation to things. Yet the body itself takes *me* into account (e.g. an erotic image immediately entails a physical modification); in this measure it is not objective in the sense defined above. In this sense I depend on its interposition; it is in the measure that I depend on it that things depend on me; in a word a real potentiality is bound up with a 'non-knowing'; my knowledge is function of something which is its very negation.

September 30th, 1922

The impossibility of accounting for experience by positing as final the distinction between a subject and an object which the subject posits to be independent of it; and this situation is not bettered by thinking an *intelligible* unity at the heart of which this subject and this object posit one another and are face to face. Our need is for an irrational unity (a unity, even, that is in some way unthinkable).

October 16th, 1922

We must ask ourselves what is meant by saying that sensation is intelligible.

Define the realism involved in this common expression 'I really love so-and-so.'

Is my body in the *third person* for me?

October 17th, 1922

These, I think, must be the general lines of my book, at least of the introduction:

1.   No inquiry is possible regarding the nature of that which is primary in metaphysics. This impossibility is bound up at one and the same time with the essence of the inquiry, and with the spirit in which it inevitably has to be carried out. The inquirer sets himself aside. He effaces himself before the result he obtains. What is the result? An answer that is valid for anyone whatsoever.

2.   Get rid of the interpretation which converts metaphysical need into a sort of transcendental curiosity. Metaphysical need is a kind of appetite—the appetite for being. It aims at the possession of being by means of thought.

3.   A mind is metaphysical inasmuch as its position[1] in relation to the real appears to it to be fundamentally unacceptable. Here we must take the word *position* almost in its physical sense. A false position.

It is a matter of stiffening (establishing) or relaxing perhaps. Metaphysics *is* this stiffening (*redressement*) or relaxation. Only watch out against metaphors. We are not concerned with stiffening or establishing a 'self' that is mobile in the midst of a so-called immobile world.

Moreover, the idea of stiffening or 'redressing' can be equivocal. Are we only concerned with establishing a judgment? Rationalism attributes to philosophy a function of exorcism. This must be examined very closely.

October 18th, 1922

I need to recall the fact that the *cogito* only gives us access to a world at whose core judgments of existence in the strict sense become meaningless. This may perhaps lead back to the ultimate phase of Schelling's philosophy.

October 24th, 1922

I have reflected at length on the feeling of inner indigence that I am experiencing so cruelly. I still think that at these moments

---

[1] In this sense Platonism is the essence of philosophy.

being reaches its lowest ebb or ceases to offer resistance to itself. And this ebbing of the self seems to be bound up with the fact that all other persons are treated as others; the *thou* disappears; even the *I* sees itself as *him*. And I wonder whether we should not see a sort of transposed instinct of preservation in the fact—I have often observed it—that when a desire, however feeble, is born at such a moment, the whole of the self becomes attached to it. The desire, though weak in itself, swells with every breath and it is only when the *I* has once more obtained a grip over itself (through conversation, reading, etc.) that the desire is reduced to its original volume. A nostalgic state of the soul; it feels itself falling below its habitual level.

May not happiness be a form of *self-presence*. The more I am present to myself, the more others exist for me. This is an example of the interior undividedness to which I referred when writing of the will—it is that which makes the will possible. To will is to succeed in avoiding self-division before performing an action. If, before acting, I look on myself in *that* particular way, my act of will is over and done with. The most I will get out of myself will be a gesture that is disavowed by all that is deepest in me.

Is ill-will possible in the metaphysical sense of the word? In last analysis I think it is not. Will is in itself a good. An act is good inasmuch as it is willed. But are there any external signs by which we can know whether an act has been willed or not? We are obliged to deny this, I think, without any hesitation. And as regards myself, am I absolutely certain that I can state at the moment of acting that I will my action? This seems to me most uncertain. I must link this up with the problem of repentance. I should say (though it needs checking) that a being whose life is frittered away in the world of successive events can have no infallible consciousness of himself as willing—at least to the extent in which his life is thus dissipated. B. was surely right when he said that my theory of the will is a central point in my philosophy; this also needs very careful re-examination. I need to review the part dealing with the will as relaxation, as active negation of the *but*. And the connection that I have pointed out this evening between will and one's own self-presence is also very important. Utilise here all that I have said about the tension within the *him*. Recapitulate it in a perfectly concrete way. As

regards this I also need to look into my question of October 16th:
Is the body in the third person for me?

October 25th, 1922

We may ask whether the operation of the will is not fundamentally
bound up with the possession of a sort of grace. At least this constitutes a very serious difficulty, for it is not possible to see how
we can depend on the will to realise a state which the will presupposes so as to be able to be exercised. Yet we must take care
not to get entangled in abstractions and myths. Can I not adopt
an attitude which is analogous to the attitude of a being who
wills? And may it not well happen that this attitude is converted
into reality?

I take up once more what I wrote several days ago on the subject of metaphysical need. For doubtless this is a key. The
appetite for being is not a desire to acquire qualities nor a desire
for self-perfection; and this is the fundamental difference between
the ethical order and the metaphysical order. The metaphysician
is searching for what is, not what will be (on this point, cf.
Hegel's complaint about Fichte). I think I made use of an
excellent metaphor when I said that the metaphysician is like
a sick person who is trying to find a 'position.' The difficulty
obviously consists in identifying the centre in relation to which
this 'position' is to be defined. As long as I move amongst objects
the question does not arise. But in the instance in question, what
can the unvarying centre be?

The fundamental datum of all metaphysical reflection is that
I am a being who is not transparent to himself, that is to say,
my being is to me a mystery. It is only in moments of interior ebb
to which I referred yesterday that I cease to apprehend myself
in this way.[1]

This afternoon I was reflecting on the relation between my
being and my task. Whatever its character, my task does not
exhaust my being. It does not provide me with a justification of
myself which can satisfy me totally. It must furthermore be

---

[1] It seems to me that interior indigence always implies the exercise of reflection in the
void: I am not this particular state, and hence this state is at bottom nothing. But I
am not anything else either; hence there only *is* this particular state which itself is
nothing. The formula of theoretical despair and pessimism is a forefeeling that there
is no appeal or recourse.

admitted perhaps that I have in me the wherewithal for transcending all possible justification. Nor can I look on others as simple agents, each with his task to accomplish, so that once their task is accomplished they have only to disappear. The more a being is *thou* for me, the less I am tempted to confound him with his task.

What I have said regarding parts or portions applies almost exactly to tasks. I am not qualified to ask myself how the existence of others is justified. But it must be noted that it is only inasmuch as I try in practice to justify myself that I can become conscious of the reality within me which surpasses all justification; this reality does not fall short of my act, it is beyond it. In that way we come back to the tragic and Christian view of life. Something is endangered from the very beginning of my existence, but this something is also capable of being saved, and it only *will be* on condition that it has been saved. This something or this reality is only an object of faith: it is my soul.

Nothing is more radically opposed to the infinite subjectivity of post-Kantian philosophers than the idea of a wager and of salvation. It is very difficult to define this wager for it is neither a timeless value nor a phenomenal content.

It seems to me, though I may be mistaken, that here we can make use of the idea of one's self-presence that I tried to unravel yesterday. We must be very careful to avoid conceiving this idea of an internal bond as a logical unity, for that would threaten to destroy the living relation between two beings, the *community* or intimacy. If we could conceive the soul as a being married to itself (this expression is apparently to be found in Lavelle's thesis but I am not sure in what context) or even as an interior city, then ideas such as those of wager, or trial, etc. would attain their full meaning. But obviously the critical conception of consciousness as the unity of the subject and of the object will not help our progress in this direction; only if we resolutely turn to ontology can we glimpse the possibility of this interpretation.

(I was wondering this afternoon whether we ought not to posit the unity of the will and of inspiration and suppose that the difference between them is only phenomenological; that is to say that this difference only has bearing on the way in which will and inspiration are data given to consciousness.)

It might be as well to show why, in concrete experience, the idea of consciousness as unity of subject and object is inadequate.

October 28th, 1922

I feel that here there is a knot or tangle of thoughts that needs to be successfully untied.

I seem to see at the centre of my metaphysics of spontaneity the metaphor of a mobile mirror set against something opaque. This mirror habitually reflects objects but owing to its mobility it is also able to reflect at least partially that which supports it. Thus the knowing subject can in some way become an object for himself. As is easy to see this way of representing the subject is absurd. To what extent is what I know still myself? What is the meaning of the supposition of the majority of philosophers that that which knows is identical with that which is known? This last postulate is probably connected with the materialistic image of a mirror attached to a wall. Here the idea of the body may function as principle of identification.

The idea that only like can know like has certainly played an essential part in the history of epistemology since Plato; and realism largely consists in a protest against this affirmation. I must admit that on this point all my sympathy goes to the realists. At the root of the idealist thesis there may be a confusion which I have not yet been able to define successfully.

October 31st, 1922

I am still thinking about my introduction—it might perhaps be called *Metaphysics and Reality*. Development of my notes of a fortnight ago. As an enquiry is impossible, it follows that a metaphysical hypothesis is likewise impossible; and this needs examining more closely. But why should an enquiry be impossible? Because it implies the subordination of thought to an object of research, that is to say the very attitude from which the metaphysician has managed to break away. In a phrase it seems that metaphysical uneasiness can be interpreted in terms of the refusal to make an abdication, the object being precisely that before which I abdicate.

From this point of view even the idea of a metaphysical problem seems rather equivocal. At this point it will be useful to turn back and examine carefully the notion of problem so as to see to what extent it has any meaning here.

But obviously this is only intelligible if we suppose that metaphysical inquiry is directed to the pure immediate (which falls short of the hypothetical[1]); irrespective of whether it attains a new reality beyond the hypothetical or whether the infra- and supra-hypothetical orders meet and are merged together.

Along such lines we obviously need to re-examine the obscure idea of 'redressment' or 'establishment' that I noted a fortnight ago.

November 2nd, 1922

Perhaps the best we could do would be to define the nature of metaphysical uneasiness[2] in relation to the problem of time and space. Here we come back I think to the reflections I made long ago on the strictly contingent character of the *here* and *now* with which consciousness, when it reflects, appears to itself as bound up. If we set out by positing a sort of equivalence of all moments of time and of all places in space, I am bound to consider insoluble the question of why I am inserted at this point rather than any other. My thought, which appears to itself as legitimately comprehending all successions and all spatial simultaneities, revolts against recognising that it belongs to a given time and space. Perhaps we could set out from here to define 'redressment' or 'establishment'. Yet I am not sure of this. Our problem in a phrase is that of the inadequate relation of the content of the ego to the form of the ego—the form is universal, the content particular. It is very interesting to note—I think I have already made this observation—that it leads us back to my theory of the lot or portion, or rather the idea of the practical impossibility of separating the person from his lot. Certainly the dualism that I have just stated is bound up with the image we form of an infinity of rôles and the inability to understand why I have been allotted one rather than any other. Why am I not a Russian musician, a Portuguese usurer, or a negro from Lake Tchad?

[1] Show the intimate bond between the notions of object and hypothesis. On this point Alain is quite simply *right*.

[2] At all events it is important to show at the outset that metaphysics always claims to be the satisfaction of an uneasiness, whereas scientific knowledge is quite different and there is no such thing as scientific uneasiness.

In other words I end up with a datum that cannot be reduced.

To express it briefly, it is meaningless to treat the spatial and temporal qualifications of my experience as a distinct fact into the cause of which we can probe. Yet this is not absolutely clear.

November 3rd, 1922

In the *Exposé du Véritable Empirisme de Schelling* I came across the profound observation that the philosopher's first task is to define the true fact (*die wahre Tatsache*) and that nothing could be less immediate than this. From my standpoint, this point is cardinal. The idea of 'redressment' 'establishment' round which my reflections have been gravitating for some time is obviously an effort to substitute an authentic fact for the appearance of a fact. Yesterday I was wondering up to what point it is possible to deny experience. Denial here would mean rejection. In this sense certain dreams can be denied or rejected. They can be effaced. May our experience not be to reality what dreams are to our experience? The impossibility of treating my experience as a *ground-plot* or as an absolute landmark. This is very important. Am I not able with certainty to discriminate within the heart of my experience, between what matters, what has an interior echo, and what is insignificant? We need to react wholeheartedly against the tendency to think that the fact that a thing 'takes place' confers reality on it.

One objection is obvious. Such discrimination—which can only be an evaluation—is purely subjective. We need to reflect on the real bearing of this objection, on the postulate that what happens (inasmuch as happening) has a sort of reality that is fundamental and universal and in opposition to the contingent evaluations to which we would submit it. Show that this postulate is bound up with a causal representation of phenomena, a chain whose links are homogeneous in relation to one another. Here we have statements that stand together.

November 4th, 1922

Once more I feel constrained to reflect on what 'to happen' means. Factual realism is not a tenable position. The fact is no more than a particular construction built on the foundation of the datum. It extends on all sides beyond the limits that we arbitrarily assign to it (this can be shown if we take as example my meeting with someone, which is destined to have distant repercussions. The encounter itself only consists in a moment of proximity. As usual we will treat as a fact what in reality is a complex). It would be a complete illusion to believe that this construction is less real than the data on which it is built. Moreover, it is important to notice that by a further illusion we extrapolate the judgment of reality by bringing it to bear on what falls short of strictly objective experience. This is rather important. Is there no means of establishing that at the root of this belief in things 'which happen' there lies a whole system of metaphors by which we are taken in and duped—and that it is the business of metaphysical reflection to deliver us from these metaphors? But that should be done without getting lost in an abstract philosophy.

February 20*th*, 1923

I think that the Christian idea of the infinite value of souls is fundamentally no more than the negation of the belief in a price, in a tariff-rate that can be applied to persons. Of course we admit quite spontaneously that a person has no commercial value (even when we transpose the meaning of those words), but we do not see clearly all that this implies. If persons themselves *have no value* what is valuable in them? Is it their qualities?

February 21*st*, 1923

As soon as we think of 'merits' we posit that they can be in some way priced. But these merits are thought to be merits of some particular person, and it is here that the uncertainties begin; how are we to conceive the *inherence* of merit in the person? What further complicates the question is the obscure idea of a merit as a quality that the subject confers on himself (this is a flagrantly vicious circle, since merit consists less in the results of effort than in effort itself). We must recognise the inconsistency that lies in the phrase 'it all depends on you . . . ', or if we wish it to have a meaning we should at least provide a coherent definition of the relation which unites a person and his qualities.

February 23*rd*, 1923

Once again I feel like someone who is vainly trying to open a door, or even like someone trying to discover what door to open.

Have I been abusing such formulae as: 'I am a being to whom his being itself appears as a mystery'? Is there not a risk that the idea of mystery, like that of the *thou*, will become a stop-gap? The distinction between problem and mystery needs more elucidation than I have provided. In my notes of January 1919 I am afraid I went too far in sacrificing the notion of divine transcendence.

February 26th, 1923

The fundamental objection that my work may have to face could be formulated as follows: 'You struggle to find in the very structure of the real a justification for particular proceedings in human thought. But are you sure that your attitude is legitimate? May it not well be that these proceedings are explained by practical conditions (of psychology, sociology, etc.) to which the human being is submitted?'

This objection presupposes that there is a radical distinction between the strict facts of experience and what is only a simple state of mind, a subjective 'disposition.' As scientific knowledge is able to get a grip on certain strata of the real, it is legitimate to ask what assures it its power of apprehension and its validity. In other words, the critical problem is only stated within the limits of what is recognised as objective.[1] But how find common ground between prayer, for instance, and some experimental operation whose effects we try to make intelligible?

We would have to begin by establishing that prayer can be useful.

Unfortunately, were we able to make a list of efficacious prayers and prayers said in vain, were it possible to determine in a statistical way the cases in which praying would be worth while and those in which 'it would be wasting time,' that would be the end of prayer as prayer. Belief in prayer implies the absolute negation of any such experiment. Were I to say: 'In this case it would be a waste of time' I would immediately be taking my stand outside the sphere of religious life. And this would also apply were I to adopt the attitude of a sick man who in despair sends for a charlatan on the grounds that nothing is lost by trying and that 'anyway there is a chance that it might work.' The sick

[1] I have in mind the disciples of Hume for whom epistemology is impossible in itself.

man in question wagers on ignorance regarding the terms of life and death and says to himself that after all the charlatan 'may do the trick.' In a word he is dominated by the idea of 'groping his way' through. Everybody 'gropes his way' and there is no reason why the charlatan should not be 'luckier' than some high priest of the medical world. As is easy to see, this sceptical way of reasoning really implies belief in the possibility of a rational technique to which mankind has not yet attained. When a sick man has lost all confidence in medicine he may think of religion as a means of getting out of the difficulty 'in case there is another world': religion considered as a system of precautions that it is better not to neglect, in case . . . etc. Against any such conception as this the objection I mentioned above certainly has its point. If religious practices are conceived of as means that permit the realisation of certain ends, the first question that obviously arises is whether they are really efficacious means. In a similar way it is only possible to ask about the metaphysical foundations for magic if magic is objective, i.e. if there is a magical experience. I note by the way that it is impossible to determine *a priori* what are or ought to be the characteristics of this experience; and furthermore that even if there is such a thing as a technique of magic, it is by no means certain that that technique can be interpreted or defined in logical terms. It may well be that the personality of the magician, or the powers of which he is possibly the agent, operate according to modalities whose conceptual equivalent we are in no position to discover. It goes without saying, moreover, that if there is no such thing as magical experience we have no ground for asking any questions about it save how the belief in magical experience has actually been able to develop.

In other words are we obliged to admit the following dilemma?—

Either there is such a thing as religious experience, and hence it is legitimate to ask how it is possible; but it is to be feared that this experience is only the sublimation of magical experience, and it is at the least doubtful whether on this ground the fundamental religious values can be safeguarded.

Or else we must agree that there is no such thing as religious experience; we remain in the order of *as if*, in the sphere of states of mind; supposing that spiritual values can be maintained from that standpoint, we must resign ourselves to viewing these values as no more than ideal expressions of personal life understood in a narrowly subjective way.

All my efforts are aimed at the rejection of this dilemma. But the problem still stands: are there grounds for supposing that my work only consists in rationalising contingent data that I find 'in myself?' This question in its turn presupposes the either-or of factual data or universal data. But what is their opposition worth?

To continue. Supposing that I recognise in myself the idea, the need of an *absolute appeal or recourse*. I will inevitably be asked whether I think of this idea or need as bound up with the nature of consciousness in general. Indeed we are always falling back on to the *Uberhaupt*. But even if we admit that this question has a meaning, why attribute ontological pre-eminence to such *Voraussetzungen?* Upon reflection do we not find that what really happens is that we transpose into another domain habits of thought borrowed from daily life, in which we are obliged to write out reports . . . the contracting parties agreeing to recognise, etc? But when we pass from this sphere into the sphere of theoretical knowledge have we any justification for the idea that the chances of error are greater from the moment at which we are no longer in agreement? If we do so it is because at bottom we are obsessed with the idea of perception as opposed to hallucination (e.g. the report of a psychical séance which on principle only *retains* that which all the spectators have seen). But if we take our stand on *inspiration* the problem changes its aspect.

It must never be forgotten that if the superiority of scientific knowledge consists in the fact that it is *for everybody*,[1] that superiority is bought at a very high metaphysical price. Scientific knowledge is only for everybody because it is, strictly speaking, for nobody.

There is a radical opposition between my knowledge—which is by essence capable of being transmitted, capable of being detached from the particular context in which it is involved—and a special experience of sentiment which is by essence incapable of transmission. What are we to say regarding the latter?

[1] Moreover we need to inquire whether a minute examination of the conditions of scientific investigation would not cause this impressive universality partially to vanish. All that can be said is that the result here obtains universally.

At first sight goods that cannot be transmitted seem so heterogeneous in comparison with communicable goods that the mind revolts at comparing one with the other. On the one side there are 'truths' and references, on the other a kind of data about whose nature it is not easy to make a statement. About some particular person I have a collection of information that I can convey to whomsoever I like because it is not attached to me. On the other hand, in relation to that person, I occupy a peculiar position that is not strictly definable—it is less definable the more essentially it is bound up with what I am. Of course I can say 'I am the friend of so-and-so,' that is to say I can express this relation under a universal form that is capable of being transmitted—but to this extent I take my stand apart from 'us'. Yet a metaphysics of the true can scarcely go beyond the schematic formula: Peter and Paul are friends.[1]

February 27th, 1923

It is impossible to reflect on myself without becoming aware of these goods that are not transmissible. It is also impossible to make out a list of them and range them next to one another; it is as though they permeated one another. The house in which I have lived with the people that I love is, so to speak, impregnated with the very quality of that affection. If this quality is not me, at least it cannot in any way be dissociated from me. Can it be converted into a 'content of thought?' No, I think it is, strictly speaking, inexpressible. We can only allude to it. If it can be sensed it is only by a sort of magic analogous to the magic of the poet and the musician. A magic to which some people may be obtuse.

Here we are very close to concrete experience, very far from 'rational thought.' And, in reality, are we not in some way tending towards a rehabilitation of the substantial forms? Is there not a danger of setting up beyond this phantom world of qualities, a pseudo-physics of 'fluids' that strengthen one another or work against one another. 'Quality' is then treated as a force—an objective entity. . . .

---

[1] Yet does not analysis as practised by Proust manage to individualise a relation of this type in an almost infinite measure? We would have to see whether it does not betray the relation when it 'details' it. I do not know.

I feel strongly that this quality cannot be treated as a predicate and that it is bound up with existence itself. Is not my relation to my body (of course the word 'relation' is wrong) essentially another possession that cannot be transmitted?

The fundamental difficulty still remains. If I speak of this unthinkable quality, I must in some way think it.

February 28th, 1923

A thought occurred to me yesterday that may dispel this difficulty at least in part. The mind is constantly confronting a determined idea with a mass of experience which is given to it as datum, but not under the form of idea: as for instance when, after reflection, I refer to someone and say 'he is no good' or 'he is intelligent.' How is such confrontation possible? Am I unable to imagine an experience that can be expressed correctly by the words *good* or *intelligent*? I *feel* my real experience to be either distinct or not distinct from this imagined experience. If that is the case the word (or idea) only serves to mediate between two experiences one of which is given as datum and the other imagined. Are we therefore obliged to suppose that this quality can be compared to a kind of 'mass' or 'quantum' that is not conceptualised? I hesitate to say that.

The example of charm occurs to my mind. Charm is surely a quality of this order, a quality immediately felt when it imposes itself on me. I note that *we have no charm for ourselves*, and that there is a tendency for charm to vanish when I, who am subjected to it, find out that the person who is employing his charm is aware that he is doing so.

Charm appears to decline with the decline of the gratuitous element in behaviour, or when a person's attention is more and more taken up with precise and specifiable ends. Thus, generally speaking, a man has less charm than a woman or a child. When J. talks of children that are lacking in charm he often says that they are 'too precise' and this well expresses the absence of a 'halo' round their acts and words. Nothing is less susceptible of being acquired than charm.[1] A manifestation of the will can exclude

[1] Charm could even be contrasted with life, in that life is acquisition and consumption. If we adopt this standpoint do we not get a glimpse of new categories? The possibility of a contrast between existence in the strict sense, and life (cf. the note of March 1st., 1923). But this is very vague.

charm radically: the manifestation of will that implies a *tension*. Charm is as it were the presence of the person round what he does and what he says.

An infant has not yet developed charm. Charm only appears where we are directly aware of the margin that separates a person from what he does. It is a 'beyond'; and hence it has no ethical equivalent. A person only has charm if he is 'beyond' his virtues if they appear to emanate from a distant and unknown source.

We can only experience charm as regards individuals as such. But by very essence it can be mistaken or ignored. The absurdity of an inquiry into charm. Considered as an element in a sketch or description the statement that 'X has (or had) charm' is self-destructive.[1]

I am fully aware that this contrast between *presence* and *action* is enormously important. It is a key.

Could there be such a thing as negative charm, an antipathy experienced positively, a repulsion whose basis lies in being itself? I cannot help thinking so. But I do not think that a person who has charm for some people can be an object of repulsion for others, unless this be in a moral sense.

The incompatibility of charm and of indiscretion, of overflowing joy: the soul becomes less present as soon as it is projected.

March 1st, 1923

Is charm more than mere appearance?

Here we need to grasp that the reality *is* the appearance. Charm cannot be dissociated from the act of charming. It would be disastrous to view it as the revelation of some particular quality that can be conceptualised.

I am being bold in attempting to link up charm with all that is most metaphysical in the personality, with the quality which is irreducible and incapable of being objectivised—the quality which is doubtless only another facet of what we call existence. What happens to this quality in a person who lacks charm? I have a confused feeling that that question is meaningless. Fundamentally

---

[1] It would be grotesque, for instance, to insert this statement into a funeral notice.

we liken this quality to a brace or a spring—but that is exactly how we should not conceive of it. This brace could only be a logical minimum of conditions, a rudiment of conception. As long as I limit myself to proceeding by means of inferences, to saying, for instance: 'Under some form or other X must also have what in Y is revealed to me as charm,' I am still only dealing with words. Whereas in reality here we can only have to do with direct experience, with revelation. Doubtless I can perfectly well say that everyone is capable, for a short moment, of grasping himself or experiencing himself as transcending his own description. But when I say this I am mainly making an act of faith. For I myself only become a complete individual through the infinite credit which I grant to other individuals.

Approximation of existence and value: there is infinite value in the fact of feeling another to be present, an infinite value in contact as such.

This word 'presence' seems to me much less deceptive than the word 'quality'. It is the conjuring of the imagination that causes my almost invincible tendency to treat as a quality, then as a predicate, what in reality is only a way in which the other is given to me myself. Here there is a sort of labyrinth of thought. For how can I fail to endeavour to attach to a special quality of the other the privileged experience I have of him? Only we do not profit by this procedure; we even run the risk in the end of distorting the experience itself. These reflections throw a sidelight on the theory of the *thou*. Note what is gratuitous and unexplainable in this experience. For instance to ask about the conditions under which a *he* can become a *thou* would be contradictory. Show also the irreducible difference between presence and objectivity. At this point I come back to my notes on interior indigence, the feeling of an absence or rather of a non-presence. The ground ceases to echo beneath my feet. The world becomes thin and transparent. There is no more resistance, no more elasticity. I do not even set up resistance to myself, I no longer expect anything either from myself or from events. Boredom bound up, if I am not putting it too boldly, with a kind of pejorative awareness of intelligibility, of the 'of course'.

But if we substitute presence for quality, is there not a risk of ending up with the purely subjectivist notion of the feeling of 'presence'? Here, again, I think we are in danger of being intimidated by fictitious dilemmas.

March 2nd, 1923

When we contrast the person himself with the attitude adopted regarding him, we represent this person to ourselves as a sort of object in face of which we ought to adopt a particular position. But the individual cannot strictly be compared with something that is capable of appearing in variable and complementary perspectives. The more a being becomes real for us and present to us, the less we think we can see all round him. It is only then that the infinite, which is enfolded in all spiritual reality, is revealed to us—though most of the time we argue about this infinite without believing in it. If this be so, we avoid the danger of subjectivism for there can no longer be any question of contrasting the invariable and global reality of the being-object and the contingent attitudes adopted by a mobile intelligence with regard to it. For this revelation to be possible, a certain internal agreement must be established between the two *beings*. The part played by *maturity or ripeness*. In the objective order there is no more place for revelation than there is for mystery: these two notions are complementary.

March 5th, 1923

As outcome of a conversation with B. I am obliged to admit that it is absurd to speak of *the* 'thou' and thus to consider as a substantive what at bottom is the very negation of all substantiality. In reality, once I have singled it out, I objectivise a particular aspect of the experience of intimacy. From the core of the *us* I subtract the element that is *not-me* and call it *thou*. This element has an automatic tendency to take on the character of the *him*. And it is only in the measure in which I succeed in re-living this experience of intimacy after the event that I am able to resist this temptation. But can I ask myself questions about the immutability of this '*thou*' without converting it into *him*? 'It is always the same!' Does not this spontaneous exclamation imply the rupture of intimacy, the escape from the *us*?

Hence we are led to ask whether intimacy does not invariably consist in breaking through the outer bark of personality, and whether it does not involve participation in a vaster life at the heart of which certain distinctions are abolished. Are we to suppose that the people whom we call our friends have the function or the privilege of liberating us in some way from our personality? When we love someone, do we elevate ourselves to a plane on which it is no longer 'somebody' that we love? For myself I am loath to accept this interpretation, for it depersonalises love and drowns it in the indeterminate.

. . . The further I proceed the more I am struck by the fact that epistemological preoccupations tend to put our minds in a state in which we can never resolve or even state the problem of love. For the theory of knowledge has the essential task of at one and the same time defining objectivity and finding a basis for it. It gravitates round the idea of the object, hence it postulates that it is at least possible for the subject to disentangle from the heart of his concrete experience everything that involves no personal contribution on his part; and this though it sets aside the *meta-physical* question of how an object can be present to a subject. The subject-object relation is presupposed in any epistemology whatsoever. But if this postulate be maintained, love is almost bound to appear to be a particular contingent attitude adopted by the subject regarding the object. But this does not resolve the real problem, it eludes it—for the real problem precisely consists in finding out how love can be referred to an individual being, and whether it is impossible in practice for a real link to be established between true love and the beloved. The impossibility of this could only be demonstrated on condition that it were not presupposed—and in this instance it plainly is presupposed.

The difficulty is increased by the fact that the reality of a fusion of feeling seems incapable of being established empirically, at least if we suppose that the only experience that is possible for me is the experience of myself, of my 'states'; in a word, that I can only grasp the object on condition that the object in some way becomes myself. But supposing it be maintained that reality and reciprocity are distinct characteristics and that a feeling should be capable of being real without therefore possessing a sort of transcendent with regard to those who experience it? But in that case how are we to distinguish between the *real* feeling and the feeling that is not real? Are we obliged to say that in this field to be real means to be experienced—and only that?

Yet we all admit that we may be misled about what we experience. Hence there is a big problem here.

March 6th, 1923

Why do we take the fact that we are able to be misled regarding our own organic condition so for granted? We get the impression that something happens within our organism other than what we think. The image, fundamentally visual, that we form of reality allows us to distinguish clearly between what is real and what is merely appearance. Then we say that *what really happens* is what an observer provided with suitable instruments would be able to observe. The same cannot be said regarding feelings. We do not imagine what really happens. The real happening cannot be represented, we do not think that it can be noted by an observer however well equipped he may be. But we must tackle the postulate itself boldly: (a) Are we to say that only that which can be inscribed on a retina really happens? As I admit that there is at least *one* psychological becoming, I do not think so. Must we then fall back on to the statement (b) that there is no definable difference between what is apparent and what is real, save in the measure in which reflection is brought to bear on events that involve representation? (or, again, in the measure in which the idea of an absolute observer can legitimately be brought in). But it is easy to see that the idea of an absolute observer involves a complete contradiction. The word observer implies the idea of a standpoint or perspective. It is of the essence of an event that it is capable of representation, that it should be able to be represented in infinitely variable perspectives, and in foreshortenings that can be infinitely graded. Every observation is a particular aspect or a particular succession of aspects of something that cannot avoid being thought as irreducibly heterogeneous in relation to these aspects themselves. None of these aspects can be called absolute. The most detailed of them is not necessarily the truest (with an impressionist painting, for instance, detail should not be perceived as detail). But the statement (b) can only be maintained if it is legitimate to admit the idea of an absolute representation. Were we to suppose that the proposition (b) is true we would need to conclude that the distinction between appearance and reality is itself dependent on an arbitrary (and fundamentally contradictory) decree of the mind. Hence we conclude that:

Either there is no absolute meaning in speaking of what really happens or in contrasting the real happening with the apparent happening,

Or else that if this formula has a meaning it cannot be regarded as indicating a succession of events to which a spatial representation can be attributed.

March 7th, 1923

We seem to be ending up by completely reversing our spontaneous conceptions about the relations between appearance and reality. If there is a real *invariant* in function of which the interpretations can be considered incorrect, it does not seem as if we can look on this invariant as capable of being represented; the invariant is rather of the order of *sentiment* or *feeling* which we can only transpose (roughly) into images. It is worth inquiring whether this does not cast light on the relations of the *thou* and the *he*. The question of whether it is possible to view this invariant as an event is secondary.

In other words, realism would only be justified as regards feeling. Feeling alone could be treated as global reality, as reality which transcends the relative interpretations to which it gives birth.

It must be admitted that this brings us face to face with a singularly embarrassing question. How can a feeling be brought into confrontation with an idea of this feeling? Only, I think, on condition that this idea operates as a suggestive power and makes us experience at least a shadow of the feeling that it claims to indicate. The meaning of this can be explained by very simple examples. Somebody asks me: 'Are you hungry?' I answer, 'No.' My coenesthetic 'state' rejects the qualification 'hunger', but that is only because the word 'hunger' suggests to me, however obscurely, a state which does not coincide with what I actually experience. It is infinitely more difficult (and perhaps not legitimately possible) to answer the question: 'Do you love him?' because here the word 'love' fails completely to evoke a simple and clearly grasped 'state' with which we can contrast the state we have experienced. This is doubtless the reason why we can be misled regarding what we experience. The error, in a word, consists in *qualifying improperly*. And this error of qualification depends on the fact that we construct a schematic idea out of a feeling. The more complex the feeling is, the more such errors in qualification are possible.

But is this after all more than a mere question of names, of words? Consider this example. I think I am experiencing for X a disinterested aversion, whereas in reality I *envy* him. I am deceiving myself about the real character of this feeling. What must we understand by that?

As soon as I begin interpreting or qualifying a way of feeling, I adopt a dialectical attitude towards it and I cease to experience it in the pure and simple sense. In the place of the feeling I substitute a particular idea of the feeling—a schema. But this brings us back to the question: how can one idea of the feeling be more exact than another? What occurs has the appearance of a reference to a catalogue or keyboard of feelings.

March 8th, 1923

All this is equivocal because we are inadequately aware of what *the idea of feeling* is, we are not even sure that such an idea is possible. It seems to me that the analogy between feeling and illness can be pushed quite far, and that the same conditions govern the diagnosis of both. This diagnostic supposes that the symptoms are defined. It is only thanks to such corroboration that recognition, i.e. subsumption, is possible. But the difficulty is not yet completely resolved. When we say subsumption we also mean concept. I am unable to say to my friend: 'What you experience for that person is not, as you imagine, respectful friendship or disinterested curiosity; it is love,' unless there is a certain universal idea of love. I may be told that this is not an idea but an experience. But that distinction is irrelevant. Experience functions as idea as soon as it is freed from the particular context that makes it 'mine.'

But these remarks are not enough to eliminate completely the idea of a 'keyboard of feelings.' For it may still happen that I qualify improperly the way in which I feel, and baptise with the name love what is only solid affection; and it is even *a priori* impossible to conceive what the conditions or the guarantees of infallibility in such a matter could very well be. Now to describe something as 'improper' only has a meaning if we suppose someone 'competent' who, when he experiences the same feeling as I myself experience, calls it by another name. What is competence save the fact of having possession of a collection of experiences with the respective designations that fit each of them? Now if we declare that the idea of a competent judge who puts himself in my place and experiences what I experience is contradictory, we are left with the conclusion that in such matters as this no mistake in designation is possible and any kind of feeling can be called by any kind of name. But this hypothesis is self-contradictory because a name is a means of communication (of making common). Thus we need to go further and maintain that feelings cannot be expressed in words and cannot legitimately serve as material for discourse. Discourse on feelings[1] is only possible if we postulate that these feelings are at least relatively independent of the subjects who experience them, and if we suppose that a feeling preserves its nature even when disengaged from its individual content. it may well be that the idea of a feeling is only the liberated feeling itself and in that case the question of how the sentiment thus liberated presents itself to consciousness would only constitute a secondary psychological problem. Yet we need to recognise that the more we make discourse on feelings which are closely bound up to the subject, the more it becomes difficult to know what we are talking about, and the consequences of this are surely important.

What are we to conclude as regards the problem that I have been examining during these last few days (the distinction between what I feel and what I think I feel)? What is the exact difference between my interpretation and the interpretation that the competent subject would give? I think we must take it that, as regards the feeling in question, the competent subject would adopt a position that differs from mine because of its *disinterestedness*. It may be that all mistakes in this field are dependent on the subject's interest in committing them. This would take us back to Freud.

Ought we to say that as soon as we succeed in thinking our feeling, that is to say, in treating it as *not-ours*, in disinteresting

---

Similarly pathology is only possible in the measure in which there are not only sick people, but that there are illnesses.

ourselves from it, we grasp it in its truth? And on the other hand is the fact that this feeling is independent of the subject (the condition of its being thought) bound up with what B. calls his reality? It is very important to examine this.

Furthermore, we must be careful about the ambiguity of the word 'independence.' Independence can be defined either with reference to the subject himself or with reference to his individual characteristics. It seems to me that we should only retain the second of these definitions here.

It follows that independence should not be confounded with transcendence. Can we proceed any further in this direction and say that a feeling is the more real the less it can be converted into its own idea and removed from its own context? I do not think this is true. There is no doubting that Romeo's love for Juliet appears to him as *love*. What is true is that the real feeling is presented as essentially new and without precedent and as incapable of being reduced to any former experience and integrated in it.

March 9th, 1923

Actually I wonder whether I am not wrestling with a commonplace. To identify a feeling we must have experienced it, if not directly and spontaneously, at least in imagination. Yet, as I have already said, the fact remains that this identification can only be effected by means of a diagnosis of the symptoms. Supposing that a pure feeling were capable of existing, which is highly doubtful, I cannot see how it could be grasped and identified. Yet this needs to be examined more closely—and it is not certain that the question is very interesting.

What is certain is that identification (and definition) are only possible in the measure in which a feeling is something that we *have* as we have a cold or measles. Hence I am led to the opinion that there must be a depth of affectivity within us which it is not possible for us to identify and hence define conceptually, still less to set face to face with ourselves and deal with objectively. It is not easy to see how feeling can fail to be in some way woven into an affective material from whose woof it then stands out. But this woof in a sense must be identified with myself[1] and the

---

[1] To use other terms we could compare this fundamental feeling to an axis of reference which itself cannot be referred to anything. Perhaps this should be examined again.

idea of it therefore cannot exist. Or at least the possibility of forming an idea of it is bound up with a capacity for interior displacement and, so to speak, of metamorphosis which is not at all common. Here I am thinking of Proust in whom the two gifts are so obviously bound together.

Are we not obliged to think that the more we succeed in converting feelings into ideas, that is to say in treating feelings as generic 'affectivities'—but 'affectivities' that are not dependent on what is most individual in our essence—the more it becomes legitimate to consider them as unreal and as non-transcendental. In other words it might well be that reflection has the power of accomplishing on feelings an operation that is strictly destructive. It could truly be said that the more reflection is exercised the more the subjectivist affirmation (which lies at the foundation of all epistemology) tends to confer on itself its own justification. What I mean is this: the relative independence of the feeling in relation to the subject who experiences it can only be an object of thought for the subject; the subject only identifies it if within himself he adopts an attitude of exteriority towards the feelings. But inasmuch as he adopts this attitude does he not by that very fact remove from the feelings in question their initial transcendence? For it must not be forgotten that we are unable to view a feeling (or *a fortiori* the bond which unites this feeling to the personality) as entirely independent of the manner in which the feeling in question is envisaged by the subject. It is impossible to look on feeling as 'taking no account' of the judgment brought to bear on it by the subject.[1] What, then, can we disentangle from these meandering reflections? Do they enable us to answer the original question of how it is possible for me to be mistaken about my feelings? I think they do. We must answer that mistakes on the nature of a feeling are possible in the measure in which we suppose that there are *ideas of feelings*, that is to say that a feeling can be treated without appreciable alteration as something that we *have*, that I *have*, for instance, but that somebody else could *have* just as I do. From this standpoint there is

[1] On the other hand I wonder whether the subject is not a complete fiction that we set up in the measure in which we treat feelings as things that 'we have', that 'somebody has'. This would explain why it is impossible to conceive a relation between the personality and a feeling that could be considered to be really fundamental (*stofflich*); to be what I have called the *Urgefühl*.

nothing contradictory about thought substituting for myself another subject who experiences the same feeling as I do and who is better able to recognise its nature (e.g. there is no essential difference between a feeling and a scent, that some other person might be better able to identify than myself). This point seems to me established beyond all discussion. On the other hand the question of what we should think of the reality of a feeling conceived in this way is still very obscure. The hypothesis I adopted this morning can be formulated as follows: As soon as I distinguish myself from my feelings, as soon as I think myself as someone who *has* these feelings, I immediately deprive these feelings of all ontological value. They are only 'related' to objects as perceptions are related. In short, this ontological character only belongs to an indivisible experience that is rent and mutilated by reflection.

March 16th, 1923

Fundamentally the whole problem comes back to the distinction between what we *have* and what we *are*. It is extraordinarily difficult to express this in a conceptual form, yet it should be possible. What we *have* evidently has a kind of exteriority as regards the self. Yet this exteriority is not absolute. In principle what one has are *things* (or what can be compared with *things* in the extent to which such comparison is possible. Strictly speaking, I can only *have* something whose existence is up to a certain point independent of me. In other words what I have is added to me; furthermore the fact of being possessed by me is added to other properties, qualities, etc. that belong to the thing I have. I only *have* that which I in some way and within certain limits have at my disposal, or to put it in other words, inasmuch as I can be considered as a potentiality, as a being endowed with potentiality. We can only transmit what we have. If it happens that a potentiality is capable of being transmitted, we are driven to conclude that that potentiality is in practically the same relation to a more substantial ego as my pen (the pen I *have*) is in to that potentiality. If the category of being is really valid it is because that which is not capable of being transmitted is to be found in reality.

May 3rd, 1923

I have been re-reading the note I made on March 16th. The idea

I expressed then scarcely seems open to criticism as such. But it is now time to ask whether it is possible for what cannot be transmitted to be individual. The question is of fundamental importance yet it is not easy to state it in clear terms. It seems to me certain that were we to succeed in elucidating the extremely confused notions that are here tangled together, we would also be successful if not in resolving problems such as that of the psychology of heredity, at least in discovering the extent to which their solution must be experimental—and that would already be no mean achievement.

One point is of primary importance at the outset. Are we capable of conceiving of a transmission being made without the use of a material vehicle? (It is plain that when we speak of hereditary psychology we conceive or imagine more or less explicitly some material basis for the qualities transmitted.) Now in last analysis it seems to me certain that it is not legitimate to do this, and that the case of the transmission of a message which involves an emission at the point of departure and its reception at the point of arrival, can be taken as typical of what we mean by transmission (on condition that we set aside the element of finality to be found in it). If this be so, a quality can only be transmitted to the extent to which it can be viewed as *attached* to an element capable of transmission, and there is little need to point out the obscurity of this idea of attachment or adhesion. Actually it is only in so far as our understanding makes a surreptitious use of it that we are capable of conceiving feeling or sensation as transmission. The 'attachment' is a kind of more intelligible equivalent of the transcription and re-transcription of the message.

It would follow that only that which can in no way be regarded as the attribute (the property that adheres) of a material basis within me is incapable of being transmitted. Were this hypothetical element that cannot be transmitted defined in terms of that which *properly belongs* to me there would be a contradiction. What belongs to me, what I *have*, is on the contrary precisely what can be transmitted.

May 24th, 1923

We need above all to solve the eternal difficulty that I mentioned at the beginning of my entry on February 2nd, 1922. I think that the elements of the solution can be found scattered throughout my notes of the last three or four years and it is only a matter of making a synthesis of them. What value are we to attribute to the statement: 'This absolute *thou* does not exist'? There could be no question, I think, of establishing that this statement is contradictory in itself and that non-existence is incompatible with the content of the absolute *thou*; but there could be question of establishing that the affirmation is insignificant because what is posited in saying 'THIS absolute thou' is itself contradictory; in such a way that non-existence is predicated of a subject which is not really thought. In brief the question would be one of establishing the nothingness of the polemical attitude when the polemical attitude is brought to bear on what I call, though improperly, the religious relation. This is extremely important. It means that as soon as we adopt a polemical attitude regarding the object of religion, the object of religion changes its nature.

This becomes clearer to me: in our metaphysical discussions we always actually set out from a symbol that is visual—the symbol of an object which remains what it is, which does not change its nature when, without ceasing to regard it, we move farther away from it. Rightly or wrongly, and without defining the idea absolutely, we even admit that there is a sort of optimum position from which we will get the best possible view of this object. Must we not make up our minds to state that the 'religious relation' can never be regarded as such an object?

To put it more concretely let us imagine that I am looking at a landscape with a friend and that my friend points out to me what he takes to be a mountain on the horizon. It may well happen that I have better sight than he has or merely that I am better informed about the topography of the region; and so I say to him '*Your mountain* is a cloud.' There I think we have the type of comparison that is inapplicable in the field of religion. It seems to me that were I to say to a believer: 'Your God . . . is a cloud' I would be guilty of a paralogism. In the first instance we are dealing with a world which is common both to my friend and to myself. My friend and I myself are talking of the same thing and in relation to this thing we have taken up positions that are comparable in the strict sense (and, moreover, our positions have the *momentous characteristic of being interchangeable*) and so as to make a correct judgment in practice I would take my friend's place and if possible would even submit myself to the same optical conditions as he (I would borrow his binoculars, etc.). Whereas in the order of religion such a change of position is by very definition impossible. I am unable to take my friend's place for a number of reasons, of which the most striking is that he *is not distinct from his place*, that he is that very place itself (and this applies equally in the instance of love: I cannot hope to see my friend's mistress through his eyes without *becoming* my friend, whereupon it becomes impossible for me to appreciate the woman in question otherwise than as he does).

It must be agreed that though this process of argument may be impressive, it leaves our minds the prey to the kind of irritation which is invariably associated with the notion of existence.

Here, as is evident, we could once more take up all the arguments that I formerly developed regarding the impossibility of the enquiry whose conclusions are summed up in every theory of atheism (this is not God's work, nor that, nor again that, hence . . . etc.). But even if we were to agree that this is valuable there is an enormous difficulty still outstanding. 'We agree,' we may say, 'that we cannot touch faith as such. But it is precisely this that makes us think of faith as a kind of residue which we are not bound to take into account. It cannot be refuted, it *cannot even be refuted*, it is below the plane on which refutation is possible, and it is negligible. In our universe what is not susceptible of becoming a common good must be relegated to the cellars of human life with those incommunicable and inexpressible feelings that a healthy man should learn always to dismiss.' Thus what is needed is the possibility of safeguarding the existence of the absolute *thou* without attributing to it an objectivity that would ruin its essence. It is at this point that my efforts to dissociate existence and objectivity attain their full significance.

Existence is not a state and that is why it is meaningless to speak of a transition from non-existence (or potentiality) to existence. This is another way of saying that it is impossible to distinguish between the existant and existence. But we need to know whether this is anything more than a mere formula. I think

I have glimpsed that there is in existence the wherewithal to dissolve the object as object; save that we are immediately held up by the element of confusion in this way of expressing it. In fact there can be no question of viewing *existence* as a quality which conflicts with the qualities that constitute the object.

However much I grapple with this idea I am forced to admit that I still find it very obscure. Formerly I identified the existant with that which can be indicated. But we must grasp that we are not dealing here with mere indication but with *identification by the senses*. What exists should be capable at one and the same time of being given as datum and of being identified. Here we must refer back to the notes I made in 1917. Those notes expressed very well what I saw so clearly at Sens. What at that time I failed sufficiently to discern was that the centre, or the immediate experience, from which these contents take their departure, is not a simple feeling—or rather that this feeling is bound up, in a way that is *unthinkable* (doubtless this unthinkableness can be demonstrated and the elements of the demonstration are even to be found in my notes), with the representation of an object which is my body: it is in relation to me as conscious of my body, that is to say as grasping it at one and the same time as object (body) and as non-object (my body) that all existence is defined. In a word, to state the existence of a being or of a thing would be to say: This being is of the same nature as my body and belongs to the same world; only this homogeneity doubtless bears less on the (objective) essence than on the intimacy that the word *my*, *my body*, involves. In this way we could explain that which in existence is incapable of definition—since the fact for my body of being my body is not something of which I can genuinely have an idea, it is not something that I can conceptualise. In the fact of *my body* there is something which transcends what can be called its materiality, something which cannot be reduced to any of its objective qualities. And the world only exists for me inasmuch as I think it (this expresses it badly), inasmuch as I apprehend it as bound up with me by the thread which also binds me to my body.

To this must be linked the fact that the world only exists inasmuch as I can act on it: for there is only action inasmuch as I am my body, inasmuch as I cease to think my body. The non-objectivity of *my body* becomes clear to our mind as soon as we remember that it is of the essence of the object as such that it does not take me into account. In the measure in which it does not take me into account my body seems to me not to be my body.

This summary is very important. It should throw some light on the problem I stated yesterday. But I will only reach my goal by roundabout ways.

At this immediate moment I am wondering whether we cannot throw light on the nature of belief by setting out from this theory of existence. Is not belief always the act by which I skip over one of the continuous series which bind up my immediate experience to a particular fact, and treat this fact as if it were given to me in the same way as my own body is given to me? It must of course be emphasised that my body is not an object of belief: all belief is based on the model of that which is not, in itself, a belief. But in that case might it not be said that all belief comes to bear on facts of a material order? No, because I can conceive infinite prolongations of the central act, unlimited possibilities of vision, etc. There is no need to underline how much this conclusion strengthens what I would like to call my 'sensualistic' metaphysics. For obviously the connection between existence and sensation is as close as it could be. Is the connection with the theory of the *thou* equally easy to grasp? As I see things at present, it is. We must set out from the *him*, from the *that*. *That* is that of which I speak to someone else, i.e. that from which I turn away, in a word that which I treat as not taking into account the act by which I think it (and here I am speaking of a concrete, detailed and present thought). Briefly, I put my emphasis on objectivity and not on existence, if we understand existence in the sense explained above. To treat a being as not taking us into account is in some way to disinterest ourselves from this being (even if we concentrate our attention on it); it is to adopt an attitude which is fundamentally opposed to the attitude implied by love. This needs defining. If I treat a being as not taking me into account, to what extent does that mean that I do not take him or it into account? The answer to this question seems to me very plain: it is that I do not treat him as a *me*, as possessing the faculty of depending on himself and taking himself into account, the faculty which is at the very root of existence.

Yet there is an obscure point here. If we say of someone that 'he will always go his own way' do we not, though treating him as a *him*, nevertheless attribute to him that self-mastery I spoke of a moment ago? I leave this subsidiary point aside. Nevertheless, we need to recognise clearly the transition from existence to presence; and I am wondering whether it is not by presence that we can effect the transition from existence to value. Is not that which has value also that which increases in us the feeling of presence (it is immaterial whether we are concerned with our presence or with the presence of the universe). In these reflections there is one essential point—they seem to make possible a transition from metaphysics to ethics; for our worth is decreased to the extent to which our affirmation of existence is limited, pale and hesitant.

EXISTENCE AND OBJECTIVITY[1]

WHEN we review the evolution of metaphysical doctrines during the last century or so we are struck by the large measure of agreement amongst idealist philosophers about reducing to a minimum the rôle of existence and of the *existential index* in the general economy of knowledge. They carry out this reduction for the benefit of all kinds of rational definitions—some people would say *values*—which confer an intelligible content on thought. Thus existence is made to appear as something on which thought is perhaps so to speak *propped up*, but of which, for the same reason, thought tends more and more to lose sight. Doubtless we could discuss further the extent to which this or that particular philosopher adopts this attitude in question. But I think there is no denying that the attitude became more and more clear in the course of the last century and it is even involved in the very definition of a certain kind of idealism. What must be noticed first and foremost is that the more emphasis put on the *object* as object, together with the characteristics that constitute it as object, and the intelligibility with which it needs to be weighted so as to provide a grip for the subject who confronts it, the more philosophers leave the existential aspect—I will not say the existential character—of the object in the shade. We can use a simple metaphor to describe the logical situation that the mind tends to create for itself; and say that thought confers on objects a sort of *insularity* in relation to itself. The object is bathed in this insularity just as it is bathed in space and perhaps fundamentally *because* it is bathed in space. And by the fact that the bonds that tie it to the hypothetical *Grund* or basis of things are to all appearances broken, it seems as though it can be tackled from every angle. Hence the tendency to establish

[1] This article is reproduced from the *Revue de Metaphysique et de Morale*. In it I disentangle several of the fundamental themes of the *Metaphysical Journal*.

between thought and the object a relation of agreement which is strictly stable and satisfying; and on the basis of this relation it is easy to build up scientific knowledge, without for this reason feeling any necessary obligation to accept the theses of Criticism in detail. But what is deliberately set aside here is the mode in which the object is *present to* the person who considers it or, which amounts to the same thing, the mysterious power of self-affirmation by which it confronts a spectator. On a deeper level there is the question of how it comes about that this object is not only a rationally articulated spectacle but also possesses the power of affecting in a thousand ways the being of the person who contemplates it and is submitted to it. This sense-presence of the 'thing' which, if it is not identified with its existence, at least appears to unbiased reflection as its immediate manifestation and revelation—it is this that a philosophy which is orientated at one and the same time towards ideas and towards objects necessarily tends to conjure away. Thus we can easily conceive how beyond this idealist theory, which though not denying existence brushes it away to an infinite distance, it is possible to construct a radical thesis which views existence as capable of being called into question and perhaps even as self-contradictory.

I would like at the outset to show that there is nothing problematical in existence and that if scepticism sets out to attack it it tends to destroy itself. To doubt existence is to say that it is not possible to affirm validly regarding anything that *that* exists. But, as we immediately see, this doubt itself presupposes a definite idea of existence that we hesitate to apply. Thus it seems that between this idea and the experience there is no guaranteed contact. We do not set out from a *this* which certainly does exist so as to ask whether *that* also exists.[1] We doubt the application of this idea considered as a whole. But how then are we to avoid being tempted to conclude that this idea is a *pseudo-idea*, that it has no hall-mark to guarantee it and that it must be thrown on to the scrapheap as a useless tool? Thus when this

---

[1] Yet it is in the second way that people generally proceed when questioning themselves about the existence of God. The statement that Tom, Dick or Harry exists is treated as a datum which is beyond all denial. Does God also exist? If we followed this train of thought we might be able to show without being paradoxical that contemporary writers and philosophers who tend to dissolve belief in the reality of Tom, Dick and Harry are indirectly preparing the way for specifically religious affirmations.

scepticism goes a little deeper, I think it is inevitably converted into a negative doctrine.

This could be shown in yet another way. Doubt is at least a provisional and recognised rupture of a particular attachment or adhesion; it is a 'disengagement' and hence it can only be exercised after the event when thought is confronted by a duality. But if existence cannot ever be regarded as a predicate we do not appear to be confronted here with anything of the kind. It is only the structure of language which obliges us to ask if there is *something* which possesses existence. In reality existence and the thing that exists obviously cannot be dissociated. We are faced here with a synthesis whether real or not on which doubt can have no grip; there is no gap or interval, so to speak, into which the sharp point of doubt can be inserted. Hence the mind can only proceed here by means of a fiat or decree. And this applies to the idealist philosophers to whom I have already alluded. They *refuse* to admit that there is any ground for applying the existential index— they proscribe its use. It would be easy to show, furthermore, that these idealist doctrines always tend to substitute hypothetical propositions in place of categorical propositions and to think the world under the form of pure legality: *if it is true that . . . it is also true that . . .* In this way existence seems to be surmounted, or reabsorbed, or simply conjured away. Now I do not believe that this enterprise is self-contradictory. Doubtless any attempt to think the world scientifically is inconceivable unless there be a fundamental decision of this kind. But on the other hand I cannot see how we can conceal from ourselves the narrow and artificial element in this decision. From this standpoint the actuality of any experience is treated as though it needs to be immediately surmounted, thanks to the mind deliberately cutting the cables: and as soon as it has got into its swing the mind owes it to itself to forget the irreducible and apparently primary element in this actuality, and hence it no longer sees it as anything more than an opportunity—which is at bottom contingent—for deploying its own immanent powers of universality.

That such a way of thinking is justified in part where the mind is involved in achieving determined ends and constituting a body or a system of truths, I have no intention of contesting. But that this constitutes the whole of philosophy and that in this way we can exhaust all speculative activity, I am quite unable to admit. The ever-widening gulf between this mode of thinking and integral human experience with its life that trembles with tragedy, is enough to show up its inadequacy. The reasons for which I am unable to accept this mutilation will doubtless become clearer in the pages that follow.

If the negation of existence is a decree or fiat, for my part I choose the contrary decree and have no hesitation in declaring that for me existence is beyond all doubt. Yet we need to be precise about the meaning of a statement that is so obviously ambiguous as this. For we risk running into the following dilemma:

Either there is *something* that exists, something in particular, whose nature we will be asked to define exactly, something that we are obliged to *indicate*;

Or else—which is beyond doubt—it is existence in general; and it seems plainly *a priori* that this is only an empty and doubtless mythical abstraction.

This is the first point that we need to clear up.

Evidently the former of these alternatives must be dismissed for reasons already mentioned. To speak of something that exists is to re-establish in a more or less explicit way the notion of existence as a predicate. Moreover, the attribution of a predicate to a subject can always raise a problem. I am unable to see how the *seal of that which cannot be doubted* can be attached to a statement bearing on the existence of any kind of particular reality.

But the second alternative seems to me just as disastrous as the former. What is existence in general? Does not this way of expressing myself set up between the fact of existing and *that* which exists, the very duality that I rejected? This would undoubtedly be so if we were obliged to regard existence in general as a concept; but it is that precisely that I think we must expressly deny at the outset. The assurance whose nature we are trying to disentangle here could no more bear on an abstract characteristic than on a *that* to which this characteristic belongs; it can only bear on the indissoluble *unity of existence and of the existant*. This assurance is of a global character and, as we have already seen, it would be dangerous to review it in detail. What is given to me beyond all possible doubt is the confused and global experience of the world inasmuch as it is existant; and here even the term 'given' fits only imperfectly. *Given* normally signifies *presented* to a subject. Now here I would not like to insinuate anything of the kind from motives which I hope to illustrate clearly in the following study. At this point I must restrict myself to pointing out that this assurance appears to us as though *constitutive* of what we habitually call the subject. It is not *added to* it or *provided* for it; without this assurance the subject ceases to be anything, it disappears or at least is reduced to a logical shadow of itself.

Hence the impossibility of introducing into our affirmation of existence a specification which is not arbitrary and therefore destructive. To say that *I exist* is only legitimate on condition that we recognise at the outset that here the word *I* does not signify the ego as normally understood; that it is not a content or a psychological system even reduced to a sort of minimum. Nor can there be any question of contrasting this existant *I* with something else which does not exist.

At this point we ought to admit that we are strictly incapable of sifting out what exists from what does not exist. And provisionally at least, perhaps also permanently, we should view as excluded the very possibility of any such discrimination. The idea of a *criterion* of existence is bound up with the notion that existence is a characteristic and that an experience of it, or a reasoned enquiry about it, will enable us to determine whether or not it is applicable to a particular content. Thus it would not be legitimate to say '*I exist*' unless the *I* is presupposed to be the express negation of any particular content and of anything that can be brought into the category of the 'this or that.'

But, as we immediately see, when the *I exist* is thus cleared of private meaning, it tends to merge with an affirmation such as 'the universe exists', the universe itself also being the negation of 'something in particular' without thereby necessarily being reduced to the general and the abstract.

Thus our first conclusion is that unless the mind deliberately *wagers* against existence it knows itself to be fortified by an unquestionable assurance regarding the existence not of any particular thing nor even regarding existence in general, but regarding the existing universe. This assurance is as little as possible external to the mind even though the mind has the singular power of detaching itself from this assurance—thereby running the risk, as must be admitted, of upsetting it and even of causing a profound alteration in its nature.

Perhaps it will be objected that all I have said so far is really more posited than proved. I am perfectly ready to agree about this, as I consider that the very idea of bringing a demonstration to bear on the primacy of existence seems to me radically contradictory. Our only possible procedure here consists in reflecting on affirmations whose titles of credit, so to speak, need to be examined.

That existence cannot be treated as a *demonstrandum* is something that we cannot fail to perceive as soon as we observe that existence is primary or it *is* not—that in no case can it be regarded as capable of being reduced or derived. Nor is the affirmation of being of the order of the *principles* which we reach by way of regression. For principles only obtain in the infra- or supra-existential world from which precisely we are trying to escape. Thus we are confronted with an assurance which coincides closely with the reality on which it bears, a reality that is as global as the assurance itself. Here once again I am constrained to put the reader on his guard against the terms I need to use. For in the words 'bear on' there is something that is not strictly applicable here, something that can only be applied to a judgment. We posit that a judgment *refers* to an object distinct from itself, that it points it out as an index does. But here there is no question of referring. In this respect I would be prepared to admit that the fundamental assurance we are dealing with here is of the order of sentiment or feeling—provided it were explicitly understood that this *feeling* must not be intellectualised and converted into a judgment, for any such conversion would not only change its nature but possibly even deprive it of all meaning.

Hence the distinction between the idea of existence and existence itself—an impasse in which philosophical reflection is always liable to get lost—must be rejected out of hand. I myself am unable to view this distinction as anything more than a fiction that derives its birth from the arbitrary act by which thought claims to transform into an affirmation of objectivity what is really immediate apprehension and participation.

Of course I am aware that to many minds a thesis of this

kind may look like a return to a pre-critical dogmatism. Later I hope to throw light on the reasons why any such accusation leaves me undisturbed. Moreover, in my view, dogmatism is more of an attitude of mind than a doctrine. There is a dogmatism in criticism, a dogmatic way of excluding dogmatism, whose internal contradictions seem to me to link it up with modes of philosophical speculation that are definitely over and done with. Whatever be the value of a discipline which bears essentially on the conditions and the criteria of objectivity I cannot see anything to dispense us—or *a fortiori* prohibit us—from identifying the limits of objectivity, and from trying to penetrate *beyond* objectivity (I hope this spatial metaphor will be forgiven) so as to reach a domain in which the classical relation between subject and object ceases to be strictly applicable.

What I have already said is doubtless enough to enable the reader to discern the position that we are obliged to adopt regarding the cogito of Descartes. The reality that the cogito reveals—though without discovering an analytical basis for it—is of quite a different order from the existence that we are trying here not so much to *establish* as to *identify* in the sense of taking note of its absolute metaphysical priority. The cogito introduces us into a whole system of affirmations and guarantees their validity. *It guards the threshold of the valid* and it is only on condition that we identify the valid and the real that we can speak—without the imprudence that is far too common—of the real as immanent in the act of thinking. Here, of course, we are in no way re-establishing an outworn distinction between matter and form. I have no hesitation in saying that the cogito is precisely the negation of this distinction and in some way the very act by which it is suppressed. But it certainly does not follow from this that the objective world to which access is opened up to us by the cogito coincides with the world of existence. The dualism established by Kant between the object and the thing-in-itself, whatever objections it raises in the form in which he states it in the *Critique*, has at least had the inestimable advantage of accustoming people's minds for over a century to making this indispensable dissociation. But it is important to be very clear in our minds that the *existant* can in no way be treated as an *unknowable* object, that is to say, as an object liberated from the very conditions that define an object as such. It is essential to the character of the *existant* that it should occupy with regard to thought a *position* which cannot be reduced to the position implied in the fact of objectivity itself. And it is this position that we must now try to elucidate.

Notice to begin with that I cannot avoid conceiving the object as 'something with which I am in communication.' The relation between subject and object is initially presented as a relation with two terms. Only, as Royce has pointed out with admirable clarity in his later philosophical work, this is only so in appearance; the relation is in reality a triad. The *object* is by character *that regarding which I converse with a real or ideal interlocutor*. It is a *third party* in a particular conversation that I carry on with X . . . a conversation bearing on it. It is in this sense interposed between me and myself and this helps to justify the use of the rather surprising term *insularity* that I employed at the beginning of this essay.

Only the *object* is not, so to speak, inert in relation to this conversation. It would be legitimate to say that I interrogate it and that it answers me. And the strength of idealist doctrines consists in the fact that, by delving deeper into the nature of this dialogue or hidden dialectic, they show that the revelations which seem to emanate from the object are closely conditioned by the active and intelligent appeals that I make to it. The idealist doctrines which put an increasingly emphatic accent on the *insular* character of the object are called upon to *minimise* the original contribution made by the object to us. This is easily explained. For the object's contribution is, properly speaking, unthinkable within the closed system that one subject here tends to form with itself. As goes without saying, the subject becomes more and more 'disindividualised' and its individual characteristics are more and more thoroughly strained away. This explains why idealist systems invariably lead to the affirmation of an *identity*—however concrete and synthetic it be—in which all that we call our experience or our universe comes to be regarded as *internal*. Of course there are plenty of obstacles on this incline leading towards identity. But when we come across a philosopher who purports to remain at one of these obstacles and build his house on it, I can never avoid a feeling of arbitrariness, though there are plenty of reasons that militate in favour of a *political system* that one contemporary thinker presents as a genuine metaphysical opportunism.

One further consideration is essential. From the standpoint we are considering, feeling or sensation is bound to seem radically unintelligible in itself. We can only treat it as a kind of priming (unthinkable in isolation) for the complex operation by which the mind brings an object before itself. Whereas we need to adopt a different attitude to sensation, or, if you like, to the *act of feeling*, if we are to be able to establish solidly and illustrate concretely the theory of existence whose first rudiments I tried to set out above.

We must get right away from the general way of interpreting sensation or feeling which is almost universally taken for granted not only by philosophers and men of science but also by common sense itself. We find it very difficult to avoid treating sensation as something which is emitted by X and received by a subject, that is to say as something which, for the sake of terminology, I shall henceforward call a message. The word 'receptivity' is particularly significant in this connection. It is very difficult for the mind to get rid of the idea that what is emitted in a form that in X is perhaps unspecifiable . . . then transmitted under conditions that, rightly or wrongly, we think we are able to represent to ourselves more adequately, is finally received and transcribed by the sentient subject. In a word, we are all irresistibly inclined to suppose that *to sense* involves a communication like the communication that takes place between two telegraph stations. Doubtless we conceive this communication differently according as to whether or not we profess a pan-psychist doctrine. Some suppose that only one of the telegraph stations is cognisant as station, or that the other is not for itself a *station* and is only apprehended as a station by the person with whom it is in correspondence. Others are inclined to believe that the accord—or analogy— is of a still more intimate kind, and that the transmitting station already has some kind of awareness, however obscure and foreign to ours it be, of the message that it addresses to us. The most suggestive example is that of a scent or smell. Between the flower garden whose effluvia reach me—and my organism—something travels, something is transmitted to me, that the physicist will simply consider to be a perturbation or commotion. People suppose, without asking themselves what the hypothesis means, that once this perturbation has been communicated to the instrument on which it is specifically qualified to cause an impression, it is *transcribed into olfactory language.* Yet one question is still open to debate, namely whether what really occurs is actually a re-transcription analogous to the one performed by the telegraphist who receives a telegram, or whether at the origin of the perturbation there was a phenomenon analogous to the phenomenon that takes place in consciousness; in other words whether what I call a flower does not enjoy a confused satisfaction regarding its existence which becomes a perfume when it is communicated to me. Admittedly we may be obliged to regard this question as devoid of philosophical meaning. It can be solved —and that in an arbitrary way—only if we suppose that we ourselves make a choice which at bottom is essentially poetical. Moreover, we need to ask ourselves whether there is any meaning whatever in the supposition that a transcription or a translation of the *sensorial message*, from whatever origin it derives, is possible.

Now, by definition, to translate means to substitute one type of *data* for another type of *data*, and for a translation to be possible these data must in some degree be an object for the mind, whereas in the present instance this is inconceivable. For my translating activity to be exercised it must be brought to bear on an *initial datum;* whereas in the case of the hypothesis we have in mind the event that I am supposed to translate into sense-language by very essence is not given to me as datum at all. We are led astray by the crude spatial image from which we cannot get away. We become victims of a confusion between the perturbation communicated *to* our organism and the fact that this commotion is given as datum *to the* subject. The simplest reflection is enough to dispose of this equivocation. The alternatives before us are: either I must recognise that this physical event is in no way given to me as datum, that it is nothing for me, whatever the modification that it may involve for my organism; and in that case it is against reason to suppose that a translation, however mysterious, can convert this event into a datum: or else we will have to have recourse to the term *'unconscious sensation'* so as to allow ourselves to view this event as in some way already given. But this second alternative may involve a very dangerous misunderstanding. For either we restrict ourselves to postponing the difficulty of inquiring how this unconscious sensation is possible in its turn, or else we have to admit that it is *primordial* which means that it is literally irreducible. In this latter case there can be no question of treating it as a message that we have received; and the interpretation which we were endeavouring to uphold straightway collapses. Nor do I see how it is possible to escape from these difficulties by declaring with the author of *Identité et Réalité* that sensation is irrational; expressions of this kind seem to me fundamentally ambiguous. It looks as if by 'irrational' M. Meyerson means a transition that cannot be effected, a sort of *No-thoroughfare*. For myself I cannot accept this admission of powerlessness and, as it were, the abdication of thought when faced with a cardinal fact. To say that sensation is unintelligible is to say that the intelligence has no grasp on reality and that in last analysis it is only a form without content. How, therefore, whatever the cost, can we avoid looking for a way of making this transition conceivable and bringing the act of feeling itself into a system of thinking?

As will be seen immediately, there is a close connection between these general observations and the thesis about the absolute priority of existence (or, if you like, of the existential) that I suggested at the outset. Both alike lead us to the affirmation of a *pure* immediate, that is to say an immediate which by very essence is incapable of mediation. And by that we must understand a *datum* in relation to which thought is not in a condition to make the necessary recoil so that it is no longer a *datum* but is apparently begotten or constructed. This pure immediate, moreover, has the paradoxical characteristic of being *incapable of specification*. Therefore it is not something that can be said to be *this* or *that*. This characteristic is doubtless incompatible with the nature of any object whatsoever—since, as we have seen, objects are always defined in function of possible dialogue—and legitimately it belongs to the infra-objective order whose reality we are trying to establish. I am quite aware that there is something at least apparently absurd about treating as a characteristic what is the very negation of any characteristic. But we must be careful to notice that this incoherence is really only verbal; the point on which I want to insist is that existence properly speaking is *incapable of characterisation*. And by this I do not mean, of course, that it is *indeterminate* but that *the mind when confronting it cannot adopt without contradiction the attitude that is needed for characterising something*. Hence existence has nothing in common with a subject that has been stripped of its predicates. For such a subject is fundamentally only an abstract schema for the subsequent specifications which alone are capable of conferring a reality and a nature upon it.

Before proceeding further with my enquiry I would like to recapitulate the preliminary results of the foregoing considerations.

Inasmuch as my metaphysical reflection is exercised I appear to myself as a being (X) who interrogates himself about his own existence. There takes place within me—or seems to take place—an interior debate which appears to separate me from my own existence by forcing me to call into question both my own existence and the existence of everything else in the world. But the meaning of this interior debate is not obvious. To doubt whether anything exists—or possesses existence—is *in appearance* to posit existence as in itself beyond all doubt (whether or not it can be legitimately *attributed*). And it is to regard it as a predicate endowed with a potentiality of application that is open to question and is perhaps equal to zero. It is easy to see how untenable this position is. A predicate which is the predicate of nothing cancels itself out. Hence the meaning of the debate is transformed. It now bears on the legitimacy of the existential judgment and can only be closed negatively if we adopt a monist theory of value and of the valid. But even supposing we could construct a monist system of this kind without contradiction there is no questioning that it must remain relative to a decree or option made by the mind. Now when I interrogate myself about existence—whether this be my existence or not—I am searching for what could be called an absolute answer: a solution which suppressed the question by depriving it of meaning would look like a trap. If I ask myself by what right or in what measure I exist I do so because I presuppose that a world exists, whatever be its structure. To object that there is no real meaning in saying of anything: 'That exists', does not answer my question. Hence, between the two extreme philosophical positions, one of which consists in rejecting existence and the other in giving it the seal of the indubitable, I do not think that any hesitation is possible. We cannot reasonably hope to suppress the question of existence *once and for all* merely because, within *certain limits*, it can be eluded or even ceases to offer an intelligible meaning. But this existence whose primacy I believe we are obliged to recognise—and that by an act of genuine *spiritual humility*—this existence which is one with the existant, could not be affirmed of anything that can be designated, not even of the ego; and we need to exercise the greatest prudence in our choice of the formulae used to express what is less an abstract immanence than an *effective presence*. This presence is neither the presence of something nor of someone; it could best be indicated perhaps, at least indirectly, by the expression *absolute presence*. Thus we are not even left with the resource of saying that the universe is present to me myself. Because that would involve reintroducing a duality, a distinction between subject and object within what by very principle can involve no such distinction. It is doubtless by an evocation of the pure act of feeling understood as an interior resonance that we will be best assisted, not to obtain an imaginative impression but 'mentally to imitate' this presence which 'subtends' the 'integrality' of our experience and of any experience whatsoever.

It may well be asked what can be the purpose of adding to the weight of a metaphysical instrument that is already so heavy. Why this out of date ontology? I think the answer is that unless thought is to abdicate when confronted with sensation, that is really to say when confronted with itself, it is obliged to look in the direction I have suggested for the way out that critical philosophy has failed to find. If sensation is to appear in some way intelligible, the mind must establish itself at the outset in a universe which is not a world of ideas. If it be possible to prove, as I think it is, that sensation is not susceptible of being conceived as a message, as a communication between different stations, it must involve the immediate participation of what we normally call the subject in a surrounding world from which no veritable frontier separates it. It can be shown, moreover, that this initial postulate enables us to account for the existence of a body that appears to the subject to be *his* body. This is the point that we must now emphasise.

★

Inasmuch as I look on myself as carrying on communications with objects or, if you like, with *things* that are distinct from me, it is perfectly natural that my body should appear to me as interposed between those things and me, or, to be more exact, that it should be presented to me as pre-eminently the instrument of which I make use both for receiving and sending messages (which may, moreover, easily be reduced to simple signs. In a world constituted by or at least marked out by stations in communication with one another, *my* body like other bodies functions as an apparatus for signalling). But when set up as an absolute this very simple and seductive interpretation gives rise to difficulties that are insurmountable.

In the first place the idea of interposition is very obscure in itself. A thing can be interposed between two things or, more exactly, a term can be slipped in between two terms. But is this logical schema applicable here? When I say that my body is interposed between me and things, I am only expressing a pseudo-idea. Because what I call *me* cannot be identified with a thing or with a term. Of course it is possible to say that my body is interposed between a body A which affects it and a body R on which it reacts. But in that case what happens to *me*, to the subject? The subject seems to *withdraw into an indeterminate sphere from which it contemplates*—without existing for itself—*the anonymous play of the universal mechanism*.

Yet if I adopt the purely instrumentalist way of representing what I call my body, I run into even worse difficulties. Note in the first place that the expression 'I make use of my body' allows for a very wide margin between itself and the rich and confused experience that it claims to translate. In the consciousness that I have of my body and of my relations with my body, there is something that this affirmation fails to *render*. Hence the protest we can scarcely repress: 'I do not *make use of* my body, I *am* my body.' In other words, there is something in me that denies the implication that is to be found in the purely instrumentalist notion of the body that my body is external to myself. And, as I see it, materialism constitutes an effort—though an unfortunate effort—to organise this protest and transform it into a positive doctrine. In this respect there is an instructive connection between materialism and sensualism. Both translate one and the same defence-reaction of thought—and all idealists are bound to recognise that this is absolutely legitimate.

It would not be enough merely to note the uneasiness with which the mind entertains the formulae of instrumentalism. The real question is whether this uneasiness can be justified rationally. An analysis closely resembling the analysis to which we have already submitted the idea of 'message' will enable us to answer this question.

When I make use of any kind of tool, in reality I do no more than prolong and specialise a way of behaving that already belongs to my body (whether to my limbs or to my senses). This is just as obvious when applied to a spade or a hammer as to a telescope or a microscope. Not only is the instrument *relative* to my body—between the instrument and my body there is a deep community of nature. But given these conditions can I treat the body itself as an instrument? As soon as we get to grips with the meaning of this question we discover that we are obliged to imagine a *physical soul* furnished with powers and faculties; and the mechanical terms, to which my body seems reduced, are really only prolongations or transpositions of these powers or faculties. But how avoid distrusting such a hybrid notion as this?

Either we are condemned to follow the ladder endlessly from physical instrument to physical instrument.

Or else we stop arbitrarily in the series of regressions and maintain that an instrument can be utilised (but how?) by a principle (?) which has a nature quite different from itself. This amounts to saying that an instrument may possibly be an instrument of nothing.

Hence there is at least an indirect justification for the repugnance I feel about looking on my body as 'something that I make use of.' I feel confusedly that it is still my body that makes use of my body and that I am involved in a dead end.

I believe that what I should like to call *instrumental mediation* can only conceivably take place within a world of objects and between bodies of which none are regarded as *my body*, that is to say, as affected by this special index which in part removes it from the order of that about which we can hold discourse either with someone else or with ourselves.

Thus, in the measure in which I speak of my body as an instrument, I treat it as an object, that is to say as *not-mine*. I adopt the position of a *third person* regarding it and any definition I am able to make of it is bound up with the *ideal disincarnation* to which I have previously had recourse, and with the act by which I delegated to a sort of fictitious *double* the 'power' of utilising this instrument. Inasmuch as I act I identify myself with this double which in this way regains the reality of which I dispossessed it when I detached myself from it. It follows that we recreate the unity that had been broken up by analysis when it substituted for this unity the duality of instrumentalist and instrument.

Thus the rôle of reflection—whether this be exercised on *feeling* or on *acting*—consists not in cutting to pieces and dismembering but, on the contrary, in re-establishing in all its continuity that living tissue which imprudent analysis tore asunder.

I will doubtless be blamed for substituting the unintelligible terms of a problem for a solution which, though perhaps imperfect, is at least clear. But at this point, as in the case of existence, our procedure must consist in asking whether thought here is not guilty of a dialectical abuse, that of positing a problem where there is not and cannot be anything problematical. What I mean is this: inasmuch as I consider my body either in its relations with other bodies or in its own structure, I am confronted with something which is essentially an occasion for a problem, and hence an object of possible knowledge, by very reason of the *detachment from myself* to which I have proceeded so as to isolate and define this totality of terms. To the extent to which my body lends itself to such treatment it is certainly converted into an object. But in submitting it to this treatment I cease to look on it as *my body*, I deprive it of that absolute priority in virtue of which *my body* is posited as the centre in relation to which my experience and my universe are ordered. Thus my body only becomes an occasion for a problem under conditions such that the very problem that we intended to state loses all meaning. This problem consists in asking how my body is bound up with the X whose body it is: it is only by a sort of mental sympathy, by identifying myself with the personality of others, that I can (or think I can) state it in universal terms. In reality this problem only has meaning for *me* (a *me* that I can expand and contract at will). But on the other hand it is precisely as regards me—and as regards my body—that this problem cannot be stated without involving a contradiction.

This point is particularly delicate and I consider it is necessary to emphasise it. So as to demonstrate its contradictory character let us consider the above formula: how is *my body* bound up (=what relation unites it to the X *of which* it is the body)? But the relation expressed by the genitive *of which* is itself formally negated by the words *my body*. To say *my body* is to refuse to attribute it *to this or that person*. At first sight this may seem outrageously paradoxical. Instead of saying my body, could I not name myself, point out the *person* to whom the body belongs?[1] But what I am maintaining is that by this operation, which is presented logically as the substitution of one term for an equivalent term, I effect a transition from a given order into an order that is irreducibly different. When I think *my body* (and not that of another person to whom I give my name) I am in a situation which it becomes impossible to account for as soon as I substitute for it the idea of a relation between terms that are hypothetically dissociated. For if I effect this substitution I place myself in conditions that are strictly incompatible with the initial state which it was my business to explain.

So as to give a more complete elucidation of the meaning of this paradox I propose to throw a beam of light all round it so as to make clearer its importance.

When I treat my body as a term which is in a certain relation to *that* of which it is the body, I misrepresent the conditions which permit the definition of a term in general. For only that which can be apprehended thanks to an act of attentive discrimin-

---

[1] It goes without saying that the whole of this discussion also bears on the *here* and the *now* (spatial and temporal *hicceity*.) I think that, taking matters rigorously and metaphysically, it is not possible to substitute for these terms other designations which would mediatise them.

ation is susceptible of functioning as term for the mind. Now this only applies to *my body* if my thought, so to speak, retires away from it to a distance and considers it as an object among other objects. But if I proceed in this way, I am operating as though I had forgotten that this body is *mine*. I disincarnate myself in idea —to use the expression already employed earlier. If on the other hand I reintegrate myself with my body, my body ceases to appear to me as a possible term or object of discourse. But to think *my body* is manifestly to throw light on this re-establishment of possession and *reincarnation;* it means that I knowingly re-establish the state of non-division that had been broken up by rudimentary reflection.

Furthermore we need, doubtless, to generalise the result we reached when we criticised the instrumentalist interpretation of the body. Whatever be the relation I pretend to establish between myself and my body, I will end up in error or, more exactly, I will in fact be speaking of something other than what I think I am speaking about; for if I mentally retrieve all that is implied by the expression 'my body' this ceases to be a term external to a further term, X, which is myself.

But what about the instance of a passer-by who is given to me as datum under the aspect of a particular organic body of which objective knowledge is possible? I cannot avoid supposing that this person, P, has a psychological nature and constitutes a particular mental system in process of development in time. Between this mental system and this physical system how can there not be a relation, X, whatever this X may be? How, in brief, if I reason by analogy, can I avoid concluding that I too must appear to other people as a particular physical system bound up with a special mental system, and that the relation that exists in the first instance must also exist in the instance of myself? At first sight such reasoning cannot fail to appear decisive.

Yet for all that it may possibly be an illusion. What am I really trying to say when I maintain that I cannot avoid attributing to P a particular mental system? I cannot insist too much that this system is not an object of possible experience in the sense in which a portion π of P's body is. Strictly speaking there is nothing there that can be an object for me. All that can happen is the production of certain material conditions that will allow me to 'sympathise' with P and embrace his 'interior becoming.' But to this extent, however fallaciously and partially, I am identifying myself with P. Hence in relation to P's mental system I cease to occupy the *external* position that I still maintain regarding his body. And it is only an illusion if I imagine things to be otherwise. Hence:

Either this mental system is discovered to me, and that means that I have for an instant become P, that P's body has ideally become my body,

Or else P's body continues to be 'that other body', an object situated in space and in a given manner in relation to 'my own body'; but in that case P's mental system remains entirely closed to me and inaccessible.

Doubtless in practice we imagine things otherwise. We construct a certain idea of P's mental system which remains 'in us', (that is to say we treat it as a piece of our psychological life); but as this idea is not P and in no way coincides with P's mental reality, we are unable, without absurdity, to question ourselves on the relation that unites it with P's body. The problem of the relations between P's soul and body thus only arises if *I take my stand*, so to speak, in an intermediary region, a sort of between worlds, which for thought should only be a point of passage— to take one's stand there is contradictory. As soon as I have attained P's mental reality (supposing that this is possible, as I for my own part believe), and have become identified with it, there can be *no longer* any question of raising this problem, and— furthermore—this problem could not be raised *before* I made the mental journey which led from myself to P.

This analysis would need to be filled out as follows: I am not satisfied with forming a mere idea (a kind of mental effigy) of *others*. By a sort of recoil I end up by executing an analogous operation on myself and establish an account of myself like the one to which I tend to reduce P. This animated account or sketch I call my soul, my spiritual reality; it tends to be converted into a personality; and it is regarding the relations of this mythical personality with my body (which is detached from me in the sense pointed out earlier) that—as a pseudo-philosopher—I embark on the vain enterprise of thinking.

These considerations lead us to make a general and very

important distinction between data that are susceptible of forming the occasion for a problem—that is objective data—and data *on which the mind must be based* so as to state any problem whatsoever. It is impossible to treat the latter data as problematic without involving oneself in the worst of contradictions. Sensation (= the fact of feeling, of participating in a universe which creates me by affecting me), and the intellectually indefectible bond that unites me with what I call my body, are data of this second kind. And it is easy to see that in all likelihood these data are confounded together at the heart of existence as we *recognised* (as distinct from identified) it at the beginning of this essay.

What is commonly—but improperly—called the union of soul and body must be considered to be a metaphysical form of *hicceity*. Like hicceity this union is indivisible and reflection can obtain no hold upon it. Of course this is not to say that it is *unknowable*, for that would amount to supposing that it conceals a mechanism with a secret operation that escapes us.

Yet here again it is difficult to deny that we seem to be not only going against the data of common sense but also against the age-long results of philosophical analysis.

I have the idea of a movement that is to be performed, I then carry out this movement. How deny that there must be a relation, X, between the idea and the movement? But in reality we are being taken in by words. What I call the idea of raising my arm is only the abstract schematisation of a particular posture that I cannot really think or represent to myself, but only adopt, i.e. mentally reproduce. But once I have placed myself in this situation, am I able to continue to consider the act of raising my arm from the outside; can I still treat it as an object? Doubtless yes. But the hybrid character of this position is obvious. Inasmuch as I identify myself with the man who 'thinks of raising his arm' this arm must appear to me as mine. Otherwise it is meaningless to declare that one and the same person *has the idea of lifting his arm* and *really lifts it*. Thus the whole question is reduced to: 'How am I going to raise my arm?' But unless this question is stated in purely physical and objective terms, it ceases to be a problem. For there is only a problem when a particular content is detached from the context that unites it with the *I*. Now here, on the contrary, I needed to re-establish that contact. Thus no physical science is possible regarding the transition which leads from the idea to the act, or rather, regarding what— by a vicious though doubtless inevitable transposition—we think we can represent to ourselves as a communication between spheres that are distinct.

THE END

INDEX